Practical Philosophy from Kant to Hegel

Scholarship on Kant's practical philosophy has often overlooked its reception in the early days of post-Kantian philosophy and German Idealism. This volume of new essays illuminates that reception and how it informed the development of practical philosophy between Kant and Hegel. The essays discuss, in addition to Kant, Hegel and Fichte, relatively little-known thinkers such as Pistorius, Ulrich, Maimon, Erhard, E. Reimarus, Reinhold, Jacobi, F. Schlegel, Humboldt, Dalberg, Gentz, Rehberg, and Möser. Issues discussed include the empty formalism objection, the separation between right and morality, freedom and determinism, nihilism, the right to revolution, ideology, and the limits of the liberal state. Taken together, the essays provide an historically informed and philosophically nuanced picture of the development of post-Kantian practical philosophy.

JAMES A. CLARKE is Senior Lecturer in Philosophy at the University of York. He has published several articles on Fichte and Hegel. He is a member of the editorial board of the *British Journal for the History of Philosophy*, with responsibility for translations.

GABRIEL GOTTLIEB is Associate Professor of Philosophy at Xavier University. In addition to publishing multiple articles on Fichte, he is the editor of *Fichte's Foundations of Natural Right: A Critical Guide* (Cambridge University Press, 2016).

Practical Philosophy from Kant to Hegel

Freedom, Right, and Revolution

Edited by

James A. Clarke

University of York

Gabriel Gottlieb

Xavier University

CAMBRIDGE
UNIVERSITY PRESS

University Printing House, Cambridge CB2 8BS, United Kingdom

One Liberty Plaza, 20th Floor, New York, NY 10006, USA

477 Williamstown Road, Port Melbourne, VIC 3207, Australia

314–321, 3rd Floor, Plot 3, Splendor Forum, Jasola District Centre, New Delhi – 110025, India

79 Anson Road, #06–04/06, Singapore 079906

Cambridge University Press is part of the University of Cambridge.

It furthers the University's mission by disseminating knowledge in the pursuit of education, learning, and research at the highest international levels of excellence.

www.cambridge.org
Information on this title: www.cambridge.org/9781108497725
DOI: 10.1017/9781108647441

First published 2021

A catalogue record for this publication is available from the British Library.

ISBN 978-1-108-49772-5 Hardback

Contents

Contributors

DANIEL BREAZEALE is Professor of Philosophy at the University of Kentucky.

JAMES A. CLARKE is Senior Lecturer in Philosophy at the University of York.

BENJAMIN CROWE is Lecturer in Philosophy at Boston University.

KATERINA DELIGIORGI is Reader in Philosophy at the University of Sussex.

GABRIEL GOTTLIEB is Associate Professor of Philosophy at Xavier University.

PAUL GUYER is the Jonathan Nelson Professor of Humanities and Philosophy at Brown University.

REIDAR MALIKS is Associate Professor of Philosophy at the University of Oslo.

ELIZABETH MILLÁN BRUSSLAN is Professor of Philosophy at DePaul University.

DOUGLAS MOGGACH is University Chair of Political Thought at the University of Ottawa.

MICHAEL NANCE is Assistant Professor of Philosophy at the University of Maryland Baltimore County.

KAREN NG is Assistant Professor of Philosophy at Vanderbilt University.

TIMOTHY QUINN is Professor of Philosophy at Xavier University.

OWEN WARE is Assistant Professor of Philosophy at the University of Toronto.

REED WINEGAR is Assistant Professor of Philosophy at Fordham University.

Acknowledgments

This volume of essays was originally conceived as part of the British Arts and Humanities Research Council research network "Reason, Right, and Revolution: Practical Philosophy between Kant and Hegel." We are grateful to all of the participants in that network and especially to Michael Beaney, Vicky Nesfield, and Elisabeth Thorsson for their help and support.

We are thankful for the support and advice of our colleagues at the University of York and Xavier University, especially Timothy Brownlee, Owen Hulatt, Chris Jay, Mary Leng, Timothy Quinn, and Tom Stoneham. We thank Sean Hamill for his editorial assistance; and we thank Mitchell Nolte (mitchellnolte.com) for creating the cover illustration for this volume. James is grateful to Sophie Gibb, Linda Clarke, and John Clarke for their love, support, and advice. Gabe is grateful to Kristen Renzi and Josephine Gottlieb for their love and support, as well as his loving family in Texas and beyond. Many, many thanks to Hilary Gaskin and the team at Cambridge University Press for their support, guidance, and patience.

Abbreviations

We have only included abbreviations for primary sources, with an emphasis on sources by Kant, post-Kantians, and Kant's critics. In the case of Kant, we follow the standard practice of citing *Kant's gesammelte Schriften* according to the volume and page number (e.g. *GW*, 4: 399), except in the case of the *Critique of Pure Reason*, where references are to the A and B editions. With other philosophers, when there is an available English translation, the English translation is cited first, followed by a reference to the German edition.

Erhard

AT	"Apologie des Teufels," in *ÜRAS*.
BA	"Betrachtungen über die Rede des Boetie und über die Alleinherrschaft, nach Anleitung der Geschichte und Erfahrung," *Der neue Teutsche Merkur*, 2:7 (1793): 209–42.
BF	"Brief an Forberg vom Dezember 1794," in *ÜRAS*.
DA	"Devil's Apology," trans. J. A. Clarke and C. Rhode, *British Journal for the History of Philosophy*, 27:1 (2019): 194–215.
DW	*Denkwürdigkeiten des Philosophen und Arztes Johann Benjamin Erhard*, ed. Karl August Varnhagen von Ense. Stuttgart and Tübingen: Cotta, 1830.
IG	"Die Idee der Gerechtigkeit als Princip einer Gesetzgebung betrachtet," *Die Horen*, 3:7 (1795): 1–30.
PA	"Prüfung der Alleinherrschaft nach moralischen Prinzipien," *Der neue Teutsche Merkur*, 3:12 (1793): 329–33.
RF	"Rezension von Fichtes Revolutionsbuch," in *ÜRAS*.
ÜRAS	*Über das Recht des Volks zu einer Revolution und andere Schriften*, ed. H. G. Haasis. Frankfurt am Main: Syndikat, 1976.
ÜRVR	*Über das Recht des Volks zu einer Revolution*, in *ÜRAS*.

Fichte

AGN — *Addresses to the German Nation*, trans. Gregory Moore. Cambridge University Press, 2008.

B — *Beitrag zur Berichtigung der Urteile des Publikums über die französische Revolution*, ed. Richard Schottky. Hamburg: Meiner, 1973.

CCS — *The Closed Commerical State*, trans. Anthony Adler. Albany, NY: State University of New York Press, 2012.

EPW — *Fichte: Early Philosophical Writings*, trans. Daniel Breazeale. Ithaca, NY: Cornell University Press, 1988.

FNR — *Foundations of Natural Right*, trans. Michael Baur, ed. Frederick Neuhouser. Cambridge University Press, 2000.

GA — *J. G. Fichte: Gesamtausgabe der Bayerischen Akademie der Wissenschaften*, eds. Reinhard Lauth, Hans Gliwitzky, and Erich Fuchs. Stuttgart-Bad Cannstatt: Frommann-Holzboog, 1964–2012.

GGZ — *Die Grundzüge des gegenwärtigen Zeitalters*, in *SW*, Bd. VII.

IW — *Introductions to the Wissenschaftslehre and Other Writings (1797–1800)*, trans. Daniel Breazeale. Indianapolis: Hackett, 1994.

R — "Reclamation of the Freedom of Thought from the Princes of Europe, Who Have Oppressed It until Now," in James Schmidt (ed.), *What Is Enlightenment?: Eighteenth-Century Answers and Twentieth-Century Questions*. Berkeley: University of California Press, 1996.

SE — *The System of Ethics*, trans. Daniel Breazeale and Günter Zöller. Cambridge University Press, 2005.

SK — *The Science of Knowledge (Wissenschaftslehre)*, trans. Peter Heath and John Lachs. Cambridge University Press, 1982.

SW — *Johann Gottlieb Fichtes sämmtliche Werke*, ed. I. H. Fichte. Berlin: Veit, 1845–6.

VBG — *Einige Vorlesungen über die Bestimmung des Gelehrten*, in *SW*, Bd. VI.

VM — *The Vocation of Man*, trans. Peter Preuss. Indianapolis: Hackett, 1987.

WLnm — *Foundations of Transcendental Philosophy: (Wissenschaftslehre) Nova Methodo (1796/99)*, trans. Daniel Breazeale. Ithaca, NY: Cornell University Press, 1992.

WM — *Über die Würde des Menschen* (1794), in *SW*, Bd. I.

Hegel

BrH	*Briefe von und an Hegel. Band I: 1785–1812*, ed. Johannes Hoffmeister. Hamburg: Felix Meiner, 1969.
D	*The Difference between Fichte's and Schelling's System of Philosophy*, trans. W. Cerf and H. S. Harris. Albany, NY: State University of New York Press, 1977.
GC	"The German Constitution," in *Hegel: Political Writings*, trans. H. B. Nisbet, ed. Laurence Dickey and H. B. Nisbet. Cambridge University Press, 1999.
HW	*Werke in zwanzig Bänden*, ed. Eva Moldenhauer and Karl Markus Michel. Frankfurt: Suhrkamp, 1971.
L	*Hegel: The Letters*, trans. Clarke Butler and Christiane Seiler. Bloomington: Indiana University Press, 1984.
LPH	"Lectures on the Philosophy of History (1827–1831)," in *Hegel: Political Writings*, trans. H. B. Nisbet, ed. Laurence Dickey and H. B. Nisbet. Cambridge University Press, 1999.
PH	*Introduction to the Philosophy of History*, trans. Leo Rauch. Indianapolis: Hackett Publishing Company, 1988.
PhS	*Phenomenology of Spirit*, trans. A. V. Miller. Oxford University Press, 1977.
PR	*Elements of the Philosophy of Right*, trans. H. B. Nisbet, ed. Allen W. Wood. Cambridge University Press, 1991.
NL	*Natural Law: The Scientific Ways of Treating Natural Law, Its Place in Moral Philosophy, and Its Relation to the Positive Sciences of Law*, trans. T. M. Knox. Philadelphia: University of Pennsylvania Press, 1975.
SL	*Science of Logic*, trans. George di Giovanni. Cambridge University Press, 2010.

Jacobi

JBW	*Briefwechsel - Nachlaß - Dokumente*, ed. Walter Jaeschke. Stuttgart-Bad Canstatt: Frommann-Holzboog, 1981–.
JWA	*Werke*, ed. Klaus Hammacher and Walter Jaeschke. Hamburg: Felix Meiner, 1998–.
MPW	*Main Philosophical Writings and the Novel Allwill*, trans. George di Giovanni. Montreal: McGill-Queen's Press, 1995.

Kant

AA	*Kant's gesammelte Schriften* (Akademie Ausgabe). Berlin: Walter de Gruyter, 1902–.
CJ	*Critique of the Power of Judgment*, trans. and ed. Paul Guyer and Eric Matthews. Cambridge University Press, 2001.
CPR	*Critique of Pure Reason*, trans. Paul Guyer and Allen W. Wood. Cambridge University Press, 1998.
CPrR	*Critique of Practical Reason*, trans. Mary Gregor in *PP*.
ETP	*Theoretical Philosophy 1755–1770*, trans. David Walford, ed. David Walford and Ralf Meerbote. Cambridge University Press, 2003.
GW	*Groundwork of the Metaphysics of Morals*, trans. Mary Gregor in *PP*.
LDPP	*Lectures and Drafts on Political Philosophy*, trans. Frederick Rauscher and Kenneth R. Westphal, ed. Frederick Rauscher. Cambridge University Press, 2016.
MM	*Metaphysics of Morals*, trans. Mary Gregor in *PP*.
PP	*Practical Philosophy*, trans. Mary Gregor, ed. Allen Wood. Cambridge University Press, 1996.
RBMR	*Religion within the Boundaries of Mere Reason*, trans. George di Giovanni in *Religion and Rational Theology*, trans. and ed. Allen Wood and George di Giovanni. Cambridge University Press, 1996.
TP	"On the Common Saying: That May Be Right in Theory but It Is of No Use in Practice," trans. Mary Gregor in *PP*.
TPP	*Toward Perpetual Peace*, trans. Mary Gregor in *PP*.
UHC	*Idea for a Universal History from a Cosmopolitan Point of View*, trans. Lewis White Beck in Lewis White Beck (ed.), *Kant on History*. New York: Macmillan, 1963.

Maimon

ANP	"Attempt at a New Presentation of the Principle of Morality and a Deduction of Its Reality," trans. Timothy Sean Quinn. *British Journal for the History of Philosophy*, 27:1 (2018): 155–82.
MGW	*Gesammelte Werke*, ed. Valerio Verra. Hildesheim: Georg Olms, 1965–76.
ÜGN	"Ueber die ersten Gründe des Naturrechts," *Philosophisches Journal einer Gesellschaft Teutscher Gelehrter*, 1:2 (1795): 141–74.

Reimarus

BE — *Betrachtungen*, trans. Almut Spalding, in Almut Spalding, *Elise Reimarus (1735–1805), the Muse of Hamburg: A Woman of the German Enlightenment.* Würzburg: Königshausen & Neumann, 2005.

FR — *Freiheit.* Hamburg: Meyn, 1791.

VN — *Versuch einer Läuterung und Vereinfachung der Begriffe vom natürlichen Staatsrecht*, trans. Almut Spalding, in Almut Spalding, *Elise Reimarus (1735–1805), the Muse of Hamburg: A Woman of the German Enlightenment.* Würzburg: Königshausen & Neumann, 2005.

Schiller

AEM — *On the Aesthetic Education of Man in a Series of Letters*, bilingual edition, trans. and ed. Elizabeth Wilkinson and L. A. Willoughby. Oxford University Press, 1967.

DGG — "Die Götter Griechenlands," *Sämtliche Werke*, Bd. I, Munich: Hanser, 1962.

LK — "Kallias or Concerning Beauty: Letters to Gottfried Körner," in J. M. Bernstein (ed.), *Classic and Romantic German Aesthetics*. Cambridge University Press, 2003.

Schlegel

ECR — "Essay on the Concept of Republicanism," trans. Frederick C. Beiser in Frederick C. Beiser (ed.), *The Early Political Writings of the German Romantics*. Cambridge University Press, 1996.

KFSA — *Kritische Ausgabe*, 35 vols., ed. Ernst Behler et al. Paderborn: Schöningh, 1958.

LF — *Lucinde and the Fragments*, trans. Peter Firchow. Minneapolis: University of Minnesota Press, 1971.

OI — "On Incomprehensibility," trans. Jochen Schulte-Sasse in Jochen Shulte-Sasse et al. (eds.), *Theory as Practice: A Critical Anthology of Early German Romantic Writings.* Minneapolis: University of Minnesota Press, 1997.

PH — *Philosophical Fragments*, trans. Peter Firchow. Minneapolis: University of Minnesota Press, 1991.

Others

AJB	*Aus Jens Baggesen's Briefwechsel mit Karl Leonhard Reinhold*, Teil I. Leipzig: Brockhaus, 1831.
BKP	Reinhold, Karl L. *Briefe über die Kantische Philosophie*, Bd. II. Basel: Schwabe, 2008.
D	Bergk, Johann Adam. "Does Enlightenment Cause Revolutions?," in James Schmidt (ed.), *What Is Enlightenment?: Eighteenth-Century Answers and Twentieth-Century Questions*. Berkeley: University of California Press, 1996.
EFN	Ulrich, J. A. H. *Eleutheriologie oder über Freiheit und Notwendigkeit*. Jena: Kröker, 1788.
GDA	Dalberg, C. Th. [K. von]. *Grundsätze der Ästhetik, deren Anwendung und künftige Entwickelung*. Erfurt, 1791.
GM	Pistorius, Hermann Andreas. "*Grundlegung zur Metaphysik der Sitten* von Immanuel Kant," *Allgemeine deutsche Bibliothek*, 66:2 (1786): 447–63; reprinted in Gesang 2007: 26–38.
KP	Pistorius, Hermann Andreas. "*Kritik der praktischen Vernunft*, von Immanuel Kant," *Allgemeine deutsche Bibliothek*, 117:1 (1794): 78–105; reprinted in Gesang 2007: 78–98.
N	Gentz, Friedrich. "Nachtrag zu dem Räsonnement des Herrn Professor Kant über das Verhältniβ zwischen Theorie und Praxis," in Dieter Henrich (ed.), *Kant, Gentz, Rehberg: Über Theorie und Praxis*. Frankfurt: Suhrkamp, 1967.
OSP	Anonymous Author. *The Oldest Systematic Program of German Idealism*, in Ernst Behler (ed.), *Philosophy of German Idealism*. New York: Continuum, 1987.
TLS	Dalberg, K. von. "Von den wahren Grenzen der Wirksamkeit des Staats in Beziehung auf seine Mitglieder," two eds., 1793/1794, Sommer: Leipzig; reproduced in R. Leroux, *La théorie du despotisme éclairé chez Karl Theodor Dalberg*. Strasbourg University Press, 1932, 45–54.
U	Bergk, Johann Adam. *Untersuchungen aus dem Natur-, Staats- und Völkerrechte. Mit einer Kritik der neuesten Konstitution der französischen Republik.* Kronberg: Scriptor Verlag, 1975.
UFR	Rehberg, August Wilhelm. *Untersuchungen über die Französische Revolution*, Erster Teil. Hannover and Osnabrück: Christian Ritscher, 1793.

ÜPF Gentz, Friedrich, "Über Politische Freiheit und das Verhältnis derselben zur Regierung," in Edmund Burke and Friedrich Gentz, *Über die französische Revolution: Betrachtungen und Abhandlungen*, ed. Herman Klenner. Berlin: Akademie, 1991.

ÜTP Rehberg, August Wilhelm. "Über das Verhältniβ der Theorie zur Praxis," in Dieter Henrich (ed.), *Kant, Gentz, Rehberg: Über Theorie und Praxis*. Frankfurt: Suhrkamp, 1967.

Introduction

James A. Clarke and Gabriel Gottlieb

1

Traditional histories of German philosophy often present the development of German Idealism as a linear, teleological progression from Kant, through Fichte and Schelling, to Hegel.[1] This approach originates in Hegel's own history of philosophy, which portrays the history of German Idealism as a cumulative, dialectical progression that terminates – rather conveniently – in Hegel's own absolute idealism. Over the past twenty years, there has been a growth of scholarship on the development of post-Kantian idealism, and a reappraisal of figures who were afforded only minor, supporting roles in the traditional narrative (figures such as K. L. Reinhold, S. Maimon, F. Schlegel, and Novalis).[2] The effects of this revisionary scholarship have been salutary: it has resulted in a more nuanced picture of the development of German Idealism that challenges the standard Hegelian narrative;[3] it has led to the recovery of important philosophical arguments and insights;[4] it has made salient previously neglected continuities with earlier traditions (e.g., the Leibnizian-Wolffian and Spinozist traditions);[5] and it has led to a deeper understanding of the philosophies of Fichte, Schelling, and Hegel by revealing their positions to be responses to hitherto unnoticed debates and questions.[6]

With a few notable exceptions, this revisionary scholarship has focused on the development of post-Kantian theoretical philosophy, neglecting the development of post-Kantian practical philosophy.[7] This is a shame, for at least three reasons. First, the development of post-Kantian practical philosophy is

[1] The classic example of this approach is Kröner 1961.

[2] See Frank 1997; Henrich 2003; Henrich 2004.

[3] See, for example, Beiser 2002.

[4] See, for example, Franks 2005.

[5] For the Leibnizian-Wolffian tradition, see Siep 2002 and Redding 2009. For Spinoza, see Förster and Melamed 2012.

[6] It is now widely acknowledged that Fichte's conception of transcendental philosophy is in part developed in the context of a debate about the nature and significance of first principles in philosophy. Central figures involved in this debate include K. L. Reinhold, S. Maimon, G. E. Schulze, and F. Niethammer. Henrich 2003, Frank 2004, and Franks 2005 address these issues.

[7] Two exceptions are Beiser 1992 and Maliks 2014.

just as philosophically rich and significant as its theoretical counterpart. In tackling the philosophical and political issues with which they were preoccupied, the post-Kantians developed sophisticated arguments and positions on topics ranging from the nature of moral agency to the justification of human rights. Second, the development of post-Kantian practical philosophy has been no less subject to misrepresentation than the development of post-Kantian theoretical philosophy. Histories of post-Kantian political philosophy typically present its development as a linear movement from Kant through Fichte to Hegel, a movement that is often interpreted as a baleful descent toward authoritarianism and "organicist" theories of the state.[8] A proper understanding of the complex and variegated development of post-Kantian practical philosophy can serve as a powerful corrective to this misrepresentation. Third, and finally, a grasp of the manifold connections and influences that constitute the development of post-Kantian practical philosophy can lead us to question and refine our understanding of those philosophers who are traditionally regarded as "central" – in other words, Kant, Fichte, and Hegel. Thus, understanding Hegel's debt to German conservatism might lead us to question "liberal" interpretations of his thought.[9]

This edited collection aims to communicate something of the richness, diversity, and complexity of the development of practical philosophy between Kant and Hegel. Each of the thirteen chapters deals with a neglected figure or issue or a neglected aspect of a well-known figure or issue. Taken together, they offer an alternative picture of the route that leads from Kant to Hegel, a route that is perhaps best conceived of not as a "royal road" but as a network of byways. In the remainder of this introduction, we provide a brief (and necessarily selective) discussion of the themes with which post-Kantian practical philosophy was concerned (Section 2) and a brief summary of the contributions to the volume (Section 3).

2

It is perhaps difficult for us to imagine the profound impact that Kant's practical philosophy – especially his moral philosophy – had upon his early followers. Two contemporary testimonies are illuminating in this regard. In his autobiography, Johann Benjamin Erhard describes his first encounter with Kant's second *Critique* as follows:

> [A]ll pleasure that I obtained in life dwindled in comparison with the stimulation of my mind that I felt in [reading] certain passages of Kant's Critique of Practical Reason.

[8] For a classic critique of authoritarian tendencies in Fichte and Hegel, see Berlin 2014.
[9] See Reidar Maliks' contribution to this volume.

Tears of the highest bliss fell from me onto this book, and afterwards even the memory of those happy days of my life moistened my eyes and consoled me every time adverse events and a sorrowful cast of mind obstructed any joyful outlook in this life. (*DW*, 20–1)

In a well-known fragment of a letter to Weiβhuhn written in 1790, J. G. Fichte describe the effects wrought on him by reading Kant's second *Critique*:

I have been living in a new world ever since reading the *Critique of Practical Reason*. Propositions which I thought could never be overturned have been overturned for me. Things have been proven to me which I thought never could be proven – for example, the concept of absolute freedom, the concept of duty, etc. – and I feel all the happier for it. It is unbelievable how much respect for mankind and how much strength this system gives us! (*EPW*, 357; *GA*, III: no. 6)

As Fichte's letter intimates, the impact of Kant's moral philosophy – its ability to open new intellectual vistas – was due in part to its reflections on the nature of human freedom and moral duty. At the risk of oversimplification, the development of post-Kantian practical philosophy might be profitably understood as a series of attempts to work out the philosophical and political implications of Kant's account of human freedom and moral duty. For the purposes of this introduction, we can identify three broad classes of implications that exemplify (but do not exhaust) the concerns of the early post-Kantians.

The first class of implications relates to the metaphysical debate between freedom and determinism and to issues concerning the ascription of moral responsibility. C. C. E. Schmid argued that Kant's claim that an action is free only if it is done from duty creates a problem for the ascription of responsibility for immoral actions since such actions would not, strictly speaking, be free, and moral responsibility presupposes freedom. Schmid also attributed to Kant the position of "intelligible fatalism," which holds that moral action is determined by the causality of the noumenal will. Intelligible fatalism was held to be problematic because it fails to appreciate the distinction between acting based on practical reason and acting based on one's own free, arbitrary choice. The attempt to respond to such worries led philosophers such as K. L. Reinhold and J. G. Fichte to offer alternative accounts of freedom and moral agency. For example, K. L. Reinhold, in response to Schmid, introduced the distinction between *Wille* and *Willkür* in his popular work *Letters on the Kantian Philosophy*.[10]

[10] See the 8th Letter in *BKP*. Daniel Breazeale's contribution to this volume addresses the "intelligible fatalism" debate, and Katerina Deligiorgi's contribution discusses J. A. H. Ulrich's deterministic critique of Kant. See also Guyer 2017 for an examination of "intelligible fatalism" that argues that Kant was committed to the *Wille/Willkür* distinction prior to Reinhold's intervention.

The second class of implications relates to legal and political philosophy (the "philosophy of right"). By the early 1790s, Kant had published only minor, albeit significant, works on legal and political issues. Absent a full, definitive statement of Kant's philosophy of right (Kant's *Metaphysics of Morals* was published in 1797), the early post-Kantians endeavored to work out the implications of Kant's account of freedom and duty for legal and political philosophy. A central concern in these endeavors is the nature of the relationship between right and morality: Are the principles and norms of right (where these norms include human rights – *Menschenrechte*) to be derived from moral principles or norms? Or are they rather to be derived independently of morality (as, say, necessary conditions of the possibility of self-conscious human agency)? In attempting to resolve this issue, the early post-Kantians developed several innovations that exerted a profound influence on subsequent thinkers and are still relevant today. Perhaps the most famous of these is the thesis, first articulated by J. G. Fichte in his 1796–7 *Foundations of Natural Right*, that a norm-governed interpersonal relationship (the relationship of mutual recognition) is a necessary condition of self-consciousness and individuality.

The third class of implications, intimately related to the second, concerns the relationship between Kant's account of freedom and morality and the French Revolution. Although Kant himself had rejected a right to revolution, early post-Kantians such as J. B. Erhard, J. G. Fichte, and J. A. Bergk drew upon Kant's moral philosophy and early political writings to justify human rights and a right to revolution. In his 1793/4 *Contribution to the Correction of the Public's Judgment of the French Revolution*, Fichte construed the people's right to revolution as its right to change its "state constitution [*Staatsverfassung*]" (*B*, Ch. 1). Such a right is justified, Fichte claimed, because morality requires that each individual possess the inalienable right to unilaterally terminate any contract he enters into, including the contract that founds a state constitution. In addition to defending the right to revolution, Fichte also provided a rhetorically powerful characterization of the opposing standpoints in the debate over the legitimacy of revolution: Defenders of the revolution occupied the standpoint of the critical philosophy, and had a lively sense of their own freedom and spontaneity. By contrast, the conservative critics of revolution (thinkers such as A. W. Rehberg) occupied the standpoint of empiricism and conceived of themselves as merely passive recipients of experience (*B*, Introduction).[11]

Fichte's defense of the right to revolution proved highly influential and secured his reputation as a radical political thinker. It is, however, vulnerable

[11] This characterization of opposing standpoints clearly foreshadows Fichte's later distinction between idealism and dogmatism in *IW*.

to criticism on several points.[12] An alternative, and arguably more sophisticated, defense of the right to revolution was provided by J. B. Erhard in his *On the Right of the People to a Revolution*, which was written in 1794 and published in 1795. Erhard argues that a people has a right to revolt if the basic, most fundamental laws of the state engender human rights violations (where the human rights that can be violated includes a human right that belongs collectively to the people – the right to enlightenment).[13]

Having provided a brief illustration of some of the themes that shaped and animated the development of post-Kantian practical philosophy, we now turn to an overview of the contributions to this volume.

3

The first two chapters, by Paul Guyer and Katerina Deligiorgi, deal with Kant's early critics. A well-known objection to Kant's moral philosophy is that the categorical imperative is merely formal and empty. The objection alleges that the categorical imperative, understood as a formal procedure of universalizing maxims, cannot generate moral norms by itself, but must surreptitiously rely on historically and socially conditioned moral norms and principles (such as, for example, the principle that there ought to be private property) or on some claim about human nature. Although this objection is usually associated with Hegel, Guyer contends that it was first advanced by Pistorius in his review of Kant's *Groundwork*. Pistorius criticizes Kant for failing to ground his moral theory on a theory of human nature that recognizes the importance of happiness in explaining the interest that subjects have in acting morally. Guyer argues that Kant has a response to Pistorius (formulated in the *Critique of Practical Reason*), a response that turns on Kant's views about the primacy of pure practical reason within human nature. *Pace* Pistorius, it is not the case that Kant disregards human beings' interest in happiness; it is simply that he does not grant interest in happiness primacy over reason's interest in morality. Pistorius offered a rejoinder to Kant's response in a review of the second *Critique*, and Guyer charts this development and considers how Kant might have replied.

In the second chapter, Katerina Deligiorgi engages with Johann August Heinrich Ulrich's critique of Kant's theory of transcendental freedom. Ulrich

[12] A trenchant critique of Fichte's defense of the right to revolution was provided by J. B. Erhard in his 1795 review of Fichte's book. Among other things, Erhard objected to Fichte's contractarian account of revolution, questioning the coherence of a conception of a contract as an agreement that can be unilaterally terminated at will. See Erhard's critique of Fichte in *RF*.

[13] Erhard's account of revolution is discussed in Michael Nance's contribution to this volume.

is committed to metaphysical determinism, and he criticizes Kant's theory of transcendental freedom on the grounds that it is unable to explain why, in any given case, an agent chose to act in one way rather than another. Given this inability, the fact that the agent chose to act as she did would seem to be a matter of indeterminism or chance. In opposition to Kant, Ulrich outlines a naturalistic and deterministic ethics that, he claims, is able to capture the absolute and categorical nature of moral imperatives. Deligiorgi identifies several flaws in Ulrich's ethical naturalism and provides a defense of Kant's conception of transcendental freedom.

The third chapter, by Timothy Quinn, considers the influence of Moses Maimonides and Kant on Salomon Maimon's ethical thought. Quinn argues that Maimon draws upon Maimonides to criticize and radically transform Kant's moral philosophy. At the heart of Maimon's critique is a claim concerning the status of theoretical reason. Whereas Kant had insisted on the "primacy" of practical reason, Maimon follows Maimonides in insisting on the primacy of theoretical reason. For Maimon, as for Maimonides, the highest good is intellectual perfection, and practical reason and morality are merely instrumental to its pursuit. According to Quinn, Maimon also departs from Kant in embracing eudaimonism and in developing a theory of motivation in which a drive (*Trieb*) for cognition plays a central role.

The fourth and fifth chapters, by James A. Clarke and Michael Nance, explore the practical philosophy of a neglected, yet highly significant, thinker – Johann Benjamin Erhard. Clarke's chapter examines Erhard's account of the relationship between right and morality. Fichte cites Erhard approvingly when presenting his own account of the relationship between right and morality in the *Foundations of Natural Right*, and it is often thought that Erhard's position is a hesitant precursor of Fichte's (*FNR*, 12; *SW*, III: 12). Clarke argues that Erhard's position is much more complex and sophisticated than is commonly assumed, and that it merits philosophical attention in its own right. Clarke also considers Erhard's position in the context of the debate between legal positivism and natural law theory, arguing that Erhard's position constitutes a compelling form of natural law theory.

Michael Nance's chapter focuses on Erhard's Kantian defense of the right to revolution. Erhard aims to establish that there are conditions under which a person is morally permitted, and hence justified, in instigating revolution. Nance reconstructs these conditions, scrutinizing them and assessing their plausibility. Nance emphasizes the centrality to Erhard's theory of the dangerous unpredictability of revolutionary action as a problem for the moral justification of revolution. Erhard's insight into the epistemic difficulties associated with consequentialist justifications of revolution is both interesting in itself, and the source of some puzzles about his theory of revolution, which Nance discusses in the second half of his chapter.

The sixth chapter, by Reed Winegar, continues the theme of political resistance by examining Elise Reimarus' account of rebellion. Reimarus' political writings were published prior to Kant's and it has been argued – by Lisa Curtis-Wendlandt – that they anticipate Kant's views on freedom and rebellion. In opposition to Curtis-Wendlandt, Winegar argues that Reimarus' position differs significantly from Kant's in offering a defense of rebellion on consequentialist grounds. Although this defense resembles Achenwall's consequentialist defense of revolution (a defense criticized by Kant), it differs from it in one crucial respect: the value to be promoted is not happiness, but freedom. Winegar suggests that Reimarus' position might prove attractive to political philosophers who endorse Kant's emphasis on freedom but are chary of his views on rebellion and his non-consequentialist approach to political philosophy.

In the seventh chapter, Daniel Breazeale explores the topic of freedom and duty in Kant, Reinhold, and Fichte. The starting point for this exploration is C. C. E. Schmid's critique of Kant's moral philosophy, which argues that Kant's claim that an action is free only if it is done out of respect for the moral law makes it hard to understand how agents could be held responsible for immoral actions; this is so because immoral actions are not, *ex hypothesi*, free, and an action's being free is plausibly thought to be a condition of an agent's being held responsible for it. Breazeale considers how Reinhold, Fichte, and Kant himself, respond to this criticism by refining and developing their conceptions of freedom, practical reason, and duty.

The eighth chapter, by Owen Ware, offers a novel interpretation of Fichte's moral philosophy. Rejecting popular interpretations of Fichte's practical philosophy that either emphasize the communitarian or individualist strands of his thought, Ware opts for a "mystical" Fichte – that is, an interpretation of Fichte's ethics that explains what it means for the subject to merge with the unity of pure spirit. Ware characterizes Fichte's position as "ethical holism," where this is the view that duties derive their material content from the social whole. Ware's interpretation helps to explain how Fichte's ethics avoids an empty formalism objection and how Fichte is able to incorporate a theory of the natural drive into his Kantian-inspired ethical system. A further, important upshot of Ware's interpretation is that it highlights the social dimension of Fichte's ethics.

The ninth chapter focuses on F. H. Jacobi. Benjamin Crowe argues that Jacobi's conception of nihilism has a practical dimension as well as a theoretical one. In its practical dimension, nihilism involves advocating a formal ideal of practical rationality and abstracting from the "way of sensing [*Sinnesart*]" that informs each agent's moral judgment and reveals the morally salient features of particular situations. This way of sensing is the source of individuality, and it is shaped and formed by social relationships. Drawing upon Jacobi's treatises and epistolary writings, Crowe shows how Jacobi's account of practical nihilism is a response to "Enlightenment" thinkers (Kant, Fichte, and the French *philosophes*) and to the French Revolution.

Elizabeth Millán Brusslan's contribution, in the tenth chapter, explores the social and political philosophy of the early German Romantic philosopher, Friedrich Schlegel. Although German Romanticism is sometimes associated with reactionary conservatism, Millán Brusslan argues that Schlegel's pluralistic conception of philosophy (and his conception of the relationship between philosophy and literature) led him to adumbrate a progressive social and political philosophy, which sought to include women and other traditionally excluded groups. Millán Brusslan discusses Schlegel's treatment of women in his fragments, correspondence, and his novel *Lucinde*, and considers his critique of Kant's condemnation of democracy in *Toward Perpetual Peace*.

The eleventh chapter, by Douglas Moggach, considers the influence of the Leibnizian-Wolffian tradition on post-Kantian political thought. Since Kantian liberals traditionally seek to defend the state's neutrality on questions of the good life, the perfectionist ethics of Leibniz and Wolff appears to conflict with Kantian liberalism. Moggach argues that if the good to be perfected consists in the conditions (both institutional and intersubjective) required for free self-determination, the appearance of conflict disappears. This conception of the good is, Moggach claims, characteristic of a post-Kantian perfectionism. Moggach explores the development of post-Kantian perfectionism by examining the debate between Wilhelm von Humboldt and Karl von Dalberg on the role of the state in promoting a perfectionist conception of the good. The central question concerns the extent to which the state should interfere in promoting perfectionist ends, with Dalberg assigning the state a prominent role, and Humboldt, an opponent of the tutelary state, recognizing that the promotion of moral perfection depends on the freedom of individuals. Moggach concludes with some remarks on how the debate influenced Fichte's economic and political thought.

The last two chapters, by Reidar Maliks and Karen Ng, offer new perspectives on Hegel's philosophy of right. Maliks adopts a "contextualist" approach to Hegel's philosophy of right, situating it within the context of a debate between the German Burkeans (a group of conservative thinkers that included Gentz, Rehberg, and Möser) and Kant and the "radical" Kantians (thinkers such as Erhard, Fichte, and Bergk). Whereas Kant and the radical Kantians championed the role of reason and a priori principles in practical philosophy, the German Burkeans condemned it, arguing that abstract theories and principles had led to the excesses of the French Revolution. Political philosophy should, they maintained, be grounded in convention, tradition, and historical experience. Maliks considers the influence of the German Burkeans on Hegel's reception of the French Revolution, and argues that Hegel's position can be read as an attempt to reconcile ("sublate," in Hegel's terminology) the two sides of the debate. This reading, Maliks argues, serves as a corrective to liberal interpretations of Hegel and sheds new light on Hegel's infamous *Doppelsatz*: "What is rational is actual; and what is actual is rational."

Karen Ng interprets Hegel's philosophy of right through the lens of critical theory. Adorno and Habermas both suggest that Hegel's account of public opinion in the *Philosophy of Right* shows that Hegel deployed a concept that is central to critical theory – the concept of ideology. In the first two parts of her essay, Ng vindicates this suggestion by arguing that Hegel's account of public opinion is an account of a form of ideological false consciousness. She further argues that a distinctive (and, indeed, attractive) feature of this account is that it conceives of ideology as embedded in social practices and social institutions. In the third part of her essay, Ng explores the origins of Hegel's social and political methodology in his 1802/3 essay on natural right. She argues that Hegel's critiques of formalism and empiricism reveal methodological commitments that constitute a nascent critical theory. Ng's interpretation provides fresh insight into the development of practical philosophy between Kant and Hegel, and sheds new light on the history of radical social philosophy.

As interest in post-Kantian philosophy grows, with new studies on Fichte, Schelling, and Hegel appearing with some regularity, there is also a quickly burgeoning interest in many of the lesser-known figures who shaped the trajectory of German Idealism and post-Kantian philosophy. Our hope is that this volume contributes not only to a better understanding of the practical philosophy of Kant, Fichte, and Hegel, but also to a greater appreciation of the contributions of neglected philosophers such as Pistorius, Ulrich, Maimon, Erhard, E. Reimarus, Reinhold, Jacobi, F. Schlegel, Humboldt, Dalberg, Gentz, Rehberg, and Möser, to name only the figures central to the chapters herein. We can only hope that scholarship on these figures and the many others we do not address will continue to flourish. It will undoubtedly enrich our understanding of the historical period, and in some cases, it might even illuminate our own moral and political predicament.

1 The Original Empty Formalism Objection
Pistorius and Kant

Paul Guyer

1 Introduction

The Rügen pastor Hermann Andreas Pistorius (1730–98) published a lengthy review of Kant's 1785 *Groundwork for the Metaphysics of Morals* in the *Allgemeine deutsche Bibliothek* in May, 1786.[1] This was not the first review of the *Groundwork* to be published – Albert Landau included nine earlier reviews, from journals all over Germany, in his compilation of reviews of books by or pertaining to Kant between 1781 and 1787[2] – but it was one of only two to which Kant referred in his subsequent *Critique of Practical Reason* of 1788, and it has been accorded a significant role in the genesis of that work.[3] Lewis White Beck, for example, saw Pistorius's charge that in the *Groundwork* "Kant had gone against the injunctions made against speculative knowledge in the first *Critique*" as a threat to "the entire critical philosophy" and as one of the major motivations for the composition of the second *Critique* in the year following the appearance of Pistorius's review.[4] And indeed, although he does not mention Pistorius's name, Kant is certainly referring to him when he says that a "certain reviewer ... who is devoted to truth and

[1] Hermann Andreas Pistorius, "*Grundlegung zur Metaphysik der Sitten* von Immanuel Kant," *Allgemeine deutsche Bibliothek*, Band 66, Stück 2 (1786): 447–53; reproduced in Landau 1991: 354–68, and in Gesang 2007: 26–38. I will quote from the latter source throughout the paper, using the abbreviation *GM*; the translations from Pistorius are my own.

[2] Landau 1991: xi–xvii.

[3] Daniel Jenisch (1762–1804), formerly a student of Kant and later pastor of the Nikolai church in Berlin, reported to Kant from Braunschweig in a letter of May 14, 1787, describing the rapid spread of interest in Kant's work following Karl Leonhard Reinhold's *Letters on the Kantian Philosophy* in the *Teutsche Merkur* and Friedrich Heinrich Jacobi's attack, and informed Kant that the reviewer of the *Groundwork* in the *Allgemeine deutsche Bibliothek* was "Provost Pistorius, the translator of [David] Hartley"; he wrote that "although for all his apparent rigor [Pistorius] did not go deep enough," but that nevertheless, "because minds in morality are distorted by popularity, he has found many followers" (Letter 297, *AA*, 10: 485–7; I owe this reference to Arnulf Zweig's biographical sketch of Jenisch in *C*: 586–7). Whether or not Kant was previously unaware either of the review or of the reviewer's identity, this letter would have brought both to his attention right at the moment he was starting to write the *Critique of Practical Reason*.

[4] Beck 1960: 16.

astute and therefore always worthy of respect" has raised the objection that in the *Groundwork* "*the concept of the good was not established before the moral principle* (as, in his opinion, was necessary)" (*CPrR*, 5: 8–9; Kant's emphasis). Kant expresses the hope that he has dealt adequately with this objection in the second chapter of the "Analytic of Pure Practical Reason," "On the Concept of an Object of Pure Practical Reason" (*CPrR*, 5: 57–71).

Pistorius's objection is the first formulation of what has come to be known as the objection that Kant's formulation of the moral law as the categorical imperative is an "empty formalism," sixteen years before Hegel made this objection more famous in his 1802 essay "The Scientific Ways of Treating Natural Law" (*NL*, 53–135; *HW*, II: 434–530). It was too late in his life for Kant to respond to Hegel's objection; but it might also be said that he really did not offer much of a reply to Pistorius. Instead of a positive argument that the categorical imperative, above all its formulation as the requirement that one act only on maxims that one could also will to be universal laws of nature, really does yield substantive moral norms non-circularly, without tacitly presupposing them, in Chapter II of the "Analytic of Pure Practical Reason" Kant seems only to repeat the negative argument of Section I of the *Groundwork* that any moral principle based on the object or aim of an action – a conception of the or a good – rather than on the form of its maxim – what is right – could only be based on an object of *inclination*, and thus would be contingent and merely empirically knowable instead of necessary and knowable a priori, as a genuine law of practical reason must be. In spite of his expression of respect, Kant does not seem to take Pistorius's criticism very seriously.

However, a careful reading of Pistorius's review and reflection on the larger argument of the *Critique of Practical Reason* can suggest that Kant's whole work is a response to Pistorius that does take him seriously. For the gist of Pistorius's objection is that Kant does not ground his fundamental principle of morality on an adequate understanding of human nature, one that grants the importance of happiness for human beings, and that Kant therefore cannot explain the interest that human beings are supposed to take in morality. In response, two of Kant's main innovations in the second *Critique*, namely his theory of the feeling of respect as the incentive of pure practical reason and his greatly expanded treatment of the highest good, can be seen as attempting to demonstrate that he does recognize the importance of happiness for human beings and the need for an interest in morality, *but on a conception of human nature that reflects the primacy of pure practical reason within human nature*. Just as in his conception of the highest good Kant recognizes that happiness is an essential part of the *complete* good for a human being but virtue, as the condition of the worthiness to be happy, is the *supreme* good, so in general the *Critique of Practical Reason* develops a conception of human nature that includes a natural interest in happiness but in which reason's own interest in virtue or moral worth is nevertheless supreme (*CPrR*, 5: 100–11). This is Kant's larger response to Pistorius.

There is more to this story, however. For Pistorius was not convinced by Kant's account of the highest good, and explained why in a review of the second *Critique* that he completed in timely fashion. However, his manuscript was apparently mislaid (*verlegt*) by the editors of the *Allgemeine deutsche Bibliothek*, and it did not appear in the journal until 1794.[5] This was six years after the publication of Kant's book, and a year after the publication of two other main works in the canon of Kant's practical philosophy, namely the essay "On the Common Saying: That May Be Right in Theory but It Is of No Use in Practice" and *Religion within the Boundaries of Mere Reason*, both of which appeared in 1793. So Kant could not have referred to or responded to Pistorius's second review in either of those works; and even though Kant's final work in moral philosophy, the "Doctrine of Virtue" of the *Metaphysics of Morals*, appeared in 1797, Kant made no reference to Pistorius there either. Yet all of these works in fact narrow the distance between Kant and Pistorius. For what Pistorius argues in the mislaid review is that Kant still too rigidly separates "pure intelligence" from the nature of the human being as a "member of the sensible world" (*KP*, 88), and thus incoherently separates the perfection of virtue, which can be accomplished only in the infinitude of an immortal life span, and happiness, which can only be understood with reference to the "present sensible nature of the human being" (*KP*, 93); further, Kant's theory of moral motivation remains unconvincing to Pistorius. In what follows, I will argue that Kant's works after the second *Critique* address these concerns even if Kant no longer had Pistorius in mind.

2 Pistorius's Review of the *Groundwork*

Pistorius makes two main objections to Kant's argument in the *Groundwork*: first, that a formal principle without an end or object cannot determine the will, and second, that on Kant's purely formal approach he cannot explain our interest in, and thus our motivation for, freely adhering to the moral law. The first of these objections is itself made at two levels: first, that in general no law can determine the will without an object, and second, that particular maxims, such as that one not make false promises in order to get oneself out of difficulties, cannot determine the will without specific presuppositions such as that promises are a useful way to achieve our goals. It might seem ironic that Pistorius brings the general objection that we "must seek the assistance of the

[5] Hermann Andreas Pistorius, "*Kritik der praktischen Vernunft*, von Immanuel Kant," *Allgemeine deutsche Bibliothek*, Band 117, Stück 1 (1794): 78–105; reprinted in Gesang 2007: 78–98 (I shall use the abbreviation *KP*).

material because the formal will not suffice for the will or the law" (*GM*, 27) against Kant, because this is precisely the objection that Kant had made against Alexander Gottlieb Baumgarten two decades earlier in his prize essay on the "Distinctness of the Principles of Natural Theology and Morality." There Kant had objected that Baumgarten's rule "Perform the most perfect action in your power" is a merely "*formal ground* of all obligation *to act*" and that "in the absence of any material first principle, nothing flows from the first formal principle" of our moral judgments, that is, the formal principle of maximizing perfection must be accompanied with a substantive account of morally relevant perfection (*ETP*, 2: 299). But Kant's revolution in moral philosophy in the critical period would generally be described precisely as his recognition that a purely formal principle could and must suffice for moral judgment, although it would not be identical to Baumgarten's principle of perfection. Pistorius's objection to Kant's formalism would only show that he was not prepared to join Kant's revolution.

As I said, Pistorius objects to Kant's formalism at both a general level and a particular level. He makes the general objection immediately in his review, in response to Kant's opening claim that the only thing that is unconditionally good is a good will, regardless of any object that it wills. Pistorius writes:

> I wished that the author had preferred before all else to explain the general concept of what is *good* and to determine more precisely what he understands by that, for obviously we would have to agree about that before we could make out anything about the absolute value of a good will . . . I do not see how one could assume anything at all to be strictly and quite entirely good, or call something good, that is in fact good for nothing, and just as little how one can assume a good will considered absolutely and merely in itself. But the will should be absolutely good only in relation to some object for it, not in relation to its principle or a law for the sake of which it acts . . . . Now we must finally come to some object or to the final end [*Endzweck*] of the law, and must seek the assistance of the material because the formal will not suffice for the will or the law. (*GM*, 27)

The idea of something that is *good* but not *good for something* makes no sense to Pistorius, so the idea of a will that is good, let alone absolutely good, but not because it is the will to bring about something good, indeed absolutely good, makes no sense to him.

At the more particular level, Pistorius objects to Kant's claim that a maxim such as that to allow oneself a false promise to get out of a difficulty is wrong *not* because of some disadvantage to which it might lead but simply because it cannot be coherently universalized by asking

> [I]s the cancellation of everything that is necessary in behalf of human life, the mutual trust that is so necessary for the need and business thereof, not a genuine disadvantage to myself and others, that must first become known to me chiefly through experience, and is this disadvantage not the sole cause why the maxim of helping oneself through lying promises does not fit into a universal legislation? (*GM*, 31)

The reason why a "universal law to lie cannot be willed" is, according to Pistorius, just that such a law "would have no relation to a presupposed interest of rational beings"; rather, if such beings "were entirely indifferent and completely insensitive to concord or discord, to truth or falsehood, to perfection or imperfection, to pleasure or pain, then it would also be indifferent to them whether a universal law to tell the truth or a universal law to lie were established" (*GM*, 31–2). For Pistorius, adherence to particular moral laws will be the means to particular ends set by our concern for concord, truth, perfection, and pleasure, which ends collectively constitute our good and the object of the most general moral law.

Pistorius's view is that the will must be connected to a law, whether the most general moral law or more particular moral laws, by some intermediary, a "third representation" of some good to be achieved by adherence to the law, and that "such a representation can be either the truth or the utility of the law, its harmony with the power of thought, or its congruence with the faculty of desire" (*GM*, 32). Our desire for truth and utility constitutes our "common nature" and determines what we find good, and grounds our interest in the moral law. Pistorius reiterates what he stated at the outset, "that moral investigation must begin with the concept of *good*, and the question must be examined whether in relation to the conduct of the human being anything could be regarded as good other than what is really good for the human being as a sensing and thinking being." Indeed, Pistorius uses the term "highest good" to characterize this good: Whatever is "universally good for sensing and thinking beings without exception, in all circumstances, must be called the highest and absolute good." Only in such a highest good, founded in the common nature of human beings, can a "universal interest of all rational beings in turn be founded," and on that in turn is the "common interest" of such beings grounded (*GM*, 33). (Pistorius switches from talking about "the human being [*Mensch*]" to "rational beings [*vernünftige Wesen*]" without comment.)

Pistorius acknowledges that his argument that the good and indeed the highest good are ends set by human nature will undermine Kant's distinction between hypothetical imperatives and the categorical imperative: The moral law or moral laws that are the condition of the realization of the highest good set by human nature will have the formal structure of a hypothetical imperative or imperatives, stating means to that end. But that does not bother him. Rather, he asks

> Why must we discover such a categorical imperative? Perhaps just to be able to assume an absolutely good will? But here I ask further: Why must we assume an absolutely good will? What is there in our moral sentiments and common knowledge of morality that necessarily leads us to the presupposition of such an absolutely good will? . . . The question remains whether such a good will is anything more than a beautiful but impossible idea. (*GM*, 33)

Pistorius is here staking his own flag on Kant's ground: By the time of the *Groundwork*, of course, Kant does not appeal to "moral sentiments" in defense of his position, but Section I of the *Groundwork* is supposed to be an exercise in the "common rational cognition" of morality, so if "common knowledge of morality" does not in fact postulate the necessity of a will that is good in itself without reference to any object, that is a strike against Kant. It is not a fatal one, perhaps, since Section II of the *Groundwork* starts the argument over again from a philosophical rather than common ground, namely, by deriving the only possible content of the categorical imperative from the very concept of such an imperative. But then again, if Pistorius is also throwing doubt on whether the idea of a categorical imperative that does not presuppose any object makes sense, then the strategy of Section II as well as Section I is in trouble.

To conclude his argument, Pistorius claims that he can only give the same response to the concept of autonomy that Kant introduces in Section II of the *Groundwork* that he has given to Kant's conception of the good will: he can give it no

> other sense than that of the double interest in truth and utility grounded in the common nature of rational beings, or the harmony of a [practical] proposition with the essential laws of our power of thought and of the interest of all rational beings resulting from the concordance of the same with our entire faculty of desire or its sum.

He can "neither conceive nor wish for any greater freedom than that which as it were results from the exercise of his own nature," which is why he feels entitled to appropriate the term "autonomy" for his own position. And he appeals to the authority of the Stoics for this interpretation of autonomy: this is what their expression "living in accordance with nature [*naturae convenienter vivere*]" means (*GM*, 36).

Pistorius's argument is thus that neither the most general principle of morality nor particular moral laws are grounded in formal considerations alone, rather they presuppose at both levels a conception of the highest good determined by our cognitive and conative nature, that our nature is the source of our interest in conformity to moral law, and that living and acting in accordance with this nature is the true meaning of autonomy. If that means that morality is expressed by a system of hypothetical imperatives, to use a modern expression, rather than by a categorical imperative or system thereof, so be it.[6]

In a way, Kant's ultimate response to Pistorius will be to agree with everything except the claim that there is no categorical imperative; he can do

[6] I refer of course to the well-known paper by Philippa Foot, "Morality as a System of Hypothetical Imperatives," in Foot 1981: 157–73.

this because on his account the "power of thinking" included in our nature is a power of *pure* practical reason, which can not only govern our faculty of desire but can also create its own interest. But he never publicly concedes an inch to Pistorius. His avowed response to Pistorius in the *Critique of Practical Reason* is particularly unyielding. Let us first examine that, and then consider how the second *Critique* as a whole can be read as a response to Pistorius.

3 The *Critique of Practical Reason*

Kant expresses the hope that he has "dealt adequately" with Pistorius's critique in the second chapter of the "Analytic of Pure Practical Reason," "On the Concept of an Object of Pure Practical Reason" (*CPrR*, 5: 8, 57). But here Kant merely repeats the argument that he had already made in Section I of the *Groundwork*, that neither inclination nor any object of inclination can be the source of the moral law, because any principle derived from such a source would be contingent and known only a posteriori, not necessary and known a priori (*GW*, 4: 400), and the similar argument for Theorem I of the first chapter of the "Analytic" of the second *Critique*, that "All practical principles that presuppose an *object* (matter) of the faculty of desire as the determining ground of the will are, without exception, empirical and can furnish no practical laws" (*CPrR*, 5: 21). He takes Pistorius's conception of the good that could precede a formal law of morality, or any such conception, to necessarily be contingent and empirically known and thus to be an inadequate source or ground for a genuine moral law. Kant allows that there may be an empirically founded distinction between well-being (*Wohl*) and ill-being (*Übel*) or woe (*Weh*), which refer, positively or negatively, to the agreeableness of our condition, but the *moral* terms good and evil (*das Güte* and *das Böse*) "always signif[y] a reference to the *will* insofar as it is determined by *the law of reason* to make something its object." They "are never determined directly by the object and the representation of it, but . . . instead [by] a faculty of making a rule of reason the motive of an action" (*CPrR*, 5: 59–60). Kant also puts his point by saying that although both good and evil are objects of desire, "by the first, however, is understood a necessary object of desire, by the second, of the faculty of aversion, both, however, in accordance with a principle of reason" (*CPrR*, 5: 58). An object of genuinely moral approbation or disapprobation must be determined to be such on a necessary rather than a contingent ground; only a rule of reason can constitute such a ground; and therefore the moral law must precede any particular conception of the object of morality. Only if "a rational principle is already thought as in itself the determining ground of the will without regard to possible objects of desire (hence through the mere lawful form of the maxim)" is a principle "a practical law *a priori* and pure reason . . . practical of itself," while if "a determining ground of the faculty of desire precedes the maxim of a will . . . such maxims can in that case never be called laws but can [only] be called rational practical precepts" (*CPrR*, 5: 62). Thus Kant insists that only his own requirement of universal validity for our maxims can satisfy the requirement that the fundamental principle of morality be necessarily true and knowable a priori.

As we saw, however, Pistorius does not accept this constraint on any possible moral law in the first place. Further, Kant does not respond in any detail to the two levels of Pistorius's attack upon formalism. He does not respond to Pistorius's general criticism by arguing that rational agency or its instantiation as humanity is itself a value to be promoted by adherence to the moral law that provides the rationale for accepting the moral law while not degenerating into a mere preference for agreeableness over disagreeableness. He could have argued this: In the lectures on natural right given in the summer of 1784 he had stated that "If rational beings alone are capable of being ends in themselves it cannot be because they have reason but because they have freedom. Reason is merely a means" (*LDPP*, 27: 1321), and what he meant by freedom in these lectures seems to be the same as what he means by humanity in the *Groundwork* and *Metaphysics of Morals*, where he defines humanity as "the capacity to set oneself an end" (*MM*, 6: 392; see also *MM*, 6: 387). The *Groundwork*'s claim that humanity is an end in itself that is the "ground of a possible categorical imperative" could thus be taken as the claim that it is through the categorical imperative as a law given by pure reason that humanity as an end in itself is realized (*GW*, 4: 428). This would have the structure of a relation between a fundamental good and a moral law that Pistorius demands: humanity would be the good realized by adherence to the moral law.[7] Kant could further have responded to Pistorius by pointing out that the categorical imperative does not work just by requiring non-contradiction between a maxim and its own universalization, but also by requiring consistency between one's maxim(s) and the human will in general, whether one's own (in the case of the duty to cultivate talents one might need to realize one's ends) or others' (in the case of the duty to assist others in the realization of their own freely chosen ends), without which "there is still only a negative and not a positive agreement with *humanity as an end in itself*" (*GW*, 4: 430). Thus, Kant could have argued that both in general and in particular his concept of humanity saves his position from being an empty formalism.

[7] Relying on *GW*, 4: 437, Allen Wood has argued that humanity is not an end to be "effected" or produced (Wood 1999: 115). More precisely, then, Kant's position is that humanity or freedom is something that must always be preserved and under appropriate circumstances promoted, where that in turn means that a human being's potential for freedom must be more fully realized by her own efforts and those of others.

Kant did not respond to Pistorius in this way. In fact, he does not employ the concept of humanity in the *Critique of Practical Reason*. We can only speculate why Kant did not appeal to his own conception of humanity as the ground of a possible categorical imperative to show that his argument does in fact have the general form that Pistorius wants, that of deriving the law from a conception of the good rather than vice versa. Perhaps he felt that the distinction between merely contingent goods and a truly necessary good would not be clear enough for readers on whom the necessity of a genuine moral law must be impressed, or perhaps he was not even clear enough himself about the difference between merely contingent goods and the necessary value of humanity as an end in itself, or clear enough about how he wanted to argue for this status for humanity, to make that the centerpiece of his response to Pistorius. So he just re-asserted his claim that only a law of reason can be truly necessary, and therefore that the moral law must precede any (particular) conception of the good.

But Kant also shortchanged himself by suggesting that his response to Pistorius is contained entirely in the second chapter of the "Analytic." For central points of the larger argument of the *Critique of Practical Reason* can also be taken to be part of his response to Pistorius: His account of respect as an incentive created by pure practical reason is an argument that reason can give rise to a genuine interest in morality, and his account of the highest good is a response to the charge that he does not have any such concept, thus that his formalism is an empty formalism.

Following the order of exposition in the second *Critique*, we can consider the issue of interest in morality first. Pistorius had objected that Kant could not explain our interest in autonomy without supposing it to be grounded in the "doubled interest in truth and utility" that is in turn "grounded in the common nature of rational beings" (*GM*, 36). Kant can be taken to be responding to this charge with the addition of an entire chapter on the feeling of respect as the incentive to morality. To be sure, in the *Groundwork* Kant had already introduced respect as a "feeling *self-wrought* by means of a rational concept and therefore specifically different from all feelings . . . which can be reduced to inclination or fear" (*GW*, 4: 402n.), but he had buried the introduction of this feeling in a footnote and, moreover, at least left open the interpretation that this feeling is merely epiphenomenal, simply the conscious "*effect* of the law on the subject" but not a cause for the actual determination of the agent to abide by the moral law; so Pistorius might well be allowed the charge that Kant had not provided an adequate account of our interest in morality. In the second *Critique*, however, Kant greatly expands his treatment of the feeling of respect, argues that it plays a causal and not merely epiphenomenal role at the phenomenal level of action, where the choice of particular maxims of action must take place even if the choice of what Kant subsequently calls our fundamental maxim must be supposed to take place at the noumenal level where freedom reigns, and then explicitly labels this account of the feeling of respect an account of "the *moral interest*" as a "sense-free interest of practical reason alone," that is, an account of a feeling and an interest *grounded* in pure reason rather than in any sense-dependent inclination (*RBMR*, 6: 36; *CPrR*, 5: 79). Kant does not mention Pistorius's name, but his intention to establish that he does have an adequate account of our interest in morality could hardly be clearer.

Kant's treatment of the feeling of respect in this chapter is intricate, the interpretation of it is vexed, and this is hardly the place for a detailed treatment of all the issues involved.[8] Here the following observations must suffice. Kant begins with the claim that "[w]hat is essential to any moral worth of actions is *that the moral law determine the will immediately*" (*CPrR*, 5: 71). But he goes on to describe how the feeling of respect "lessens" the "hindrance to pure practical reason" and as a "representation" of the "relative weightiness of the law (with regard to a will affected by impulses)" removes the "counterweight" of such impulses and "supplies authority to the law, which now alone has influence," and further how this happens in the choice of maxims (*CPrR*, 5: 75–6). Both points are made in the statement that

> respect of the moral law must be regarded as also a positive though indirect effect of the moral law on feeling insofar as the law weakens the hindering influence of the inclinations by humiliating self-conceit, and must therefore be regarded as a subjective ground of activity – that is, as the incentive to compliance with the law – and as the ground for maxims of a course of life in conformity with it.

It is from this that there arises "an *interest*, which can never be attributed to any being unless it has reason and which signifies an *incentive* of the will insofar as it is *represented by reason*" (*CPrR*, 5: 79). I suggest that these comments may be reconciled with Kant's opening statement that for moral worth the moral law must determine the will immediately by taking the latter to refer to the noumenal determination of the will and the former to the phenomenal etiology of morally worthy action. At the noumenal level, the free will simply elects the moral law as its fundamental maxim, but this produces the complex phenomenal phenomenology in which self-conceit is painfully humbled but a positive feeling toward the capacity of our own reason to do that compensates for and outweighs the effect of other inclinations and allows the phenomenal agent to choose the morally correct path of action, which takes the form of choosing a morally correct maxim fitting the situation at hand. There are two pieces of evidence for this interpretation. First, Kant states that the hindering influence

[8] For my fuller account and some reference to the extensive literature on the subject, see Guyer 2010, reprinted in Guyer 2016: 235–59.

of the humiliation of self-conceit is a "positive though indirect effect of the moral law on feeling"; indirect because it is the phenomenal effect of a noumenal choice. Second, Kant remarks that all this is the ground for a "choice of maxims of a course of life in conformity with" the moral law, for such maxims, such as never to make false promises or take advantage of others in weaker positions than oneself or to cultivate one's talent and help others when one can, are maxims that presuppose facts about the empirical conditions of human existence, such as that our intentions are not automatically transparent to others and that our potential talents do need to be cultivated. Thus the choice of such maxims can only be supposed to take place in the phenomenal world, even if the fundamental choice whether to be moral or not may be supposed to take place noumenally.

Pistorius might well not have been convinced by this expanded account of the feeling of respect as the ground of an interest in morality, because it relies upon what he considered Kant's "problematic concept of freedom, transposed from the sensible world into the intelligible world, and takes from this world, according to [Kant's] own principles fully unknown to us, the grounds of the possibility and necessity of his categorical imperative" and of our interest in living up to it as well (*GM*, 37). Of course, Pistorius was not to succeed in persuading Kant to give up his *transcendental idealist theory of the freedom of the will, but the question might remain open* whether much of Kant's complex theory of the intermediation of the feeling of respect between choice of fundamental maxim and choice of particular maxims and the performance of actions upon the latter might not survive the elimination of Kant's theory of noumenal freedom.

Be that as it may, we can turn now to the second main addition to Kant's explicit response to Pistorius, namely, his lengthy account of his conception of the highest good in the *Critique of Practical Reason*. Obviously, Kant did not invent his theory of the highest good in order to respond to Pistorius; it is already present in the *Critique of Pure Reason* (see A 810–11/B 838–9). But that Kant gave the doctrine such extensive treatment in the second *Critique* could be taken to be a response to Pistorius's objection that Kant had not explained "for what" adherence to the moral law is good, that "we yet must finally come to an object or a final end [*Endzweck*] of the [moral] law, and must seek the assistance of the material, since with what is merely formal we cannot arrive at either the will or the law" (*GM*, 27). Kant specifically says that through reason's search for the unconditioned pure practical reason "seeks the unconditioned totality of the object of pure practical reason, under the name of the *highest good*" while also insisting that "although the highest good may be the whole *object* of a pure practical reason, that is, of a pure will, it is not on that account to be taken as its *determining ground*" (*CPrR*, 5: 108, 109). This could be intended to admonish Pistorius that although he, Kant, does have an account of the complete object or "final end" of adherence to the moral law, and it does involve human happiness as a goal of moral action, it also does not impair the purity of moral motivation.

Kant's presentation of his conception of the highest good in the second *Critique* could be taken as both a concession to Pistorius's insistence that the final end of morality must be grounded in a conception of human *nature* and as a critique of it. Kant introduces his concept with the statement that "pure practical reason ... seeks the unconditioned for the practically conditioned (which rests on inclinations and natural needs), not indeed as the determining ground of the will, but even when this is given (in the moral law), it seeks the unconditioned totality of the object of pure practical reason, under the name of the *highest good*" (*CPrR*, 5: 108). This suggests that the highest good is a composite of what each individual sees as his own good, that is, his own happiness and that of those others in whose happiness he happens to take an interest, combined with the determination of the individual's will by the moral law, which restricts his pursuit of happiness to what is allowed by his acceptance of the moral law. Kant's ensuing argument against both Epicureans and Stoics that the connection between virtue and happiness is synthetic rather than analytic likewise suggests that the highest good is a composite conception of the individual's natural and moral good (*CPrR*, 5: 111–13). Such a model of the highest good could be taken as a concession to Pistorius in its allowance that the desire for happiness is a part of human nature that must be must be acknowledged in the formation of any concept of the complete good for any human being, but also as a critique of Pistorius in its insistence that the pursuit of individual happiness is "practically conditioned" by the "unconditioned" validity of the moral law; Pistorius's own account of the highest good does not make the subordination of the pursuit of happiness to virtue clear. Kant's further claim that for the "whole and complete" good "*happiness* is also required, and that not merely in the partial eyes of a person who makes himself an end but even in the judgment of an impartial reason, which regards a person in the world generally as an end in itself," a claim that is based on the premise that "to need happiness, to be also worthy of it, and yet not to participate in it cannot be consistent with the perfect volition of a rational being," might be thought to be an even further critique of Pistorius: It states not merely the negative thesis that the individual pursuit of happiness must be constrained by the condition of compatibility with the demands of morality, but is a positive, moral rather than merely natural claim that any virtuous individual, not just oneself, *ought* to be happy because he or she is *worthy* of happiness (*CPrR*, 5: 110). This is a normative claim; thus, Kant could be agreeing with Pistorius that the highest good including happiness as well as virtue is the complete object of morality, but insisting that the ground for this fact is itself moral, the moral recognition of the worthiness of the virtuous to have their natural desire for happiness satisfied. In this way the moral would still be the ground of the good rather than vice versa. Kant would thus be responding to Pistorius that he does have a complete conception of the human good, but that this conception is still founded upon the moral law, not merely upon any natural conception of the human good.

Of course, this response depends upon the assumption that morality does itself require the interpretation of virtue as worthiness to be happy, an assumption that Kant takes for granted rather than explaining. But that is not the objection that Pistorius in turn makes to Kant's account of the highest good. His objection is rather that it still turns on "the present sensible nature of the human being," something that is no problem for Pistorius himself, who makes no pretense to an a priori moral theory, but which he thinks to be inconsistent with Kant's own premises (*KP*, 93). This is in his review of the *Critique of Practical Reason*, which as mentioned was mislaid and not published until Kant had published his own final statements about the highest good. Let us now look at Pistorius's review and then consider how Kant's further thoughts about the highest good might bear upon it even if, because of the delayed publication of the review, they could not have been intended to do so.

4 Pistorius's Second Review

Pistorius begins by correctly observing that the two main issues on which Kant intended to expand in the *Critique of Practical Reason* were "whether and to what extent pure reason is practical, [and] whether it has any relation to the faculty of desire," that is, the issue of our freedom to act in accordance with the moral law and that of the relation between the moral law and the desire for happiness (*KP*, 78). After a brief exposition of Kant's treatments of freedom and the highest good in the new book, Pistorius began his criticism with a renewed attack on the formalism of the categorical imperative. Here he argued that "the merely rational or consistent [*das bloße Vernunftmäßige oder Consequente*]" is not a sufficient condition for the determination of what is morally right, because both a "Christian" ethic of treating one's enemies kindly or a "Huronic" ethic of treating them with unrelenting hostility can be exercised in an equally "consistent and non-contradictory" way (*KP*, 86).[9] Since consistency is not a sufficient condition for morality, Pistorius maintains, the Kantian project of grounding morality solely on a conception of the "human being considered merely as a pure intelligence, merely on the rational part of his nature, without reference to the sensible part and its needs and

[9] The name "Huronic" is obviously derived from the Hurons, an Iroquoian-speaking confederacy of tribes of the indigenous peoples of northeastern North America. The peoples and their language are now properly referred to as "Wyandot."

inclinations," is doomed (*KP*, 88). In his view, a conception of the final end (*Endzweck*) of human beings cannot be established without reference to the "entire natural disposition of the human being [*die ganze Naturanlage des Menschen*]," and that is no problem for him; but in view of Kant's insistence that both the fundamental principle and the object of morality must be entirely a priori, it is inconsistent of Kant to appeal to the "present sensible nature of the human being" to establish his conception of the highest good (*KP*, 91). Here is the crucial passage:

> by happiness the author chiefly means external well-being and sensible gratification. Now if such happiness is reckoned as part of the highest good, thus also to the object and end of the moral law ... then the author evidently takes account of the present sensible nature of the human being in the determination of the concept of the highest good, in that he counts what only that demands (external well-being and sensible gratification) as part of the highest good, and here it must appear very inconsistent that in the determination of the law and the will in accord with it, which is to yield the highest good, he nevertheless does not want to take account of the sensible nature of the human being ... in a word ... he has not made his theory of happiness and his theory of virtue consistent ... in the theory of virtue he would seem to be stricter than *Zeno* yet in the theory of happiness more lax than Epicurus. (*KP*, 93)

Kant wants his moral principle to be entirely a priori and yet in his conception of the highest good he is forced to make empirical assumptions about human nature.

Still unaware of Pistorius's review, Kant returned to the issue of the highest good in both his essay on "Theory and Practice" and in the Preface to *Religion within the Boundaries of Mere Reason*. He still made no reference to it in the *Metaphysics of Morals*. Nevertheless, these works can be regarded as containing Kant's further response to this criticism from Pistorius. First, Kant shows how a conception of the highest good, perhaps revised from that of the second *Critique* in one crucial regard, can be generated by the application of the moral law to the single empirical assumption that human beings do seek their own happiness, thus requiring no appeal to the mysterious conception of worthiness to be happy. Second, in his own doctrine of virtue, Kant shows how to take account of more empirical information about the human situation without sacrificing anything of the purity of the fundamental principle of morality. In other words, Kant's final work in moral philosophy shows how his own combination of the a priori principle of morality and empirical facts about the human condition is *not* a violation of his own methodological principles, and in this way answers Pistorius's final criticism of his work.

5 Kant's Defense against Pistorius

Kant's first step is to clarify both his conception of the highest good as the necessary object of morality and his derivation of it. While the *Critique of*

Practical Reason allowed the interpretation that the complete object of morality is the perfection of *one's own* virtue combined with the realization of *one's own* happiness, the latter being restricted by the former but not grounded in it, Kant's 1793 essay "On the Common Saying: That May Be Right in Theory but It Is of No Use in Practice" makes clear that the highest good is rather "universal happiness combined with and in conformity with the purest morality throughout the world," so that from the point of view of the individual agent "the determination of will which limits itself and its aim of belonging to such a whole to this condition is *not selfish*;" divine authorship of the laws of nature must then be postulated so that the realization of both the purest morality and universal happiness "throughout the world" can be regarded by us as at least possible, since it would be irrational for us to strive to realize a goal the realization of which we cannot believe to be possible (*TP*, 8: 279, 280n.). Kant's characterization of the highest good in the Preface to *Religion within the Boundaries of Mere Reason* also makes clear that universal rather than individual happiness must be the goal of the highest good. Here Kant begins by premising that a rational will cannot act without an end or object, although the idea of such an end must "rise out of morality and is not its foundation" (*RBMR*, 6: 5); he then makes clear that this end must be universal happiness rather than merely one's own happiness by contrasting the "objective end (i.e., an end which we ought to have)" as "one which is assigned to us as such by reason alone" with "one's own happiness" as the merely "subjective ultimate end of rational beings (they each *have* this end by virtue of their nature which is dependent upon sensible objects)" (*RBMR*, 6: 6). If one's own happiness is a merely subjective end, which each naturally has, that leaves the happiness of all as the only possible objective end, which can be assigned to each of us by reason rather than by nature.

But while these formulations clarify Kant's concept of the highest good, they still do not clarify how he proposes to derive the necessity of this end, and thus do not clarify what his alternative to Pistorius's naturalistic argument is supposed to be. The essay on theory and practice hints at Kant's argument by stating that "duty is nothing other than the *limitation* of the will to the condition of a giving of universal law possible through a maxim adopted, whatever the object of the will or the end may be (thus happiness as well)" (*TP*, 8: 279–80). But it takes the Doctrine of Virtue of the *Metaphysics of Morals*, four years later, to make completely clear Kant's thought that the only *morally* permissible way to will one's *natural* maxim to seek one's own happiness with whatever assistance in the pursuit of it one might be able to obtain from others is to will the universalization of that maxim, in other words, to will that *all* should assist whatever others they can in their individual pursuits of happiness. Kant makes his argument most clearly in his discussion of "duties of love":

[E]very morally practical relation to human beings is a relation among them represented by pure reason, that is, a relation of free actions in accordance with maxims that qualify for a giving of universal law and so cannot be selfish [*ex solipsismo produentes*]. I want everyone else to be benevolent toward me [*benevolentiam*]; hence I ought also to be benevolent toward everyone else. But since all *others* with the exception of myself would not be *all*, so that the maxim would not have within it the universality of a law, which is still necessary for imposing obligation, the law making benevolence a duty will include myself, as an object of benevolence, in the command of practical reason. (*MM*, 6: 451)

The first two sentences of this passage clearly state that if I apply the moral demand for universal legislation to my natural maxim of seeking benevolence from others (for the realization of my own happiness), I must will benevolence toward everyone else – that is, I must will that *I* be benevolent to others but also that *others* be benevolent to others. The last sentence allows two possibilities: first, even though I cannot *morally* will benevolence toward myself, *others* can and must, so my own happiness will be included in the total object of morality willed by all; or, second, that once I have universalized I can properly will *my own* happiness along with that of all others, so that in particular circumstances in which I can either only or else most effectively promote my own happiness, I have moral permission or even a moral command to do so. But either way, it is clear that morality requires that collectively all promote the happiness of all: thus, even though Kant does not use the term "highest good" here, he has made clear how the application of morality's requirement of universalizability to *everyone's* natural maxim of seeking their own happiness gives rise to what the other works of the 1790s have clarified is the happiness component of the highest good, namely universal happiness. Kant's argument thus shares with Pistorius the premise that human beings have a natural interest in *their own* happiness, but shows how morality itself, and only morality, requires the generalization of this goal, a morally grounded pursuit of the happiness of all.

A further clarification of the relation between morality and human nature is provided by Kant's general method of deriving duties in the *Metaphysics of Morals*. Kant's method in this work is to "take as our object the particular *nature* of human beings, which is cognized only by experience, in order to *show* in it what can be inferred from universal moral principles," which "will in no way detract from the purity of these principles or cast doubt on their *a priori* source" (*MM*, 6: 217). In other words, the duties specific to human beings are to be derived by showing what follows from the fundamental, a priori principle of morality, grounded in pure practical reason, for beings, like ourselves, who have such reason, but also have certain basic characteristics and live in circumstances that can only be known empirically. This is Kant's concession to but refinement of Pistorius's approach: The empirical nature of human beings has to be recognized in order to derive their duties, but the fundamental principles of these duties is rational and therefore knowable a priori.

We can focus here on ethical duties, those that, unlike duties of right, morality itself does not allow to be enforced by external constraints, so must instead be self-enforced only by respect for the moral law itself on the part of individual human beings (*MM*, 6: 218–19). Ethical duties include the subcategory of duties of virtue, which are those duties that can only be self-enforced by respect for the moral law, which in turn requires that each human be treated as an end and never merely as a means, but also require the pursuit of an end that is also a duty (*GW*, 4: 429). At the most general level, there are two categories of ends that are also duties and therefore of duties of virtue, namely the perfection of oneself and the happiness of others (*MM*, 6: 385–6). One example of the duty of self-perfection is the duty to develop one's "natural perfection," one's potential powers of "spirit" such as the ability to reason, "soul" such as memory, and "body," through appropriate mental and physical training and practice (*MM*, 6: 444–5). This duty is based on the obvious yet only empirically known facts that human beings need these capacities to be able to pursue various ends with a reasonable prospect of success, and therefore to be able to reasonably *set* such ends, but also, unlike various other species, are not born with all the capacities they will ever have already fully developed.[10] It is an empirical fact that humans need a lengthy process of education and self-development to achieve their full potential, but given this empirical though incontrovertible fact the a priori principle that the full development of our freedom is an end in itself then gives rise to the duty of self-perfection. Likewise, to return to the duty of benevolence to others, the fact that no human being can reasonably think that he could ever realize any end he could freely yet reasonably set for himself solely out of his own resources, and therefore must naturally adopt the maxim of seeking the assistance of others on appropriate occasions, is contingent and empirically known; but it is the a priori principle of morality that requires the universalizability of our maxims that anyone who wills the assistance of others when he needs it and it is in their ability to provide it must also be prepared to render assistance to others when they need it and he can supply it. This is a consequence of applying the fundamental principle of morality to a basic fact about human capabilities and circumstances.

This then is the ultimate form of Kant's defense against Pistorius's searching critique, based on an empirical conception of the human good. Kant's practical philosophy does specify a conception of the human good that takes into

[10] See my "Setting and Pursuing Ends," in Guyer 2016: ch. 6.

account the contingent but incontrovertible facts of human physiology, psychology, and ecology, but it derives the human obligation to promote this good, whether subsumed under the general concept of the highest good in the world or parceled out into the full complement of specific juridical and ethical duties, from a fundamental principle of morality that is grounded in pure practical reason and therefore can be known entirely a priori.

2 Freedom and Ethical Necessity

A Kantian Response to Ulrich (1788)

Katerina Deligiorgi

Kant presents his argument about transcendental freedom, in the first *Critique*, not just as a new solution to an intractable metaphysical problem, but also as a vital part of his moral philosophy: freedom in the transcendental sense is essential for moral agency, because only possession of such freedom can secure governance by the moral "ought" as a genuine possibility for human beings.[1] Transcendental freedom is necessary for the moral "ought," as Kant conceives it, that is, as a command of pure reason. Given this conceptual link between the "ought" and transcendental freedom, any problems with Kant's theory of freedom would directly affect his ethics. On the other hand, and unlike most traditional metaphysical treatments of the topic of freedom, in Kant's account it is the reality of the moral "ought" that secures the truth of the claim that human beings are transcendentally free. Skepticism about the "ought" would then stand to damage the claim to freedom. The idea of a command that belongs, as Kant puts it, to an "order" that pure reason creates itself in "complete spontaneity" is vulnerable to doubts about its reality and its efficacy within the network of causes to which all beings and things are bound (*CPR*, A 548/B 576).

The aim of the paper is to examine these issues through a set of arguments presented by Johann August Heinrich Ulrich in his 1788 book *Eleutheriology*

The paper has improved enormously thanks to the meticulous attention and helpful suggestions of the editors, James A. Clarke and Gabriel Gottlieb, and the anonymous referee. An early version of the paper was presented at the "Morality after Kant" workshop, held at the University of York in 2017, and benefitted from discussion with the participants in that workshop.

[1] Kant makes the connection between the solution to the antinomy that yields the transcendental conception of freedom and morality explicit in the section on the "Clarification of the cosmological idea of a freedom in combination with the universal natural necessity" (*CPR*, A 542/B 570). He hints at this connection in an earlier section when he introduces the idea of "pure morals" in the context of explaining that certain metaphysical problems cannot be simply ignored (*CPR*, A 480/B 508). Relevant here is also Kant's note on the "Clarification" section: "What speculative philosophy could not succeed at, bringing reason out of the field of sensibility to something real outside it, practical reason is able to do, namely, giving an existence that is not sensible, [and] through laws that are grounded on reason. This is morality, if one admits it through freedom" (cited in *CPR*, 537; *AA*, 23: 41).

or On Freedom and Necessity.[2] I devote the first part of the paper to presenting Ulrich's views, focusing on his criticism of Kant's theory of transcendental freedom. Ulrich uses what has come to be known in the contemporary literature on the metaphysics of freedom as the problem of luck. Critics of libertarianism argue that the denial of deterministic causation leaves choices fundamentally undetermined and, therefore, on libertarian assumptions, what agents do is a matter of luck.[3] The criticism presents an interesting challenge. In the second part of the paper I show how this challenge can be met from a Kantian perspective. Ulrich's critical argument, however, is not the only element of his engagement with Kant's philosophy that warrants attention. Equally interesting is his treatment of the Kantian thesis about the categorical nature of moral imperatives, which Ulrich endorses while rejecting Kant's commitment to the idea of a pure ethics. While Ulrich's naturalistic conception of ethical necessity is ultimately flawed, it helps bring into view the relations between practical and theoretical claims in Kant's defense of transcendental freedom.

1 Freedom: A Problem about Determination

In his opening dedication, Ulrich asserts that "properly understood, determinism does not abolish ethics, rather it protects it" (*EFN*, not numbered in the original). In the introductory sections of the book, he defends this claim mainly by appealing to common sense – for example, he points out that nobody worries whether or not a man of "reformed and ennobled character" can "still act, think, or will badly"; what matters is that such a man does not want to do anything other than what is right – and to philosophical tradition (*EFN*, 7, 11–15). He presents the systematic defense of his position in the main part of

[2] The book was a textbook for Ulrich's lectures in Jena. Kant responds to the book in a letter to C. J. Kraus (notes of which are in *AA*, 23: 79–81) . Kraus's review, which was indebted to Kant's notes, was published in 1788 (*PP*, 8: 453–60). On the historical significance of Ulrich's book, see Di Giovanni 2005: 108–18.

[3] The problem of luck in the form that is relevant to Ulrich's argument is in Mele 2006; for discussion, see Coffman 2010 and Franklin 2011. Mele, like Ulrich, argues that the libertarian cannot explain why a free agent on the libertarian account chooses option *a* rather than some alternative *b*. The libertarian cannot give such an explanation because the libertarian position presupposes that the agent is free and no facts can be given that show why the agent's choice is determined in the way it is rather than in some other way. This indeterminism amounts to chance. Libertarian responses to the problem of luck include probabilistic explanations, which cite the conditions that raise the probabilities of specific actions performed by specific agents, and singular case explanations, which require that the agent is able to cite reasons for her actions. Whether either of these is available to Kant is something I discuss in the final section of this paper. The probabilistic account is generally associated with Kane. See Kane 1989 and 1996; but see too the event-causal position defended in Clarke 2005. The main contemporary agent-causal account is due to Tim O'Connor; see O'Connor 2007 for specific engagement with Mele.

the book. Chapters 1–5 are devoted to a systematic defense of determinism, while the last two chapters, 6–7, focus mainly on the ethics of the position. The core theoretical thesis, defended in the early chapters and essential for Ulrich's criticism of Kant, is presented as follows. Determinism, on Ulrich's definition of it, is belief in the existence of "determining [*entschiedene*] and universal necessity" (*EFN*, 8). The advantage of the position is that it secures everyday and scientific cognitions, by justifying our expectations that what we experience is explicable by reference to causes or "grounds [*Gründen*]" (*EFN*, 8). Epistemic expectations of "order, lawfulness and intelligibility" depend on deterministic necessity and the thoroughgoing application of natural laws (*EFN*, 8). Before I turn to Ulrich's engagement with Kant's arguments, from both his theoretical and practical philosophy, I want to discuss briefly the notion of "ground," a notion that plays a key role in Ulrich's theoretical argument, which includes his criticism of Kant's theory of freedom.

As we have just seen, the central thesis in Ulrich's defense of determinism is that our expectations of the intelligibility, order, and lawfulness in nature depend on the existence of regularity of ground/grounded relations among natural phenomena, which is secured only by deterministic necessity. Although it is evident, from the presentation of the position in the introduction, that Ulrich believes this to be an easily graspable and uncontroversial claim, it is worth examining further his use of "ground" in the opening statement of his views. This is because it is important to distinguish different senses of the term according to whether it features in everyday requests for explanation or in metaphysically ambitious explanatory projects. In the context of everyday explanatory demands, "ground" stands for the reasons that explain people's actions and also, like the more usual "*Ursache*," for the causes cited to explain natural phenomena. In the book, Ulrich uses "grounds" and "causes" interchangeably. He only differentiates between the two when he claims that the search for specific causes (*Ursachen*) is justified on the assumption that there are determining grounds (*Gründe*), which permit thoroughgoing connection between phenomena without exceptions (*EFN*, 21, 41–2). While it is plausible to assert that there is a relation between the fulfillment of everyday explanatory needs and assumptions about how the world is, where these assumptions guide the search for explanation, this thought alone cannot support Ulrich's claim about unexceptionally determining grounds (*EFN*, 21). The thesis about unexceptionally determining grounds requires a more demanding conception of ground than is used or needed in everyday explanations. To reach the deterministic position about natural necessity that Ulrich advances here, the search for explanation must be guided by a different set of expectations. In other words, the more demanding conception of ground that justifies determinism has a counterpart that guides and sustains ambitious explanatory expectations, by guaranteeing, for example, the application of the principle that similar effects have similar causes (*EFN*, 16) and that given some state of affairs an explanation is available why it is so and not otherwise (*EFN*, 17). This more demanding conception is given by the principle of sufficient reason (PSR), especially as formulated by Leibniz, who is mentioned in the brief bibliography Ulrich provides in the introduction (*EFN*, 13).[4]

Ulrich's reliance on Leibniz's formulations of PSR is key to understanding his criticism of Kant. Leibniz gives two versions of PSR. The first formulation, following Aquinas's conception of the principle, serves to justify a regressive quest after what is ontologically prior and foundational. Adherence to this version of PSR is needed for Ulrich's claim that the causal relations cited in explanations depend, or have their ground, in thoroughgoing natural necessity, which functions as the foundational and ontologically prior ground. The second formulation elaborates the demand for a *sufficient* reason in terms of a demand for a form of explanation that is, in the contemporary terminology, "contrastive," that is, it is an explanation that gives a reason why something is such and such and not otherwise.[5] Leibniz presents the contrastive

[4] In his introduction, Ulrich focuses on the so-called causal principle, which stands for the idea that there is no effect without a cause. As Ulrich rightly points out, the use of this principle is widespread. In appraising Ulrich's arguments, however, it is important to specify what the principle entails. Usually, it entails a substantive conception of causal relations, where this is to be contrasted with a semantic relation between the meanings of "cause" and "effect," as discussed in Hume, for example. Importantly, having such a substantive conception of causal relations is compatible with modest explanatory demands, which are satisfied once antecedent causes for observed phenomena are identified. To motivate the regress needed to launch a metaphysically ambitious explanatory project, a notion of cause is needed according to which the cause is qualitatively different and superior to that which it explains. Formative for the tradition to which Ulrich belongs is Thomas Aquinas, who relies on the causal principle in the search for an explanation of the existence (*esse*) of non-necessary beings. This search leads to a consideration of hierarchical relations of ontological dependence, leading up to a cause that is necessary. This philosophical inheritance is discernible in Ulrich's argument in his demand for a complete explanation of actions.

[5] Leibniz presents contrastive PSR in the following extract, using "cause" and "reason" interchangeably:

> the reason [*causa*] why some particular contingent thing exists, rather than others, should not be sought in its definition alone, but in a comparison with other things. For since there is an infinity of possible things which, nevertheless, do not exist, the reason [*ratio*] why these exist rather than those should not be sought in their definition ... but from an extrinsic source. (Leibniz 1989: 19)

That the explanation is not in the definition means that it is not a feature of the substance itself as would follow from Leibniz's principle of predicate-in-notion, which states that: "The nature of an individual substance or of a complete being is to have a notion so complete that it is sufficient to contain and to allow us to deduce from it all the predicates of the subject to which this notion is attributed" (Leibniz 1989: 41). A clear case of the dual use of PSR is the following from the *Principles of Nature and Grace*: "the first question we have the right to ask will be, *why is there something rather than nothing*? For nothing is simpler and easier than something" leads to "a necessary being, carrying the reason for its existence within itself. Otherwise, we would not yet have a sufficient reason where one could end the series. And this ultimate reason for things is

interpretation of PSR as: "nothing happens without it being possible for someone who knows enough to give a reason sufficient to determine *why it is so and not otherwise*."[6] An illustration of Leibniz's use of this interpretation of PSR can be found in his correspondence with Clarke about absolute space. Leibniz is critical of absolute space because it violates PSR: if the orientation of the world is God's free choice, as Clarke claims, then for Leibniz this freedom is senseless because it explains nothing. Most clearly and famously, the contrastive sense of PSR is used by Leibniz to explain God's choice of the actual world over the many possible worlds that he could have chosen instead. Optimality, the idea that the actual world is the best of all possible worlds, explains by giving a reason why this world is the case and not others. The originality of Ulrich's criticism of Kant's theory of freedom consists in his use of the contrastive version of PSR.

1.1 Chance

Ulrich's critical discussion of Kant's theory of freedom comes immediately after the introductory sections. It contributes to a general argument intending to show that there are no philosophically credible defenses of freedom, or, as the title of the chapter has it, that "[t]here is no middle way between necessity and chance, between determinism and indeterminism" (*EFN*, 16). The first subsection, entitled "Necessity," contains Ulrich's views on the categorical imperative, which anticipate his positive argument about the ethics of determinism. It is the second section, entitled "Chance," that contains his criticism of transcendental freedom. I start with the latter partly because it is the centerpiece of Ulrich's argument against libertarian freedom and the basis of his defense of determinism, the truth of which is presupposed by and sets the metaphysical context for the ethics.

The purpose of the argument is to show that Kantian freedom reduces to chance. Ulrich starts by defining chance as a happening without determinate grounds (*EFN*, 19). He then asserts that a metaphysical defense of freedom that is plausible can be given provided freedom is understood as chance or as

called *God*" (Leibniz 2004: 5). Then supposing that there are some things, "we must be able to give a reason for *why they must exist in this way*, and not otherwise" (Leibniz 2004: 4). Aside from the contrastive version of PSR, Ulrich is also relying on a principle that follows Leibniz's PSR, possibly in conjunction with the predicate-in-notion, that has a criterial role for explanations and states that one explanation cannot be used for two incompatible phenomena. This principle has gained currency in contemporary philosophy of science as "Leibniz's principle": "It is impossible that, on one occasion, circumstances of type *C* adequately explain an outcome of type *E* and, on another occasion, adequately explain an outcome of type *E′* that is incompatible with *E*" (Salmon 1998: 155; see also 329).

[6] Leibniz 2004: 7; my emphasis.

radical indeterminism, which Ulrich treats as equivalent to chance. However, Ulrich argues that the metaphysical plausibility of such a defense is offset by its epistemic costs – namely, that the appeal to chance or indeterminism leaves us without explanations based on "causes" (*EFN*, 41–2, 102). As well as pressing the general point about explanatory inadequacy, he argues that the position is morally unsustainable: indeterminism undermines morality because it makes impossible what is essential for moral accountability, namely, the identification of the determining grounds of the action (*EFN*, 87–8). Ulrich, therefore, concludes that chance or indeterminism should be rejected and proposes an ethics that is based on deterministic assumptions. The criticism of Kant's theory of freedom plays an important role in this argument, because it aims to show that the doctrine of "transcendental freedom or absolute spontaneity" fails to explain free actions in a way that "unites freedom and natural necessity," and that transcendental freedom is, consequently, nothing more than chance (*EFN*, 19).

The main tool Ulrich uses in his criticism of transcendental freedom is the contrastive interpretation of PSR or what he calls "the causal principle." He puts the Kantian doctrine to the test by asking whether transcendental freedom allows for an explanation why the agent acted in this way and not otherwise. At first, this looks like an unfair demand, because the concept of freedom that would seem more relevant to the topic of contrastive explanation is that of practical freedom, the freedom to do or to refrain from doing, what is traditionally called a "two-way power." The concept of transcendental freedom, by contrast, is mainly a negative concept, signifying absence of necessitation by antecedent causes. Kant's connection of practical and transcendental freedom, however, makes Ulrich's question appropriate. Kant argues that the practical idea of freedom, which describes the human power of choice, is "grounded" on the transcendental idea and that "the abolition of transcendental freedom would also simultaneously eliminate all practical freedom" (*CPR*, A 533/B 561). If this ground proves problematic in the way Ulrich claims, then indeterminacy will be transmitted to the practical level.[7] So Ulrich's concern with explanation is perfectly legitimate.

Ulrich presents Kant's position aiming to show that his concern with explanation cannot be met. He identifies two sides to the Kantian position. On the phenomenal "side," human actions and decisions obey natural necessities (*EFN*, 22). So from this perspective, Kant is a "strict determinist"

[7] At the practical level, reason-giving is undermined because although reasons can be cited by the agent to explain the chosen course of action, such reasons *ex hypothesi* are the upshot of a free process, grounded on transcendental freedom, which means that at some point there is no reason that can be cited as a reason for the reason.

(*EFN*, 22).[8] On the "other side," however, Kant posits an extraordinary "*neutrum*," which does not seem to fit existing classifications. By "other side" Ulrich presumably means what Kant calls the intelligible character of actions. It is with respect to this intelligible character that Kant argues that human actions are free in the transcendental sense: "in its intelligible character (even though we can have nothing more than merely the general concept of it), this subject would nevertheless have to be declared free of all influences of sensibility and determination by appearances" (*CPR*, A 540–1/B 568–9). Ulrich's calling the side of freedom a "*neutrum*" anticipates his critical argument that transcendental freedom is neither one thing nor another.[9]

Ulrich's argument is based mainly on an analysis of the following passage from the first *Critique*, which he quotes in full (*EFN*, 23–4):

> By freedom in the cosmological sense, on the contrary, I understand the faculty [*Vermögen*] of beginning a state **from itself**, the causality of which does not in turn stand under another cause determining it in time in accordance with the law of nature. Freedom in this signification is a pure transcendental idea, which, first, contains nothing borrowed from experience, and second, the object of which also cannot be given determinately in any experience, because it is a universal law – even of the possibility of all experience – that everything that happens must have a cause, and hence that the causality of the cause, as itself having happened or arisen, must in turn have a cause; through this law, then, the entire field of experience, however far it may reach, is transformed into the sum total of mere nature. But since in such a way no absolute totality of conditions in causal relations is forthcoming, reason creates the idea of a spontaneity, which could start to act from itself, without needing to be preceded by any other cause that in turn determines it to action according to the law of causal connection. (*CPR*, A 533/B 561)

Ulrich then proceeds to examine the plausibility of the concept of a "faculty" – or, better, "power" (*Vermögen*) – that allows the beginning of a state from itself in a way that is genuinely independent of all grounds (*Gründe*).

Starting with the negative characterization that Kant provides, namely, that the power signifies an idea that contains nothing borrowed from experience, Ulrich proposes that we understand the freedom in question as independence from sensuous causes, which are identifiable as temporally preceding appearances (*EFN*, 24–5). This suggests that the power is a property of the human being qua thing in itself. Since the causal chains that are produced by this supra-empirical agent are part of the phenomenal world, they must *also* follow normal natural causal laws, just as Kant himself asserts. But if the products of this power obey causal laws, then the supposition that there is such a power

[8] Kant makes the claim explicitly: "In its empirical character, this subject, as appearance, would thus be subject to the causal connection, in accordance with all the laws of determination; and to that extent it would be nothing but part of the world of sense" (*CPR*, A 540–1, B 568–9).

[9] The anonymous reader's comments were particularly helpful in helping me clarify this point.

seems superfluous since the actions it purportedly produces are already explicable in terms of temporally preceding appearances. Ulrich makes this point by paraphrasing Kant: "all actions of men as appearances [*in der Erscheinung*] are with respect to their empirical character and the other co-operating causes determined in accordance with the natural order" (*EFN*, 25). Therefore, Ulrich's first line of attack, his criticism of explanatory superfluity, follows simply the implications of Kant's negative characterization of freedom.

Ulrich then reconsiders, arguing that the faculty of beginning a state from itself cannot be thought of as "mere independence from empirical causes," because, if it were just that, it could not determine appearances (*EFN*, 30). But the point of introducing the "cosmological" sense of freedom is to establish the determining power of this faculty and thereby ensure that actions are free. Therefore, the freedom in question must be "positive" and describe the power to "initiate a series of happenings from itself" (*EFN*, 30). In this case, Ulrich argues, we need to know what the determining ground for this power is, the nature of its causality.[10] If this cannot be established, then Kant's position is a *neutrum*, neither determinism, because while determining power is claimed no determining grounds are given, nor freedom, because without an account of its originating character, all that is left is chance.

Ulrich argues that the determining ground of freedom in the positive sense cannot be established. Contrastive explanation is key to the argument. Ulrich asks for a contrastive account of the causality of freedom or, as he also calls it, causality of reason. He asks why, for any action *a*, the faculty of beginning a state from itself determines appearances through its causality in one way rather than another. Kant, he states, has no answer to this question (*EFN*, 31). Once we leave behind the thought that the phenomenal character of the action is all there is, we also leave behind the possibility of adducing facts from the circumstances of the action to explain its occurrence contrastively. The idea of transcendental freedom is there to ensure that actions are not predetermined and that agents have the possibility of choosing which action to perform. Hence it is the ground for the exercise of practical freedom or freedom of choice. At the same time, transcendental freedom undermines the very idea of choice between alternatives and therefore the possibility of explaining agential causality contrastively because it is "the persisting [*beharrliche*] condition of all free [*willkürlich*] actions" (*EFN*, 29). All free actions have the same explanation, they are all products of the same causality. Therefore, for

[10] Ulrich is not after an explanation of freedom as such, because this would not address his worry about determination and explanation of actions. One can explain human freedom by claiming, for example, that God made us free. One can be committed to this, just as one can be committed to the existence of transcendental freedom, without having thereby answered Ulrich's question about the ground of free actions in the contrastive sense of reason Ulrich demands.

transcendentally free exercises of the practical freedom of choice, there is no determining fact that can explain why an agent performed one action rather than another. Hence, Ulrich concludes:

> Overall I do not see how the question can be avoided: why is this power used with respect to some actions and not others? Either something is present in one instance that contains the ground for its use and in another instance the ground for its omission, or not. In the first case, we have necessity, in the other chance [*Zufall*]. (*EFN*, 34)

Under pressure from the contrastive PSR, Kant's position is revealed to be reducible to indeterminism or chance.[11] If Ulrich's criticism is sound, then the doctrine of transcendental freedom fails on three counts: it cannot satisfy a reasonable request for contrastive explanation, it does not reconcile freedom with natural necessity, and it cannot show how the moral ought determines actions. So, on the basis of the last two points, the doctrine is damaging for both Kant's transcendental philosophy and his ethics.

Ulrich's final critical move is to consider and reject a possible solution to the problem of explanation and of the ethical determination of actions. Since, on Kant's account, the determining ground for practical freedom is cosmological freedom, if a determining ground for cosmological freedom were to be identified in order to address these problems, then it would have to be located in the noumenal realm. The moral ought is a plausible candidate for such a ground since it has a non-empirical origin. So the moral ought would be the determining power of the noumenal self who in turn determines the actions attributed to the phenomenal self. To avoid the obvious problem with this solution – namely, that it only explains morally good actions – morally flawed actions must have as their ultimate determining ground a weakness in a person's intelligible character.[12] This position is noumenal determinism: it states that what determines the exercise of an agent's causal powers is the unalterable nature of their intelligible character. Because the ground of the actions is

[11] A clear contemporary statement of this criticism is given by Mele as follows:

> [I]f the question why an agent exercised his agent-causal power at *t* in deciding to *A* rather than exercising it at *t* in any of the alternative ways he does in other possible worlds with the same past and laws of nature is, in principle, unanswerable – unanswerable because there is no fact or truth to be reported in a correct answer, not because of any limitations in those to whom the question is asked or in their audience – and his exercising it at *t* in so deciding has an effect on how his life goes, I count that as luck for the agent. (Mele 2006: 70)

[12] Ulrich believes that his account, premised on the continuity between ethical and natural necessity, helps explain both why an agent acts the way she does and how some actions show law-likeness while others do not (*EFN*, 39–40). Generally, he is hostile to the idea of attributing moral relevance to a supra-empirical power – which is how he reads spontaneity – not just because of the problem of determination discussed here, but also because it is unclear how such a power can be cultivated and perfected through "practice and effort" (*EFN*, 37). On how Ulrich anticipates the problem of noumenal determinism or fatalism see Gardner 2017.

beyond the agent's control, the position cannot accommodate the normative aspects of ethics, which include advice, correction, direction and so on. In addition, the position has revisionist implications for the use of terms such as "wicked" or "virtuous"; while such terms retain their evaluative meaning, such evaluations serve to identify the moral lot of different agents as their conduct manifests the moral valence of the noumenal necessities they fall under. From the perspective of ethics then, noumenal determinism is hardly preferable to chance.

1.2 Necessity

Under "Necessity," Ulrich sets out his views about the relation between ethics and determinism. Central to this discussion, and for Ulrich's ethics more generally, is the concept of "ethical necessity." Ethical necessity stands for the idea that what is morally commanded "ought to happen [*geschehen solle*]" (*EFN*, 16). Ulrich elaborates on what he means by ethical necessity in a discussion of Kant's "absolute or so-called categorical imperative," which he treats as a predecessor concept, presenting Kant's ethics very favorably and sympathetically (*EFN*, 17). Ulrich's claiming common ground with Kant is intriguing, because ethical necessity is part of a deterministic ethics, whereas the categorical imperative is the presentation of the moral law for human agents, the distinct thought of which is the *ratio cognoscendi* of freedom (*CPrR*, 5: 5). As we shall see, Ulrich's aim is to show that Kant's ethics can be recast in a deterministic framework without loss.

The argument hinges on the sense Ulrich gives to "ethical necessity." As he first introduces it, the term is used to explain the importance of moral considerations in human life by reference to a distinctive ethical necessity, which Ulrich also calls, following Kant, an "absolute ought" (*EFN*, 18; see *GW*, 4: 421). In support of this claim, he cites Kant's distinction between categorical and hypothetical imperatives, arguing that categorical imperatives are not reducible to hypothetical ones (*EFN*, 17). On one interpretation of these passages, which fits with Ulrich's appeal to Kant, what Ulrich presents here is a claim about the normative authority of moral commands. The idea, which has become dominant in the contemporary discussion of Kant's notion of a "categorical" imperative, is that moral considerations – for example, that something is right, or obligatory – override other kinds of considerations.[13] On this interpretation then, Ulrich's claim about ethical necessity translates into a claim about the authoritative nature of ethical commands, such that an

[13] The claim that moral considerations are overriding is used widely, though with slight variations in usage and emphasis, to explain the sense in which the moral imperative is "categorical" for Kant; see Hanna 2006: 302; Hill 2000: 289; Wilson 2008: 373.

agent who is aware of them cannot fail to take them into account and accords them priority over other considerations when deliberating about what to do.

However, this interpretation stands to mislead. Ulrich's aim is to show that the necessity Kant claims on behalf of the moral law, as the ground of authoritative commands (e.g., in *GW*, 4: 389), must be thought of as a species of natural necessity, indeed, as the "true natural necessity" (*EFN*, 17, 94–5). So Ulrich's argument does not aim to establish the claim that essentially different types of necessity exist, but rather to provide a unified account of necessity that fits our understanding of nature. The advantage Ulrich claims for his view is that it can better serve substantive theses of Kant's ethics, especially regarding the practical efficacy of the moral ought and the discipline demanded for moral conduct (*EFN*, 38, 48). The reason he gives is that on his account the exercise of moral agency does not depend on free will, but is rather the product of the different determining forces influencing the will (*EFN*, 51–2). Ulrich goes as far as to say that notions such as "ought" and "duty" and "legislation" mislead us insofar as they tend to obscure the unified character of moral and natural forces (*EFN*, 65).

Ethical necessity, then, signals the assimilation of moral imperatives to naturally determining forces in the context of a defense of deterministic causation. The position does not lead to moral determinism, because, Ulrich argues, ethical necessity is but one of the many forces that are exerted on individuals and shape their lives and therefore it is manifested in different ways and to different degrees in people's actions (*EFN*, 18, 37, 66–7). By putting ethical necessity on an equal footing with other forces, Ulrich avoids moral determinism, but makes it very hard to maintain that it is also a "true natural necessity" (*EFN*, 17, 94–5). If "true" is meant as an honorific, then the justification for awarding this honorific is unclear. Relatedly, if contextual and gradual qualifications are admitted to the notion of ethical necessity, then it is not as easy to maintain the early claim that ethical necessity is an "absolute ought."

To better understand Ulrich's position, we need to consider his rejection of pure reason as "necessary for cognizing the categorical imperative" (*EFN*, 17). The main argument in support of this, besides his criticism of the causality of pure reason, concerns the objectivity and efficacy of ethical principles. Ulrich introduces the topic by citing Kant's distinction between subjective and objective principles of willing, adding that the moral "ought" is, strictly speaking, a "will" that holds for "every rational being" (*GW*, 4: 449, cited in *EFN*, 38). He then interprets this to mean the rational pursuit of goals human beings share, such as gaining approval, attaining well-being, and pursuing various interests (*EFN*, 39, 57–9). On Ulrich's interpretation, then, moral laws express the rationally discernible principles for the perfection of human abilities displayed in the pursuit of these general goals. In effect, then, categorical demands are reduced to or absorbed by demands of prudence. What differentiates natural from ethical necessity is that the former is "blind or brutish" while the latter is internally accessible to rational agents as a moral "insight" (*EFN*, 16, 66). In light of this distinction, it is possible to understand the idea that ethical necessity is a "true" natural necessity, on the grounds that it is rationally perspicuous and this feature warrants the honorific "true."

The accessibility of rational principles is not convincing as a justification for the qualitative distinction Ulrich seems to want to draw between general natural necessity and ethical necessity. This is because his defense of determinism has at its basis the idea that expectations of intelligibility regarding natural processes are justified and secured through universal determinism. So natural necessity is not blind and brutish after all; it is simply accessible through observation, rather than insight. Equally, the objectivity and efficacy of ethical principles – the rules concerning the perfection of one's natural talents, faculties, and dispositions, which Ulrich defends in the end – do not support the claim to absoluteness he uses to introduce the notion of ethical necessity – we cultivate this talent or that faculty provided we have good reasons for doing so, not because we are under an unconditional obligation so to do.[14]

2 A Kantian Response: Grounds Revisited

Ulrich's key critical claim is that, despite being presented as a power of determination, transcendental freedom is no such thing and therefore reduces to chance or indeterminism. The argument supporting this conclusion relies heavily on the contrastive version of PSR, which asks for an explanation why an agent chooses *a* rather than *b*. Under conditions of transcendental freedom, such an explanation is not available. This is because the very idea of transcendental freedom precludes reference to explanatory facts (or states of affairs), or what Ulrich calls "grounds." The advantage of determinism is that facts of that sort are readily available and discoverable within the deterministic chains of causation that antecede the action. Were Kant's theory adjusted to include reference to a noumenal ground that determines actions, it would be in a position to respond to the explanatory demand, but it would no longer be a theory of freedom.

[14] In the Schulz review Kant expressly criticizes a perfectionist position very close to Ulrich's and more generally in the *Groundwork* (*PP*, 8: 12; *GW*, 4: 410). Kant's own views contain perfection of one's talents as a moral aim (*GW*, 4: 430, 443), but the moral sense of perfection mainly refers to efforts of the will (*CPrR*, 5: 127; *MM*, 6: 387) rather than to what Ulrich describes, which, on Kant's account, is still a natural perfection (*MM*, 6: 382).

Ulrich's use of PSR supports a relation of ground to grounded that is characterized by ontological dependence – specifically, the grounded exists and is the way that it is because of the ground. The relation can be illustrated again with Leibniz's account of divine creation. That God is the ground for the actual world means the world exists because God created it and, in addition, that it is this world, rather than some other possible world, because this particular world-configuration is the best among the alternatives available to God and His creative choice is guided by what is best. This ontological picture underpins Ulrich's conception of what it takes to explain actions, in particular, that successful explanations track grounds that are not just necessary but also sufficient for the action's occurrence and specific character. I want to show that Ulrich's assumptions concerning ground and its function in explanation need not be accepted and, indeed, that there are good reasons for rejecting them.

An easy way to answer Ulrich's demand for contrastive explanations of free actions is by focusing on Kant's psychological account of human choice (*arbitrium*), and specifically his characterization of choice as free, yet also "affected" (*CPR*, A 534/B 562; *MM*, 6: 213). "Affected" describes how agents exercise their choice – they choose on the basis of facts about what they believe, hope, fear and so on (*CPrR*, 5: 100).[15] None of these facts, however, suffices to determine the object of choice, the end the agent is to pursue; therefore, choice is free (*MM*, 6: 381, 384–5). Still, once an end is chosen, it is possible to identify the facts that became determining for the choice and, thus, to provide contextual contrastive explanations for one's actions. Explanations of that sort are what reflective agents are ordinarily able to offer in answer to the question why they chose as they did, or why they chose one course of action rather than another one that was available to them.

One reason to remain dissatisfied with this solution is that the explanation given is not complete, that is, it does not tell us why at this juncture, this set of reasons prevailed and became determining for the agent. To say that one set of reasons is granted determining power over another *by* the agent simply redescribes the situation, leaving indeterminate the agent's exercise of their choice. Therefore, while it satisfies the contrastive explanatory demand, the account of the free and affected exercise of human choice leaves an explanatory gap.

The Kantian question is whether the demand for closing the gap is a reasonable one. The gap results from the absence of some determining factors. A complete explanation could be provided, if such determining factors are identified. Such identification could be possible only if a comprehensive account were available that tied every circumstance in which the agent acts to specific deliberative steps that link given intentional contents to determinate

[15] The interpretation presented here relies on a more detailed discussion given in Deligiorgi 2017.

ends. Such an account would be possible, however, only if thoroughgoing metaphysical determinism is the case. Consequently, the demand for a complete explanation depends on a presupposition with considerable substantive metaphysical commitments, which the defender of the account of free choice may justifiably resist.

On the other hand, the psychological account of free choice simply assumes that the agent has the ability to pursue or not some option. The possession by the agent of such freedom, traditionally described as a "two-way power," is not argued for. Such argument is needed, however, since ordinary instances of the exercise of such power, empirically ascertained through introspection, may well be illusory. In addition, from Ulrich's perspective, appealing to freedom as a two-way power amounts to evasion, since it does not touch his argument about transcendental freedom.

The Kantian response to the points just raised is to grant them fully. A key step in Kant's theoretical defense of transcendental freedom is his argument that the only way to block skeptical doubts about whether human beings possess freedom as a two-way power is by asserting transcendental freedom. Transcendental freedom does not designate some extra power agents possess; it serves simply to spell out the condition that is needed to secure the possession of the two-way power of freedom, whether the power is exercised or not. The condition for the possession of the two-way power of freedom, which defines free choice, the freedom to do or to refrain from doing, is absence of necessitation by antecedent causes. The claim that absence from necessitation by antecedent causes is a condition for the possession of free choice can be viewed and assessed in a number of ways. As a statement of a conceptual dependence relation, it is obvious and therefore uninterestingly true: if antecedent causes determine what the agent does, then the agent does not possess a two-way power of freedom and so cannot be said to possess free choice. Taken now as a statement relating to empirically accessible facts, it is again true though again relatively uninteresting, because it is vague about what matters most in judging particular cases, namely what counts as "antecedent necessitation," for example, whether social pressure is to be treated on a par with manipulation or brainwashing and so on. The claim gains significance only when asserted as a transcendental thesis of what is *metaphysically* necessary, but not sufficient, for free choice.

One missing element from the interpretation of transcendental freedom just given is spontaneity, which is also the feature that Ulrich considers most problematic. The assumption underpinning Ulrich's criticism is that Kant uses spontaneity to designate the grounds of free action. Spontaneity would then do service as generic *explanans* for transcendentally free actions, that is, actions that are not caused by antecedently necessitating causes. This assumption is erroneous. At the very least, paying attention to Kant's argumentative strategy allows us to discard it without loss.

Kant's strategy is shaped by his perception of the failure of traditional metaphysical arguments aiming to prove (or disprove) freedom and by his meta-ethical commitments. On the interpretation of transcendental freedom given here, Kant asserts, as a transcendental thesis, what is a metaphysically necessary condition for the possession of psychological freedom, or freedom as a two-way power. The assertion of the transcendental thesis about freedom marks the conclusion of Kant's carefully hedged metaphysical investigations into the topic. In light of this methodological consideration, "spontaneity" cannot attach to a metaphysically substantive thesis. In any case, as Ulrich observes, "the idea of a spontaneity, which could start to act from itself," is obscure (*CPR*, A 533/B 561). If we consider it in a practical rather than a theoretical context, however, we can get a better sense of this claim. To act is to pursue some end. End-setting, as we saw, is the task of choice. The theoretical condition for free choice is given with the idea of transcendental freedom. Spontaneity is the same idea presented in a way that serves a forward-looking perspective, the practical perspective of an agent choosing ends. The shift in directionality allows the argument to focus on the ends that are the object of free choice. This change of focus is essential for the Kantian response to Ulrich's question about determination of free actions. To clarify, once the demand for complete explanations is shown to be resistible, all that is needed is to show that and how free end-setting is compatible with determination. This can be shown for actions that aim to realize rationally demanded ends, that is, ends that are in accordance with the moral law. The determining ground of such actions is a law of pure reason, or an "ought" that expresses a "connection with grounds which does not occur anywhere else in the whole of nature" (*CPR*, A 547/B 575). Because the moral "ought" expresses a kind of determination that is only possible for beings who are not fully bound by natural causality, moral agency is also a transcendentally free agency. Therefore, moral actions represent a class of actions that are free transcendentally by virtue of being free morally, that is, by virtue of their determination and so they are both free and have an identifiable ground for their determination.[16]

3 Conclusion: Ethical Necessity?

As we saw, one motivation for Ulrich's naturalization of ethical necessity is to establish its objectivity and efficacy. As a result, Ulrich is forced to revise the

[16] It is important for Kant that we are not mere passive recipients of the ought, mere copyists of the moral law. Kant writes that the agent *knows* the constraint of her free choice "through the categorical nature of its pronouncement (the unconditional ought)," adding that human beings are "rational natural beings, who are unholy enough that pleasure can induce them to break the moral law even though they recognize its authority" (*MM*, 6: 379).

claims to absoluteness he originally attaches to the moral "ought." Kant's position is exactly the reverse: "[a] principle of duty," Kant claims, "is a principle that reason prescribes to him absolutely and so objectively (how he *ought* to act)" (*MM*, 6: 225). The objectivity that reason guarantees is of a different order to the objectivity of the laws of nature. The question now is whether Ulrich's suspicion of the pure rational provenance of moral commands is justified, that is, whether the objectivity of reason is plausible and plausibly efficacious within the world of appearances that is explicable by reference to natural laws.

Quite simply stated, the objectivity Kant defends for moral principles is unconditional validity. To solve the efficacy problem, a way must be found for that sort of objectivity to apply to practical attitudes of rational agents. Kant and Ulrich agree that rational agents can apply rules to their conduct and direct their practical attitudes in accordance with such rules. Where they differ is in their accounts of how an objective principle can be adopted as a subjective rule of conduct. Ulrich uses the notion of ethical necessity for that purpose. Ethical necessity is objective and efficacious because it is natural: it describes a connection between rational agents and ethical rules that parallels the connection between massive bodies and the law of gravity. Kant, by contrast, uses the notion of ethical necessitation. Ethical necessitation stands for the fact that the objective principle makes an action necessary for agents whose will is contingently determined by that principle. The conceptual point about necessitation can be easily conveyed by reference to the phenomenology of duty and of obligation. To do one's duty, or to see something as obligation, carries the sense of having to constrain one's practical attitudes in accordance with what is presented as dutiful or obligatory.

My aim here is not to offer a comparative assessment of Ulrich's and Kant's arguments, but rather to identify an important difference in their respective approaches to the issue of objectivity and of efficacy.

Ulrich treats both as topics in metaphysics. What the notion of necessitation shows is that they can be fruitfully treated as topics in moral epistemology and moral psychology, that is, by showing how agents have access to objective principles and how they can act on principle. The proximity of metaphysics to moral psychology and epistemology illustrates how theoretical and practical philosophy can play a mutually supportive role in Kant's system. This is advantageous when it opens up new ways of looking at a problem, such as the problems of efficacy and objectivity. It can also be a disadvantage. The argument about freedom examined previously shows the limitations of a purely theoretical treatment of the topic, which at best shows transcendental freedom to be a condition for other types of freedom, freedom of choice and moral freedom. The reality of transcendental freedom can be known practically, that is, in the exercise of one's moral agency. But, as Ulrich rightly saw, making sense of such exercises of moral agency depends on showing how unconditional commands can feature in rational deliberation and inform choice of context-bound natural beings. Though flawed, Ulrich's account of ethical necessity is valuable for drawing attention to these important aspects of Kant's theory of freedom.

3 Maimonides and Kant in the Ethical Thought of Salomon Maimon

Timothy Quinn

One of the shop windows he paused before was that of a second-hand book-shop, where, on a narrow table outside, the literature of the ages was represented in judicious mixture . . . That the mixture was judicious was apparent from Deronda's finding in it something that he wanted – namely, that wonderful bit of autobiography, the life of the Polish Jew, Salomon Maimon . . .

– George Eliot, *Daniel Deronda*[1]

1 Introduction

Daniel Deronda's fortuitous discovery of Maimon's *Autobiography* in George Eliot's novel leads him gradually back to the faith of his fathers. By contrast, Maimon's discovery of Maimonides' *Guide of the Perplexed* led him in a rather different direction: away from Judaism, smack into the arms of philosophy, and eventually Immanuel Kant. Of course, as his *Autobiography* explains so delightfully, Maimon made a few other important stops along the way, through Wolff, Leibniz, Spinoza, and Mendelssohn, before arriving at Kant. Yet even a cursory account of Maimon's philosophical development makes plain a process of emancipation from early Jewish influences, toward a life-changing encounter with Kantian philosophy.

However true in outline, though, this account does a disservice to Maimonides' lasting influence upon all precincts of Maimon's thought. As Maimon makes clear in his *Autobiography*, Maimonides' *Guide of the Perplexed* (hereafter, *Guide*) was both an inaugural and a lasting influence on his philosophical development, as his decision to change his surname attests.[2] In one of his earliest writings, a collection of essays under the title *Hesheq Shelomo*, or *Solomon's Desire*, Maimon attempted to harmonize Maimonidean philosophy with what he had learned from his youthful Kabbalah studies.[3] Somewhat later, in 1791, the same year Maimon published

[1] Eliot 2014: 323. [2] Maimon's given name was Shlomo ben Yehoshua.
[3] Maimon 1778. Of particular interest is "Ma'ase Livnat ha-Sapir," Maimon's essay on Maimonides and Kabbalah. See Freudenthal 2012.

his *Philosophical Dictionary*, and one year after the publication of his important criticism of Kant, *Essay on Transcendental Philosophy*, Maimon published a Hebrew commentary on Maimonides' *Guide*, *Give'at ha-Moreh*, or *The Hill of the Guide*.[4] Even while his Kantian critique was flourishing, Maimon remained deeply engaged with Maimonides.

To be sure, Maimonides' influence on Maimon is not news; much recent scholarship has mapped Maimonidean influences on Maimon's critiques of Kantian epistemology.[5] Less familiar, though, is the Maimonideanism of Maimon's ethical writings. This Maimonidean influence is both general and particular. In general, it leads Maimon to reject the primacy Kant wishes to award the practical sphere in favor of theoretical or intellectual perfection as the goal of moral life. In particular, it compels Maimon to attempt a "new deduction" of the Kantian moral principle, an attempt that, at the close of his life, he abandons in the face of his own moral skepticism.

The goal of this essay is to show the role played by Maimonides in shaping the basic themes of Maimon's critique of Kant's moral philosophy. After a brief excursus into the interplay between Kantian and Maimonidean elements of Maimon's epistemological critiques, I will attempt to describe the development of his ethical critique of Kant, in order to trace out its Maimonidean elements. Although this essay will offer but a skeletal account of this rather rich and complex series of interrelationships, my hope is that it will at least set the matter of Maimon's ethical debt to Maimonides into relief.

2 A Maimonidean Kant or a Kantian Maimonides?

The signal problem Maimon attempts to resolve in Kant's *Critique of Pure Reason* concerns Kant's justification for the possibility of synthetic a priori judgments, a central assumption of the *Critique*. Maimon calls into question both the possibility and even the existence of such judgments.[6] The problem of justifying synthetic a priori judgements depends upon our ability to justify the application of intellectual categories to the world in a way that yields demonstrable knowledge: in Kantian terms, to demonstrate how the forms of understanding can be applied to the forms of intuition, apart from which synthetic a priori judgments are impossible. In the "top-down" approach Maimon criticizes (and of which he accuses Fichte), these categories – for example, cause and effect – represent basic concepts ordering our experience and intuition, but exist in our minds a priori, independent of either experience or intuition to

[4] For a fine French translation of *Give'at ha-Moreh*, see Maimon 1999.
[5] Some recent studies include Franks 2007, Fraenkel 2009, Socher 2009, Freudenthal 2012.
[6] See Freudenthal 2003b: 144ff.

which they are applied.[7] By contrast, according to Maimon, "for a cognition to be true, it must be both given and thought at the same time: *given* with respect to its matter (that must be given in an intuition), and *thought* with respect to the form that cannot be given in itself."[8] Kantian philosophy fails to bring together the thought and the given – or, in the Aristotelian language he imbibes from Maimonides, the matter and the form of cognition – and to that extent fails to answer the twin questions to which transcendental philosophy gives rise, *quid juris* and *quid facti*. At bottom, the issue is one of overcoming dualities that Maimon sees at the heart of the Kantian system: between what Maimon labels the "form" and "matter" of cognition, between sensibility and understanding, and, finally, between theory and practice, the central duality involved in Maimon's critique of Kantian morality.[9] Importantly, it is Maimonides who guides Maimon to an answer.

Two particular works serve as useful indices for this influence. The first, Maimon's *Probe Rabbinische Philosophie*, or *Example of Rabbinic Philosophy* (hereafter, *Example*), originally published in the *Berlinische Monatschrift* in 1789, offers what appears to be a Kantian interpretation of Maimonides' remarks concerning a brief passage from *Mishnah Avot*, 3:17.[10] For Maimonides as well as Maimon, the issue in this passage is the relationship between cognition and understanding, an issue familiar from Kant's epistemological project. Maimon's explanation of this interrelationship draws together an Aristotelian-Maimonidean account of active intellect with a Kantian account of concept formation. In brief, from Maimonides Maimon acquires a thesis concerning the unity of divine intellect with the form of an object, which results in the act of cognition. In this case, cognition depends on our power "to attain concepts from abstracted forms." At the same time, intellect may recognize that the concept attained is already in accord with cognition: cognition leads to concepts, and concepts presuppose acts of cognition. There is, in short, no *Da'at* (cognition) without *Binah* (understanding), and no *Binah* without *Da'at*.[11]

[7] *MGW*, VI: 449–50: "you wish to travel from top to bottom (from the concept of a science as such to the concrete sciences), but I wish to travel it from bottom to top."

[8] Maimon 2010: 36.

[9] See Franks 2007. Note Maimon's use of Aristotelian terminology, inherited from Maimonides, in place of the more familiar Kantian language.

[10] *MGW*, I: 589–97. The passage runs: "Rabbi Eliezar states … without Da'at (cognition) [*Erkennen*] there is no Binah (comprehension, understanding) [*Begreifen*, *Verstehen*]; and without Binah there is no Da'at." The entire passage runs: "Without Torah there is no way of life; without a way of life there is no Torah; without wisdom there is no fear; without fear there is no wisdom. Without knowledge there is no understanding; without understanding there is no knowledge. Without bread there is no Torah; without Torah there is no bread." The passage indicates the interplay of all aspects of human life in light of the divine; Maimonides, and Maimon with him, focus only on the epistemological statement.

[11] See Freudenthal 2005.

For Maimon, this brief exegesis of a few lines of Maimonides leads him to a correction of Kant: to attain a concept from the abstracted form of an object is the equivalent of arriving at a cognition based on intuition, which at the same time must be subsumed under a priori categories that determine the unity of the cognized object. If so, then the Kantian categories, "which receive their reality through judgments," are "discovered in the objects of perception." Although Maimon has yet to articulate this particular Kantian distinction, we find here an early attempt to reconcile the problem, *quid juris* – the categories of the understanding – with *quid facti* – the objects of perception.

Setting aside the details of Maimon's argument, the essay reveals a curious nesting of influences: is Maimon a Kantian Maimonides or a Maimonidean Kant? That is, does Maimon intend to amend Maimonides' thought by means of Kantian epistemology? Or does he wish to reorient the goals of Kantian thought by means of Maimonides? On the one hand, we may note that Maimon frames his interpretation of Maimonides in the alien tongue of Kantian epistemology. On the other hand, the extent to which Maimon's debt to Kant transcends the terminological remains, in this early essay, unclear. In fact, Maimon was well aware of this ambiguity in his argument, indicating that his essay was bound to offend in equal measure both traditional rabbinic authorities, deeply suspicious of Maimonides, and proponents of the *Haskalah*, or Jewish Enlightenment, "as if I wished thereby to curtail the deserving fame of our contemporaries, while trying to show that someone in the twelfth century had already thought as they do."[12] The statement is revealing: in Maimon's view, there is enough affinity between Maimonides and Kant to allow for a blending of concepts – a blending at work in Maimon's use of the terms "form" and "matter" for "understanding" and "sensibility."

A second writing useful for gauging Maimon's assimilation of Maimonides to Kant is his commentary on Maimonides' *Guide*: *Give'at ha-Moreh*, or *The Hill of the Guide*. In his commentary on I.68 of the *Guide*, the theme of which is the unity of divine intellect, Maimon takes aim at the dualism implicit in Kant's account of cognition. According to Kant, Maimon writes, the act of cognition requires sensibility (*Sinnlichkeit*) to receive the "matter" of cognition, while intellect produces through itself the "form" of the cognition.[13] By itself, understanding fails to unite the form of cognition with the matter of cognition, because it grasps only general representations that possess universal validity; it orders our perception of objects without giving us knowledge of the objects it orders in light of logical categories. It therefore fails to culminate in cognition. For that, sensibility is also required. On the other hand, if only sensibility existed, we would be able to reach a sensible perception

[12] *MGW*, I: 590. [13] Maimon 1965: 107.

(*Wahrnehmung*) but not a cognition. Both are therefore necessary. Maimon concludes: "the intellect, the subject, and the intelligible object will become one thing in itself from the point of view of the form of cognition, when it in itself is the object of cognition [*Objekt der Erkenntnis*]."[14] The language of this solution is Maimonidean.[15] In brief, according to Aristotle, god as intellect (*nous*) is the act of intellection (*noesis*) that knows itself as a "by product" (*par erga*), that is, god is the object of its own act of intellection (*noesis noeseos*). Aristotle's god, in short, thinks of nothing lesser or lower than itself. As Maimonides renders it: God is "the intellect (*al-áql*) as well as the subject of intellection (*al-'aqil*) and the object of intellection (*al-ma'qul*)."[16] Maimon discovers in this formula a way to resolve Kant's inability to unify the form of cognition with the matter of cognition. But to do so, he interprets Maimonides' account of divine intellect in such a way that it can be understood to contain not only self-consciousness, but also knowledge of all the real existing objects that human sensibility takes as given. In this way, for Maimon, the unity of divine intellect provides a paradigm for human intellection, containing in actuality what human intellects contain potentially: a unity of intellect with cognized object in the act of cognition itself.

As Maimon clarifies in his *Essay on Transcendental Philosophy*, it is necessary "to assume an infinite mind, at least as an idea, in relation to which all forms are at the same time objects of thought," since "our human mind is of the same nature as the infinite mind, although in a restricted and limited manner."[17] In other words, for Maimon, Maimonides' account of the unity of divine intellect explains "the true reality of every intellect." In short, the question, *quid juris*, requires, in Maimon's view, the assumption of an infinite intellect producing all possible relations between objects, therefore explaining how concepts can be applied to objects given through the forms of sensibility. We note in passing how the structure of Maimon's argument mimics that of Kant's regarding the practical postulate of God's existence, except that Maimon transposes it from the plane of morality to that of theoretical philosophy.[18]

Of course, much more would need to be said to clarify Maimon's argument concerning Maimonides' account. For now, it suffices to say that these two selections, from the *Example* and from *Give'at ha-Moreh*, were not chosen at

[14] Maimon 1965: 107.

[15] See Aristotle's *Metaphysics* XII.7, 9 and *On the Soul* III.1–5. For a commentary on Maimon's interpretation of this chapter of the *Guide*, compare Lachterman 1992 and Fraenkel 2009. In what follows, I am particularly indebted to Fraenkel's analysis.

[16] Maimonides, *Guide*, I.68. [17] Maimon 2010: 64.

[18] In the second *Critique* and in *Religion within the Limits of Reason Alone*, Kant argues that the existence of God is the practical postulate for morality, since moral action implies the existence of an intelligent being who exactly proportions happiness to moral worth.

random. First of all, between them, they show two faces of the interplay between Kant and Maimonides in Maimon's theoretical philosophy: in the case of the *Example*, a Kantian clarification of Maimonides, while in the case of his interpretation of Maimonides' *Guide*, a Maimonidean solution to a problem endemic, in Maimon's view, to Kant's epistemology. Second, and of particular importance for Maimon's moral thought, both writings address in related ways the problem Maimon saw at the core of both Kantian theoretical and practical philosophy: the *quid juris* and *quid facti*.

3 Maimonides and Kant: A Moral Synthesis?

Although they occupy considerably less space in his *oeuvre* than do his critical reflections on matters of Kantian epistemology, Maimon's critiques of Kantian morality are not correspondingly insignificant, especially given the way he at times weaves them into his critiques of Kant's theoretical project. For example, in his *Essay on Transcendental Philosophy* of 1790, Maimon indicates the need "to remark that the moral good is good only because it is true."[19] Three years later, in his *Disputations in the Area of Philosophy*, Maimon writes: "justifying a necessary and universally valid morality is surely the most important issue for anyone seeking truth."[20] These statements are particularly telling; as will become evident, they indicate the influence of Maimonides on Maimon's ethical thought in a manner that mirrors Maimonides' influence on his theoretical critiques.

Maimon, at first blush, appears to accept the basic framework and nomenclature of Kantian moral philosophy: the familiar opposition between duty and inclination, and the corresponding problem of avoiding motives that would either seduce or coerce moral action, in order to preserve the intrinsic goodness of the will apart from what it may or may not accomplish; the corresponding demand (against Spinoza, to whom Maimon is elsewhere indebted) for freedom of the will; the identification of the categorical imperative as the supreme principal of morality, and the problem of establishing its universal validity. Maimon's divergences from Kant in matters of morality are however more numerous than his affinities. These divergences arise principally in two interrelated ways. First, as was mentioned at the outset, Maimon rejects Kant's subordination of the theoretical to the practical. Second, and connected to this rejection of the "primacy of the practical," Maimon attempts to restore a material element to Kantian morality by grounding duty in a universally valid "impulse" or "drive" (*Trieb*) toward truth. In both instances, Maimon seeks a ground for moral duty that would establish its universal validity without

[19] Maimon 2010: 209. [20] *MGW*, IV: 256.

abandoning the connection between morality and the various inclinations that shape human nature, inclinations that ultimately compel the pursuit of truth. In short, Maimon seeks a reconsideration of the "why" of moral action that would unite what Maimon deems the formal and material elements of morality, in other words, the twin questions *quid juris* and *quid facti*. In this connection, Maimon revives notions of happiness and perfection Kant had banished from the charmed circle of moral worth.

In the first case, Maimon's rejection of the "primacy of the practical" in Kant's thought is based on a view that intellectual perfection is the highest good. Explaining the origins of his moral convictions in his *Autobiography*, Maimon writes:

> My own morality, back then, was genuine *stoicism*: striving to achieve freedom of will and the dominance of reason over subjective impressions and passions. This view also meant believing that the highest calling of man was the assertion of his *differentia specifica – knowledge of truth*. All other drives that we share with the animal world should be employed to that end. For me, there was no distinction between knowledge of the *good* and knowledge of the *true*. Following Maimonides's lead, I held knowledge of the truth to be the highest good worthy of man.[21]

For Maimon, morality is instrumental, "set down merely as a means to the highest good . . . knowledge of truth" (*MGW*, I: 177–8). In so arguing, Maimon takes his bearings from Maimonides' account of the four species of perfection in the ultimate chapter of the *Guide* (III.54), a passage Maimon summarizes in the ultimate chapter of his *Autobiography*. The highest species of perfection, which consists in "the acquisition of rational virtues," is the "ultimate end" of human life – through it, "the human being is a human being." By comparison, morality is "a preparation for something else and not an end in itself." As Maimonides states earlier, "to ultimate perfection there do not belong either actions or moral qualities" (*Guide*, III.27). This strict separation of moral and intellectual virtues or "qualities" reduces morality, for Maimonides, to "commonly held opinion" necessary to support human community; it aims at "cultivating the disposition to be useful to people," and therefore, unlike intellectual perfection, aims at the good of human community rather than to what is essential to the human as human. Thus, in an early passage from I.34 of the *Guide*, Maimonides exhorts the young to acquire moral virtue, but only as a means to acquire intellectual virtue: its sole value is to prepare the soul to pursue intellectual perfection.[22]

[21] Maimon 2018b: 210.

[22] Maimonides' subordination of moral to intellectual virtue follows Aristotle's *Nicomachean Ethics* X.8, where he designates practical virtue as virtue "in a secondary sense." In fact, there exists an important debate regarding the restriction of happiness or *eudaimonia* to contemplation, or what Maimon would consider "intellectual perfection." See Kraut 1979. Maimon,

Maimon embraces this view, closely paraphrasing these Maimonidean passages in his interpretation of the *Guide* at the end of his *Autobiography*. Thus, the "lowest sort" of perfection, pursued by most human beings, is the "perfection of possessions [*Vollkommenheit des Besitzes*]." The second, "perfection of the body [*Vollkommenheit des Körpers*]" belongs to human beings insofar as they are animals (men are strong, Maimon points out, but elephants are stronger; therefore, human beings have little to take pride in). The third perfection is that of morality, which Maimon allows is not the highest end (*Hauptzweck*) for human beings, but rather "merely a preparation for it [*bloß Vorbereitung zu demselben*]," important for establishing human community. The final and highest perfection, and the final end of human being (*der letzte Zweck des Menschen*) is "perfection of knowledge [*Vollkommenheit der Erkenntniß*]." By means of this perfection, Maimon writes, one "receives one's being as a person" (*er bloß durch sie sein Wesen als Mensch erhält*). Of particular significance is his endorsement of Maimonides' view that moral perfection is but the penultimate human perfection, important for establishing human community, but in the end "merely a preparation" for and therefore inferior to the ultimate, intellectual perfection, or "perfection of knowledge." This Maimonidean-inspired goal allows Maimon not merely to subsume the moral under the theoretical or intellectual. It renders the intellectual the end for the sake of which moral virtue *is* virtue, a view that roughly parallels Maimon's earlier explanation of the assumption of an infinite intellect as a basis for solving the *quid juris* question. In a deliberate reversal of Kant, a critique of pure reason no longer serves as propaedeutic for establishing the sovereignty of pure practical reason; rather, practical reason serves as propaedeutic for the perfection of knowledge.

It is important to note that Maimon's interpretation of Maimonides renders the latter as a "radical Aristotelian" of the school of al-Farabi and Averroes. Although the motives compelling Maimon to this interpretation are not clear, they are nonetheless at work in his earliest writings, a handwritten manuscript titled *Hesheq Shelomo*, "Solomon's Desire," composed during his time in Posen.[23] It consists of five separate treatises: "Ma'ase Nissim," a commentary on the medieval Talmudist Nissim of Gerondi; "Eved Avraham," a supercommentary on Avraham Ibn Ezra's commentary on Torah and Psalms; "Ma'ase Livnat ha-Sappir," his essay on Maimonides and Kabbalah; "Ma'ase Hoshev," an algebra textbook; and "Avachecha Bahya," an exposition of Bahya Ibn Pakuda's biblical commentary. A cursory look at the scholars on which he comments – Nissim of Gerondi, Ibn Ezra,

following Narboni's commentary on Maimonides' *Guide*, ascribes to Maimonides and to Aristotle a strict view of the subordination of practical to intellectual virtue.

[23] Maimon 1778.

Maimonides, and Bahya Ibn Paquda – show Maimon's inclination toward thinkers all of whom rejected mystical interpretations of Torah in favor of rational explanation. By including Maimonides with this group of authors, Maimon implies an intellectual kinship. Ibn Ezra was crucial for Spinoza's later denial of the Mosaic authorship of Torah, while Ibn Paquda was one of the first Jewish thinkers to attempt to weave together an accord between reason and revelation. All were rationalists of a sort, a fact implicit in Maimon's choice of title.[24] As Abraham Socher points out, the Hebrew word *hesheq* derives from the Arabic *ishk*, a term used by Ibn Sinna, Maimonides, and other Arabic and Jewish Aristotelians of the Middle Ages to specify a philosophical *eros*. This *eros* culminates in intellectual perfection.[25] Intellectual perfection, in turn, requires participation in divine intellect. Although Maimon would exchange "infinite intellect" for divine intellect, his convictions about the teleology of philosophical *eros*, convictions he shared with his medieval forebears, remained throughout his career. They in part inform Maimon's eventual rejection of the Kantian "primacy of the practical."[26]

With this reversal in the status of theoretical and practical reason comes a revision of Kant's notion of the role played by incentives in morality, and in particular, by pleasure and happiness. In his *Philosophical Dictionary* of 1791, Maimon asserts his deviation from Kant, writing that what appears to be the fulfillment of a duty may well be caused by an inclination. If so, obedience to duty on purely rational grounds is not the sole motivation to act in accordance with duty.[27] Maimon writes: while "no one claims that he is obligated to follow one's inclinations," there is in fact "nothing apart from inclination that can provide a ground for duty other than reason mediated by its necessary form." At the same time, Maimon criticizes Reinhold's notion of a

24 Nissim of Gerondi (1310–76); Avraham Ibn Ezra (1089–1167); Moses Maimonides (1135?–1204); Bahya Ibn Paquda (first half eleventh century).

25 Socher 2006.

26 Important for Maimon's own "radical" reading of and commentary on Maimonides was the work of Moshe Narboni (d. 1362?). See Holtzman 2013 and Ivry 2015.

27 *MGW*, III: 92; Maimon also writes:

> Duty is the objective necessity that is grounded in the form of reason (the principle of identity). Namely, the form of conduct of a rational being must be obtained so that it can be thought as a universal law ... Now one must indeed admit, first, that this explanation of duty is in accord with the uses of language, since duty signifies a compulsion to act against inclination. No one says that he is obligated to follow one's inclinations; however, there is in fact nothing apart from inclination that can provide a ground for duty other than reason mediated by its necessary form. (MGW, III: 116)

Kant's elevation of practical over theoretical reason is at odds with Aristotle's assertion of the superiority of intellectual over practical virtue (see *Nicomachean Ethics*, Book X.6–9), as well as of contemplation over action (see *Metaphysics*, Book I.1–2). This Aristotelian view is adopted by Maimonides in his *Guide* (III.27, 32). For an overview of this issue, see Shatz 2005.

"disinterested drive" as the motive for moral action as an alternative to Kant's notion of "respect for law." In Maimon's view, Reinhold fails to connect this drive to rational concepts of duty and virtue, so that it remains little more than "illusion."[28] On the other hand, Maimon concedes that Kant's notion of respect for law, while doubtlessly one of the motives for morality, cannot be the sole motive, given its inevitable conflict with other possible feelings (*ANP*, 10; *MGW*, VI: 405). "Why," asks Maimon, "ought this artificial feeling determine me more than all other natural feelings" which may claim our attention?

As an alternative both to Reinhold and to Kant (who shared aspects of Maimon's criticism of Reinhold), Maimon proposes that the motive for moral action must involve some "pleasurable feeling" (*angenehmes Gefühl*), the basis of which lies in an analogy between the common human understanding and the "drive (*Trieb*) for cognition."[29] His argument, in sum, runs as follows. All motives, Maimon states, are or involve pleasant feelings, because they derive from drives; a drive, as Maimon states in "On the First Grounds of Morality," is "the inner tendency to exercise a force [*Kraft*] accompanied by a pleasant feeling" (*MGW*, VII: 455). Drives, in short, insist on their satisfaction. Against Reinhold, Maimon asserts that "every drive is selfish and unselfish in the same way, since . . . no drive precedes the idea of a pleasant feeling, and the pleasant feeling accompanies every drive in general."[30] But not all these pleasant feelings are material and particular: some are formal and universal. The drive to cognition constitutes one such motive; the pleasure we take in it is not in the object known but arises from the drive itself, in "the form of cognition."[31] Maimon concludes that every "actualization of this form" (*Wirklichmachung dieser Form*, a phrase using conspicuously Aristotelian nomenclature) involves a similar pleasure. It follows then that morality, which is a determination of the will by a formal law, must be accompanied by "an original pleasurable feeling."

It is not entirely clear what Maimon means by an *original* pleasurable feeling; Maimon states only that it does not arise as a result of custom. Invoking this original pleasurable feeling however leads Maimon to distinguish between "higher" and "lower" pleasures. Again, taking his bearings from Kant, Maimon argues that while all pleasure belongs to the genus "self-love" or "one's own happiness," sensuous pleasures remain "lower," given their inseparability from the material order, and are therefore not of the same

[28] *ANP*, 10; *MGW*, VI: 406–7. See also "Letter from the Author to Herr Professor Reinhold" (*MGW*, IV: 225–34). While no date is given with this letter, it is likely to have been composed in 1791. Across his career, Maimon's relationship with Reinhold became increasingly vexed. Although Reinhold was an early champion of Maimon's work, he broke with Maimon after Maimon published their correspondence, airing his disagreements with Reinhold.

[29] *MGW*, VII: 241 ff. [30] *MGW*, VII: 457. [31] *MGW*, VII: 241.

"species" as pleasures in the act of cognition or in moral action. Even though Maimon concedes that the pleasure accompanying cognition of truth may admit of degrees – truths concerning principles are more satisfying to know than particulars – the fact of pleasure remains identical for knowledge of all truths, because it depends upon the form and not the object of cognition. We note in passing that, given the need to distinguish higher and lower pleasures, Maimon's Stoicism becomes all the more significant, as the instrument for discrimination.

In its details, Maimon's argument here is not conspicuously Maimonidean. In particular, Maimon's reliance on the "drive" has antecedent origins not in Maimonides, but in Spinoza's notion of *conatus*. For Spinoza, drive or conatus is the force intrinsic to beings to act for their own preservation and welfare. It is therefore universal not only to human beings, but to all beings. Maimon defines a drive as the development of a power in the subject accompanied by a consciousness of that development, rather than of the end toward which it is directed (*ANP*, 16; *MGW*, VI: 422).[32] Consequently, the drive for cognition of truth, as our paramount drive, cannot be limited by any conditions; only its actual fulfillment is subject to conditions. In this respect, though, the drive for cognition of truth is in no way different from the "compulsion" (*Zwang*) to duty, which is limited in its own exercise by the condition that it possess the force it needs to secure its end.

The notion of drive does bring with it a second departure from Maimonides. Even though, as Maimonides explains in his account of human perfections, only the few can attain intellectual perfection, Maimon shares with Kant the aim of universalizing the attainment of the highest good, a universalizing that follows from the claim that both cognition and the moral law make to universal validity.[33] This drive to universalization however does not obviate the elitism implicit in Maimon's Maimonideanism; while the justification for moral principles inevitably involves establishing their universal validity, it remains the case that only a few will be able to attain the highest level of moral and intellectual perfection. The concept of drive embeds this universalizing within nature, since a drive in general belongs to beings by dint of their natures, as Maimon makes plain later in his essay: caterpillars, he instructs us, "sense a drive within themselves" to become butterflies. In human beings, this drive involves not only a consciousness of the drive toward cognition, but also of "the state of the subject directly determined by it . . . and of the laws according to which [cognition] is exercised." Unlike caterpillars, we are not merely conscious, but self-conscious. Thus, "what drives me to discover the Pythagorean theorem is not the representation of the property of a right

[32] See also *MGW*, VII: 237.

[33] Maimonides, *Guide*, III.54.

triangle . . . but rather the consciousness of the *activity of my power of cognition, in conformity to its laws*" (*ANP*, 17; *MGW*, VI: 423). Consequently, the drive "cannot cease with the discovery of this truth"; its aim is not particular truths, but truth in general. Yet, even though the drive for intellectual perfection, like the compulsion to duty, is part and parcel of human nature, it is not reducible to natural processes: while every natural drive has an end, the drive for cognition of truth is an end in itself. While every other natural drive is subject to the laws of the sensible world, only the drive for cognition of truth is subject to the laws of the intelligible world, and therefore independent of temporality and the temporal succession of events. In this way, the drive to cognition of the truth constantly renews itself.

Yet, even though absent from Maimonides, the concept of drive commits Maimon to a central element of Maimonidean-Aristotelian thought, that is, to eudaimonism, which is implicit whenever a drive is satisfied. Maimon's acceptance of eudaimonism is clearly in opposition to Kant. For Kant, happiness and morality are famously at odds. While morality must possess universal validity, happiness, as an "empirical principle," is inseparable from instances of private gratification. Concepts of happiness are thus invariably tainted by self-interest; as Kant puts it in the *Groundwork*, "the principle of happiness . . . is the most objectionable" of all empirical principles, because it bases moral obedience "on incentives that undermine and destroy all its sublimity" (*GW*, 4: 442). Maimon, by contrast, is led to rehabilitate the place of happiness in moral action owing to his commitment to Maimonides' elevation of intellectual perfection to the status of the highest good. According to this Aristotelian argument, intellectual pleasure is the greatest pleasure, since it completes our most characteristically human potential, for the excellence of rational activity.[34] For Aristotle, happiness and the acquisition of virtue therefore go hand in hand. Maimon embraces this argument as well, but not without some important modifications. In the first instance, Maimon admits, with Kant, that happiness has an empirical dimension that would appear to disqualify it from the domain of moral motives. However, Maimon holds that happiness "cannot be called empirical in itself, but only in its application" (*ANP*, 19; *MGW*, VI: 429). To the degree to which happiness transcends the empirical, happiness is a "practical law" that resembles the role played by "the principle of causality" in uses of theoretical reason. Maimon further argues that the same pleasure accompanying the drive for intellectual perfection through the cognition of truth also accompanies actions in obedience to the categorical imperative, both "extensively" – that is, it accompanies all moral actions – and "intensively" – that is, it belongs to us by virtue of our human nature.

[34] See Aristotle, *Nicomachean Ethics*, I.7.

A particularly striking indication of this elision of will and reason is Maimon's playful rephrasing of the first sentence of the first part of Kant's *Groundwork*: "It is impossible to think of anything at all in the world, or indeed even beyond it, that could be considered good without qualification except *the striving after cognition of truth*" (ANP, 11; MGW, VI: 407–8). Maimon therefore confesses that he must "take the liberty of departing from this great philosopher" – Kant – in arguing that a "material principle" compels the drive for cognition of truth and intellectual perfection, even though it remains entirely of a different sort than the drive for sensuous pleasure (*ANP*, 19; *MGW*, VI: 430). Happiness, in short, is the end of intellectual perfection.

The association of intellectual perfection and happiness therefore brings with it a correction of Kant's demotion of Aristotelian notions of virtue. While Kant, in his *Groundwork*, presents virtue as at best instrumental, Maimon indicates that virtue rightly understood consists in perfection, specifically, in perfection of the will. Maimon therefore understands virtue and duty to be compatible: the concept of virtue follows, according to Maimon, from duty conceived as a general "compulsion" (*Zwang*) to determine the will against the influence of inclinations, but not from any specific duty. Rational moral law henceforth sets "the conditions for the possible use of virtue." In this way, Maimon believes that "all moral principles, which can be advanced here are . . . bound up with one another." Again invoking Stoicism, Maimon writes in "On the First Grounds of Morality": "According to me (as according to the Stoics) there is only one virtue: self-control, or the acquired power, to determine the will against all sensuous drives and inclinations" (*MGW*, VII: 457). Self-control, the key virtue, does not depend upon an absolutely good will; rather, it makes it possible. Thus,

> The concept of virtue as self-control is Stoic; and since this is a perfection of the will, the doctrine of virtue agrees with the doctrine of perfection as well as with the doctrine of happiness (in so far namely as happiness is not determined by chance, but rather by a genuine causality of the subject). The doctrine of duty however is derived just as well as Kant's doctrine of virtue, from rational laws. (*MGW*, VII: 459)

In this curious nesting of assertions, Maimon professes Stoic virtue as a vehicle for liberating the will and for pursuing the sovereignty of intellectual perfection. Maimon's profession of Stoicism is therefore at home, at least in part, in Kant's own rejection of the influence of passion and inclination on the formation of an unconditionally good will. At the same time, the severity of Maimon's Stoicism is mitigated by his Maimonidean-Aristotelian commitment to pursuit of intellectual perfection as the highest good, since the pleasure of happiness accompanies this pursuit. Maimon's concept of virtue becomes, in short, a meeting point for Maimonidean eudaimonism and Kantian abstention from inclination. In Maimon's practical philosophy, Maimonides and Epictetus, Aristotle and Kant join hands.

As in his doctrine of intellect, the central issue emerging in Maimon's moral thought is the problem of unity, a problem of human consciousness reflected in his own interweaving of historical influences. At the core of this issue is the more fundamental interweaving of reason and will. In his *Attempt*, Maimon puts the matter this way:

> Truth and duty in fact possess a common essential characteristic, namely, *universal validity*. I cannot recognize as true what cannot hold as true for every other rational being. I could not will as a *duty* what another rational being is unable to will. I therefore generalize both propositions by making the characteristic common to both a *predicate*. From this results the following proposition: *a rational being* can, as such a being, only determine itself by *modifications that it recognize to be universally valid*. But this proposition, in regard to the *cognition of truth*, is given to us as a fact of consciousness, and its possibility is proven by its actual use. Its reality must therefore also be admitted with regard to *duty*. (*ANP*, 15; *MGW*, VI: 419–20)[35]

Given Maimon's desire to ground the universal validity of duty in the universal drive for truth, the ensuing parallelism of truth and duty reveals the unity of human moral and intellectual consciousness. He writes: "It is there, from the drive to cognition of truth, that the moral law is derived, obedience to which belongs therefore to the acquisition of the moral good" (*ANP*, 27; *MGW*, VI: 452). Will, which now means "the drive for cognition of the truth belonging to the power of cognition"; action, "producing the truth according to the laws of the power of cognition"; and end, "the truth produced," are all "intimately united." This unity of will, action, and end should remind us once more of Maimon's appropriation of Maimonides' concept of divine intellect, whose inner unity of being, action, and end ensures the unity of understanding with sensibility. The motto with which Maimon concludes his essay, "*vitam impendere vero*," holds both for intellect and for will.[36] It is, as Maimonides himself might indicate, our only share in the eternal.

4 Concluding Thoughts

From Kant, in sum, Maimon gleans his fundamental orientation to morality and its nomenclature. From Maimonides, however, he acquires its end. This Maimonidean end, in turn, requires a virtual overturning of central aspects of

[35] In his undated letter to Reinhold, Maimon writes: "You appeal, in view of moral feeling, to the healthy human understanding. But should one not ask: what is the criterion for this healthy human understanding? And how can one label that claim, which psychology explains as illusion, a claim to healthy human understanding?" (*MGW*, IV: 250–5).

[36] "Devote one's life to the truth." The passage is from Juvenal, *Satires* IV: 91. The passage also appears in a portrait of Jean-Jacques Rousseau by the artist Maurice Quentin de la Tour (1704–88). The inscription appears as well on the frontispiece to Maimon's *Philosophisches Wörterbuch*.

Kantian morality. Three aspects of this overturning in particular merit our attention. First, by identifying intellectual perfection or cognition of truth as the highest good, Maimon rejects the primacy of practical philosophy in favor of theoretical philosophy. That is to say, Maimon rejects the sharp distinction between practical and theoretical philosophy in order to establish that practical philosophy exists for the sake of theoretical philosophy, and culminates in its goals, intellectual perfection. Second, for Maimon, moral action is an issue only owing to one's relationship to others, that is, morality matters only in community. It is therefore at least in part a matter of convention, obedience to mores necessary for sustaining community, and guided by the sole virtue of self-control. Finally, while Kant rejects pleasure and happiness as legitimate influences on the will, Maimon draws them back in; for Maimon, happiness and satisfaction ought to accompany action in accord with duty, and therefore motivate them. This last point shows most clearly the evidence of the eudaimonism Maimon inherits from Maimonides.

In these respects, Maimon's moral philosophy diverges in important ways from Kant's, ways that display the influence of Maimonides on his critiques of Kantian moral thought. In fact, it remains ambiguous whether Maimon believes that the elements of Kantian ethics are at least in sum true, or whether they merit a Maimonidean critique merely because they represent conventional moral opinion, that is, they constitute the prevailing point of view.[37] Be that as it may, at the heart of these departures from Kant is Maimon's dedication to a Maimonidean-Aristotelian understanding of mind, a dedication that demands a reworking of Kantian morality in ways consonant with this Maimonidean-Aristotelian account. It is for this reason that Maimon's theoretical critique of Kant and his moral critique bear such a strong affinity with one another.

However potent these Maimonidean commitments, however, Maimon still attempts to preserve Kantian forms of moral analysis. A useful illustration of Maimon's attempt at a synthesis between Maimonides and Kant emerges in his view of Moses, in his late essay, *Der große Mann*, composed one year before his death.[38] Moses, Maimon's summary illustration of human greatness, understood (unlike the Patriarchs, who according to Maimon remained in the grip of pagan anthropomorphic illusions) that "the agreement of the moral with natural orders was not empirical . . . but rather through merely my pure reason, on the basis of which moral laws could be postulated." God now is not the "the cold concept of a first cause," nor a being "determined anthropomorphically," but "a God wisely and correctly postulated by pure reason a priori, for the

[37] In *Give'at ha-Moreh*, Maimon makes clear his agreement with Maimonides' view that moral issues are a function of convention, rather than reason; see Maimonides, *Guide*, III.27: overall, morality consists in "commonly held opinion." See Socher 2006: 103.

[38] *MGW*, VII: 520.

purpose of postulating his [Moses's] moral laws as an a priori fact" (*MGW*, VII: 517). Maimon's explanation is telling. On the one hand, it recalls Maimonides' account of Moses' intellectual perfection, which rendered him not merely a prophet, but the exemplary prophet, capable of entering the mind of God. On the other hand, Maimon's explanation of Mosaic rationality is Kantian.

As Maimon's moral thought evolves throughout the rest of his brief life, however, it is the tension between these two poles of his thought, Kantian and Maimonidean, that overtakes his thinking. Eventually, though, this would lead Maimon, in his last writings, to temper the Kantian moral project in favor of a skepticism that returned to premodern notions of virtue Maimon associates with Aristotle and the Stoics. In fact, by the end of his career, Maimon seems to abandon the various unities – epistemological, moral, historical – he sought to establish; and in so doing, he dispenses with his life-long project to offer firmer ground for Kant's moral principles. Maimon leaves us instead with a stand-off between moral skeptics and moral dogmatists: the former, seeing the promised land they cannot enter, and the latter, believing they can enter, but remaining, with the skeptics, only on its verges. Maimon writes: "A *comforting* yet *humiliating* voice calls to him: *you may see the desired land from afar, but you may not come!* Fortunately, *seeing* and *coming there* do not matter: for those who boast about it can do nothing more than show that they are legitimated by the distant *vision*."[39] As Abraham Socher has observed, the Kantian moral philosopher and the moral skeptic resemble Moses, gazing into a land neither can enter. The image is apt, not the least owing to its Mosaic inspiration.[40] Moses' fate becomes, for Maimon, a sort of cautionary tale about the limits of transcendental philosophy, but more trenchantly, about the perils of human finitude. However pessimistic this assessment, though, Maimon still offers a glimmer of hope. At the close of his *Autobiography*, Maimon admonishes his readers regarding this highest end: "Therefore, strive! . . . The highest end of human being is knowledge of the truth. God fulfills his promise to us. The people who wander in darkness have seen a great light" (MGW, I: 454). The verse Maimon excerpts here, alluding to the exodus and therefore also Mosaic inspiration, also concludes Maimonides' *Guide*. For both Maimon and Maimonides, the "great light" is the light of intellectual perfection, the new promised land, to which we might emigrate, through the perfection both of thought and of action.[41]

[39] *MGW*, VII: 554; see also *Deuteronomy* 34:4. [40] Socher 2006. [41] *Isaiah* 35:5.

4 Erhard on Right and Morality

James A. Clarke

In his 1796/7 *Foundations of Natural Right*, J. G. Fichte advances the innovative thesis that the theory of right is independent of, or separate from, moral theory: the "philosophical doctrine [or theory – *Lehre*] of right . . . ought to be a separate science standing on its own" (*FNR*, 11; *SW*, III: 10). Although Fichte is concerned to stress the originality and heterodoxy of his approach, he refers approvingly to some "excellent hints" by Johann Benjamin Erhard in "several of his most recent writings" (*FNR*, 12; *SW*, III: 12).[1] Given the recent scholarly interest in Fichte's account of the relationship between right and morality,[2] and in the topic of the relationship between right and morality more generally, it is surprising that there has been very little discussion of Erhard's position. Where Erhard's position is discussed, it is often presented as nothing more than a hesitant precursor of Fichte's more fully developed and more radical position. Thus, Luc Ferry claims that Erhard "manages to sketch" Fichte's position in the *Foundations*, and Xavier Léon describes Erhard as "glimpsing" a kind of independence of right in relation to morality.[3] Léon further claims that Erhard conceives of the independence as "partial" or "relative," thereby inviting an invidious comparison with Fichte, who, it is sometimes thought, argues for full independence or "complete separation."[4]

In this paper, I attempt to show that Erhard's account of the relationship between right and morality constitutes a distinctive and compelling position in its own right that merits philosophical attention. In Sections 1 and 2, I reconstruct Erhard's account of the relationship between right and morality. I argue that Erhard's position should not be characterized simply as the claim

Drafts of this paper were presented at the "Right and Morality" workshop at the Humboldt University, Berlin and at the German Idealism seminar at Aarhus University, Denmark. I am grateful to participants at both events for their comments, criticisms, and suggestions. I am also grateful to Gabriel Gottlieb for critical feedback and discussion. The research for this paper was supported by the Arts and Humanities Research Council (grant reference: AH/R001847/1).

[1] Fichte also refers approvingly to Salomon Maimon's 1795 essay "On the First Grounds of Natural Right." I briefly discuss Maimon's essay in footnote 14 below.

[2] For recent discussions of Fichte's position, see: Clarke 2016; Kosch 2017; Neuhouser 2016.

[3] Ferry 1981: 294; Léon 1954: 484.

[4] Léon 1954: 485. Ludwig Siep cited in Neuhouser 2016: 32, n. 1.

that the theory of right is partly independent of morality; rather, it is best characterized as focusing on the dynamic *interplay* between the theory of right (which is internally complex, comprising a hierarchically ordered set of disciplines) and the requirements of morality as articulated by Kantian moral theory. In Section 3, I demonstrate the coherence and significance of Erhard's position by considering it in relation to a central debate in the philosophy of law – the debate between legal positivism and natural law theory.

Before beginning, a note on terminology is necessary. It is standard among commentators to speak of "the relationship between right and morality" in connection with Fichte and Erhard. I think that both Fichte and Erhard are interested primarily in the relationship between the *theories* or *doctrines* of right and morality. However, they often slide from talking about the relationship between the theories of right and morality to talking simply about the relationship between the object domains of those theories – viz., right and morality. This slide is warranted because the relationships between the theories that they are interested in hold primarily in virtue of the relationships between the norms and principles that constitute the object domains of those theories. Thus, for Erhard, many of the relationships between moral theory and the theory of right are grounded in the relationships between the norms and principles of morality and those of natural right.

1 "Devil's Apology"

Discussions of Erhard's account of the relationship between right and morality tend to focus – often exclusively – on his 1795 essay "Devil's Apology [*Apologie des Teufels*]."[5] This focus is liable to result in a truncated and misleading view of Erhard's position. To see why, we need to discuss the argument of "Devil's Apology."

"Devil's Apology" attempts to contribute to Kantian practical philosophy by providing a discussion of the concept of the devil and of the grounds for postulating his existence. Drawing upon Kant's practical philosophy, Erhard argues that the devil should be conceived of as the "ideal of wickedness" – the polar opposite to, or inverted mirror image of, the ideal of morality, where an ideal is here understood, following Kant, as the personification of an idea (*Idee*). (For Kant, the Stoic sage is the ideal of wisdom [*CPR*, A 569/B 597].) When conceived of in this way, the devil is an extremely powerful and completely self-interested being who strives to dominate every other rational being.

The moral ideal (and every human agent who acts morally) acts on the categorical imperative, which Erhard formulates as: "Act in such a way that the

[5] See Léon 1954: 484–5 and Ferry 1984: 292–4.

maxim in accordance with which you act can be followed by all other human beings at all times without conflict" (*DA*, ¶ 15; *AT*, 118).[6] The fundamental principle – the "wicked intention" – on which the devil acts is: "I want to act in such a way that my self is the only possible end of my action and appears as the only free being" (*DA*, ¶ 20; *AT*, 122). The categorical imperative entails interpersonal "peace" and the coordination of agents' behavior. The wicked intention entails interpersonal conflict and the subordination of all agents to the devil.

Most of "Devil's Apology" is devoted to providing an account of the concept of the devil. However, Erhard devotes several paragraphs to considering the implications of his account for Kantian moral theory and the philosophy of right. It is here that he discusses the relationship between the theory of right and moral theory.

To understand Erhard's account of the relationship, we obviously need to understand his account of the relata – that is, we need to know how Erhard characterizes the theory of right and moral theory. Erhard states that "morality," understood as a rigorous discipline or "science," is not a doctrine (*Lehre*) of virtue and does not aim to make human beings virtuous (*DA*, ¶ 16; *AT*, 119). It rather aims to make human beings *just* by providing a theory of what does not contradict virtue. It does this by telling us how our maxims (the subjective principles on which we act) must be constituted so that they do not contradict a virtuous disposition. Since the categorical imperative is the principle that allows us to determine whether or not our maxims contradict the virtuous disposition (by determining whether or not they can be acted on by *all* agents without conflict), we can assume that it constitutes the core of morality qua science. This is a fairly thin conception of moral theory and of morality. However, Erhard gestures toward a richer conception of morality, when he refers, at a later stage of the essay, to the requirements that morality imposes on human beings and to the "fully developed idea of morality" (*DA*, ¶¶ 43, 45; *AT*, 131–2).

Despite its brevity, Erhard's characterization of moral theory and its object domain is fairly comprehensible. By contrast, his characterization of the theory of right and its object domain is unclear. He refers briefly to "natural right" and to the "doctrine [*Lehre*] of right" in its capacity as the "science of rights"; unfortunately, his characterizations of both are uninformative, and it is not clear how they are related (*DA*, ¶¶ 16, 45; *AT*, 119, 132). (Are they different descriptions of the same discipline, or do they pick out two different disciplines? If the latter, is one a part of, or based on, the other?) From the little that Erhard says, it seems that the central task of the theory of right is to identify the

[6] The paragraphs of the English translation of *Apologie des Teufels* are numbered for ease of reference. All of my references to the translation cite the paragraph numbers.

norms – the rights and laws – that must obtain if self-interested human agents are to coexist peacefully in community with each other, develop their capacities, and satisfy their needs. Such norms prevent interpersonal domination by coordinating the behavior of agents so that their "selfish drives" are "reciprocally compatible" (*DA*, ¶¶ 48, 44, 45; *AT*, 133, 131–2, 132).

Having discussed Erhard's account of the relata, let us consider his account of the relationship between them. Erhard claims that the theory of right is dependent on morality in some respects, and independent of it in others. The theory of right is dependent on morality because morality exerts normative authority and control over the theory of right's object domain – viz., right. This happens in two ways. First, morality imposes normative side-constraints on right in that rights or laws are valid only if they are morally permissible and would not, when acted upon, "annul" the capacity for morality in "any human being" (i.e., harm or hinder those capacities that are necessary for moral agency) (*DA*, ¶¶ 43; *AT*, 131). Insofar as it is subject to these constraints, right is "answerable before the tribunal of morality." Second, right "receives its sanction" from morality because a social order governed by law is the "only possible condition . . . in which morality can successfully appear in external actions and does not remain restricted to inner consciousness alone" (*DA*, ¶¶ 43; *AT*, 131). In other words, laws, rights, and legal-political institutions are sanctioned by morality because they are the necessary, enabling conditions of its realization in the world. Implicit in this idea is the claim that morality *demands* that laws, rights, and legal-political institutions be so configured that they enable the realization of morality. The normative authority and control that morality exerts over right carries over to the theory of right: the theory of right must not derive laws or rights that violate the side-constraints that morality imposes on right; and the theory of right must satisfy the moral demand that it derive laws, rights, and legal-political institutions that enable the realization of morality in the world.

Although the theory of right is dependent on morality, it is also independent of it in one important respect. This independence relates to the distinctive task of the theory of right: to coordinate the behavior of human agents so that their free actions are "reciprocally compatible," thereby ensuring peaceful coexistence and preventing domination. Erhard suggests that this task can be carried out *independently* of any appeal – whether explicit or implicit – to moral concepts or principles. This is so because the principle that is used to identify and allocate rights – the "principle of right [*Grundsatz des Rechts*]" – requires nothing more than *consistency* in our judgments about right. Erhard characterizes the principle as follows:

> The *principle of right* is the following reciprocal proposition: what has once provided the reason for an action that was recognized by me as right (or morally possible), must always provide the reason for my judgement about this action, and what has once provided the reason in another's judgement about my action must always provide the

reason for the same. – Thus right arises from the demand for complete consistency which human beings reciprocally make on each other (*volenti non fit iniuria* [to a willing person, no injury is done]). (*DA*, ¶ 42; *AT*, 131)

Erhard's account of the principle of right turns on the thought that self-interested agents will be motivated (provided their self-interest is sufficiently enlightened) to establish a system of rights and laws that protects each agent's pursuit of her self-interest and does so equally for all agents. To establish this system, agents reason collectively, making judgments about which actions are rightful and which not. In this process of reasoning, each agent demands of each other agent that she reason consistently, and these demands generate a principle that governs collective deliberation – the principle of right. The principle of right stipulates that anyone who judges an action to be right in *her* case must judge it to be right in *all* cases (and must therefore accept any adverse consequences that might arise for her from other people performing the action), and that anyone who condemns an action performed by another as unrightful must condemn it in *all* cases, including her own. The point of this deliberative constraint is to ensure that no one can advance her self-interest at the expense of others by arrogating to herself a privilege that she alone can enjoy. The upshot of this constraint is that a right can be a right only if it is a right "reciprocally" (*DA*, ¶ 43; *AT*, 131).

The principle of right requires consistency in deliberation about the identification and allocation of rights. Now, the concept of consistency is, Erhard argues, a theoretical concept, not a moral one, and discerning whether judgments are consistent across relevantly similar cases is an exercise of theoretical rationality. Such reasoning need not appeal to, or rely on, moral concepts such as justice or fairness or moral principles based on those concepts (e.g., the principle that fairness requires that I judge consistently across my case and the cases of others); and while one might be motivated to reason in this way by moral concerns, one might equally well be motivated by prudential ones. Indeed, Erhard thinks that *self-interested* rational agents will judge in this way because they realize that a legal order that assigns rights equally to everyone will best protect and secure their self-interested pursuit of their goals.

According to Erhard, then, the theory of right discharges its distinctive task by using a deliberative procedure (stipulated by the principle of right) that does not appeal to, or rely on, moral concepts or principles. In this respect, the theory of right is independent of morality and moral theory.

Erhard's discussion in "Devil's Apology" suggests that his position is simply that the theory of right is *partly* dependent on morality and moral theory and *partly* independent of them. It therefore seems that Xavier Léon is warranted in characterizing Erhard's position solely in terms of "relative independence."[7]

[7] Léon 1954: 485.

However, although this characterization gets something right, Erhard endorses a much more sophisticated and complex position than that which is immediately suggested by "Devil's Apology." (Elements of this position are, I think, implicit in "Devil's Apology," but this will become apparent only once the position is reconstructed in full.) I now want to reconstruct that position by discussing writings by Erhard that were written either shortly before or after "Devil's Apology." My discussion will draw primarily upon Erhard's review of Fichte's 1793/4 defense of the French Revolution (the *Contribution to the Correction of the Public's Judgment of the French Revolution*), a review that Erhard claims – in a 1796 letter to Karl Leonhard Reinhold – contains many of his ideas on natural right (*DW*, 418). I will supplement my discussion where necessary by drawing upon Erhard's own defense of the French Revolution – *On the Right of the People to a Revolution* (written in 1794 and published in 1795) – and his writings on "autocracy [*Alleinherrschaft*]" and on the theory of legislation.

2 The Review of Fichte

In my discussion of "Devil's Apology," I noted that Erhard's account of the theory of right lacked clarity. Erhard's review of Fichte (hereafter, "Review of Fichte") remedies this defect, providing a clear account of the nature and structure of the theory of right. A striking feature of this account is that the theory of right turns out to be internally complex, comprising three disciplines: natural right; the theory of legislation; and jurisprudence (*Rechtsgelahrtheit*).[8] Let us consider each in turn.

Natural Right

Natural right derives the general norms – the rights and laws – that are necessary, given some very general facts about human nature, to enable human beings to coexist peacefully, satisfy their needs, and develop their capacities in a community. These norms are the necessary, enabling conditions of human agency, and they include human rights (*Menschenrechte*), which include the

[8] Here the English term "jurisprudence" is to be understood in its original sense as "knowledge of or skill in law" – the literal translation of "*Rechtsgelahrtheit*" is "legal learnedness" – rather than as "philosophy of law." In *On the Right of the People to a Revolution*, Erhard claims that the doctrine of right comprises two disciplines: natural right and jurisprudence. Natural right "examines only what can be a right in virtue of morality and what should be declared as such on account of the relations into which human beings must enter in order to live most happily and peacefully with each other while developing their powers" (*ÜRVR*, 14). As Erhard's discussion makes clear, natural right provides an account of human rights. Jurisprudence determines what rights are actually recognized in a historically existing state and is closely related to the study of positive law. It is not clear where the theory of legislation fits into this schema.

right to acquire property. Natural right derives these norms by considering the human being in the state of nature. For Erhard, the state of nature is not a real, historically existing community that existed prior to civil society; it is a heuristic "fiction" that is used to discover the norms of natural right (*RF*, 156–7, 160–1).[9] Although the state of nature is a "mere fiction," the norms derived with its aid serve a regulative, guiding function for legislation and, taken together, constitute an "ideal" that societies should strive to realize (*RF*, 155).[10] (I return to the fictional status of the state of nature in Section 3.)

The Theory of Legislation

The norms derived by natural right constitute a regulative ideal that societies should strive to realize (*RF*, 160; see also *PA*, 333). Now, the norms of natural right are abstract and indeterminate, and cannot, precisely because they are abstract and indeterminate, effectively govern and coordinate human behavior (or, as Erhard puts it, "have causality"). If they are to effectively govern and coordinate human behavior, they must be endowed with "legal force" or the "force of law" (*Rechtskraft*), but this can happen only if they are made concrete and determinate by being authoritatively laid down (i.e., posited) in the positive laws of a community. (The concept of *Rechtskraft* denotes the binding force of law and is closely related to the concept of legal validity.) Erhard calls the condition in which a community is governed by positive law "civil society," and he therefore claims that "[t]here must be civil society so that natural right can have causality" (*RF*, 156; see also 158).

Erhard rejects the thesis that civil societies emerge historically through a contract in which legitimate authority is transferred to a government.[11] He holds instead that civil societies emerge through an act of "arrogation [*Anmaßung*]," in which a person or group claims "supreme power [or "supreme authority" – *Obergewalt*]" and imposes "civil order" on the other members of society; the other members of society acquiesce (realizing that civil order promotes their self-interest) and come to recognize the judgments of those who impose order as authoritative and binding (*RF*, 140; *ÜRVR*, 81; *BA*, 212–18, 221–3; *BF*). With this, civil society and positive law are established. This account of the historical origins of civil society implies that nascent positive law is in large part a codification of preexisting inequities and asymmetrical power relations. But this means that nascent positive law is "impure" when judged from the perspective of natural right. If the ideal of

[9] Cf. Perrinjaquet in Erhard 1993: 254, n. 51.

[10] On the regulative function of natural right, see *PA*, 333, 339–40.

[11] Erhard thinks that such explanations of the emergence of civil society are viciously circular (see *RF*, 140; cf. *ÜRVR*, 81 and *BA*, 217).

natural right is to be realized, positive law must undergo a gradual process of purification in which states and legal systems are progressively transformed in accordance with the regulative ideal of natural right (*RF*, 157; *IG*, 14).[12]

Now, the theory of legislation guides the activity or "art [*Kunst*]" of legislation, which has two interrelated tasks: (1) it must facilitate the realization of natural right (or, equivalently, the purification of positive law) by transforming the positive laws of a given state so that they better approximate the ideal of natural right; (2) it must convert the abstract and indeterminate norms of natural right into concrete and determinate positive laws, thereby endowing them with legal force. The theory of legislation guides and informs the activity of legislation by providing insight into the nature of its task and the means for achieving it (*IG*, 1–2, 14).

Jurisprudence

Jurisprudence studies the legal systems and positive laws of historically existing communities. Alain Perrinjaquet points out that whereas natural right and the theory of legislation are "*normative*" disciplines, specifying what ought to be the case, jurisprudence is a "*descriptive*" discipline, which merely surveys the positive law of societies.[13] Because it is descriptive, jurisprudence does not participate in the complex norm-governed interaction that, as we shall see, takes place between the other disciplines. I will therefore ignore it in what follows.

***

Having discussed Erhard's revised conception of the theory of right, let us consider its relationship to morality. The first thing to consider is the dependence of the theory of right on morality. In "Devil's Apology," Erhard claimed that the theory of right is dependent on morality because morality exerts normative authority and control over right in two ways: (1) right is "answerable" to morality in that any proposed legal norms are valid only if they do not violate moral side-constraints; (2) morality "sanctions" right and demands that laws, rights, and legal-political institutions be so configured that they enable the realization of morality.

The account of dependence in "Review of Fichte" is consistent with this. However, as one might expect, Erhard's revised conception of the theory of right makes the dependence relationship far more complex and involved. For we are now dealing with *three* disciplines and their object domains: moral theory; natural right; and the theory of legislation. These disciplines are

[12] Cf. *DA*, ¶ 43, n. *; *AT*, 131, n. *: "Right is always positive in its origins [*ensteht allezeit positiv*], and positive right is not based on a right that is natural . . . but is purified through enlightenment to the level of natural right."

[13] Perrinjaquet in Erhard 1993: 248, n. 43.

hierarchically ordered: moral theory occupies the top of the hierarchy; natural right is immediately below moral theory; and the theory of legislation is immediately below natural right. A discipline's position in the hierarchy is determined by its normative authority relative to the other disciplines. Moral theory, at the top of the hierarchy, exerts its normative authority over natural right and, by means of natural right, over the theory of legislation.

Natural right is immediately subject to the normative constraints of morality (and hence "answerable" to it) in that it ought not to derive any norms that permit actions that are morally impermissible. The theory (and activity) of legislation is immediately subject to the normative constraints of natural right in that it ought not to propose the enactment of positive laws that conflict with the norms of natural right (e.g., by permitting the violation of human rights) (*RF*, 157; see also *PA*, 372). Since the normative constraints that natural right imposes on legislation are themselves determined by morality, the theory of legislation is mediately, and ultimately, constrained by morality.

As well as being subject to moral constraints, natural right and the theory of legislation are subject to positive demands on the part of morality and moral theory. Morality demands that it has "causality" in the world of appearances by being realized in human actions; it therefore demands that the necessary conditions for that realization obtain (*RF*, 156). If human beings are to act morally, they must be able to exercise their capacity for free agency; but they can do this only if they coexist peacefully with each other and their fundamental needs are satisfied (*ÜRVR*, 68; *RF*, 156). The task of the theory of natural right, which is mandated by morality, is to derive a set of norms that enables peaceful coexistence and the satisfaction of needs. (These norms include human rights, which include the right to acquire property.)

The theory of natural right derives the norms that enable the realization of morality. If morality is to have causality in the world, the norms of natural right must themselves be given "causality" by being converted into positive law (*RF*, 161). Consequently, morality demands that this conversion take place. It is the task of the theory and activity of legislation to satisfy this demand.

The account of the dependence of the theory of right on morality in "Review of Fichte" suggests that it is very far-reaching. Indeed, it creates the impression that the theory of right is *completely* constrained and controlled by the requirements of morality. Has Erhard simply dropped the claim that the theory of right is partly independent of morality?

The answer to this question is "No." Erhard is still committed to this claim; he has simply provided a different account of independence. This account is not formulated in terms of "consistency," but in terms of "necessary exceptions."[14]

[14] The language of "necessary exceptions" is also used by Maimon. In his 1795 essay "On the First Grounds of Natural Right," Maimon defines the theory of natural right as "the science of

Erhard deploys the terminology of "necessary exceptions" in his discussion of the three disciplines that constitute the theory of right. He characterizes "natural right in its entirety" as "the science of the necessary exceptions to the complete [*durchgängigen*] determination of our way of acting by the moral law, exceptions which are necessary for its implementation [or "introduction" – *Einführung*] in human life" (*RF*, 156). He characterizes the theory of legislation as "[t]he doctrine of the necessary exceptions to the laws of natural right for the sake of the legal force [*Rechtskraft*] of natural rights themselves" (*RF*, 157). Finally, jurisprudence is characterized as "[t]he doctrine of those exceptions [to the laws of natural right] that are deemed to be necessary" (*RF*, 157).

Clearly, Erhard thinks that each discipline in the hierarchy derives or studies "necessary exceptions" to the norms derived in the discipline immediately above it. What is less clear is what this is supposed to mean and precisely how the derivation of necessary exceptions involves independence from morality and moral theory. Let us try to make sense of this by first considering the way that natural right derives necessary exceptions to the norms derived by moral theory. We will then consider how legislation derives necessary exceptions to the norms derived by natural right. (I ignore jurisprudence for the reason given earlier.)

The Exceptions of Natural Right

As we saw, Erhard claims that morality demands that natural right derive the necessary conditions for its realization in the world. These necessary conditions are the necessary conditions of human agency, and they consist of a system of norms – laws and rights – that regulate human interaction so as to

the necessary and universally valid *apparent exceptions* to the moral law that are determined by it *a priori*" (*ÜGN*, 142). Maimon is especially concerned with the "right of coercion" and the "right to acquire ownerless things." These rights constitute "exceptions" to the moral law because they authorize agents to override the wills of other agents in certain circumstances (using force if necessary), something that is normally prohibited by the moral law. However, these exceptions are ultimately justified by the moral law because they are either (in the case of the right of coercion) indirect consequences of it, or (in the case of the right to acquire ownerless things) necessary conditions of its "use [*Gebrauch*]" or application to experience. Because they are ultimately justified by the moral law, they are only apparent exceptions to it.

Erhard was aware of Maimon's essay, and it is probable that his choice of terminology was influenced by it. However, Erhard's account of necessary exceptions is a good deal more developed and sophisticated than Maimon's. Whereas Maimon thinks that there is one "level" of necessary exceptions (the exceptions to morality derived by natural right), Erhard's account of the structure of the theory of right leads him to think that there are two levels: the necessary exceptions to morality derived by natural right and the necessary exceptions to natural right derived by the theory of legislation (see Oncina Coves 1997: 69). For helpful discussions of Maimon's essay, see: Léon 1954: 479–84; Schottky 1995: 299–311; Nance and Yonover 2020.

guarantee peaceful coexistence and the satisfaction of needs. These norms include the human right to acquire property. In what sense are they "necessary exceptions" to morality?

Erhard explains his terminology in the following footnote:

> No exception to the rule [viz. the moral law] occurs here in the sense that a case falling under it would not be determined by it; an exception occurs only in the sense that something that first makes its application possible is determined without it. The principle of natural right is the greatest possible causality of the moral law in [the realm of] appearance. (*RF*, 156, n. *)

There are, I think, two distinct ideas in play here. The first idea is that moral theory does not itself possess the conceptual resources to derive the necessary conditions of its realization in the world. These conditions are to be derived by reflecting on the necessary conditions of human agency, a process of reflection that is informed and guided by certain very general facts about human nature and the world. Such reflection, Erhard thinks, need make no reference to moral concepts or principles. Consequently, something that first makes the realization of morality possible is "determined without it." But to say that it is determined without it is, of course, to say that it is independent of it. We might dub this first idea the "derivational" or "theoretical" sense of "exception."

That is one idea. However, Erhard has another idea in mind, which explains why the necessary conditions derived by natural right are "exceptions" to the "*complete determination of our way of acting*" by the moral law (*RF*, 156; my emphasis). The theory of natural right derives the human right to acquire property (the right of appropriation – *Zueignungsrecht*) as a necessary condition of human agency. Now, as Erhard conceives of it, this human right allows me to justify an action *simply* on the basis of features of a situation that pertain solely to me and my individual circumstances: the bare fact that *I* need *this* to live is a sufficient justifying reason for my taking exclusive possession of it. Erhard thinks that this mode of justification is normally ruled out by morality, which does not allow me to be determined "wholly by chance and need" (*RF*, 153; see *ÜRVR*, 68). However, although morality normally rules out this mode of justification, it is sanctioned and licensed in this case because the human right to acquire property is a necessary condition for the realization of morality in the world. We might dub this the "practical" or "normative" sense of exception insofar as what is at issue is the introduction of a mode of practical justification (a species of reasons for action) that is normally ruled out by morality.

There are thus two, related, ways in which natural right constitutes an exception to, and is thus independent of, morality and moral theory: (1) natural right derives the necessary conditions of human agency independently of moral concepts or principles; and (2) this introduces a needs-based mode of practical justification that is independent of morality insofar as it is not directly subject to its normative constraints.

The Exceptions of the Theory of Legislation

In what sense are the positive laws derived by the theory of legislation exceptions to natural right? Again, I think that two ideas are in play here.

The first idea turns on Erhard's claim that legislation ought to be a process of the purification of positive law. As we've seen, Erhard holds that natural right (and morality) demand that the ideal of natural right be realized or "given causality" in the world. Since the ideal of natural right can be realized only through legislation, this generates the demand that the theory and activity of legislation derive and enact laws that realize the ideal of natural right. Now, as we've also seen, Erhard holds that nascent positive law is, when judged by the standard of natural right, "impure" in its origins and must be purified by legislation until it realizes the ideal of natural right. This process of purification is a piecemeal affair – a gradual, cumulative process of amelioration. The legislator cannot hope to realize the ideal of natural right wholesale: her society stands at a specific point on a developmental continuum, and although she can make changes that bring her society a step closer to purity, she must leave certain inequities intact. The upshot of this is that the theory and activity of legislation will involve the derivation and enactment of laws that do not fully satisfy the requirements of natural right and are thus "impure." Since natural right demands that the norms of natural right be fully realized, such laws constitute "exceptions" to it. Such exceptions are "necessary" because the realization of the ideal of natural right can be achieved only through the enactment of such positive laws. That is the first idea.

The second idea concerns the way that the abstract and indeterminate norms of natural right are realized in positive law. The task of the theory and activity of legislation is to make the abstract and indeterminate norms of natural right concrete and determinate by converting them into the positive rights and laws of an actually existing state. Now, it is Erhard's view that the norms of natural right are *multiply realizable* in that they can be made concrete and determinate in a variety of ways, each of which counts as a realization of the relevant norm. This view is expressed most clearly in the following discussion of positive law or right (*das positive Recht*) in *On the Right of the People to a Revolution*:

> Positive right may never be contrary to natural right because it would thereby also be against morality; but among the rights that are possible in natural right, it can determine some as actual *without having decisive reasons for this selection* [*Auswahl*]. The moral

possibility of different laws in different states is based on this. (*ÜRVR*, 14; my emphasis)[15]

The task of the legislator, then, is to select one of the possible ways of realizing the norms of natural right. The theory of natural right does not itself possess the conceptual resources to determine this selection. It imposes requirements on legislation – there must be a regime of property; there must be laws governing contracts, etc. – but it cannot determine and is silent on which of the many ways of satisfying those requirements should obtain. The legislator does this by making a selection from a range of alternatives. It is here that a degree of independence enters, for the legislator's selection will involve considerations that are not dependent on or guided by natural right. (To say that the legislator lacks "decisive reasons" for selection is not to say that she need have *no* reasons for selection, that the legislative choice is arbitrary.) She will, as Erhard makes clear in his writings on the theory of legislation, be concerned to legislate consistently. But she will also consider utility, past practice, feasibility, and the customs, culture, and mores of the community for which she is legislating.

***

The preceding reconstruction has, I hope, shown that "Review of Fichte" offers a much richer and more complex account of the relationship between the theory of right and morality than "Devil's Apology." "Devil's Apology" is usually read as maintaining that the theory of right is partly independent of morality and partly dependent on it. The richer account reveals something that was only implicit in "Devil's Apology" – namely, that morality is itself profoundly dependent on the theory of right for its realization. Moreover, by conceiving of the relationship in terms of "necessary exceptions," the richer account also suggests that the relationship between the theory of right and morality should be understood not as a static relation, but as a dynamic, conflictual *interplay.*[16]

[15] Cf. *RF*, 158:

> There is only one morality, one natural right, and one state, just as there is only one human species; but since the state is a mere means for the legal force of natural right, it is determined only with regard to its end, and the means [*die Mittel*] depend on insight [*Einsicht*]. There are thus different modifications of the [one] state, and these constitute what one calls *different* states.

Zwi Batscha identifies Erhard's "*Einsicht*" with "Aristotelian phronesis," understood as the capacity to answer "technical-practical questions" (Batscha 1972: 58, n. 22).

[16] It is interesting to note that Schottky discerns something similar in Maimon's account of the relationship between natural right and morality. According to Schottky, Maimon's definition of the science of natural right suggests "a sort of dialectical relationship between ethics and natural right: as 'exceptions,' natural rights stand in a certain opposition to the moral law; but, on the other hand, the moral law itself determines that exceptions of a specific kind are necessary in the relevant respects, and thus the exceptions are again only apparent" (Schottky 1995: 300).

Morality demands that natural right derive the necessary conditions of the realization of morality, but the independent derivation of those conditions exerts normative pressure on morality by introducing a needs-based mode of justification. Morality responds to that pressure by justifying and sanctioning that mode of justification. Natural right demands that the theory and activity of legislation convert the abstract norms of natural right into positive law, thereby "purifying" positive law to the level of natural right. However, the theory and activity of legislation exerts normative pressure on natural right by deriving and enacting laws that do not fully satisfy the requirements of natural right and thus conflict with it. Natural right responds by justifying and sanctioning these "impure" laws as necessary for the progressive realization of the ideal of natural right. Note that although the relationship can be described as an *interplay*, morality is the dominant partner in the relationship and the whole interaction is ultimately constrained and controlled by it.

3 Erhard and Natural Law Theory

Having reconstructed Erhard's account of the relationship between right and morality, I now want to consider it in relation to a central debate in the philosophy of law: the debate between natural law theory and legal positivism. This debate is often characterized as a dispute between those who maintain that there is a necessary, conceptual connection between law and morality (natural law theorists) and those who deny that there is such a connection (legal positivists).[17]

To say that there is a necessary, conceptual connection between law and morality is to endorse the thesis that conformity with the standards of morality (or practical rationality) is criterial for law and legal validity, so that a putative law that failed to satisfy those standards would in some sense not be a law. (This thesis is often associated with the slogan "*lex iniusta non est lex*" – an unjust law is no law at all.) The legal positivist rejects this thesis, arguing that laws are legally valid simply if they satisfy the de facto criteria of legal validity – the "source tests" – of a given legal system, where these criteria might violate the requirements of morality.[18]

Erhard's emphasis on the normative authority of morality and his claim that legislation should not conflict with the requirements of morality and natural right would seem to suggest a commitment to the central thesis of natural law theory. And, indeed, we find him explicitly endorsing this thesis. Thus, in *On the Right of the People to a Revolution*, he states that "[i]t is the inner condition [of the validity] of any law ... that it not contradict the moral laws," and he

[17] See, for example, Alexy 2002: ch. 1. [18] Beyleveld and Brownsword 1984: 3.

asserts that "[w]hat contradicts reason cannot be called a law for human beings; it is the dictum of a fool or the threat of a robber" (*ÜRVR*, 15, 16; see also 17 and *RF*, 158).

There are, however, aspects of Erhard's work that might be thought to be congenial to legal positivism. Thus, Erhard places considerable emphasis on the positivity of law – that is, its nature as a humanly created, socially constructed fact;[19] and he endorses the view (often taken to be characteristic of legal positivism) that laws depend for their existence and legal validity (their legal force) on social facts such as legislation, judicial precedent, and custom.[20] (Recall that for Erhard the norms of natural right can have legal force only if they are instantiated in positive laws.) Finally, Erhard's claim that natural right is based on a "mere fiction" might be taken to suggest that no universal, context-transcendent norms of natural law exist, a view that is often associated with legal positivism and that is thought to entail the rejection of natural law theory.[21] Does the presence of these apparent concessions to legal positivism mean that Erhard's position is an inconsistent and confused hybrid of the two approaches to theorizing about law?

I don't think that it does. I think that Erhard's position is perfectly consistent and represents a compelling and innovative approach to natural law theory. To see this, we need to examine those aspects of his work that might be thought to be congenial to legal positivism and inconsistent with natural law theory. I begin by discussing Erhard's claim that natural right is based on a "mere fiction."

As noted, Erhard's use of the term "fiction" might be taken to suggest that he thinks that no context-transcendent norms of natural right exist. It should be clear from my discussion of Erhard's position that he is committed to no such view. The state of nature is a heuristic device that is used to derive a set of abstract and indeterminate norms – the norms of natural right. To say that the state of nature is a "mere fiction" is *only* to deny the possible existence of a "primitive condition" corresponding to the state of nature, in which the abstract and indeterminate norms of natural right effectively govern human behavior. It is *not* to claim that these norms lack directive, normative force and cannot guide legislation and serve as a standard for it. (Recall that Erhard thinks that

19 This emphasis is noted by Gustav A. Walz, who claims that "[i]t is above all Erhard who, through his emphasis on the positivity of law [*Recht*] and its independence in relation to morality clearly influenced Fichte's conception" (Walz 1928: 466).

20 Finnis 2018: §§ 1, 1.5.

21 Hans Kelsen argues against natural law theory on the grounds that it relies on the assumption that a universally valid morality exists, an assumption that Kelsen considers to be wholly unwarranted (Kelsen 1967: 64–8; see Alexy 2012). Alexy has dubbed this the "argument from relativism" (Alexy 2012; Alexy 2002: 53–6).

the norms of natural right serve a regulative function for legislation.) Erhard makes this clear in the following two passages, which are worth citing in full:

> The state of nature, in contrast to [*im Gegensatz*] the state, is a mere fiction, just like the Leibnizian kingdom of grace in contrast to the current condition of man. But because the ruling [*Entscheidung*] [pronounced] under this fiction becomes universally valid, *it is the rule for the analogous judgment in reality. Just as the moral law has primacy in relation to natural right, so natural right has primacy in relation to the state.* (*RF*, 157; my emphasis)

> Since the primitive condition is a fiction, yet natural right must absolutely have causality if human beings should live, preserve themselves, and manifest themselves as moral beings, *this fiction must be transformed into something actual*, a [certain] condition [*Zustand*] of human beings must be established [*festgesetzt*] and accepted as primitive, certain signs must be determined which must indubitably demonstrate to everyone the reality of a fact from which a right follows, and the rules of rights [viz. the rules that determine positive rights] must be removed from personal examination [literally, "self-examination" – *Selbstprüfung*] and established as unconditionally valid. There must be civil society so that natural right can have causality. (*RF*, 156; my emphasis)

Clearly, if the norms derived by considering the state of nature are to be "transformed into something actual," they must exist in some sense, even if they do not, prior to such transformation, enjoy the same kind of existence as positive law (viz., institutional existence). Erhard's use of the term "fiction" therefore does not commit him to the claim that no context-transcendent norms of natural right exist.[22]

Let us turn now to Erhard's emphasis on the positivity of law and his endorsement of the view that laws depend for their existence and legal force on social facts such as legislation, judicial precedent, and custom. This emphasis and endorsement are congenial to legal positivism. Are they also inconsistent with natural law theory?

The idea that there is an inconsistency here relies on a particular view of natural law theory that is often espoused by critics of natural law theory, and that is clearly and canonically formulated by Hans Kelsen. On this view, natural law theory conceives of the principles of natural law as existing in a transcendent realm that is quite separate from the realm of positive law. The principles of natural law fully specify how law ought to be, and the task of the legislator is simply to transpose the requirements of natural law into positive law. As Kelsen puts it:

[22] Although I cannot pursue this line of inquiry here, it might be illuminating to compare Erhard's account of the fictional status of the state of nature with Fichte's claims (in the *Foundations of Natural Right*) about the status of "original rights [*Urrechte*]" and of natural right (see *FNR*, 102, 132–3; *SW*, III: 112, 148–9).

> [T]he natural-law teachers contend, in a version which has remained a stereotype from the Church Fathers down to Kant, that positive law derives its entire validity from natural law; it is essentially a mere emanation of natural law; the making of statutes or decisions does not freely create, it merely reproduces the true law which is already somehow in existence . . .[23]

This view of natural law theory would, if endorsed, have several implications for the treatment of positive law and legislation. First, positive laws would derive none of their validity from their being posited – that is, their being authoritatively laid down by legislation, judicial precedent, and custom. Second, positive law would be regarded as merely ancillary to natural law and of little interest as an object of study in its own right. The only thing that would matter would be the compliance of positive law with natural law; and compliance would require only that the principles of natural law be straightforwardly transposed into positive law. Third, and relatedly, the activity of legislation, when conducted correctly, would involve none of the creativity and ingenuity that we often associate with it. The task of the legislator would be simply to descry the requirements of natural law (visible by the light of reason) and to convert them into positive law. This would mean, finally, that the diversity and variety of positive laws in different communities would have to be explained in terms of a *failure* to instantiate the requirements of natural law. These implications are problematic, for they all devalue or dismiss aspects of positive law and legislation that we ordinarily take to be important.

If this view of natural law theory were accurate, and if it were the *only* view of natural law theory, Erhard's emphasis on the positivity of law would be inconsistent with natural law theory. Fortunately, the view is little more than a bowdlerized caricature of natural law theory. It has been forcefully dismissed as "travesty" by John Finnis, who argues that natural law theory can accommodate the "truth" in legal positivism, and that it is just as concerned as legal positivism is with the positivity of law and the study of systems of positive law.[24] (According to Finnis, this concern can be traced back to Aquinas' natural law theory, a central innovation of which was to see positive law as an object worthy of study in its own right.[25]) A brief discussion of Finnis' argument will help us to address the worry about inconsistency.

Finnis claims that natural law theory, insofar as it is plausible, is not committed to the account of the derivation of positive law from natural law that is associated with the view criticized by Kelsen. Finnis substantiates this claim by drawing upon Aquinas' natural law theory, which distinguishes between two modes (*modi*) of derivation.[26] The first mode is characterized as

[23] Kelsen 1961: 416; cited in Finnis 2011: 28.
[24] Finnis 2011: 28; see Finnis 1996.
[25] Finnis 1996: 195.
[26] Finnis 1998: 266–71; Finnis 1996; Finnis 2011: 281–90. Aquinas 2002: Book I–II, Question 95, Article 2.

derivation by entailment from the principles of natural law. The idea is that certain positive laws are entailed by these principles (typically in conjunction with certain non-normative facts) and can be regarded as conclusions from them. (So, in a Kantian theory of natural law, a law prohibiting murder would be entailed by the Formula of Humanity.) The second mode of derivation is called "*determinatio*," and the positive laws derived are called "*determinationes.*" Finnis sometimes translates "*determinatio*" as "implementation" or "concretization," but one might think that "determination" best captures the idea; for the laws derived determine, give shape to, and specify practical principles that are indeterminate and general and – this is crucial – could not effectively govern and coordinate human behavior unless they were so determined.

The idea of *determinatio* can be illustrated by a simple example: the rule of the road. It is a requirement of practical reason that we respect our own and others' physical safety and this, in conjunction with certain non-normative facts (e.g., that traffic is dangerous) entails the requirement that there be laws governing traffic. Considered in itself, this requirement is indeterminate and cannot, in virtue of its indeterminacy, effectively govern and coordinate human behavior. If the requirement is to effectively govern and coordinate human behavior, it must be made *determinate* by being posited – authoritatively laid down – as a specific positive law or set of positive laws. Now, there are various ways that the requirement could be made determinate (it is multiply realizable): all traffic could be required to drive on the left or the right; the speed limit could be set at 60 or 65 miles per hour, etc. The legislator must select one of these ways to lay down as law, but the *specific way* that she selects is not determined by the requirement itself.[27] The legislator enjoys a degree of freedom and independence in drafting the law comparable to that enjoyed by an architect who exercises creativity within the confines of his brief (he must, for example, design a school with certain features – classrooms, doors, courtyards, etc. – but he has considerable creative latitude and freedom with regard to each of those features – the courtyards could be square, round, etc.).[28]

Finnis emphasizes Aquinas' doctrine of *determinatio* because it allows the natural law theorist to respond to Kelsen's objection, to capture the "truth" in legal positivism, and to do justice to the positivity of law. This is so for the following reasons. First, on this conception of the derivation of positive law from natural law, natural law turns out to be profoundly dependent on positive law and legislation for its realization and concretization. Second, although

[27] This is the standard, textbook example (Finnis 2011: 285). A richer example, with obvious political ramifications, would be the requirement that there be a regime of property. The principles of natural law entail that there be a legal regime that organizes the ownership, transfer, and distribution of property, but they do not themselves specify what form that regime should take – e.g., whether it should be a regime of private property or communal ownership, etc. (cf. Finnis 2011: 285–6).

[28] Finnis 2011: 284–5. Cf. Aquinas 2002: Book I–II, Question 95, Article 2.

determinationes are required by the principles of natural law, their legal validity and legal force is derived partly from the fact that they have been authoritatively laid down or posited.[29] (What gives "drive on the left and at no more than 65 miles per hour" legal force rather than some other rule is simply the fact that it was posited by an authoritative source.) This shows that the natural law theorist is *not* committed, *pace* Kelsen, to the view that positive laws derive their "entire validity" from natural law; and it allows the natural law theorist to capture the positivist insight that legal validity depends on social facts. Third, and finally, the doctrine of *determinatio* emphasizes the creativity of the activity of legislation and can make sense of "the patent and multiple diversity of positive laws at different times and places."[30]

It should, I hope, be apparent that there is considerable affinity between the doctrine of *determinatio* and Erhard's account of the relationship between natural right and positive law and legislation. As we have seen, Erhard holds that (1) many of the requirements of natural right are multiply realizable, that (2) the legislator enjoys a degree of creativity and autonomy in realizing them, and that (3) the diversity of positive laws in different states is explained and justified by (1) and (2). But this is precisely the position endorsed by Aquinas and Finnis. If this is correct, Erhard's account is consistent with a compelling conception of natural law theory.

None of this is to suggest that Erhard is a pale imitator of Aquinas or a mere precursor of Finnis. Erhard's natural law theory goes beyond both thinkers in important ways. First, Erhard introduces a pronounced historical dimension into natural law theory, conceiving of the development of positive law and legislation as the progressive pursuit of a regulative ideal that is constituted by the norms of natural right. Insofar as this ideal exists in the future, we might describe Erhard's natural law theory as "future-oriented."[31] Second, Erhard conceives of the relationship between natural right and positive law as a dynamic, conflictual one in which the attempt to realize the requirements of natural right in positive law necessarily involves deviations from and exceptions to those requirements. These aspects of Erhard's natural law theory strike me as sufficiently interesting to warrant a detailed study of it in relation to the tradition of natural law theory. Unfortunately, such a study is beyond the purview of this paper.

[29] Finnis 2018: §1.5. Aquinas 2002: Book I–II, Question 95, Article 3.
[30] Finnis 1996: 203.
[31] Cf. Batscha 1972: 57.

5 Erhard on Revolutionary Action

Michael Nance

1 Introduction

At the height of the German debate about the French Revolution, the philosopher, physician, and public intellectual Johann Benjamin Erhard offered a broadly Kantian defense of the right to revolution under conditions of structural injustice.[1] Erhard's theory of revolution is of continuing interest, for central themes of Erhard's heterodox Kantianism – for example, Erhard's emphasis on the duty oppressed people owe to respect humanity in their own person by resisting their oppression – resonate with contemporary appropriations of Kantian ethics for emancipatory purposes.[2] Furthermore, Erhard's theory touches on difficult practical questions related to what we might call the *ethics* of revolutionary action. Erhard is especially focused on the fact that revolution is an inherently risky endeavor, with potentially enormous downsides for society, and for those on whose behalf revolutionaries purport to act. How must a would-be revolutionary balance the risks of revolution against the reality of oppression?

Erhard's theory is spread across two main texts: Erhard's 1795 book *Über das Recht des Volks zu einer Revolution* (henceforth *Revolution*), and Erhard's lengthy critical review of Fichte's 1793 text on the French revolution, published in Niethammer's *Philosophische Journal* in 1795.[3] In these texts,

For critical feedback and discussion of drafts of this paper, I am grateful to the audience at a workshop on "Reason, Revolution, and Rights," the University of York, UK, December 2018, and to the following individuals: James A. Clarke, Gabriel Gottlieb, Steve Yalowitz, Jessica Pfeifer, Whitney Schwab, Blake Francis, Lisa Cassell, Jim Thomas, Mavis Biss, Laura Papish, Tim Jankowiak, and Alex Englert. Research for the paper was partially funded by the Alexander von Humboldt Foundation.

[1] A useful overview of Erhard's project can be found in Batscha 1972. Haasis 1970 focuses more on Erhard's life and politics. For a detailed look at the left-Kantian school of which Erhard was a member, see Maliks 2012.

[2] Duties to the self are central to Erhard's account of human rights. See *ÜRVR*, 27, 30. For a contemporary discussion of Kantian self-respect as a basis for a duty of resistance, see Hay 2013.

[3] Per Haasis 1970: 210, Erhard did not read Fichte's book on the revolution until after composing *Revolution* in 1794. Thus, although both the Fichte review and *Revolution* appeared in 1795, the review must have been written after the book. The relation between the two texts poses problems

Erhard develops a detailed theory that aims to explain the conditions under which an individual can be morally justified in revolutionary action – in trying to trigger a revolution, or engaging in insurrectionary activities that may lead to revolution.[4] The method of this paper is to move through Erhard's arguments, collecting and analyzing necessary conditions for justified revolutionary action as I go. By the end of the paper I will have outlined the complete set of necessary conditions that are for Erhard sufficient to justify revolutionary action. The primary aim of the paper is thus reconstructive; I aim to give a philosophical account of the overall shape of Erhard's theory.

Erhard holds that individuals are morally permitted to instigate a revolution only if they are morally required to do so. I explain his argument for this claim in Section 3. This thesis of Erhard's in turn raises the question as to whether, and if so under what conditions, revolution is morally required. The following section (Section 4) argues that in *Revolution*, Erhard develops the outline of a theory of what I call *structural injustice* in order to explain the conditions under which revolution is, as he puts it, "morally authorized." Perhaps surprisingly, as Erhard uses the term, individual "moral authorization" is not sufficient to justify revolutionary action.[5] What is required in addition is "specific authorization," which is in part a function of the "political possibility" of revolution for a given agent in a specific time and place. Section 5 reconstructs and critically discusses Erhard's complex account of specific authorization. Section 6 argues that Erhard's review of Fichte adds in yet another set of conditions for individuals to be morally justified in revolutionary action. These conditions derive from the fact that individuals who attempt revolution take on fiduciary responsibilities in acting on behalf of others. In the course of my reconstruction of these arguments, I focus especially on the central role of epistemic limitations regarding the consequences of revolutionary action in Erhard's account. Erhard takes the problem of revolution's dangerous unpredictability very seriously as an obstacle to the justification of revolutionary action. This is both a merit of his account, and the source of some interpretative and philosophical puzzles, which occupy me in the last three sections of the paper.

2 Erhard's Concept of Revolution

Before beginning the main argument of the paper in Section 3, I first need to clarify some basic distinctions and definitions. In his social theory, Erhard

of interpretation. Some of the central doctrines of the book stand in apparent tension with various claims of Erhard's in the review, as I discuss in more detail in the last few sections of the paper.

4 The main task of the treatise is to develop an account of the *people's* right, as a collective agent, to revolution. But Erhard also extensively treats the question of an individual's right to begin a revolution, which is my focus here.

5 See my critical discussion of Erhard's terminology toward the end of Section 5.

distinguishes between three possible institutional sources of injustice: the administration, the constitution (*Verfassung*), and society's basic laws (*Grundgesetze*) (*ÜRVR*, 49).[6] At the most abstract level, the basic laws are the fundamental normative infrastructure that defines the community of right.[7] Erhard defines *revolution* as the transformation of this fundamental infrastructure (*ÜRVR*, 43). Because the constitution and administration are dependent upon the basic laws, revolution entails the destruction of society's political institutions (administration, constitution) and their reconstruction on a new normative basis – a new set of basic laws (*ÜRVR*, 43).

One important way in which basic laws are distinct from the other two kinds of political institution concerns the availability of avenues for legal *reform*, which Erhard defines in contrast to revolution (*ÜRVR*, 49). Erhard's intuitive idea is that revolutionary action is justified only if there are no non-revolutionary means available for rectifying the wrongs done to human rights by society's political institutions. Non-revolutionary means of reform include, for example, the passage of new laws or the reform of the constitution, which themselves can be spurred by the exercise of rights of free expression in criticizing existing practices and institutions. As Erhard argues, an unjust administration (a government in the narrower sense) can be replaced in accordance with constitutional rules, and a constitution can be reformed by appealing to society's basic laws. But basic laws are rock bottom, in terms of institutions and socially accepted principles. If the basic laws are corrupt, society is rotten all the way down, leaving no normative or institutional basis for reform. Thus injustice caused by basic laws can be functionally defined as just that injustice for which there is no legal remedy or legal reform possible within the parameters of the existing system of right, and this definition suffices for present purposes.[8] Such injustice can by definition only be remedied by the transformation of society's basic laws – by revolution.

[6] Erhard also sometimes refers to society's "*Grundverfassung*," which seems to be equivalent to *Grundgesetze*. See *ÜRVR*, 50, 91.

[7] Although Erhard does not explicitly define the concept, "basic laws" are most likely implicit or explicit juridical principles that are functionally equivalent to the French Declaration of the Rights of Man or the US Bill of Rights, which provide the normative foundation for the rest of the constitutional system. But one might also interpret "basic laws" more sociologically, as the most basic normative principles that are built into the social fabric and regarded as legitimate by the populace.

[8] When legal reform is and is not possible is a complicated question on which Erhard does not take a clear position. On a minimal construal of what is necessary to make legal reform possible, any constitution that contained within its provisions a mechanism for changing its terms, no matter how difficult to exercise in practice, would thereby block the possibility of legitimate revolution. For one could argue that within such a constitutional system legal reform is always possible, in some sense of that term. I doubt that such merely juridical possibility would suffice for Erhard, but he does not address the issue.

Erhard further distinguishes in his social theory between *revolution* and *insurrection*. Erhard invites us to consider a case "in which the people is roused to sudden revolt due to the appearance of an obvious injustice or a great harm. This is what one understands by 'insurrection'" (*ÜRVR*, 44). Later in the text, Erhard further clarifies what he has in mind: "It is necessary for an insurrection that the judgment: 'I must prevent this with violence' occurs simultaneously in many human beings. The deed [*Faktum*] which occasions this judgment must therefore seem so clear, and the necessity of opposition must be so clearly acknowledged, that there can be no marked difference about it in the minds of the masses" (*ÜRVR*, 55). According to these passages, an insurrection is a violent, spontaneous, mass uprising in response to a specific triggering event. Erhard further argues that there are three types of insurrection, which he labels *antagonistic*, *sympathetic*, and *moral* insurrection (*ÜRVR*, 57–9). The first two kinds of insurrection result from material suffering and natural feeling, respectively. The last type, by contrast, is motivated by the moral enlightenment of the agents of insurrection, who respond to their recognition of the injustice of the existing order (*ÜRVR*, 59). Unlike revolution, insurrection need not aim to transform society's basic laws. For example, an insurrection might demand the removal of a corrupt official, the release of an unjustly imprisoned person, or more affordable bread. Each of these demands can be met without transformation of society's basic laws. But clearly insurrection can lead to revolution under certain circumstances. Erhard's view is that individuals cause revolution by instigating insurrection, either spontaneously or through planning (*ÜRVR*, 59–60).[9] Indeed, although insurrection itself is not necessary for revolution, Erhard holds that the *fear* of insurrection – the belief on the part of political authorities that it is possible – *is* necessary for revolution to be politically possible (*ÜRVR*, 60). Unsurprisingly, then, Erhard's treatment of individuals' right to begin a revolution deals extensively with questions related to insurrection.

3 Deontic Modalities, Consequences, and Revolution

This section explains Erhard's argument in support of the claim that revolution is permitted for individuals only if it is required by duty. Here is Erhard's argument (*ÜRVR*, 46):[10]

[9] Since an insurrection is a spontaneous uprising, a planned insurrection might seem like a contradiction in terms. But Erhard holds that the pre-conditions – dissatisfaction in the populace, say – and the triggering event itself can be prepared in advance. Erhard surely has in mind Danton here.

[10] This argument is attributed by Erhard at *ÜRVR*, 46 to *opponents* of revolution. But he makes clear at *ÜRVR*, 48 that he grants the soundness of this part of his opponents' argument.

1. "In actions that the law commands, consequences are not at all to be considered; and in those [actions] that [the law] allows, the evaluation of consequences is left to us."
2. An action with consequences that are (a) completely indeterminate and nonetheless (b) extremely important must either be done from duty (because the law commands it), or else it must not be done.
3. Revolutionary action meets the characterization of (2).
4. "A revolution, therefore, if it is to be possible morally speaking, can only be thought as an action from duty."

Erhard holds the standard view that "the law" – which I here take to mean the deontological moral law familiar from Kantian ethics[11] – sorts actions into three categories: those that are forbidden by the law, those that are required by the law, and those that are permitted but not required (merely permitted). In the case of an action required by the law, for Erhard, the action is justified without consideration of consequences; it must be done simply because the law commands it. In the case of a merely permitted action, though, consideration of consequences must come into our determination of the justification of the action. Erhard thus holds that the fact that an action is merely permitted by the deontological moral law is a necessary but not a sufficient condition for that action to be justified, all things considered. One additional necessary condition is captured by Erhard's principle forbidding actions with unknown but potentially very bad consequences.[12] Within the domain of actions that are permitted but not required by the deontological moral law, Erhard is thus committed to a kind of non-maximizing consequentialism.[13] We need not choose the action with maximally good consequences, which explains why Erhard can say that within the domain of the merely permitted, the "evaluation of consequences is left to us": individuals are normatively free to choose from a range of possible courses of action, not all of which maximize the good. But within the domain of the merely permitted, Erhard's view rules out actions whose possible bad consequences meet an unspecified threshold of "importance" and yet cannot be calculated in advance. Practically, I take the latter requirement to amount to the imperative to avoid risking catastrophe under conditions of uncertainty. Consequentialist considerations thus determine a floor for justified action – no action with an unknown risk of catastrophic consequences can be justified if

[11] Compare Erhard's account of moral personality at *ÜRVR*, 16–17. See also Erhard's remarks on the moral law at *DA*, 10; *AT*, 118–19.

[12] A similar principle is often invoked in contemporary applied ethics. In that context it is referred to as the "Precautionary Principle." See, e.g., Manson 2002. Thanks to Blake Francis for pointing out the connection.

[13] Those who prefer to reserve the term "consequentialism" for maximizing conceptions may substitute another term.

it is deontologically optional – but do not require maximization of good consequences above that floor. Although Erhard does not give criteria for the threshold of importance above which the consequentialist principle takes effect, for our purposes it suffices that Erhard's main application of the principle – his claim that revolutionary action is an action-type with extremely important possible consequences that are difficult or impossible to predict in advance – seems very plausible.

One question for the account just sketched is whether the consideration of consequences in such cases is internal to Erhard's account of *moral* justification, or whether moral permissibility is merely one component in a broader account of "all things considered" justification, which would also take into account non-moral considerations. I favor the former option for the simple reason that, when Erhard writes that a person who undertakes a politically impossible revolution (i.e., one destined to fail) acts wrongfully due to the bad consequences of failed revolution (*ÜRVR*, 53), I take him to be making a *moral* claim. And here the wrong-making feature of the action is not its motive but rather its consequences. This reading of Erhard's normative theory results in a blend of deontological and consequentialist moral theorizing. Erhard's view of morally justified action turns out to be disjunctive: *either* an action is required by the deontological moral principle, in which case it is justified irrespective of consequences; *or* the action is merely permitted by a deontological moral principle, in which case it is justified only if its possible negative consequences either fall below the threshold of importance, or meet the importance threshold but can be calculated well enough in advance to know that the action does not risk catastrophe.

Having established this framework for thinking about deontic modalities and consequences, Erhard next observes that it is in the nature of the case that revolutionary action cannot meet the condition that the foreseeable consequences should not be bad, for the simple reason that the practical consequences of radical political action are not easily foreseeable at all. As Erhard points out, revolution quickly escapes the control of those who instigate it (*ÜRVR*, 46), which means that indeterminacy regarding the eventual outcome is built into the revolutionary enterprise.[14] One cannot say at the outset that the very important consequences of revolutionary action will not be (very) harmful (*ÜRVR*, 46). Thus if under conditions of uncertainty we must not risk catastrophe, then revolutionary action cannot be justified. Therefore, revolutionary action can be justified only if it is morally required, in other words, a duty.[15]

[14] Compare Rehberg's reflections on the tendency of revolution to (disastrously) outrun the control of those who begin it, at *UFR*, 78–9.

[15] As Batscha notes, the duty of revolutionary action encompasses a duty to wage war, if necessary, on behalf of human rights. See Batscha 1972: 70.

Further, in the passage discussed above, Erhard states that revolutionary action must, as in Kant's account of morally worthy action, be done not merely in accordance with duty, but *from duty*. There is thus an internal motivational requirement in Erhard's account of justified revolutionary action. If objective circumstances and moral requirements determine that there is a duty of revolution in a specific time and place, that state of affairs does not by itself justify an agent's revolutionary action. The agent must in addition be motivated to act by the consideration *that* revolutionary action is required by duty under those circumstances.

4 Structural Injustice and Moral Authorization

So far, then, we have two necessary conditions for justified revolutionary action: such action must be necessitated by duty, and it must be done from the motive of duty. But when is revolutionary action a duty? This section argues that on Erhard's account, for there to be a duty of revolution, revolutionary action must be necessary to counteract structural injustice against humanity. In connection with Erhard's arguments, I discuss what it might mean for *humanity*, as opposed to individual human beings, to be wronged by structural features of society. This section thus seeks to explicate Erhard's theory of humanity and structural injustice as these ideas relate to the moral necessity of revolution.

After constructing a strong case against revolution on behalf of his conservative opponents, Erhard responds by arguing that revolution is morally required when the basic laws of a state violate individuals' human rights.[16] It is important to Erhard's account that the state's basic laws are the causal factor, for it is only in such a case that the resulting injustice counts as *structural.* To clarify what he has in mind, Erhard distinguishes two cases (*ÜRVR*, 49–50). In the first case, we are to imagine a miscarriage of justice: a person is unjustly convicted of a crime, robbed of his freedom, and sentenced to a life of slave labor. This is clearly a horrible injustice; indeed, on Erhard's account, it is a violation of the individual's human rights. But it does not warrant revolution because the problem is not, according to Erhard, with the constitution itself or with society's basic laws, which (let us suppose) guarantee individuals a fair trial, but rather with the application of the law in this particular case.[17] By

[16] Erhard gives his summary of *Menschenrechte* in part one of the text at *ÜRVR*, 37. There are nine types of human rights that fall into three broad categories: rights of independence, rights of freedom, and rights of equality. For discussion, see Colbois and Perrinjaquet 1994.

[17] Contemporary readers will likely think that lifetime indentured servitude is not an appropriate criminal punishment in any case. But what is important for Erhard's purposes is that the cause of the injustice of wrongfully convicting the innocent is specific to this case, not a structural feature of society's basic institutions.

contrast, imagine someone *born* into servitude in a nation whose constitution allows slavery or indentured servitude at the level of its most basic laws. Here, too, an individual's human rights have been violated. But in this case, Erhard wants to say that *more* than an individual's rights have been violated. Rather, it is "humanity" itself, or "reason" that is wronged.[18] Only in the latter kind of case is a radical response necessary. The basic intuition behind Erhard's two cases is supposed to be that one involves an individual injustice while the other involves a deeply structural injustice. Revolution is not appropriate as a response to individual injustice, but it is necessary as a response to structural injustice. How can we capture this intuition about the cases in more systematic terms?

After describing the contrast between his two cases of indentured servitude, Erhard writes that in the case in which indentured servitude is written into the constitution itself:

> [I]t is not I alone who suffers injustice, but rather at the same time the humanity in my person. My sufferance is therefore not to be valued unconditionally, because it contains the possibility of wrong that will be suffered by many thousands after me. It is the same if I am persecuted due to the forthright communication of truths believed by me, [or] if it is completely forbidden according to the state's basic constitution to make further progress in the cognition of the most important affairs of human beings – right, religion, ethics, and the institution of a civil constitution. For there the party that suffers is not I, but rather reason in general. (*ÜRVR*, 50)

Erhard clearly wishes to draw a sharp contrast between cases in which "I alone" suffer a rights violation, and cases in which "humanity" in my person or "reason in general" is violated. Furthermore, according to Erhard's account, the *cause* of the violation of an individual's human rights determines whether the *object* of that violation is the individual alone or humanity or reason in general. Based on the passage's overall context, Erhard holds that humanity is wronged only if the cause of the rights-violation lies in the basic constitution of the state (i.e., the basic laws). And he gives an explanation for why this should be so: in a case in which the basic laws of the state cause my human rights to be violated, my sufferance of the violation "contains the possibility of wrong that will be suffered by many thousands after me."

I have been referring to human rights violations caused by basic laws as cases of *structural injustice.* Erhard says that in such cases, not only individual persons, but also humanity itself is harmed. What must "humanity" be for

[18] Haasis (1970: 211) points out that, with this claim, Erhard is referring implicitly to Article 34 of the revised Declaration of the Rights of Man in the 1793 "Jacobin" constitution, which states: "There is oppression against the social body when a single one of its members is oppressed" (quoted from Anderson 1908: 174).

Erhard, such that it can play the role he assigns it in his theory of revolution?[19] First, Erhard's account implies that, if the cause of an individual rights-violation is not *structural* (i.e., if the cause is not the basic laws), then although the *individual's* rights are violated, *humanity* in the individual's person is not violated. The latter kind of violation is therefore something over and above the former, and the causal profile of the property "humanity" turns out to be highly peculiar: *humanity* cannot be touched, causally speaking, by individual actions, but it can be impacted by society's basic laws.[20] Although I do take him to be self-consciously adopting Kantian language here and at other points in his account, Erhard is clearly not operating with Kant's account of humanity. The standard cases of treating people as mere means that Kant describes in the *Groundwork* would evidently not qualify for Erhard as cases of wrongs against humanity, although (one assumes) they would still be wrongs. Second, for Erhard, my humanity is not just mine, but *ours*. A wrong to humanity in my person is, therefore, at the same time a wrong against other members of the human community. How can we make sense of this claim theoretically? Erhard's text suggests the following account: in cases of the "containment" of the possibility of a wrong to thousands of others in the sufferance of a wrong against one person, the same causal forces involved in actual wrong against one person put thousands of others at *risk* of being wronged. This would explain Erhard's language of the "possible wrong" to others contained in our toleration of the actual wrong to the one. It would also go some way toward explaining why only society's basic laws can violate humanity: Erhard likely holds that individual actions do not pose the same large-scale threat to human rights as do basic laws. But it is important to note that on the analysis I just offered, the *actual* wrong to the single person plays at most an epistemic role in bringing it to our attention that the basic laws pose a threat to citizens' human rights; the risk would have been there irrespective of whether the individual person had actually been wronged or not.[21] Revolution is required to defend humanity from the possibility of the wrong to the thousands.

[19] Colbois and Perrinjaquet argue that "humanity" is equivalent to "moral personality," i.e., the capacity to act according to self-legislated maxims (Colbois and Perrinjaquet 1994: 559). Violations to human rights wrong humanity by preventing the expression of one's moral personality in one's actions. This is indeed the account Erhard offers at *PA*, 372. But it fails to account for the necessary connection in *Revolution* between society's basic laws and wrongs to humanity.

[20] One possible analogy here might be hate-crime legislation. One way to spell out what is especially wrong about such crimes would be to say that the crime in fact targets the entire group, with the individual standing as a mere placeholder for the whole. I thank Elaine Miller for the suggestion.

[21] Actual wrongs do, however, play a central role in Erhard's social theory of insurrection, since actual cases are required for individuals to recognize their shared feelings and interests. See *ÜRVR*, 58.

In sum, structural injustice has two features that make revolution necessary. First, structural injustice is *pervasive*: it involves large-scale actual or possible violations of individuals' human rights, where the explanation of these widespread wrongs lies in society's most basic laws. Structurally grounded human rights violations wrong not only individual persons, but humanity as a whole. Second, structural injustice is *unreformable*: revolution is the only possible remedy to the injustice, since injustice caused by basic laws is by definition injustice that cannot be reformed via a constitutionally prescribed legal process. I take both of these conditions to be necessary for there to be a duty of revolution. For Erhard, then, there can be a duty of revolution only under conditions of what I am calling structural injustice.

5 Specific Authorization

So far, we have two results. First, there is a right of revolution only if there is a duty of revolution, and the revolutionaries act from duty; and second, there can be a duty of revolution only under conditions of structural injustice. One of the consequences of Erhard's insistence that structural injustice wrongs *humanity* is that, at least in principle, it seems to morally authorize everyone – not only the individual person or persons wronged – to respond to injustices. Or, to put it somewhat differently, since structural injustices against others wrong not only these specific others but also our common humanity, it follows that these unjust acts against others wrong *me* as well. And since individuals whose human rights are violated are generally morally required to resist the injustice perpetrated against them (*ÜRVR*, 27, 30, 53), it seems to follow that under such conditions each person may resist structural injustice, even if it has not yet affected that person *specifically*. Indeed, Erhard draws just this conclusion: "For each person it is thus equally morally possible to bring about a revolution … Now that we have investigated the *moral* possibility of a revolution, we can transition to an explanation of the *political* possibility, in order to show who can first hope to bring about a revolution" (*ÜRVR*, 52). This passage gives the impression that, with the claim that revolution is equally morally possible (because morally required) for all under conditions of structural injustice, the *moral* component of Erhard's argument is complete, and all that remains is the working out of some practical details.

Yet this impression is misleading. As I will show, Erhard does *not* hold that all human beings are morally required to make a go at revolution under conditions of structural injustice. And this is a good thing, for as Erhard acknowledges (*ÜRVR*, 52), such a "categorical imperative" of revolution would be imprudent, socially destabilizing, and in all likelihood counterproductive. In response to such concerns, Erhard distinguishes carefully between the moral judgment *that revolution is required*, and the question as to *who*, specifically, is authorized to engage in revolutionary action (*ÜRVR*, 50). He takes his argument about structural injustice to have established only the general moral necessity of revolution under such conditions, which underwrites the equal "moral authorization" of all to resist, not the "specific authorization [*spezielle Befugnis*]" of any specific person to engage in such activity (*ÜRVR*, 50). Thus it is conceivable on Erhard's view that revolution could be generally morally necessary, and yet *no specific person* could be justified in acting. "Moral authorization," as Erhard uses that term, turns out to be necessary but not sufficient to justify individual revolutionary action, a claim to which I return toward the end of this section.

If moral authorization is not sufficient to justify revolutionary action, what more is required? Erhard answers this question with his account of "specific authorization." In this section and the next, I argue that, assuming background conditions of structural injustice that morally authorize revolution, Erhard holds that one is *specifically* authorized to instigate revolution if and only if either (1) one's human rights have been directly violated and one acts to resist this injustice, or (2) one is certain that one *can* instigate a successful revolution (in other words, one is certain that revolution is politically possible).[22] In both cases, one must further act from the motive of duty. The two cases differ because in case (1) certainty that revolution is politically possible for the agent is not required as a justification. Case (2), by contrast, requires morally authorized agents to act only if they are certain that revolution is politically feasible. Given Erhard's view about the uncertainty of the consequences of revolutionary action, cases of type (2) are theoretically but not practically possible. I include the second disjunct here anyway because, as I discuss in Sections 6–7, it is worth considering whether the epistemic standard Erhard endorses (certainty) is the correct one, and how that epistemic standard fits (or does not fit) with some arguments from the review of Fichte.

Before turning to Erhard's account of specific authorization, we must first consider Erhard's argument for the claim that moral authorization by itself is not sufficient to justify individuals in attempting revolution. He writes:

[22] I here formulated the condition in the second disjunct subjectively, in terms of the agent's beliefs, as opposed to objectively, in terms of what is actually politically possible in the world. Erhard, though, tends to put the point objectively. Erhard writes: "he who attempts a politically impossible revolution … acts without right" (*ÜRVR*, 53). On the latter formulation, what matters to the wrongfulness of the action is not what the person *believes* about the possibility of revolution, but rather whether revolution is *in fact possible*. Erhard's objective way of formulating the condition makes his account vulnerable to the following kind of counter-intuitive case. Suppose that there is no reason available to an agent to believe revolution to be possible, and yet revolution is nonetheless objectively possible. Should the agent foolishly set in motion a revolution in the absence of any reason to believe their action could succeed, they would nonetheless turn out to be justified – but only because of luck.

An unsuccessful revolution is always a most harmful thing. It casts much into ruin, arouses the suspicion of the government, and makes despotism more careful. He, therefore, who undertakes a politically impossible revolution without a specific instigation [*Veranlassung*] acts wrongly; and since no one can be sure that a revolution will succeed, each person who wants intentionally to bring forth a revolution, and acts solely in order to bring forth a revolution, acts wrongly. Each person acts rightly only in this: that he defends his human dignity, that he provides others an example, that he teaches them their rights, and that he instructs them in the dutiful use of these rights. Should he be the cause of a revolution merely because he spoke and acted as a truthful person, then his conscience will comfort him regarding all consequences, and he will not regret his conduct . . . (*ÜRVR*, 61)

A second passage from earlier in the text makes a similar point: "Since, however, the oppression [*Druck*] of the unrightful party is strengthened through its victory, he who attempts a politically impossible revolution without a specific, excusing reason acts without right, and he is not to be pitied if he is chastised" (*ÜRVR*, 53). Each of these passages states that it is prima facie wrong to instigate a politically impossible revolution, even under conditions of structural injustice. Since Erhard emphasizes both here and elsewhere that the course of a revolution is very difficult to predict, he maintains that it is difficult prospectively to know, or even to form reasonable beliefs about, whether it is politically possible for one to instigate a revolution. Erhard puts the point in terms of the difficulty of achieving certainty: "no one can be sure that a Revolution will succeed" (*ÜRVR*, 61). It follows that it is very difficult to know or to form reasonable beliefs about whether one is specifically authorized to instigate revolution. These commitments combine to push Erhard toward a skeptical view of specific authorization: people might be generally *morally* authorized to instigate revolution under conditions of structural injustice, but if no one can believe with any degree of certainty that they are *specifically* authorized, the general authorization would turn out to have no practical import. Revolution would be de facto prohibited.

Yet each passage cited in the previous paragraph mentions an exception to the rule that one acts wrongly if one sets in motion a politically impossible revolution:[23] one does not act wrongly in so doing if one is responding to a "specific instigation" or has a "specific, excusing reason." The following passage describes the kind of "excusing reason" Erhard has in mind:

If the defense of my human rights is the basis for a revolution, then I do not need to occupy myself with investigating its political possibility. I am bound to maintain my human dignity, whatever the consequence may be . . . If I am arbitrarily mistreated with

[23] Without attempting to address the issue, I note once again the difficulty in the notion of "political possibility" here. Suppose I set in motion a revolution, but it fails. Plausibly, failure by itself would not be sufficient to show that my attempted revolution was impossible. What else would be necessary to demonstrate impossibility?

no regard for right, then I can and ought to do everything I can to rescue myself and others who are threatened with the same treatment from this condition. I may loudly rebuke the injustice committed against me, and call upon everyone to defend with me the dignity of humanity, and employ all means to gain the freedom required for this call. (*ÜRVR*, 53–4)[24]

Here Erhard claims that one is permitted to bypass consideration of the political possibility of revolution if one acts in defense of their human rights. This text is the basis for the first disjunct in my interpretation of Erhard on specific authorization. The first disjunct holds that direct violation of a person's human rights suffices for specific authorization to act. Since violations of one's human rights and dignity are the only cases Erhard discusses that excuse people for instigating revolution without "investigating its political possibility," I take his view to be that *only* violations of one's human dignity justify one in so acting, and this is what disjunct (1) says. This interpretation is reinforced by a passage at *ÜRVR*, 61 in which Erhard draws a contrast between the person who "acts solely in order to bring forth a revolution" and the "truthful" person who only "defends his human dignity." Again, only the latter individual has an "excusing reason," should their actions trigger a politically impossible revolution. Although the text is not entirely clear, I take Erhard's thought to be that there are two distinct actions at issue here. The first is something like: instigating insurrection and revolution to defend one's human rights and dignity. The second is something like: instigating revolution as an end in itself. The problem is not with acting to instigate revolution, but with acting "*solely* in order to bring forth a revolution" (my emphasis). Only in the first case is one justified in acting without regard for consequences, for in attempting to rouse people to insurrection and revolution, one has the excuse that one is merely fulfilling the duty to defend one's human rights.[25] The "truthful" person's excuse amounts to the claim that they instigated a revolution only as a by-product of speaking and acting according to their conscience in defending their dignity, which is, in Erhard's framework, a categorical duty to self.

While this argument prevents Erhard from sliding into an anti-revolutionary position due to epistemic difficulties with the consequences of revolutionary action, the account that results is not without problems or ambiguities. First, although in my reconstruction so far I have followed Erhard in holding "moral" and "specific" authorization apart, I am not convinced that Erhard's

[24] Here again, Erhard is following the lead of the 1793 Declaration. Article 11 states: "Any act done against man outside of the cases and without the forms that the law determines is arbitrary and tyrannical; the one against whom it may be intended to be executed by violence has the right to repel it by force" (Anderson 1908: 172).

[25] Compare Erhard's account of the three "grounds of excuse" for revolution at *ÜRVR*, 49.

use of this distinction is well-founded. We have seen that, as Erhard uses the term, moral authorization is necessary but not sufficient for justified revolutionary action. For although all persons are equally morally authorized to act under conditions of structural injustice, as the account of specific authorization shows, not all persons are thereby justified in acting. In my view, Erhard's position would be better formulated as follows: one is morally authorized to attempt revolution only if one is morally required to act[26]; and one is morally required to act just in case (1) there is structural injustice, and (2) one is either (a) the direct victim of such injustice, and acts to defend one's human dignity; or (b) one is certain that one can counteract structural injustice via instigating revolution. Erhard puts condition (1) under the rubric of "moral authorization" and condition (2) under the rubric of "specific authorization," which is supposedly concerned only with the "political possibility" of revolution. But this way of presenting the view is confusing, since Erhard evidently also holds acting without satisfying condition (2) to be *morally* wrong. It seems tidier, then, to build both conditions (1) and (2) into a unified account of moral authorization. This would have allowed Erhard to clarify and streamline his presentation. It also makes clear that, since in practice no one can meet the very difficult epistemic standard described in (2b), the existence of a duty of revolution is conceptually parasitic on the more basic duty to self to defend one's human rights and dignity (as captured in (2a)). According to the argument I analyzed in Section 3, there is a right of revolution only if there is a duty of revolution. According to the argument here, there is a duty of revolution only if there is structural injustice, and one has a duty to defend one's human dignity in response to a direct attack on one's human rights.

Second, according to the first disjunct of Erhard's account of specific authorization, one who acts to defend their human dignity may be excused if their action triggers an unsuccessful revolution. But why should this form of excuse be limited to defending one's *own* dignity? The examples he gives, such as the imprisonment of an innocent person without due process, suggest that Erhard has in mind cases in which a specific person's human rights are directly and egregiously violated by an oppressive state. Only in such cases does this specific person have an excuse for ignoring difficult questions about the political feasibility of radical political action. But in light of the account of common humanity Erhard offers, the restriction of this excuse to the direct violation of one's *own* human rights seems arbitrary. What is it about the actual violation of my own human rights, as opposed to the actual violation of others'

26 Justified revolutionary action additionally requires that (3) the revolutionary agent correctly judges that conditions (1) and (2) obtain, and is motivated to act by the judgment that under such conditions there is a duty of revolution; and (4) the agent of revolution satisfies the moral and epistemic criteria for justified acting-for-others (see Section 6 below).

human rights or the possible violation of everyone's human rights, that especially justifies me in fomenting rebellion despite uncertainty regarding the outcome? On the one hand, Erhard needs some such restriction of the scope of the duty of revolution to avoid the excessively permissive scenario described at the outset of this section, in which all have an immediate and unconditional duty to revolt under conditions of structural injustice. Erhard's position, that the duty of revolution ought to be restricted at least in part by considerations of political possibility, seems sensible. But on the other hand, it is not clear that Erhard has a principled reason for avoiding the excessively permissive scenario. He seems conflicted on the question as to whether there is something normatively unique about wrongs to one's own person, sometimes emphasizing the unique status of the duties we owe to ourselves, while in other cases emphasizing our obligations to our common humanity.

6 Acting for Others

The previous section showed that for Erhard there is a prima facie prohibition on attempting politically impossible revolution. Erhard's account of specific authorization states that there are, at least in theory, two ways to override this prima facie prohibition. One way (the first disjunct, discussed in the previous section) is to urge others to insurrection and revolution only as part of the overall project of defending one's own human dignity, which is a duty that justifies one in acting without regard for considerations of political possibility. The other way (the second disjunct) is by being certain that revolution is politically possible under present conditions.[27] Of course, we have seen that Erhard denies that such certainty is possible. But this section argues that Erhard's account in his review of Fichte of acting for others in revolution *commits him* to the possibility of "guaranteeing" the beneficial consequences of revolution for those upon whose behalf one acts.

In the Fichte review, Erhard says that the standard dialectic in discussions of the Revolution is that defenders of the Revolution such as Fichte argue that each individual or group has the right to decide for themself about whether and when they should submit to political authority, and that therefore the Revolution is justified on the basis of this right; while critics such as Rehberg argue that no one has the right to decide that question *for others* outside of the revolutionary individual or group, which amounts to unilaterally imposing new political conditions on others, and therefore revolution is

[27] I assume that the notion of "political possibility" here is agent relative: it is a matter of what is politically possible *for me*, as a downstream consequence of actions that are available to me under present conditions.

unjustified. Erhard thinks the critics of revolution have a point. But he does not hold that the critics' point entirely rules out the possibility of morally justified revolutionary action. It does, though, introduce an additional justificatory burden, an extra condition that must be met by would-be revolutionaries. In his account of the burdens of revolutionary action, Erhard claims that revolutionaries must – and here the "must" again appears to be moral – consider the consequences of their actions if they are to be warranted in acting for others. Consider this passage:

> . . . there can be actions where it is a duty to pay attention to the consequences. This is the case whenever the discussion concerns what I ought to do for others. The question: how ought I to act toward others, can admittedly not be answered from experience, but it is also not the main question in a revolution. As soon as I act for another without his explicit instruction, then I guarantee [*verbürge*] to him that the consequences shall be good for him; and if I do not foresee the latter, then it is not right that I presume to take on this business. (*RF*, 136)

Here we find Erhard claiming that, when we act on behalf of others, we take on the burden of guaranteeing to these others that the consequences of our actions will be good for them. Without this guarantee of beneficial consequences, the action is "not right."

There is an important insight here, namely that the "acting-for" relation typical of revolutionary action, in which one purports to act on behalf of others' interests without their explicit instruction (or even against their expressed will), poses special ethical issues. However, the fact that Erhard holds the acting-for relation to be a necessary feature of revolutionary action as such puts him in a bind. Putting together premises from the Fichte review and from *Revolution*, we could formulate the following argument against the very possibility of justified revolutionary action:

1. Revolutionary action necessarily involves acting on behalf of others without their "explicit instruction" (*RF*, 136–9).[28]
2. For action on behalf of others to be justified without the others' explicit instruction, the agent must guarantee to the others that the consequences of the action will be good for them (*RF*, 136).
3. But we cannot predict the consequences of revolutionary action (*ÜRVR*, 46).

[28] An agent of revolution might act on behalf of two categories of people: those who support the revolution and those who do not. In the case of the latter group, it is clear that they do not authorize or instruct the agent's revolutionary action. In the case of the former group, even if they generally authorize the agent's activity, they cannot explicitly instruct the agent regarding each specific action or decision in advance (*RF*, 137–8). Therefore, revolutionary action necessarily involves action-for-others without their explicit instruction.

4. Thus the necessary condition for acting on behalf of others expressed in premise (2) cannot be met in the case of revolutionary action.
5. Revolutionary action therefore necessarily involves unjustified action on behalf of others.
6. Therefore revolutionary action cannot be justified.

Erhard went to a great deal of trouble in *Revolution* to show that one could be justified in instigating revolution without being certain in advance of its political possibility, so long as one acts under conditions of structural injustice, from the motive of duty, in order to defend one's human rights. This argument provided Erhard with a way to avoid the inherent epistemic difficulties with justifications of revolution that depend on its consequences. Yet the first two premises of the argument just sketched bring the problem of consequences right back into Erhard's picture. We seem, then, to have arrived at a contradiction in Erhard's commitments. On the one hand, *Revolution* argues that the consequences of revolution are "completely indeterminate." Given the prohibition on actions with very important but completely indeterminate consequences, revolutionary action can be justified only if agents have a reason for action that warrants bypassing consideration of consequences entirely. On the other hand, the Fichte review argues that revolutionary action can be justified only if agents of revolution can guarantee to others that the consequences of revolution will be good for them. As Erhard points out, this requirement involves two types of empirical knowledge: knowledge about the wishes of those on whose behalf one acts (*RF*, 138), and historically informed knowledge about the likely consequences of various courses of action (*RF*, 140). But given the alleged "complete indeterminacy" of the foreseeable consequences of revolution, how could the latter kind of knowledge be possible?

7 Revolutionary Action and Uncertainty

This section begins the task of sorting through this tangle of issues regarding revolutionary action, acting for others, and uncertainty about the consequences of revolution. I argue for two claims: first, that Erhard's claim about the "complete indeterminacy" of the consequences of revolution in *Revolution* is too strong, and in fact undermined by other arguments he makes. Second, after describing the interpretative options available for making sense of Erhard's position, I suggest that relaxing the epistemic standard required for an agent to be justified in revolutionary action under some conditions may be the best route available.

My interpretation thus far has focused on those passages in Erhard that emphasize the epistemic difficulties in predicting the course of a revolution.

But the epistemic situation of would-be revolutionaries is perhaps not quite as dire as Erhard sometimes makes it out to be. For there are other passages in *Revolution* and in the Fichte review where Erhard writes that the study of history and social theory provides useful guidance regarding the triggering conditions of insurrection and the political possibility of revolution (see *ÜRVR*, 54–9 and *RF*, 140). In fact, in *Revolution* Erhard outlines a social theory of insurrection that allows him to categorize the various precipitating causes and hindrances of revolution. Erhard identifies at least three supports of oppressive government: religious ideology, lack of education, and mutual mistrust among the oppressed, which I take it produces a collective action problem (*ÜRVR*, 56). There are likewise three precipitating causal factors of insurrection: suffering, enlightenment, and communication. Erhard's account of the causes of insurrection emphasizes the insufficiency of material deprivation alone in explaining insurrection. As evidence, Erhard offers various historical examples of people's stoic endurance of enormous suffering, from which he draws the conclusion that suffering alone, no matter its quantity or intensity, is not sufficient for insurrection; what matters is not the quantity of suffering per se, but rather people's *judgments* about that suffering. If people, for example, judge their enormous suffering to be a natural inevitability, then that suffering will not lead them to revolt against existing authorities. Instead, they will hold that nothing is to be done but endure. If, by contrast, people judge a qualitatively and quantitatively lesser degree of suffering to be brought about by the unjust actions of the powerful; and they judge that they can influence the actions of the powerful in the future via revolt; then in comparison with the former case, an objectively lesser degree of suffering will be far more likely to lead to insurrection. That is why enlightenment and the possibility of effective communication are, on Erhard's theory, crucial causal factors in the explanation of insurrection. In this sense, Erhard's view could be seen as offering a rudimentary version of ideology-critique: enlightenment reveals social suffering to be largely the consequence of human agency, not natural necessity, and therefore at least in principle something that can be remedied by political action.

There is much more to be said about the account just sketched. But already it should be clear that, according to Erhard, people are *not* condemned to complete ignorance regarding the likelihood of success in instigating revolution. For he believes we can say something about the conditions under which insurrection is more or less likely to take hold. One immediate consequence of this point is that the argument I discussed in Section 3 turns out to be unsound, for premise (3) of that argument is, according to Erhard's own social theory, false. Taken together with premise (2), premise (3) states that revolutionary action is a kind of action with completely indeterminate and nonetheless very important consequences. But Erhard does not in fact hold the consequences of revolutionary action to be completely indeterminate. This result need not be a major problem for Erhard. His argument could simply be reformulated to state: revolutionary action is a kind of action with uncertain and nonetheless very important consequences, and such actions must either be done from duty or else they must not be done. This reformulation would bring Erhard's argument in line with the epistemic condition in his argument about specific authorization, which I discussed in Section 5. What is at issue in both cases is (un) certainty about the consequences of revolutionary action. To be justified in acting for others, must we likewise be *certain* that the consequences of our action will be good for them? The text of the Fichte review provides indirect support for this interpretation, since a revolutionary must be in an epistemic position to provide others with a guarantee about the consequences of action on their behalf.

Erhard argues that, if we cannot be certain that revolutionary action does not risk catastrophe, then we can engage in such action only if it is a duty; and if we cannot be certain that revolution is politically possible for us, then we can be specifically authorized to act (and therefore have a duty to act) only if our human rights have been directly attacked. Lastly, if we cannot be certain that our actions will benefit those on whose behalf we act, then we are not justified in acting, apparently *even if* the previous conditions are met. I conclude by posing the question: in each of these three cases, does Erhard have a good reason to insist on certainty as the relevant standard?[29] Recall that Erhard's justification for the certainty norm is consequentialist: given the moral weight of the possible consequences of revolution, we must be certain that specific types of consequences will or will not follow from our revolutionary action. But within a broadly consequentialist framework, whether it is rational to risk certain types of bad consequences ought to depend, not just on the possible consequences of action, but also on the likely consequences of *inaction*. Now suppose the status quo of structural injustice is extremely oppressive. If the point of avoiding the risk of revolution is to avoid risking catastrophe, but the status quo which will be perpetuated by inaction is itself a moral catastrophe, then why insist on certainty about the consequences of action? Intuitively, the worse present conditions are, the more risk one should be willing to tolerate in efforts to improve them. This suggests an alternative view about risk and revolution, according to which the relevant epistemic standard should be indexed to the badness of the status quo. Revolutionaries should not insist on certainty about the political possibility of revolution if they have nothing left to lose, a point with which Erhard would surely agree.

[29] Thanks to Lisa Cassell and Jessica Pfeifer for prompting me to think more about this question.

6 Elise Reimarus on Freedom and Rebellion

Reed Winegar

1 Introduction

There is a well-known tension in Kant's political philosophy. On the one hand, he bases his political philosophy on the concept of freedom. For example, in the *Doctrine of Right*, Kant claims that freedom "is the only original right belonging to every man by virtue of his humanity" (*MM*, 6: 237).[1] But on the other hand, Kant claims that people must live in obedience to unjust states and may not rebel against them. There is a long list of critics, beginning in Kant's own day, who have felt that Kant's emphasis on obedience to unjust states and opposition to rebellion stands in tension with his emphasis on freedom.[2] Indeed, the list of such critics is so long that one might well think that Kant must have stood alone amongst his immediate contemporaries in both embracing freedom as the central concept of political philosophy and rejecting rebellion. However, Lisa Curtis-Wendlandt has recently claimed to find a similar position in the political thought of Kant's contemporary Elise Reimarus (1735–1805). Reimarus was an important figure in the German *Aufklärung*, whom historians have identified as the author of two political works: (1) the anonymously published 1791 dialogue *Freedom* (*Freiheit*) and (2) a text, left unpublished during Reimarus's lifetime, titled *Attempt at a Clarification and Simplification of the Concepts of Natural Civil Law* (*Versuch einer Läuterung und Vereinfachung der Begriffe vom natürlichen*

I would like to thank James A. Clarke, Wiebke Deimling, Gabriel Gottlieb, Paul Guyer, and Lauren Kopajtic for detailed comments on earlier versions of this paper. I would also like to thank the audience at the 2017 Morality after Kant conference and the members of Clark University's Early Modernists Unite group for their questions and comments. Finally, I would like to acknowledge the support of a Fordham Faculty Research Grant that facilitated research on the Reimarus family.

[1] The translations of Reimarus are my own, although I have consulted the translations of select passages in Curtis-Wendlandt 2012, Curtis-Wendlandt 2013, and Spalding 2005.

[2] See Maliks 2014: 112–43 for discussion of early criticisms. Although Kant's view of rebellion has attracted much criticism, see Ripstein 2009: 325–54 for a sympathetic defense of Kant's view.

Staatsrecht).[3] Reimarus wrote both works before Kant started the serious publication of his own political philosophy, beginning with the 1793 *Theory and Practice* essay and concluding with the 1797 *Doctrine of Right*.[4] However, like Kant, Reimarus posits freedom as the basis of her political philosophy and, according to Curtis-Wendlandt, anticipates Kant's views regarding both membership in and rebellion against the state.[5] Thus, Curtis-Wendlandt suggests that Reimarus anticipated key elements of Kant's political philosophy.

It would, of course, be of significant historical interest to learn that Reimarus anticipated Kant's position. However, I think that we should be careful about assimilating Reimarus's position to that of Kant. In fact, I will argue, contrary to Curtis-Wendlandt, that Reimarus's attitude toward rebellion differs significantly from Kant's own. In particular, I will argue that Reimarus's views regarding rebellion are, unlike Kant's, consequentialist in nature and that her position leaves significantly more room for permissible rebellion than Kant countenances. Indeed, I will argue that Reimarus's view of rebellion resembles that of the eighteenth-century philosopher Gottfried Achenwall, which Kant singles out for criticism in the *Theory and Practice* essay.[6] However, Reimarus's account of rebellion also comes with a notable twist – namely, whereas Achenwall suggests that people may rebel against the state to protect

[3] See Curtis-Wendlandt 2012; Curtis-Wendlandt 2013; Green 2014: 239–46; Green 2017: 86; Spalding 2005: 280–98, and Spalding 2006. The German text of Reimarus's *Attempt* is published in Spalding 2005: 504–13. Earlier commentators attributed *Freedom* to Reimarus's brother, Johann Albert Hinrich Reimarus; for example, see Alexander 1985. Spalding 2005: 280–98 persuasively argues that Elise Reimarus is the more likely author. The manuscript of the *Attempt* is written in Elise Reimarus's own hand (Spalding 2005: 280–98). In 1803 Johann Albert Hinrich published a book titled *Sketch of a General Civic Education for Future Citizens* (*Entwurf eines allgemeinen Staats-Unterrichts für künftigen Bürger*) that resembles (and incorporates some aspects of) Elise Reimarus's prior works.

[4] Some earlier works like *Idea for a Universal History with a Cosmopolitan Aim* and *An Answer to the Question: What Is Enlightenment?* anticipate parts of Kant's mature political philosophy, but he began to publish extensively on political philosophy only during the 1790s.

[5] Curtis-Wendlandt identifies numerous potential similarities between Reimarus's position and that of Kant: (1) endorsement of a hypothetical social contract; (2) acknowledgment of a duty to enter into a state; (3) rejection of rebellion within a state; (4) advocacy of freedom of thought and freedom of speech; (5) defense of a distinction between moral right and legal right; and (6) acceptance of social inequality in the form of relative equality (Curtis-Wendlandt 2012; Curtis-Wendlandt 2013). In this essay, I focus on (1–3), which are all relevant to Kant's views regarding rebellion.

[6] Kant used the 1763 edition of Achenwall's *Jus Naturae* as the textbook for his lectures on natural right. See Guyer 2020 for a general overview of the similarities and differences between Kant's political philosophy and that of Achenwall. I do not claim that Achenwall directly influenced Reimarus, although she could have read his *Jus Naturae*, which was available prior to the writing of *Freedom* and the *Attempt*. Spalding suggests that Reimarus's political texts are a "distillation of political works" by Hobbes and Locke (Spalding 2005: 285). However, Reimarus clearly draws on elements of other social contract theorists, such as Rousseau's notion of a general will.

their lives and promote their happiness, Reimarus suggests that people may rebel against the state to promote their freedom. Thus, political philosophers who are attracted to Kant's emphasis on freedom but skeptical of his views regarding rebellion can find in Reimarus's writings an interesting eighteenth-century alternative to Kant's own position.

2 Elise Reimarus's Political Philosophy

Because Reimarus remains a relatively obscure figure, I will begin with an overview of her biography and political thought before examining the topic of rebellion. Elise Reimarus was born in Hamburg to a prominent intellectual family.[7] Her father, Hermann Samuel Reimarus, was a well-known philologist and philosopher, whom Kant singles out for praise in the *Critique of the Power of Judgment* (*CJ*, 5: 476). Today he is best known as the author of the radical deist text *Apology or Defense for the Rational Worshippers of God* (*Apologie oder Schutzschrift für die vernünftigen Verehrer Gottes*). Unpublished during his lifetime, this book sparked the infamous Fragment Controversy when G. E. Lessing (with the permission of Elise Reimarus and her brother) published several anonymous excerpts from it.[8] Elise Reimarus's brother, Johann Albert Hinrich Reimarus, was a well-known physician. He brought smallpox inoculation to Hamburg, installed the first lightning rod in the German countries, and wrote several philosophical works. He was also the target of Kant's short essay "Settlement of a Mathematical Dispute Founded on Misunderstanding."[9] Johann Albert Hinrich's second wife Sophie, known as *die Doktorin*, ran a high-profile intellectual salon called the Tea Table, whose visitors included such illustrious figures as Lessing, Jacobi, and Klopstock.[10] Elise Reimarus was an active member of the Tea Table and also carried out an extensive correspondence with associates like Lessing, Jacobi, and Mendelssohn.[11] In addition, Elise Reimarus was a prolific translator and writer. She translated several plays, including such Enlightenment classics as Addison's *Cato* and Voltaire's *Zaïre*, for the Hamburg stage. She composed poetry, and she wrote pedagogical works for children, many of which were published anonymously

[7] See Spalding 2005 for full biographical details.

[8] For details on Elise Reimarus's involvement in this controversy, see Sieveking 1940 and Winegar 2021.

[9] See Alexander 1985 for an overview of J. A. H. Reimarus's life and accomplishments. See Spalding 2006 for an overview of the likely collaborations between Elise Reimarus and her brother.

[10] For details on the Tea Table, see Spalding 2005: 177–98.

[11] Elise Reimarus was the intermediary for the letters between Jacobi and Mendelssohn that sparked the Spinoza Controversy, when Jacobi revealed that Lessing had confessed to being a Spinozist. See Sieveking 1940 and Winegar 2021 for Elise Reimarus's involvement in the Spinoza Controversy.

in J. H. Campe's influential *Kinderbibliothek*. And, most importantly for our purposes, she wrote two works of political philosophy: *Freedom* and *Attempt at a Clarification and Simplification of the Concepts of Natural Civil Law*. These two works differ greatly in style. *Freedom* is a readable dialogue between two characters A and H (which presumably stand for "America" and "Hamburg"), whereas the *Attempt* is a terse treatise divided into numbered sections. But despite these differences in style, both works develop a consistent political philosophy based on the central concept of freedom.

Reimarus's political thought begins with acknowledging a "fundamental concept of right" – namely, that the "external freedom of a person may be limited by the external freedom of other persons only in that deed [*thun und lassen*], which is not compatible with the deeds of other persons" (*VN*, §5).[12] Reimarus defines this "external freedom" as "the capacity of a person to be able to carry out his resolutions" (*VN*, §1). According to Reimarus, people differ from mere things, because people possess external freedom and, thus, may not be used arbitrarily by others. For Reimarus, then, freedom is foundational. It is both an inalienable right and an original right in the sense that it is not derived from any prior right. Reimarus maintains that external freedom is the only original right, but she also claims that external freedom gives rise to two further inalienable rights – namely, the right to one's own existence and the right to one's own body. Specifically, Reimarus derives these two further rights from the original right of freedom by plausibly arguing that people have inalienable rights to those things that the exercise of external freedom requires and that the exercise of external freedom requires both existence and control over one's own body.

Reimarus believes that people's external freedom is not secure outside of the state. For example, the character A in *Freedom* describes how his life on the American frontier beyond the reach of the state exposed him to attack from others (*FR*, 4f.). Embracing a social contract theory, Reimarus argues that people enter into a "civil social contract" for the purpose of securing their external freedom from such dangers (*VN*, §8). Because people join together into a state to secure their external freedom, Reimarus claims that the "general will [*der allgemeine Wille*]" of the people is that all citizens be treated according to the fundamental concept of right and that the state take the proper means to achieve this end. Reimarus writes: "Hence no state can be conceived without a general will, which though insofar as it is presupposed for the lawful existence of a state in general can exist in nothing other than the resolution of all to secure the external right of each and to apply the indispensable means thereto" (VN, §8). Reimarus does worry, however, that some people might interpret membership in the state as a limitation or restriction of freedom. And

[12] All of the underlining in the quotations from Reimarus's *Attempt* is Reimarus's own.

one of her chief aims in *Freedom* is to argue that the freedom people have in the state of nature is a wild, lawless, insecure freedom and that people can have a more desirable form of freedom – namely, "freedom, in the social condition" – only as members of a state (*VN*, 21).[13]

Although the civil social contract joins people into a state, it does not determine the form of government. Thus, Reimarus claims that the civil social contract is supplemented with a "contract of subjection" [*Unterwerfungs Vertrag*] that determines the state's rulers (*VN*, §13). Reimarus holds that monarchy, aristocracy, and democracy are all reasonable forms of government. On Reimarus's view, monarchy might be well suited for some nations, aristocracy well suited for others, and democracy well suited for still further others. The form of government best suited to a particular nation depends on empirical facts regarding a particular country's circumstances, national character, and culture (*VN*, §25).[14] Yet, although Reimarus claims that democracy can be a reasonable form of government, she does reject a form of democracy that she refers to as "pure democracy." According to Reimarus, "pure democracy" is incompatible with the concept of a state. She writes, "The so-called pure democracy, in which the entire highest authority in all of its constitutive parts is found in the hands of the people, contradicts the determinate concept of a state" (*VN*, §20). Reimarus does not define "pure democracy," but she appears to have in mind a system where each state action requires the unanimous agreement of the people. Such a system contradicts the concept of a state, for people join together into a state because they are unable to coordinate their individual wills in the state of nature and, consequently, run into conflicts with one another. Thus, a pure democracy, where each state action requires the unanimous consensus of the entire populace, does not differ from a state of nature.[15] Accordingly, on Reimarus's view, the concept of a state requires that a subset of the population serve as rulers. She writes, "The choice and execution of the means of the security of right, which is absolutely impossible through the will of each individual, is at least to a certain degree possible through the united will of some" (*VN*, §11). Of course, one might worry that Reimarus overlooks a version of direct democracy where state actions are decided and carried out through majority rule, rather than requiring unanimous agreement. However, I take it that this type of direct democracy would not

13 Green emphasizes this aspect of Reimarus's view (Green 2017: 86). Similar views are found in a wide range of social contract theorists, including Locke and Rousseau. Kant endorses a similar view: "One does not lose any rightful freedom but only the lawlessness of the *status naturalis* since the coercive law restricts freedom to conditions of universal security" (*LDPP*, 19: 510).

14 In *Freedom*, Reimarus defends enlightened monarchy in particular against potential criticisms (*FR*, 20f.). However, it is also worth noting that in conversations during the 1790s, Elise Reimarus harshly criticized the actual European aristocracy (Spalding 2005: 293f.).

15 Reimarus's brother makes the same general argument in his *Sketch* (Reimarus 1803: 15f.).

qualify as pure democracy in Reimarus's sense, because the majority would count as the relevant subset of rulers.

Reimarus does place some restrictions on eligible rulers. She claims, for example, that the rulers of the state need to be knowledgeable experts. Thus, in *Freedom*, the character A compares rulers to sea captains, and argues that no reasonable person would willingly travel with a sea captain who lacked nautical knowledge.[16] Additionally, Reimarus seems to endorse the common eighteenth-century view that only property owners should be eligible to serve as rulers (*FR*, 13f.).[17] One interesting question is whether Reimarus thinks that women should be eligible to serve as rulers. Unfortunately, she addresses this issue in neither *Freedom* nor the *Attempt*. But she does consider it in a series of notes written several decades earlier (*BE*).[18] In these notes, Reimarus imagines a conversation between two people, one of whom suggests that women should serve in official posts. In reply, the other conversation partner argues that women are just as talented and capable as men but that women have further talents and abilities that makes them more suitable than men for domestic life. Reimarus writes:

> It is not because I believe that we possess not so many abilities, not so many gifts of nature, not so many merits as the other half of the human race, the men, this is not my opinion, no I believe we possess all of this just as well as they . . . [S]till more I believe we even possess merits which they do not possess and which indeed have a great value. (*BE*, 329)

According to this conversation partner, it is best that men are active in the public world, while women are active in the domestic world, because women have useful domestic talents that men lack. With this arrangement, the conversation partner argues, no arena of human life will be neglected: "nature itself actually made amongst people the division to two different modes of life, and in particular imprinted on us the calling to domestic matters" (*BE*, 329). The view expressed in these passages is, of course, lamentable. But it was also common during Reimarus's time. And although it is hard to know for sure, I suspect that Reimarus meant to endorse it. If this is true, then Reimarus's views on this topic were less progressive than we might like today. Nevertheless, it is worth emphasizing that Reimarus (unlike Kant) emphasizes in these notes that women are just as talented and intellectually capable as men.

[16] Reimarus (*FR*, 13f.); this comparison likely draws, either directly or indirectly, on Plato's *Republic* (Plato 1997: 488a–489d).

[17] However, Reimarus also stresses that a just constitution must allow all people the chance "to acquire more through diligence and skill," such that all people can, in principle, acquire property (*FR*, 14f.).

[18] See Green 2014 and Spalding 2005: 109–33 for opposing interpretations of these notes; my interpretation is closer to that of Green 2014.

She also does not go so far as to explicitly claim that women should be barred from serving in official posts, even though she seems to suggest that women should opt not to do so in favor of domestic pursuits. Of course, one might feel a tension between Reimarus's eighteenth-century attitude toward the role of women in society and her own norm-defying decision to write about political philosophy. But we should also remember Reimarus was reluctant to fully challenge the conventions of her day.[19] In particular, she did not want to be identified publicly as a writer. And with the exception of her correspondence, her literary output was almost entirely anonymous.

Given that Reimarus rejects neither monarchy nor aristocracy as reasonable forms of government, she is clearly willing to accept significant social inequality. Indeed, Reimarus maintains that freedom is compatible with significant social inequality. She notes that servants freely enter contractual relationships with their employers and that such contracts are accordingly just. Reimarus takes this to hold even in cases of indentured servitude (*FR*, 8f.). In her view, indentured servants have certainly entered into contracts with stringent conditions but have done so with reasonable knowledge of those conditions and their consequences. Thus, the contracts are just (*FR*, 8f.). However, Reimarus does distinguish between indentured servitude and serfdom (*Leibeigenschaft*), which she rejects (*FR*, 15).[20] According to Reimarus, serfdom has arisen in human society through "violence" and "deceit" (*FR*, 15f.). Reimarus argues that no reasonable person with adequate knowledge of serfdom's conditions would willingly consent to be a serf. Rather, anybody who did so would be regarded as "immature [*unmündig*]" – that is, legally incapable of representing his or her own interests (*FR*, 16f.). According to Reimarus, serfs should be viewed as oppressed and exploited, and she claims that the rulers of a state have every right to abolish serfdom (*FR*, 16f.). Additionally, Reimarus rejects slavery, which relies on violence and clearly contradicts the inalienable right to external freedom (*FR*, 7f.).

3 Kant and Reimarus on Rebellion

Now that I have introduced the general contours of Reimarus's political philosophy, let us compare her views regarding rebellion to those of Kant. As noted above, Reimarus composed her works on political philosophy prior to Kant's major writings in this area, and there is no evidence that her political philosophy was directly inspired by Kant. Moreover, although Kant was familiar with some of the Reimarus family's writings, there is no evidence

[19] Spalding 2005 illustrates that Reimarus remained concerned with publicly abiding by social conventions throughout her life.

[20] It is important to note that serfdom remained widespread in the German countries at the time.

that he read these particular texts. Nevertheless, Lisa Curtis-Wendlandt has recently argued that Reimarus's attitude toward rebellion closely resembles Kant's own and that Reimarus, thus, anticipated an important aspect of Kant's political philosophy. However, in opposition to Curtis-Wendlandt, I will argue that Reimarus's views regarding rebellion differ significantly from those of Kant. In fact, Reimarus endorses a consequentialist position similar to that of Achenwall, which Kant criticizes in the *Theory and Practice* essay. However, Reimarus's position differs from Achenwall's in one key respect – namely, in its focus on freedom, rather than happiness. As I will close by suggesting, this difference provides Reimarus with an interesting alternative to Kant's own philosophy of freedom.

Kant's views regarding rebellion are closely intertwined with his theories regarding people's membership in a state. In his political writings, Kant famously maintains that people are obliged to enter into a civil condition. For example, in the *Doctrine of Right*, Kant writes:

> [H]owever well disposed and law-abiding human beings might be, it still lies a priori in the rational idea of such a condition (one that is not rightful) that before a public lawful condition is established individual human beings, peoples, and states cannot be secure against violence from one another, since each has its own right to do *what seems right and good to it* and not to be dependent upon another's opinion about this. So, unless, it wants to renounce any concepts of right, the first thing it has to resolve upon is the principle that it must leave the state of nature, in which each follows its own judgment, unite itself with all others (with which it cannot avoid interacting), subject itself to a lawful external condition, and so enter into a condition in which what is to be recognized as belonging to it is determined *by law* and is allotted to it by adequate *power* (not its own but an external power); that is, it ought above all else to enter a civil condition. (*MM*, 6: 312)

Here Kant argues that no circumstance in a state of nature can count as a rightful condition. In the state of nature, no person can guarantee that he or she will not be subject to the unilateral will of another person. But if one is subject to the unilateral will of another, then one's own "right to do *what seems right and good*" is violated. Indeed, even if we were to assume that people are generally well-disposed and law-abiding, the state of nature can never count as a rightful condition, because people in the state of nature are always potentially subject to the unilateral will of others. Accordingly, Kant maintains that people are obliged to enter into the civil condition, where law governs conflicts and disputes between people (*LDPP*, 27: 1382). Moreover, Kant argues that people may compel others to enter into the civil condition with them. Kant writes, "each may impel the other by force to leave this state and enter into a rightful condition" (*MM*, 6: 312).[21] After all, if other people do not enter into the civil

[21] Cf. *LDPP*, 19: 503.

condition, then our relations to them will not be rightful, violating the obligation to establish a rightful condition. And I am thus wronged when other people do not enter into a rightful condition with me: "I am *laesus per statum* [wronged through the condition] by other human beings who are in the state of nature. For I have no security and property is always endangered. I am not obligated to endure this fear" (*LDPP*, 19: 476).

Because people who are compelled to enter into the civil condition do not consent to do so, Kant denies that one's membership in a state depends on one's actual consent. Thus, for Kant, the notion of a social contract is merely an Idea of reason that governs our concept of a just state, rather than an actual agreement among people. More specifically, the Idea of an original contract mandates that laws should be evaluated in terms of whether they are consistent with the Idea of the rational agreement of all. As we read in the *Naturrecht Feyerabend* lectures, "The *contractus originarius* [original contract] is an idea of the agreement of all who are subject to the law. One must test whether the law could have arisen from the agreement of all; if so then the law is right" (*LDPP*, 27: 1382).

Kant's views regarding the obligation to enter into a rightful condition underlie his negative attitude toward rebellion. Kant famously condemns rebellion against the state. For example, in the *Doctrine of Right*, he writes:

> Therefore a people cannot offer any resistance to the legislative head of a state which would be consistent with right, since a rightful condition is possible only by submission to its general legislative will. There is, therefore, no right to *sedition* (*seditio*), still less to *rebellion* (*rebellio*), and least of all is there a right against the head of a state as an individual person (the monarch), *to attack this person* or even his life (*monarchomachismus sub specie tyrannicidii*) on the pretext that he has abused his authority (*tyrannis*) . . . The reason a people has a duty to put up with even what is held to be an unbearable abuse of supreme authority is that its resistance to the highest legislation can never be regarded as other than contrary to law, and indeed as abolishing the entire legal constitution. (*MM*, 6: 320)[22]

Here Kant argues that people cannot justifiably rebel against the state, even in the face of unbearable abuses. According to him, rebellion against the state occurs when people assert their own wills against that of the sovereign. As such, rebellion returns people to a condition where there is a conflict of wills and no recognized authority to lawfully resolve the conflict. Consequently, rebellion takes people out of the rightful condition. Because people are obliged to remain in a rightful condition, people may not justifiably rebel. One might, of course, wonder why the people could not have established the state in such a way that they gave themselves the right to evaluate the sovereign and to rebel

[22] Cf. *MM*, 6: 371f.; *TP*, 8: 298–303.

against the sovereign if deemed necessary. But Kant claims that this is impossible. In such a case, the people, rather than the sovereign, would retain the ultimate power, which would mean that the sovereign was not actually sovereign. Kant writes, "If the people hand sovereignty over to someone they cannot limit it for otherwise it is not sovereignty. All limitation presupposes that the people retain supreme power" (*LDPP*, 19: 511).[23]

Now, it is important to stress that Kant does think that people have rights against the state. A state that violates these rights treats its citizens unjustly. However, Kant maintains that these rights are not "coercive rights" (*TP*, 8: 303).[24] In other words, the state has a duty to respect these rights, but the people do not have a right to coercively force the state to respect these rights if it fails to fulfill this duty. Kant maintains, instead, that people have two options when confronted with unjust state laws. First, Kant argues that people have a right to complain to the state in hopes of encouraging reform: "Thus *freedom of the pen* . . . is the sole palladium of the people" (*TP*, 8: 304). Second, Kant argues that people can decline to obey laws that violate the moral law so long as they accept the state's sanctions. He writes, "they can never oppose but only resist, i.e. refuse to do what is in itself morally impossible and endure the consequences" (*LDPP*, 19: 487).[25] Additionally, we should note that Kant's philosophy also leaves room for accepting some apparent cases of rebellion on the grounds that they are not technically rebellions against the state. For example, Kant maintains that the French Revolution was not actually a rebellion against the king, because Louis XVI's decision in summer 1789 to recognize the National Assembly, which then formed a committee to write a new constitution, had ceded sovereignty back over to the people (*LDPP*, 19: 582). Thus, the subsequent conflict was not actually a rebellion against the king's sovereignty. Kant writes:

> In France the National Assembly was able to alter the constitution though it was, to be sure, called together only to bring order to the nation's credit system. For once the king had allowed it to make decrees in accordance with indeterminate authority, they were the representatives of the whole people . . . Thus the misfortune of the king comes directly from his own sovereignty, after he had once allowed all the people's deputies to assemble, then he was nothing; for his legislative power was founded only on his representing the whole people. (*LDPP*, 19: 595f.)

Moreover, although Kant himself does not make the argument, several commentators have argued that in some cases the state may be merely an apparent

[23] Cf. *LDPP*, 19: 524, 575; *MM*, 6: 372. [24] Cf. *LDPP*, 19: 523.

[25] This is the meaning behind Kant's remark in the doctrine of right: "*Obey the authority who has power over you* (in whatever does not conflict with inner morality)" (*MM*, 6: 371); cf. *MM*, 6: 322.

state or impostor state, rather than an actual state.[26] Given that an impostor state lacks sovereignty and, thus, is not actually a state, revolt against an impostor state would be a case of war in a state of nature, rather than a case of rebellion against a state. But in any case, it is clear that Kant rejects rebellion against an actual state, even in the face of extreme abuses, on the grounds that rebellion contradicts the people's obligation to enter into a rightful condition.

Up to this point, I have isolated three key elements of Kant's views regarding membership in a state and rebellion. First, Kant claims that people are obliged to enter into the state. Second, Kant denies that membership in a state relies on one's actual consent. Third, Kant rejects rebellion against the state. According to Curtis-Wendlandt, Reimarus agrees with Kant on these three points. I will argue, however, that Reimarus actually denies all three. To begin with the first point, Curtis-Wendlandt argues that Reimarus acknowledges a duty to enter into a state. Now, there is no passage where Reimarus explicitly states that people have such a duty. But Curtis-Wendlandt presents two rationales for why Reimarus might be committed to such a duty. On the hand, she suggests that, for Reimarus, people would have a duty to enter into a state because the state is a prerequisite for the enforcement of justice and, thus, a prerequisite for rightful relations between people. Curtis-Wendlandt writes: "Accordingly, *if* legality is taken as a precondition for securing the outer law (or of rightful relations between people), and *if* people could not achieve justice on their own, Reimarus may also have held ... that people actually have a *duty* to enter (and remain in) the civil condition."[27] Second, Curtis-Wendlandt suggests that people have a duty to enter into a state, because they have a duty to secure their own freedom and can do so only by entering into a state.[28]

However, Reimarus's texts support neither rationale. Recall that Kant defends a duty to enter into a state on the grounds that people in a state of nature are always potentially subject to the unilateral will of others. Kant maintains that there is, therefore, always the potential that one's own freedom will be violated in a state of nature. However, he does not think that the probability of such violations is relevant. Instead, he maintains that the mere potential for such violations grounds a duty to enter into the state, even if people are generally well disposed and lawful. In contrast, Reimarus stresses that violations of one's external freedom are highly probable in a state of nature. For example, in *Freedom* the character A explains in detail how his freedom was threatened and violated by others during his time living on the American frontier beyond the reach of the state (*FR*, 4f.). Through her character A, Reimarus aims to convince her readers that violations of their freedom are likely if they choose to live outside the state. As such, Reimarus

[26] For example, see Maliks 2014 and Ripstein 2009. I will not evaluate this interpretation here, but I mention it for its relevance to Curtis-Wendlandt's interpretation below.

[27] Curtis-Wendlandt 2012: 766.

[28] Curtis-Wendlandt 2013.

suggests a consequentialist position – namely, that people who want to secure their own freedom against likely violations should enter into a state. Thus, her character A says that the "pressing" reason to enter into the state is so that a person "will be protected from violence, and may enjoy the fruits of his labor in peace and safety" (*FR*, 5). Here Reimarus suggests that entering into society will protect the exercise of one's freedom against violence and, thus, is generally desirable. But Reimarus never claims that people living on the frontier beyond the reach of the state are violating a duty to enter into a rightful condition, and her character A never claims that moving to America proved to be a violation of such a duty. Rather, the character A suggests that his choice was not prudential, because it made violations of his freedom highly likely, and that life in a state better protects his freedom against such infringements. Additionally, contrary to Curtis-Wendlandt's suggestion, Reimarus does not claim that people have a duty to secure their own freedom. Curtis-Wendlandt takes Reimarus's claim that people should not be used arbitrarily to entail that people have a duty to secure their own freedom. But this does not follow. One can consistently hold that people have a duty not to infringe on the external freedom of others while also holding that people lack any duty to secure their own external freedom. Thus, Reimarus's remarks are consistent with the view that people have the right to secure their external freedom from interference by others if they want to but do not have a duty to do so. Of course, Reimarus thinks that people are generally interested in securing their external freedom and that entering into the state is, thus, rational for most people. But she does not commit herself to the view that people who put their own freedom at risk by refusing to enter into the state have violated any duty.

Further confirmation for my interpretation can be found in Reimarus's own views regarding the conditions of membership in a state. As we have seen, Kant maintains that the obligation to enter into a civil condition entails that one's membership in a state does not require one's actual consent. Instead, one can be compelled to enter into the civil condition. Consequently, Kant's social contract theory does not entail that people must actually agree to enter into a state. Instead, the notion of an original contract is merely an Idea of reason. Curtis-Wendlandt describes this position as a hypothetical social contract theory and suggests that Reimarus endorses a similar position: "The formation of the common will is thus assumed to be merely hypothetical: people's agreement or consent (whether tacit or explicit) does not actually 'happen' in historical time, but can only be stipulated or presumed on the basis of some rational principle that Reimarus here leaves undefined".[29]

Now, Curtis-Wendlandt is right to note that, for Reimarus, the initial creation of the state does not normally take the form of an actual agreement

[29] Curtis-Wendlandt 2012: 766.

between people. Instead, Reimarus claims that historically states have arisen through the "mastery of the strong and the indolence of the weak" (*VN*, §23). But unlike Kant, Reimarus claims that one's membership in a state *does* rely on one's actual consent. In particular, Reimarus argues that one's membership in a state relies on one's express or tacit consent to the authority of the state. For this reason, she denies that people can be compelled to enter into the state: "No person can be compelled through a social union to secure his external right" (*VN*, §7). On Reimarus's view, one can expressly consent to the state's authority by swearing allegiance to the state. But one can also tacitly consent to the state's authority by choosing to remain inside the state's territory, rather than emigrating (*FR*, 6f.). However, these are both versions of actual, rather than merely hypothetical, consent. And Reimarus denies that others can rightfully compel one to be a member of a state against one's consent.

Given my interpretation up to this point, we can see that Reimarus could not endorse Kant's own argument against rebellion. As noted previously, Kant's argument relies on the claim that rebellion against the state violates one's duty to remain in a rightful condition. But Reimarus does not recognize a duty to be in a rightful condition. For Reimarus, somebody who does not consent to the state and leaves the civil condition by immigrating to the American frontier might be said to act imprudently but does not violate any obligation. Thus, somebody who rebels against the state and, consequently, exits the rightful condition cannot, on Reimarus's view, be said to have violated an obligation on this ground. Accordingly, if Reimarus were to agree with Kant that rebellion against the state is not justified, she would need to do so on different grounds.

Now, the main textual support for Curtis-Wendlandt's interpretation of Reimarus's view of rebellion comes from *Freedom*, where Reimarus writes:

> [T]hose means [namely, rebellion] to achieve right for yourself are in no case permissible, and if you thereby win one time, so do you yet lose on the whole . . . because you then as well as others are given over to contingent authority and could not rely on the same protection, which the social union should secure for all. (*FR*, 11f.)

Reimarus later adds, "We must thus hold this union as unbreakable" (*FR*, 12f.). In these passages, Reimarus argues that rebellion poses a significant danger to freedom, because it turns things over to the arbitrary power of people's individual wills. Moreover, phrases like "in no case" and "unbreakable" in these passages might seem to suggest that Reimarus's alleged rejection of rebellion against the state is categorical. Based on these passages, Curtis-Wendlandt writes, "*Freedom* argues that violent revolt can never be a legitimate means to an end, even if the end is worthy."[30]

[30] Curtis-Wendlandt 2012: 756.

There are, however, good reasons to question Curtis-Wendlandt's interpretation here. Granted, we know that Reimarus published *Freedom* in response to the events surrounding the 1791 Locksmith's Uprising in Hamburg. This uprising, which grew violent, centered on the Hamburg journeymen's protests against the power of the guilds.[31] One might, thus, think that the pamphlet aims to show that proper freedom is had within the state, rather than outside it, so as to discourage such conflicts. But the Reimarus family does not seem to have held a negative view of rebellions in general. Rather, the family celebrated the French Revolution and even threw a party commemorating the first anniversary of the storming of the Bastille.[32] Of course, we saw above that Kant also sympathized with the French Revolution. But while Kant felt compelled to reconcile his rejection of rebellion against the state and his sympathy for the French Revolution by subtly arguing that the start of the French Revolution was not actually a rebellion against the state at all, we find no similarly nuanced arguments in Reimarus. This suggests that she approved of the French Revolution as a rebellion against the state. Moreover, the cited passages from *Freedom* need to be interpreted against the background of Reimarus's more general views regarding unjust states in the *Attempt*. In the *Attempt*, Reimarus denies that any state is perfectly just. She writes, "But this perfection is not reachable under any form of government other than through an approach into the infinite" (*VN*, §26). However, the *Attempt* distinguishes between different levels of injustice, some of which are more tolerable than others. In particular, the *Attempt* divides states into those with "despotic" and those with "republican" constitutions. In a state with a despotic constitution, a single person or group of people both legislates and executes the law, and there is no legal check on this group's power. In a state with a republican constitution, the legislative and executive functions of government are assigned to different people, who check one another through their political power. Reimarus maintains that states with despotic constitutions are always unjust. She writes, "In so far as in every despotic constitution the right of each to the highest authority is relinquished, such a constitution can neither <u>originate</u> nor <u>persist</u> in a just manner" (*VN*, §24). However, Reimarus argues that some states with republican constitutions are, in fact, despotic due to further circumstances. Thus, she refers to a despotism that is "through <u>external circumstances</u> (always more or less) <u>limited</u>" (*VN*, §24). Reimarus contends that a limited despotism need not be counted as unjust (even though it is not perfectly just) because it "contains in itself the <u>inner</u> condition of its future external destruction" (*VN*, §24). More specifically, Reimarus maintains

[31] Spalding 2005: 280.

[32] Spalding 2005: 283f. It would not be unusual for a thinker like Reimarus to look favorably on the French Revolution, which (at least until the Terror) many people in the German countries viewed as promoting Enlightenment ideals; see Aris 1965: 21–62 for an overview of early German reactions to the French Revolution.

that the republican constitution of a limited despotism will naturally promote political reform.

Now, the state that Reimarus's characters are discussing in the above passages from *Freedom* is a limited despotism, rather than a full despotism. The characters do not describe the state's constitution as itself unjust; instead, they regard the state in question as reasonably just but imperfect. In fact, the character A describes the state under discussion as a "well-ordered state, where one is not subjected to mere caprice" and where there are higher courts to which a party can appeal if one loses a legal case (*FR*, 12). The characters A and H are discussing a situation where, in such a state, one party to a legal proceeding loses and rebels by overthrowing the results of the proceeding through force. Even if Reimarus's characters maintained that such rebellion would be impermissible in a limited despotism, they could still accept that rebellion against a full despotism, where the constitution itself violates freedom, could be justified. Thus, the passages from *Freedom* do not show that Reimarus rules out rebellion against the state under all circumstances. Moreover, in the *Attempt*, Reimarus claims that a limited despotism will count as just only "insofar as right itself would by means of its cancelation have more to lose than to win" (*VN*, §24). Here Reimarus claims that a state is only just if freedom is more secure in that state than it would be with the state's cancelation. Obviously, Reimarus's claim that a full despotism is unjust is based on the idea that a full despotism threatens freedom more than its cancelation would. But Reimarus's claim also indicates that even a limited despotism that threatens freedom more than its cancelation would qualify as unjust. Granted, in a limited despotism reform might be possible, but it might also be hindered or frustrated for any number of reasons. And people might be forced to suffer serious injuries to freedom while waiting for those hindrances and frustrations to pass. Thus, even in a limited despotism, the people might reasonably decide that canceling the state through rebellion would promise more to win than to lose. As we can see, Reimarus suggests a consequentialist evaluation, where one must decide whether obeying a state or rebelling against the state will, in the end, promise more freedom. And this view of rebellion is obviously consistent with Reimarus's suggestion in *Freedom* that a single legal decision that fails to go one's way in a generally well-ordered state is not a sufficient violation of freedom to justify rebelling against the state and, consequently, undermining the system of law that secures people's freedom.

There is, then, no persuasive reason to rule out that Reimarus's position leaves room for rebellion against the state. Is there, however, any evidence that she actually endorses such rebellion? Yes. In *Freedom*, Reimarus writes:

> H. However you cannot deny, that there is much injustice in human society. Should one simply endure all of this?
>
> A. Well now: those are not consequences but instead deviations from our union, and if this were overstepped in essential parts by one part of society, then admittedly the other part would not be held to it. (*FR*, 7)

In this passage, Reimarus's spokesperson A explains that in cases of significant injustice that overstep essential parts of the social contract, people are no longer obligated to obey the state and may, instead, rebel. Additionally, Reimarus writes that slaves, who have been "placed in their condition" merely "through violence," may free themselves "if they ever receive the upper-hand" (*FR*, 7). This strongly suggests that slaves would be justified in rebelling against a state that kept them in chains.

Curtis-Wendlandt is aware that the last block quotation above presents a prima facie problem for her interpretation, and she attempts to accommodate it by drawing a distinction between rebellion within the social contract and rebellion outside the social contract. She writes:

> If some parties to the contract violate it to the point where external right can no longer be secured, and where the laws of the state defy even hypothetical approvability by reason, there remains no obligation to obey ... [T]his is a consequence of the dissolution of the condition of external right, and thus outside the domain of the social contract itself.[33]

Curtis-Wendlandt suggests that this position resembles Kant's view that rebellion *within* a state is never justified.[34] At first, some readers might balk at Curtis-Wendlandt's apparent suggestion that Kant would accept rebellion in cases where the state fails to secure external right. But perhaps Curtis-Wendlandt has in mind the aforementioned interpretation of Kant, according to which some alleged cases of rebellion against the state are, in fact, cases of fighting a war in the state of nature against an impostor state that is not actually a state at all. If one were to accept this interpretation of Kant,[35] then perhaps one might be able to suggest that both Kant and Reimarus condemn rebellion within the state but sanction war against an impostor state in a state of nature. Moreover, although Curtis-Wendlandt does not directly address rebellion in the case of slavery, she might suggest that a slave rebellion against the state should similarly be regarded as a war in the state of nature against an impostor state.

But does Reimarus's position actually resemble Kant's own? I do not think so. To see this, consider the position of Gottfried Achenwall, a defender of rebellion whom Kant singles out for criticism in the *Theory and Practice* essay. Kant quotes from Achenwall as follows:

> If the danger that threatens a commonwealth as a result of continuing to endure the injustice of the head of state is greater than the danger to be feared from taking up arms against him, then the people can resist him, for the sake of this right withdraw from its

[33] Curtis-Wendlandt 2012: 767. [34] Curtis-Wendlandt 2012: 768.

[35] Again, I do not mean to evaluate this interpretation here.

contract of subjection, and dethrone him as a tyrant ... In this way the people (in relation to its previous ruler) returns to the state of nature. (*TP*, 8: 301)[36]

Achenwall's suggestion that in some cases the danger of enduring injustice outweighs the danger of rebelling against the state is, of course, similar to Reimarus's own claim that one must consider whether one has more to win or lose from canceling the state through rebellion. Thus, Reimarus's overall position seems more similar to a view that Kant explicitly criticizes than it does to Kant's own position.

Now, Kant criticizes Achenwall on two counts. First, Kant claims that Achenwall's defense of rebellion results "in part from the common mistake, when the principle of right is under discussion, of substituting the principle of happiness for it in their judgments" (*TP*, 8: 301).[37] And Kant routinely insists that the state exists to secure right, not to promote happiness.[38] Kant's characterization of Achenwall is simplified, for Achenwall thinks that the state fundamentally aims to promote *both* the right to self-preservation *and* happiness. But in any case, Achenwall does not base his theory of state on the value of freedom as such. Unlike Achenwall, Reimarus never substitutes the principle of happiness for that of right. On her view, the state does not primarily aim to promote the happiness of citizens but, instead, aims to secure their external freedom. However, one might think that Kant's main complaint is not aimed at happiness per se, but rather at Achenwall's willingness to forgo a rightful condition in favor of some consequential good. Reimarus's position similarly seems to express a willingness to exit a rightful condition in favor of a consequential good – namely, freedom. Kant is unwilling to accept this consequentialist calculus, because he believes that people are obligated to enter into a rightful condition and that exiting the rightful condition is, consequently, a violation of one's duty. But as I have argued above, Reimarus does not share Kant's view that people have an obligation to enter into a rightful condition. Instead, people have the freedom to enter into a state on the grounds that doing so promises to better secure the beneficial consequence of upholding one's external freedom. Thus, Reimarus suggests that people may rebel against the state on consequentialist grounds – namely, in order to promote the security of their freedom.

Second, Kant claims that people like Achenwall take "the idea of an original contract, which is always present in reasons as the basis [of a commonwealth], as something that must *actually* have taken place, and so think they can always save for the people authorization to withdraw from the contract as it

[36] Cf. Achenwall and Potter 1995: §791 acknowledges that resistance to the state is unjustified when such resistance harms the public welfare.

[37] The view that the state should act to maximize the happiness of its citizens was widespread amongst German Enlightenment thinkers; see Aris 1965: 67f.

[38] E.g., *LDPP*, 19: 535, 554, 564; 27: 1383.

sees fit if, though by its own appraisal, the contract has been grossly violated" (*TP*, 8: 302). Now, as noted previously, Reimarus does not think that states have historically arisen through an actual contractual agreement to join together for the sake of securing freedom. But she does think that once a state exists, people can then choose whether to consent to the state's authority or not. And this consent is actual consent, be it explicit or tacit. According to Kant, the (allegedly mistaken) claim that the state's authority relies on actual consent entails that people can withdraw their consent if the social contract is violated. Reimarus endorses this conclusion, when her characters in *Freedom* concede that one group in society may justifiably decide that it should no longer be held to the social contract if another group violates it. This position is for all purposes identical to Achenwall's own view that one part of society might decide that it can extricate itself from the contract of subjection. Of course, Kant criticizes Achenwall's position. But we can use Reimarus's position to illustrate that Kant's criticism of Achenwall is not fair. More specifically, Kant argues that Achenwall's position presupposes that people actually agreed to a contractual relationship, even though no such event historically occurred. But our discussion of Reimarus's position clarifies that we need to distinguish between the original formulation of a social contract and later generations' subsequent consent to the state's authority. Like Kant, Reimarus denies that states historically arose through actual contractual agreements. But she maintains that the authority of the state over its current members, nevertheless, depends on those members' actual consent. And one can withdraw one's actual consent on the grounds that the state has violated the notion of a social contract, even though the state did not originate through any contractual agreement. In other words, Kant's criticism of Achenwall confuses the view that the state's authority relies on people's actual consent with the view that the state's original founding resulted from an actual, historical social contract.

4 Conclusion

In this essay, I have outlined Elise Reimarus's political philosophy and have argued that Reimarus's view of rebellion differs more significantly from Kant's own than others have recognized. This allows us to draw two conclusions. First, Reimarus did not anticipate Kant's views regarding membership in a state and rebellion. Thus, regardless of whether one dislikes or sympathizes with Kant's views, they should be seen as Kant's original theories, not as Reimarus's. Second, Reimarus's position is consequentialist and similar to that of Achenwall. However, unlike Achenwall, Reimarus believes that the relevant consequence to consider is freedom, rather than happiness. Thus, for those who are attracted to Kant's own emphasis on freedom as the basis of a just state but find themselves reluctant to accept Kant's views on rebellion or the non-consequentialist tenor of his political philosophy, Reimarus's position offers an interesting contemporary alternative, for Reimarus proposes a consequentialist position, where the aim of the state is not to maximize happiness but, instead, to maximize the external freedom of all.

7 Freedom and Duty

Kant, Reinhold, Fichte

Daniel Breazeale

In what follows, I will be painting with a very broad brush and addressing the following questions: What is the relationship between practical reason and moral obligation? What is the relationship between freedom, and, more specifically, the human power of free choice [*Willkür*] and duty? What are the requirements for holding someone responsible for failing to act in accordance with duty? What is the basis of our conviction that we are free at all? And how can a non-sensible faculty such as pure practical reason or the pure will have any efficacy in the empirical world?[1]

I propose to address these issues historically, by considering how they were addressed in turn by Kant, Reinhold, and Fichte during an especially fertile period of German intellectual history during the final decade of the eighteenth century. This decade featured intense debate concerning the issues mentioned above, debate largely initiated and certainly stimulated by Kant's views, as first presented in his first and second *Critiques* and as subsequently refined and defended in the *Metaphysics of Morals* and other writings. Among the more trenchant critics of Kant's moral theory was C. C. E. Schmid, who insisted that by identifying genuinely "free" actions exclusively with morally obligatory ones, Kant was incapable of explaining how one might bear responsibility for immoral actions. Schmid's challenge to Kant stimulated K. L. Reinhold to defend Kant by introducing a sharp (non-Kantian) distinction between practical reason (and the associated faculty of pure will) and the power of free choice or *Willkür*. Reinhold also went well beyond Kant in arguing that a free choice must involve not just the intelligible or pure – according to Reinhold, the "unselfish" – drive but also the natural or "selfish" drive; indeed, our "freedom" consists precisely in choosing between the demands of these two drives. But Reinhold's new doctrine raised problems of its own, which stimulated Fichte to develop, in his *System of Ethics*, a new moral theory, one that would follow Reinhold's lead in resolving the Kantian issue of imputability by distinguishing practical reason from the power of choice, but would also

[1] All translations in this paper are by the author.

(unlike Reinhold) distinguish different types of freedom ("formal" and "material"), as well as different degrees or levels of the latter. Breaking from both Kant and Reinhold, Fichte would relate these types of freedom to one another in an explicitly *genetic* manner, thus explaining how moral imputability is ultimately rooted in the innermost nature of I-hood itself, while also indicating how a pure or intelligible drive for complete self-sufficiency could become a mixed or "ethical" drive, thereby acquiring empirical efficacy. My hope is that this narrative may illuminate what is at stake in these disputes and suggest the price that must be paid in order to bring our theories into line with our practices.

1 Kant

From a strictly theoretical or naturalistic view, the most Kant believes we can know is that freedom – here understood as the capacity to initiate a new causal series in the sensible world[2] – is not utterly *impossible*, even if there is no way we can *know* it to be actual, since every naturally cognizable event must have a prior cause, and there is no way we can *understand* how a *noumenal* choice could have a *sensible* effect.

It is only in the *Groundwork of the Metaphysics of Morals* and in the *Critique of Practical Reason* that Kant, in an effort to explain how pure reason can be truly "practical" – that is, how it can determine the human will a priori – articulates a *positive* conception of the freedom of the will, the most distinctive characteristic of which is its intimate relationship to the moral law. Indeed, for Kant, the will is nothing other than our capacity for determining our actions in conformity with the thought of certain laws, whether categorical or merely prudential (*GW*, 4: 396, 412, 427). A particular determination of the will deserves to be called unconditionally "good" only when it is not merely *in accord with* the moral law but *motivated solely by respect* for the same (*GW*, 4: 394, 400–1), and the distinctively categorical character of such a law is grounded in its *universal form*.

Obviously, no action of this sort can be empirically *caused*, since that would eliminate the freedom (and hence the responsibility) of the moral agent; instead, it can only be *commanded*, leaving the agent *free* to obey it or not (*GW*, 4: 400). In this context, Kant appears to have viewed willing as a peculiar sort of causal power possessed by rational creatures, a power that

[2] Cf. the Third Antinomy of Pure Reason in the *Critique of Pure Reason*, where freedom is defined as a "special kind of causality according to which the events of the world could happen: viz., a power of absolutely beginning a state, and hence also of absolutely beginning a series of consequences thereof" (*CPR*, A 445/B 473).

can be said to operate *freely* if and only if it is determined by no *external* causes, but is instead *self-determined* and *spontaneous* (*selbsttätig*).

Combining Kant's negative definition of freedom as not being determined by anything outside of the agent's will with his analysis of the supreme principle of morality, it follows that any genuinely free action (i.e., any exercise of the will's power of spontaneous self-determination) must always involve reference to a non-empirical, a priori law governing that exercise. Genuine freedom is never lawless. To be sure, it operates independently of *natural* laws, but it freely subordinates itself to the *moral* law, as determined by the faculty of pure practical reason. If the will did not possess this capacity to "be a law unto itself," the concept of a "free will" would, says Kant, be an "absurdity [*ein Unding*]," inasmuch as "*a free will and a will under moral laws are one and the same*" (*GW*, 4: 446–7; emphasis added). If the *negative* conception of freedom is "independence from the determining causes of the world of sense," then the *positive* sense of the same is acting autonomously in obedience to supersensible moral laws.

The kind of "freedom" in play here is described by Kant as "transcendental freedom,"[3] the "unconditioned" or "absolute" power spontaneously to initiate a new causal series of events in the empirical world (though in these texts Kant remains prudently silent concerning precisely *how* such an "effect" can be thought to be *possible*). To act freely in this sense, the agent must simultaneously occupy *two standpoints*: the *phenomenal* or *empirical* standpoint, from which one views oneself as one more (necessary) "appearance" within the phenomenal world of events and another *noumenal* or purely *intelligible* standpoint, according to which one is immediately conscious of oneself not as an appearance but as an "I in itself" or as a "pure activity" (*GW*, 4: 451). Additionally, one must view some of one's empirical actions as expressions of noumenal choices.

But *how* does one become conscious of one's true, free, purely noumenal self? In the *Groundwork* Kant tentatively suggests that freedom is *analytically* connected with the very concept of human *action*, in the sense that one cannot really "act" at all except "under the idea of freedom" (*GW*, 4: 448). However, as his contemporary critics quickly pointed out, this establishes merely that one must *presuppose* or *think* that one is free, but not that one really *is* free. Sensitive to such criticisms, Kant conceded that the reality of freedom can never be demonstrated theoretically, while insisting upon the incontrovertible *practical* evidence for the same. Thus, in the second *Critique*, he argues that we must believe – or postulate – ourselves to be free whenever we find ourselves bound by a categorical, moral law, since such a law can only be

[3] This term is introduced in *CPrR*, 5: 4–5.

freely or autonomously *self-imposed*. If – *ex hypothesi* – we *are obliged* to act in accordance with such a law, then we *are also obliged* to consider ourselves to be free, even if this is merely a "postulate of practical reason."

That we consider ourselves bound by the moral law is, for Kant, an indisputable "*factum*" – not, to be sure, an empirical fact, or "fact of understanding [*Tatsache des Verstandes*]," but instead a "fact of reason [*Faktum der Vernunft*]."[4] Unlike the former, such a *factum* is not something that can simply be discovered to be the case; instead, it is an *accomplishment* of reason itself, something that *is* the case only because reason *freely makes* it so.[5] Hence Kant's well-known contention that morality is the *ratio cognoscendi* of freedom, whereas freedom is, in turn, the *ratio essendi* of morality (*CPrR*, 5: 4n.). Just as empirical (or "conditioned") causality is a condition for the possibility of phenomenal experience, so is transcendental (or "unconditioned") causality a condition for the possibility of purely practical – that is, of moral – experience. Only a *free* being can have an obligation to *impose upon itself* categorical obligations.

An obvious difficulty with Kant's account concerns the problematic *imputability* of *immoral* actions. If an action is truly "free" only when it is undertaken out of respect for the demands of the moral law, then what should one say about actions that *violate* those demands or are motivated by something *other than* such respect? It would appear that such acts cannot really be "free" at all, but if that is so, then how can one be *held responsible* for such heteronomously determined actions? If, on the other hand, one *can* be held responsible for immoral actions, then must there not be some *gap* between acting "freely" (and thus responsibly) and acting in accordance with the demands of practical reason?

Kant, of course, appears to deny any such gap and to identify free action narrowly with moral action and to treat such actions as governed by a non-empirical, hence "intelligible" law. This is what led C. C. E. Schmid to describe Kant's position as "intelligible fatalism," since it appears to imply that there is some intelligible (and unknowable) reason or cause why some human beings act freely and others do not. Though this might seem to be a *reductio ad absurdum* of Kant's position, since it appears to result in the abolition of human freedom (and hence responsibility) for both moral and immoral actions, Schmid nevertheless viewed it as the true import of the

[4] Thus, Kant rehabilitates the strategy of treating the concept of freedom as presupposed by that of action, but he applies this conclusion solely to cases of *moral* action: "As a rational being, and thus as a being belonging to the intelligible world, the human being can never think of the causality of his own will otherwise than under the idea of freedom" (*GW*, 4: 452).

[5] For an illuminating discussion of the meaning of the term *Faktum der Vernunft*, see Franks 2005.

same.[6] Schmid's colleague at Jena, K. L. Reinhold, was sufficiently annoyed by this interpretation of Kant's ethics to propose his own interpretation of the same, one that avoids "intelligible fatalism" by introducing a sharp distinction between "practical reason" (closely associated with *Wille*) and "freedom of choice" (*Willkür*), thus acknowledging the role of *contingency* in human agency.

2 Reinhold

Reinhold first attracted widespread attention with a popular series of "Letters on the Kantian Philosophy." He then achieved brief fame for his boldly innovative *Elementary Philosophy*, in which he attempted to recast Kant's Critical philosophy as a rigorously unified system derived from a single first principle.[7] What interests us here however, is the second volume of his *Letters on the Kantian Philosophy*, which was published in 1792 and included a new and highly original theory of the relationship between practical reason and free choice.[8]

The biggest innovation in Reinhold's theory is its razor-sharp distinction between freedom and practical reason. As he explained to his friend and correspondent Jens Baggesen in March 1792, "I distance myself entirely from Kant and the Kantians concerning the concept of the will, which I regard neither as the causality of reason nor as the capacity to act in accordance with represented laws, etc., but instead, as a *capacity of the person* to determine himself equally independently of reason and of sensibility" (*AJB*, 168; emphasis added).

According to Reinhold, practical reason is a spontaneously self-legislating and purely intelligible faculty. The product of such self-legislation is the moral law, which is immediately present within empirical consciousness in the form of concrete *feelings* of right and wrong and duty. These feelings are experienced by the individual as promptings of his "unselfish" drive, which is Reinhold's name for the pure, non-empirical drive to act in accord with the universally applicable moral law. Further reflection upon this same drive yields a rule of conduct requiring that one always subordinate the demands of the

[6] Recently, Paul Guyer has argued (in Guyer 2017) that Schmid never really embraced the doctrine of "intelligible fatalism" at all, but only employed it as a device for criticizing what he took to be the misinterpretation of Kant's moral theory by critics such as J. A. H. Ulrich. This claim, however, is difficult to reconcile with Schmid's actual writings.

[7] Reinhold articulated his *Elementarphilosophie* or "Elementary Philosophy" in three books: *Versuch einer neuen Theorie des menschlichen Vorstellungsvermögen* (1789); *Beyträge zur Berichtungen bisheriger Missverständnisse der Philosophen, Band I* (1790); *Ueber das Fundament des philosophischen Wissens* (1791).

[8] This important volume has recently been re-edited and published as Band 2/2 of Reinhold's *Gesammelte Schriften*. See *BKP*.

opposing, sensible or "selfish" drive to pure reason's own law and hence to the demands of the unselfish drive. Though the legislative power of practical reason is *negatively free* in the sense that it is determined by nothing *outside* itself, its own spontaneous operation occurs with *necessity* and is experienced as such by the moral agent, for whom there is nothing "voluntary" about a demand of the moral law.

Freedom in the *positive* sense, on the other hand, refers to one's ability to determine one's will in response to the demands of these two opposing drives. Since such self-determination is supposed to occur *freely*, nothing outside of one's own *Willkür* or faculty of choice can possibly lie at the basis of such a decision, which might very well therefore be described as "groundless" – even if Reinhold himself preferred to say, somewhat gnomically, that "the ground of *Willkür* is freedom." So understood, willing is a property or power only of *human agents* and not of practical reason.

The will is said to be "pure" when it is determined in accordance with the moral law (or unselfish drive), and "impure" when it wills in violation of that law's requirements. According to Reinhold, therefore, an impure – or immoral – will is no less free than a pure one. Even though the maxims of practical reason are promulgated as absolutely necessary, the power of free choice is precisely the power to obey or not to obey such maxims:

> *My freedom* [explained Reinhold to Baggesen] *is elevated above all laws*, even though it apprehends through itself the practical law . . . Even though *practical reason pertains to my innermost self* and I can obtain harmony with myself only by obeying the law of practical reason, such obedience is nevertheless possible only though my freedom. I am indebted only to myself for this harmony, *and I could never create it if I were unable to destroy it.*[9]

An obvious advantage of Reinhold's theory of freedom is the ease with which it can answer the question concerning one's *responsibility* for immoral choices and action. An immoral act is simply an act in which one freely elects *not* to subordinate a demand of the selfish drive to that of the unselfish drive, despite one's awareness that one's own power of practical reason demands that one do precisely that. It follows that one is absolutely and equally responsible for *every* act of free choice – whether "moral" or "immoral" – since the determining ground of every free act is one's own power of choice.

A further implication of Reinhold's theory is that no truly free act can be morally indifferent, since every free decision must always include consciousness of a demand of one's pure drive, as well as of the demands of one's sensible, or selfish drive. Although he draws a much sharper distinction than Kant had yet drawn between practical reason and free will, Reinhold agrees

[9] Reinhold to Baggesen, July 23, 1792, emphasis added (*AJB*, 221).

that any free choice must include some *reference* to the demands of the moral law – even if the choice is to ignore those demands or is one that is merely morally permissible but not demanded.[10]

Practical reason is not a power *distinct from* the person of the free agent, though it is distinct from his faculty of free choice. It is still *his* practical reason, and the laws it issues are *issued by* and *addressed to him.* In contrast, he recognizes that precepts grounded upon his selfish drive do not really have their origin *within him* at all, but are *given* to him by nature. He also recognizes that, as a finite agent, he too is a part of nature. His sensible drive is therefore *his* as well, though not in the same intimate sense in which this can be said of his unselfish drive, for the former is not a product of his own rational spontaneity. According to Reinhold, every person has an innate longing (rooted in reason's supreme demand for non-contradiction) to *unify* the various aspects of his self and to reconcile the often-opposing demands of his two basic drives. In the eyes of the free agent himself, however, these are in no sense "equal" powers, since only one of them tells him how he *ought* to determine himself. Thus, the only way one can succeed in actually "unifying oneself" is by *subordinating* the demands of the selfish drive to those of the unselfish drive. Hence there is little if any role for "practical deliberation" in Reinhold's account. One need only become clearly aware of these conflicting demands and then act in accordance with the aforementioned rule requiring the demands of the selfish drive to be subordinated to those of the unselfish drive.

Concerning the *reality* of the radical freedom of the human will and power of choice, Reinhold explicitly denies that this is a postulate or a matter of practical belief, and instead maintains that we each have immediate empirical *knowledge* of our own freedom "as a fact of consciousness [*Tatsache des Bewusstsein*]" and that this is universally acknowledged by "healthy common sense." We *know* that we are free in the same way we know we possess a lower and a higher power of desire; in other words, we know this *through experience.* But whereas our knowledge of our own higher and lower powers of desire is *indirect* and derived from *reflection* upon immediately present *feelings* of duty, pleasure, and pain, our knowledge of our power of free will or choice is *immediate* and *direct.* We are aware that we *can* determine ourselves

[10] This is not to say that Reinhold anticipates Fichte in insisting that there are no "morally neutral" actions. Though he insists that every genuinely free choice must at least *make reference* to the demands of the unselfish drive, he concedes that there may well be situations in which more than one empirical course of actions is *consistent with* the pure drive and, therefore, morally *permissible.* See Letter Six of volume two of his *Briefe* where Reinhold describes actions as "right in the narrower sense" when they are not "the only possible" actions in accord with the unselfish drive and thus not "necessary," but "merely possible" (*BKP*, II: 145). His point seems to be that in every case the unselfish (moral) drive either *requires* or simply *permits* a certain concrete action, and that in order to choose freely I must always *take into account* its relationship to the moral law. See *BKP*, II: 194, 198–200.

through the undeniable *fact* that we *do* determine ourselves. We are immediately conscious of this power, however, only when we actually make a choice between satisfying some natural desire and satisfying a demand of practical reason. (So in this sense, Reinhold affirms Kant's claim that duty is the *ratio cognescendi* of freedom.) From all of this it follows that moral *philosophy* and moral *practice* are both grounded upon precisely the same "knowledge" – our factually based conviction that we are, at least in certain cases and circumstances, truly free.

As for explaining *how* a noumenal law for willing can have any effect in the sensible world, Reinhold maintained that one of the great advantages of his theory over Kant's lay precisely in the way that his new account of freedom bridges the gap between these two realms. It does this, first, by connecting the intelligible faculty of practical reason to a drive that expresses itself in consciousness through moral *feelings*, and, second, by connecting freedom of choice to *both* sensibility and reason, inasmuch as the function of *Willkür* is strictly limited to the choice between satisfying the demands of the selfish or of the unselfish drive. In other words, Reinhold sought to reconcile transcendental with empirical freedom by showing that the power of free will could not be intelligible without also being sensible and could not be sensible without also being intelligible. This was precisely the point of his declaration that "I distance myself from Kant's concept of sensibility, inasmuch as I cannot think of any morality [*Sittlichkeit*] apart from sensibility [*Sinnlichkeit*]" (*AJB*, 168). It is the duty and function not of practical reason but of the power of *Willkür* or individual freedom of choice *freely* to subordinate the demands of the selfish to the unselfish drive. Hence only a creature endowed with such a power possesses such "autonomy."

Yet Reinhold explicitly declined to offer any *explanation* of *how* a free choice between the demands of the selfish and unselfish drives is possible. Perhaps, he surmised, some future philosophical system might be able to explain the fact of human freedom, but in Vol. 2 of his *Letters*, he explicitly eschews such a task and treats the freedom of the will not simply as an undeniable empirical fact or *Tatsache* but also as an impenetrable mystery or *Geheimnis* (*BKP*, II: 237). And this, he claims, is a good thing too, for if philosophy (or natural science) could ever successfully "explain" this fact – that is, explain *why Willkür* determines itself in one way rather than another – then freedom, as both philosophy and common sense understand it, would be *abolished*, since, in Reinhold's view, the only way to "explain" the choice in question would be by deriving it from some ground or principle lying outside of and determining it.

For Reinhold, the conclusion is inescapable: a free choice is by its very nature inexplicable; yet we are fully and personally responsible for such a choice, since it is in the deepest sense *ours*. A properly Reinholdian rejoinder to the objection that such an account makes free choice radically unintelligible would be similar to the reply he is reported to have made to complaints concerning his failure to explain how intelligible freedom can produce any sensible appearances: namely, "this is simply how it is, *no matter how absurd this may be*!"[11]

3 Kant (Again)

Without mentioning Reinhold by name, Kant responded to his proposal and directly addressed the issues that motivated it in subsequent writings, beginning with *Religion within the Boundaries of Mere Reason*. Here he appears to be in at least partial agreement with Reinhold, inasmuch as he introduces a new, much sharper distinction between *Wille* (or "pure will," which he now identifies specifically with the legislative power of practical reason and thus with the moral law) and *Willkür* or the power of free choice. The latter is the power freely to incorporate some desire or feeling – whether this is a purely natural desire or a feeling of moral obligation – into a *maxim* for action (*RBMR*, 6: 23–4). Such a choice, he stoutly maintains, is *free* in the sense that it is not determined by anything external to the agent. This does not mean that the choice in question is *arbitrary* and not determined by anything at all, but only that it is "completely within the power of the subject at the moment that it occurs" and therefore occurs "with absolute spontaneity," by virtue of which alone "an act as well as its opposite must be within the power of the subject at the moment it takes place" (*RBMR*, 6: 49–50n.).

According to *Religion*, therefore, an action can be both "freely chosen" and not in conformity with the moral law. Indeed, Kant now insists that such independent freedom is necessary in order for the action in question to be *imputed* to the agent. But he also maintains (again, like Reinhold) that an exercise of the power of free choice cannot be called genuinely free unless this involves some *explicit reference* to feelings of duty, inasmuch as the very concept of the free power of choice is first inferred from one's awareness that this power can be determined by the moral law and that one is commanded to do just this (*RBMR*, 6: 49n.). A free choice is therefore always a choice between acting in accord with a maxim that incorporates the demands of the moral law or with one that rejects this demand.[12]

In this same essay, Kant places a striking new emphasis upon the distinction between one's original or intelligible *character* or *disposition* (*Gesinnung*) and

[11] See the report by Reinhold's student Herman Coch in a letter to his fellow student Johann Smidt, January 10, 1794, in Fuchs 1992: 31, emphasis added.

[12] Kant concedes that there is a sense in which a human being, considered as a purely natural and sensuous being, can be said to "choose" which desire to satisfy, but he denies that this is real freedom of choice, which can only be found in a being who is also aware of his capacity to act in accordance with the intelligible demands of the moral law. See *RBMR*, 6: 31.

one's empirical character. He describes the former as the "inner principle" of one's maxims, something that underlies and therefore *explains* all of one's empirical choices and actions, including those made in obedience to the moral law. The person of good character is one who has freely made respect for the moral law into his supreme maxim, whereas the person of bad character subordinates the demands of morality to those of his sensible nature.

The kind of choice Kant is talking about here is clearly a higher-order choice of one's supreme maxim for choosing, and he maintains that such a choice must be understood as a *purely intelligible* exercise of *Willkür*. Such a choice is not bound by the formal conditions of phenomenal experience, including the form of inner sense, *time* (*RBMR*, 6: 40). Through a purely subjective and *intelligible* act of choosing, one freely determines one's own original or noumenal character, which, in turn, determines one's empirical character, choices, and actions (*RBMR*, 6: 25–7, 31–2). Though one is never empirically conscious of making such an original choice, one can nevertheless recognize that one *must* have done so or be doing so. Why? Because otherwise one could not hold oneself responsible for one's own empirical actions. On this point Kant seems unequivocal: possession of an "evil" disposition is not to be understood as some sort of *privation*, but *positively*, "as a consequence of a real and contrary determination of the power of choice [*Willkür*], i.e. of an *opposition* to the law" (*RBMR*, 6: 22–3n.).

To be sure, Kant continues to maintain that the evidence that one actually possesses such a remarkable power of free choice is always only *indirect*. One is never immediately aware that one is *free* to overcome one's sensuous incentives to transgress the moral law, but only that one has a categorical *duty* to do so, and from this, he says, one "rightly *concludes* that one must be *able* to do so, and that one's *Willkür* is therefore free" (*RBMR*, 6: 49n.). "Ought," after all, implies "can."

Why might someone freely "choose" an "evil" character – or, for that matter, a "good" one? What are the "subjective grounds" that might lead one to adopt one maxim rather than another? Such questions, insists Kant, are, strictly speaking, *unanswerable*, inasmuch as something can be "comprehended" or "explained" only by referring it to something else, as its ground, whereas a spontaneously free act has – by definition – no such ground. This is also why he condemns efforts to explain anyone's basic character in terms of empirical circumstances or past experience (*RBMR*, 6: 40). For finite intellects such as ourselves, one's free choice to become the kind of person one is must remain forever *inscrutable*, inasmuch as "there is for us no conceivable ground from which the moral evil in us could originally have come."[13] Kant thus concedes

[13] *RBMR*, 6: 43. Similarly, though we must always concede the possibility – and indeed, the moral necessity – of a radical change in one's character and thus in one's original choice, "how it is

that his entire doctrine concerning our radically free power of choice regarding our own character must always harbor an insoluble *mystery* (*MM*, 6: 21n.).

But even this does not represent Kant's final word on this subject, since he returned to it again in 1797, in the *Metaphysics of Morals*. Here he once again attempts to elucidate the fraught relationship between the morally legislative power of *Wille*, here described as the self-determining "higher power of desire," and the spontaneously active power of free choice or *Willkür*. In reconsidering this issue, Kant appears to retreat from the standpoint of *Religion*, for he reiterates more unequivocally than ever the controversial position implied by his earlier writings: namely, that *only* actions motivated by respect for the moral law can be described as truly free. Accordingly, he explicitly rejects the definition (proposed by Reinhold and apparently endorsed by Kant himself in *Religion*) of *Willkür* as "the freedom to make a choice for or against the moral law" (*MM*, 6: 226).

Negatively construed, "freedom" refers to *Willkur*'s capacity to determine itself independently of any sensible drives or inclinations. Positively construed, "freedom" refers to the capacity of pure reason itself to be practical, that is, to legislate laws for the actual employment of *Willkür*, which is, in turn, genuinely "free" if and only if it is in fact determined by the a priori legislation of practical reason (*MM*, 6: 226–7).

This, of course, by no means resolves the previously indicated problem of the *imputability* of immoral acts; on the contrary, it makes it even more explicit and unavoidable; and, once again, Kant's response is to insist that this is a *puzzle* that no finite intellect will ever solve. The issue here is similar to one first raised in the Third Antimony: namely, how can the spontaneity of the will be reconciled with the "pre-determinism" of the natural order, in which every event is determined by preceding ones. This too, declares Kant, is something that is simply *incomprehensible* for the human intellect.

The closest he ever came to addressing this issue is in the second part of the *Critique of the Power of Judgment*, in which he entertains the possibility of a cosmic, teleological perspective upon *both* the intelligible and the sensible worlds, according to which the latter is purposive for ends determined within the former, since both are subsumed under a single, still higher principle. But alas, such a principle, however necessary we may find it to be, can be no more than *regulative*, a way of looking at the world "as if" it were designed to further our noumenal ends. Consequently, such a perspective can never be

possible for a naturally evil man to make himself a good man is something that wholly surpasses our comprehension," as does the occurrence of a "lapse from good into evil" (*RBMR*, 6: 45). Though the possibility of such a moral rebirth cannot be denied (indeed, it is demanded by the moral law), we still cannot *comprehend* how this is possible and can obtain no *insight* into the same (*RBMR*, 6: 50).

occupied *cognitively* and must remain a matter of rationally necessary practical *belief* – in this case, belief in the sensible efficacy of our conscientious moral choices.

4 Fichte

The *Wissenschaftslehre*, boasted the young Fichte, is "the first system of human freedom." By this, he explained that it was the first philosophy to free man from bondage to things in themselves and indeed from external circumstances in general. Accordingly, the Jena *Wissenschaftslehre* begins by postulating the unconditioned occurrence and reality of a self-grounding and utterly inexplicable F/Act or *Tathandlung*, in which the I spontaneously posits itself for itself qua unified subject-object, an act that engenders a fact and a fact that is the product of an act. (The parallels between this Fichtean *Tathandlung des Ichs* and the Kantian *Faktum der Vernunft* are striking.)

The I – or rather, the concept of pure I-hood, described in the first, utterly unconditioned *Grundsatz* of the *Foundation of the entire Wissenschaftslehre* – is, by definition, self-determining, unconditioned, and "absolute," in the sense that both *what* it is and *that* it is are determined by nothing beyond its own spontaneous activity. Such a concept of pure I-hood contrasts sharply with the constrained condition of every empirical – which is to say, of every *actual* – I, which always finds itself to be *limited*, not only by the causal forces of the natural world, but also by the demands of other finite I's for mutual recognition, as well as by the categorical obligations of the moral law.

Fichte's central and perhaps most original philosophical claim is that in order to posit itself as an I at all – whether as a cognizing intellect or as practical agent – every I must, at least implicitly, posit itself as sharing the same spontaneously self-reverting structure that is characteristic of pure I-hood in general (which Fichte, in his *System of Ethics*, calls "formal" or "external" freedom).[14] The task of the Jena system is to show – by means of what Fichte describes variously as "*a priori* construction in intuition," "genetic derivation," or "pragmatic history" – that the absolutely posited self-positing with which such an account commences can *actually occur* if and only if the I encounters

[14] The terms "formal" and "material" freedom are first introduced in Fichte's *Foundation of Natural Right* and then employed extensively in the *System of Ethics*, where they acquire a rather *different* meaning. Generally speaking, in both texts Fichte associates "formal freedom" with the original spontaneity characteristic of I-hood as such. Such freedom is "external" in the sense that the pure I is entirely self-determined. In the *Foundation of Natural Right*, "material freedom" refers to the domain of an individual's efficacious action in the sensible world, but in the *System of Ethics* it refers instead to one's freedom to determine the *ends* of one's actions and not just the means for pursing naturally given ends. For a detailed discussion of this topic, see Breazeale 2020.

"certain incomprehensible limits, within which [it] simply finds [itself] to be constrained" (*IW*, 149; *SW*, V: 184). The I can actually succeed in positing itself, therefore, only by positing itself as a *finite individual.* Hence, only a *limited* I can posit its own *absoluteness* – first, as constituting its own original formal character as an I, and secondly, as the material goal of its endless striving to overcome its own original limitations.

First in the *Foundation of the entire Wissenschaftslehre* and then in his lectures on *Wissenschaftslehre nova methodo*, Fichte sought to demonstrate (or rather to describe) how the "limitations" of the finite I are first encountered simply as an *Anstoß* or check upon its own original striving (a striving implicit in the very concept of the I as a self-posited *Tathandlung*) – a striving to realize its self-posited independence. Such a check is first present within consciousness in the form of certain involuntary *feelings*. When the I turns its attention toward, or, in Fichte's idiom, "reflects upon" these same feelings (something which, according to Fichte, it is compelled to do by virtue of its distinctive character as a self-reverting activity), this stimulates its spontaneously productive power of imagination to re-posit these feelings, first as sensations, then as intuitions and concepts, and finally as full-fledged "representations" of causally interacting material things.

Or consider Fichte's celebrated demonstration, in the *Foundations of Natural Right*, that the I cannot posit itself as an *individual I* without at least implicitly acknowledging the freedom of *other* individuals and hence recognizing a domain of reciprocal "rights," by which all finite I's are at least hypothetically bound. This demonstration too begins with the finite I's encounter with another of its original limits: in this case, the unbidden presence of a summons or *Aufforderung* to recognize and to respect the freedom of the other. Less familiar, perhaps, is Fichte's even more audacious effort, in his *System of Ethics*, to show how the finite I is, as it were, originally "limited" by the very fact that it is – and posits itself as – a spontaneously self-positing I, a "pure I" or "pure will," which possesses no end or goal beyond the efficacious affirmation of its own independence and utter self-sufficiency. This original determinacy of the pure will – namely, that it wills its own self-sufficiency and is obliged to do all it can to make it actual – is the final and highest limitation discovered by the finite I and, as we shall see, facilitates Fichte's novel solution to the problem of reconciling human freedom with categorical moral obligation.

This limitation too is discovered by means of a *feeling*, in this case a feeling of harmony between some possible course of action in the natural world and the categorical insistence of the pure I upon its own utter self-sufficiency, a demand present to the finite I in the form of a pure drive to self-sufficiency in the face of myriad obstacles to the same. This, according to Fichte, is the origin of the unerring inner voice of *conscience*, a voice that dictates not what any finite I actually *is*, but rather what it *ought to strive to become*.

It is widely recognized that Fichte sought to establish a more radical and thoroughgoing system of transcendental idealism than either Kant's or Reinhold's, but it is not always appreciated that his primary motive for doing this was precisely to overcome some of the paradoxes implicit in Kant's doctrine of free will in its relation to practical reason, as well as to provide a transcendental account of the *empirical efficacy* of noumenal freedom. The original I of self-consciousness (that is, the I of which we are empirically first aware) is, declared Fichte, always the practical, that is, the willing I. But this practical power cannot operate independently of the theoretical or cognitive power, since choice and action always presuppose a consciously posited *concept* of the goal or end of the action in question (*FNR*, 20; *SW*, III: 19–20).

This, however, seems to lead to an impasse: on the one hand, the theoretical activity of the intellect *presupposes* the practical activity of the same, since empirical feelings originally arise within and for the I only in consequence of some limit or check upon its practical striving; on the other hand, the practical striving of the I is unintelligible without some prior cognition of the goal to be accomplished by the action in question.

Fichte's solution to this problem, which is most clearly enunciated in his lectures on *Wissenschaftslehre nova methodo*, is to describe the finite I as possessing an original, pure will to assert, preserve, and extend the domain of its own *Selbstständigkeit* or self-sufficiency. Such a material end is determined pre-deliberatively and pre-reflectively. It is not the product of any choice or cognition on the part of the finite I, but is originally given to it by its formal character as a *spontaneously* self-positing and *self-active* pure I.

"Formal freedom," which is implicit in the unconditioned, original self-positing of the I, constitutes the "true essence" or "original being" of the latter. (*SE*, 30, 35; *SW*, IV: 24, 30).[15] Such "freedom" designates, as it were, the self-productive power of the I as such, which must always posit for itself anything ascribable to it. Yet such freedom applies merely to the I "as such," which is

[15] One must, however, exercise caution in interpreting such remarks, inasmuch as Fichte repeatedly insists that the I, precisely because it is free, cannot be understood as any sort of "being" or "thing" at all and explicitly denies that the finite I possesses an "essence" or "nature," in the sense of a substantial determining ground of its spontaneous actions and choices. If it is to be understood as *free*, insists Fichte, the rational being, the I, must not be thought of as any sort of "thing" or "being" at all, but purely and simply *an acting* (*ein Handeln*) and not even a "thing that acts [*ein Handelndes*]" (*FNR*, 3; *SW*, III: 1). Willing is defined by Fichte as "an absolute transition from a state of indeterminacy to one of determinacy, accompanied by consciousness of the same" (*SE*, 149; *SW*, IV: 158); therefore, if the I is to be understood primarily as an *act of willing*, it must also be understood as originally *indeterminate*, and this applies to the individual human being as well, who is memorably described by Fichte as "originally nothing at all. He must become what he is to be; and since he is to be a being for himself, he must become this through himself" (*FNR*, 74; *SW*, III: 80).

utterly lacking in any determinacy beyond what is implicit in the bare notion of an unconditionally occurring self-reverting and self-positing F/Act.

The "spontaneous" activity of the intellect, by means of which the finite I's practical encounter with its own limits is transformed into theoretical cognition of representations of external objects, involves a similarly "formal" freedom of the I.[16] Fichte's collective name for these spontaneously and unconsciously occurring activities of the intellect is "reflection," a term designating the I's capacity to attend to its own actions and states in accordance with the "laws" of its own nature. Since such "reflections" occur "spontaneously" and have no foundation outside of the I itself, they can be described as "free," albeit only as "formally" so. This kind of purely formal freedom is, according to Fichte, "the root of all freedom," inasmuch as it designates the "external" freedom of every I from all that is not-I (*SE*, 129; *SW*, IV: 135).

Formal freedom is posited along with I-hood itself or "immediate self-consciousness" and can therefore always be *presupposed.* It is not, however, necessary that any particular finite I be explicitly *aware* of its own formal freedom, though Fichte insists that it is always *possible* to obtain such an awareness. How? By means of a new, freely and consciously initiated, *act of reflection* upon one's own I-hood and intellectual activity – precisely the kind of reflection characteristic of transcendental philosophy. Moreover, insists Fichte, the person who engages in such reflection will also *become free* in a new and highly significant sense, since he will now explicitly *recognize* that he is *not* in fact determined by those "external objects" of cognition that seemed to oppress him, since it is he, qua free intellect, that first posits these objects as such. This marks the all-important transition from "formal" to "material" freedom.

The finite I is, of course, never merely – or even primarily – a knower; it is also an actor, an agent in the external world. At first, however, the "agency" of the finite I is barely recognizable as such, since it appears to consist simply in acting in obedience to the promptings of natural forces and desires. Nevertheless, the I is never directly *caused* to act in this manner. On the contrary, it must always "bring about" its own actions, employing for this purpose a force that stems from nature, but one that is no longer *nature's* force. Instead, declares Fichte, this natural force now comes "under the sway" of a principle that lies above all nature, namely, the formal freedom of the I. Whatever one *does* with consciousness, one does with this kind of formal freedom, even if what one actually does is fully in accord with a natural desire,

[16] These activities are described in detail in Part Two of the *Foundation of the entire Wissenschaftslehre*, in *What is Distinctive of the Wissenschaftslehre with Regard to the Theoretical Power*, and the lectures on *WLnm.*

for the ultimate ground of such acting is no longer any natural drive, but rather one's *consciousness* of the same.

Such a thin notion of freedom is obviously inadequate for understanding moral willing and acting, for the latter presupposes a consciousness not only of one's *desires* but also of one's *freedom of choice*, as well as an awareness of some kind of non-sensible or non-natural *norm* for *freely choosing* how to act in a particular situation. What is required in this case is precisely what Fichte calls *internal* or *material* freedom – that is to say, the freedom not merely to lift oneself above natural determinacy but the freedom to determine for oneself the *goal* or *end* of one's actions.[17]

In order to elucidate the I's capacity to *choose* between various ends, Fichte provides a complex *genetic* account of the development from formal to material freedom: from the freedom to choose among *means* to a predetermined natural end to the freedom to choose the *ends* of one's actions. In the manner of a *Bildungsroman*, *The System of Ethics* narrates the progress of the individual I, first toward awareness of its own formal freedom and then toward full material freedom. Such progress proceeds by means of a series of spontaneously generated *reflections* upon one's character as an I and what that entails.

Such a reflection, Fichte assures his readers, must lead to a new and clearer recognition of what is actually implicit in the concept of the original and merely formal freedom of the I. The intellect that engages in such reflection will therefore take "self-sufficiency as a norm, in accordance with which the intellect charges itself to determine itself freely . . . [The] concept of self-sufficiency thus contains both the power and the law demanding that one employ this power steadfastly. You cannot think of the concept of self-sufficiency without thinking of these two, [the power and the law,] as united" (*SE*, 54; *SW*, IV: 52). The materially free individual takes the aim of reason itself as his own and, in all his decisions and actions, strives to advance "the self-sufficiency of reason as such," thereby transforming himself, in Fichte's infelicitous phrase, into "a tool of the moral law" (*SE*, 248, *SW*, IV: 259).

Such is the schema that underlies Fichte's profoundly unKantian account of conscience (an account that owes much more to Kant's account of aesthetic judgment in the third *Critique* than to his description of moral judgment in the

[17] In *WLnm*, Fichte identifies "internal" or "material freedom" with the individual I's "freedom of choice" [*Freiheit der Wahl*]," which he describes as the "ideal activity of the practical power" (*WLnm*, 168; *GA*, IV/2: 58). Whenever we elect a determinate goal we are exercising our material – which is to say, our "practical" – freedom in this sense. But in the purely foundational portion of his system he makes no distinction between the various ways in which the material self-determination of the I may occur nor does he further illuminate the relationship between the purely formal freedom of the self-positing I and the material freedom of the practically volitional individual subject. This deficiency is remedied in the *SE*.

second). For Fichte, conscience is an unerring feeling that arises whenever a particular possible course of action in the sensible world is discovered to be in harmony with the pure will's demand for complete self-sufficiency.

Fichte often claimed that the *Wissenschaftslehre* is the only philosophical system compatible with a "moral way of thinking," and by this he meant, first, that it is the only system capable of reconciling freedom with natural necessity and explaining the real possibility of efficacious free action in the material world, and, secondly, that it is the first system to *demonstrate* that and why genuine or material freedom can never conflict with but must always coincide with the demands of moral duty. This is because the moral law is nothing other than the expression within human consciousness of the ultimate demand made by the formal freedom of I-hood as such, now considered as a norm for material action in the sensible world.[18] Material freedom is thus the same thing as self-legislation or "autonomy" (*SE*, 58; *SW*, IV: 56). Such a law does not *determine* or *necessitate* the individual I to act in any particular way; instead, it stipulates what one *ought* to do in a particular situation. Though the force of such a moral ought can certainly be described as a kind of "compulsion," such compulsion, Fichte insists, is not only compatible with the freedom of the I, it is the highest expression of the same. Accordingly, there is no irony in his claim that anyone who has elevated oneself to the reflective standpoint required for full material freedom simply *cannot help but do* what duty commands, for at this point freedom and duty are finally in perfect sync with one another (*SE*, 181–2; *SW*, IV: 191–2).

In the end, Fichte believed that everyone should be held responsible for failing to act in accord with the moral law (though, like Kant, he cautioned his readers against judging the morality of others' actions and advised them to focus upon their own transgressions). This means that he thought one could be held responsible for failing to accomplish the complete series of free acts of reflection described above. Every finite I, just because it is an I, possesses formal freedom, and is therefore, just because it is an I, potentially capable of freely reflecting upon this freedom and transforming it into the much more robust and concrete kind of freedom in harmony with duty that Fichte called material freedom. By distinguishing *degrees* and *kinds* of freedom in this way, Fichte avoids the Kantian paradox of imputability. On this point he is clearly on the side of Reinhold in his dispute with Kant concerning the independence of the power of free choice from the legislation of practical reason. But he goes

[18] See *SE*, 244, 250, 258, 295–9; *SW*, IV: 255, 261, 270, 310–15. Since the determining ground of the act that ought to occur lies entirely in the original freedom of the I, it is one "that ought to occur purely and simply because it ought to occur. This ought is therefore an absolute, categorical ought, and the rule in question is a law that is valid without exception, since its validity is simply subject to no possible condition whatsoever" (*SE*, 57–8; *SW*, IV: 56).

well beyond Reinhold's position (and in this respect draws closer to Kant's) by distinguishing formal from material freedom and identifying the latter alone with acting in accord with the dictates of morality.

Though he duly notes the important role played in one's moral development by the examples and contributions of others, Fichte always concludes by insisting that at best such education can merely *prepare* one for something that one must always accomplish entirely on one's own: namely, freely reflecting upon one's own formal freedom as an I. thereby elevating oneself to full material freedom or the standpoint of morality. As a spontaneously occurring act, such a reflection cannot really be *explained* at all; it is, says Fichte, something that "occurs through absolute freedom." The "fact *that* such an act of reflection occurs – i.e., its form – is something absolute. It is not a product of nature; *it occurs simply because it occurs, because I am I*" (*SE*, 126; *SW*, IV: 132; emphasis added).

For Fichte, as for Kant and Reinhold, there is something mysterious and incomprehensible about the finite I's path from formal to material freedom and thus about the link between freedom and duty. The acts of reflection that propel one along the path from formal to material freedom possess no ground beyond themselves and are therefore, strictly speaking, *inexplicable*. *Why* do some people succeed in realizing their material freedom whereas others do not, and why do some who have realized it then relapse into immoral behavior? To such questions Fichte responds candidly: "there is something incomprehensible here, and it cannot be otherwise, since we are now standing at the boundary of all comprehensibility: namely, the doctrine of freedom as it applies to the empirical subject." Moreover, anyone who has failed to achieve the requisite reflective standpoint cannot be aware of his obligation to achieve it, since, as Fichte puts it, he "cannot have a concept of what [he is] supposed to do before [he] actually do[es] it . . . The situation could not be otherwise, for an act of freedom *is* purely and simply *because it is*. It is what is absolutely primary [*ein absolut erstes*], something that cannot be connected to anything else or explained on the basis of anything else" (*SE*, 172–3; *SW*, IV: 182).

Here we detect a certain ambivalence in Fichte's account. He insists that one can – and indeed absolutely ought to – lift oneself by one's own bootstraps, as it were, and achieve material freedom purely through one's own spontaneous efforts.[19] In accordance with his original being as an I, every human being is "free and independent of nature, even if he is not free in actuality." Moreover,

[19] It is true that Fichte also recognized the vital role played by one's "upbringing," or education in the widest sense, in preparing one for one's moral vocation, and several recent commenters have strongly emphasized this feature of his thought. See, e.g., Kosch 2018 and Wood 2016. However, Fichte remained adamant that no amount of ethical training or exposure to moral exemplars could every *make* one moral or free. In every case, he insisted, this is something for which each individual always bears final responsibility.

"he always ought to tear himself loose from this state; and if one considers him to be absolutely free, then he is also *able* to do this," declares Fichte. Yet this conclusion seems to harbor a paradox, one that he does not even pretend to conceal: "Before [a human being] can freely tear himself loose, he must first be free. But it is precisely *his freedom itself* that is fettered; the very force through which he is supposed to help himself is allied against him." Though it is true that he *ought to* "tear himself loose" from his apparent bondage to nature and realize his material freedom, it seems impossible to explain how such an act of willing could occur or even be possible. In the end, concludes Fichte, with a note of ironic wistfulness, "only a miracle could save him – *a miracle, moreover, which he himself would have to perform*" (*SE*, 191; *SW*, IV: 201; emphasis added).

5 Concluding Observations

1. Perhaps it is best to think of freedom not as a black and white, either/or issue, but as a matter of *degree*. For Fichte, for example, everyone is always formally free, but material freedom is an achievement that few, if any of us can ever be said to have accomplished, but for which we are all obliged to strive. As he wrote in the "Personal Meditations" in which he first tried to formulate his new philosophy, "one should never have said 'the human being *is* free,' but rather 'the human being necessarily strives, hopes, and assumes that he is free.' – The proposition, 'the human being *is* free' is not true."[20] Freedom, in other words, is not an innate property of human beings; it is something that one has to *acquire*, to *become*. Thinking of freedom as an *achievement* rather than an *endowment* may well prove to be illuminating.
2. From the naturalistic standpoint of ordinary human understanding and the natural sciences there appears to be something profoundly mysterious, incomprehensible, and even "absurd" about the alleged "fact" of human freedom, which cannot be easily reconciled with all the other "facts" we accept. Fichte, of course, thought he could do just this, but only by *starting* with transcendental freedom and then deriving empirical necessity as a condition for its possibility. Such a systematic philosophical idealism is, however, not without substantial difficulties of its own. And even after offering his own idealistic "explanation" of the ultimately compatible relationship between freedom and nature, Fichte still agreed with Kant and Reinhold that there is something profoundly *inscrutable* about every *actual* free decision – and above all, about the possibility of the "free

[20] *Eigene Mediationen über Elementar-Philosophie/Practische Philosophie*, *GA*, II/3: 183.

decision" to "become free" – a mystery that even the *Wissenschaftslehre* could not hope to eliminate.

3. Kant, Reinhold, and Fichte all agree that without constant reference to the categorical feeling of moral obligation it is impossible to defend the claim that any of our choices and actions are actually "free," in the sense of being spontaneously and autonomously self-determined, rather than determined heteronomously by natural drives and circumstances. However one understands moral obligation – even in its more recent, profoundly debased guise as "anxiety" or "dread" or "guilt" – it seems impossible to defend the universality and necessity of the same without endorsing a robust notion of human freedom as the *ratio essendi* of moral obligation, and of moral obligation as the *ratio cognoscendi* of freedom.
4. Even supposing that the great majority of what we normally think of as our "free choices" – including most of our everyday "moral" decisions – are really not *free* at all, since we seldom actively consider the fact that we are utterly, radically free to obey or disobey the moral law in any particular case, but simply continue to act as we previously have: this does not imply that direct experiences of radical freedom *never* occur or are *impossible.* Perhaps what is called for is something entirely lacking in Kant's practical philosophy, something that might be described as an "aesthetic of practical reason." Such a doctrine, like the transcendental aesthetic of theoretical reason, would involve no deductions or derivations, but would be an explication or *Erörterung* of how moral obligation (and hence human freedom) is actually experienced. In this case, however, we would be dealing not with a priori intuitions of space and time, but with categorical, immediate consciousness of desiring and willing. Perhaps what is needed and appropriate is not a *demonstration* of the reality of freedom but a *rigorous description* of our actual *experience* of freedom and of the *varieties* of the same. In search of such descriptions one might turn to the writings of philosophers such as Kierkegaard, Heidegger, Scheler, and Sartre, though an even richer lode of inspiration and evidence might well be found in authors such as Dostoevsky, Melville, Musil, Gide, or Camus.

8 Fichte's Ethical Holism

Owen Ware

The error of the mystics is that they represent the infinite, which cannot be attained in any time, as something that can be attained in time.

– Fichte (*SE*, 143; *SW*, IV: 151)

1 Introduction

If one casts a glance to the reception of Fichte's moral philosophy during the past 200 years, one can discern the outlines of three distinct figures: the individualist who bids us to listen to the "voice of conscience" within, the communitarian who bids us to engage in open dialogue with others, and the mystic who bids us to merge into the "one great unity of pure spirit" (*WM*, 1: 416).[1] Among these figures, the first has exerted the longest and, in my view, most distorting impression. The second figure has many advocates in the literature and is witnessing a revival among some prominent English scholars today. I shall argue that the least popular of the three, Fichte the mystic, in fact captures what is most essential to his moral philosophy: what I shall call its ethical holism.

The figure of the individualist joins hands with another popular image of Fichte as basing all reality on the activity of "the ego."[2] Coleridge's "burlesque" on Fichte from his 1847 *Biographia Literaria* (which begins with the opening line, "Here on this market-cross aloud I cry: / I, I, I! I itself I!") presents us with an amusing illustration of this view.[3] But this image would in fact color Fichte's reception well into the twentieth century; and by the time of

[1] Throughout this paper I have modified the English translations of Fichte's works and, in some cases, I have provided my own translation.

[2] This was a long-standing convention of translating *das Ich*, which may have contributed to the vitality of the figure of Fichte-the-individualist who wished to put forth one's own finite, limited, or empirical I at the center of all reality.

[3] "Here on this market-cross aloud I cry: / I, I, I! I itself I! / The form and the substance, the what and the why, / The when and the where, the low and the high, / The inside and outside, the earth and the sky, / I, you and he, and he, you and I, / All souls and bodies are I itself I!" (Coleridge 1847: 160n).

Bertrand Russell's *History of Western Philosophy* Fichte is portrayed as a kind of metaphysical solipsist who believed that "the Ego is the only ultimate reality," a view Russell correctly judged as approaching "a kind of insanity."[4] While most scholars would agree that Russell's portrait is a false one, the status of Fichte's subjectivism remains largely unquestioned in historical studies of post-Kantian Idealism.

My aim here is to move beyond this old tradition of interpretation. In speaking of Fichte's ethical holism, I wish to capture the idea that our duties acquire their material content in relation to the social whole of which we are parts, as finite, limited, and empirical agents. This idea comes out most clearly in Fichte's claim from the *System of Ethics* (1798) that our duties to others not only enjoy primacy over self-regarding duties, but are in a sense the only duties we have, given the set of relations making up our existence as individual agents. One difficulty of interpretation, however, is that Fichte ends up offering two derivations of moral content in the *System of Ethics* without leaving much of a clue to explain their connection. The first proceeds to derive the content of our duties from our "natural drive [*Naturtrieb*]," which Fichte defines in terms of our striving for enjoyment. The second proceeds to derive the content of our duties from what Fichte calls the conditions of our selfhood, namely, our embodiment, intelligence, and sociality. In this essay I wish to show that a careful rereading of Fichte's notion of a *Naturtrieb* is consistent with his second derivation of moral content. As we shall see, there is a form of reciprocity inherent in the natural drive itself, such that our ethical vocation to unite with others in community amounts to a preservation of what is, for Fichte, originally present in our nature.

Before proceeding further, one caveat is in order. Talk of our "nature" and "natural drive" might lead one to think that Fichte's moral philosophy is naturalistic, or at least friendly to forms of naturalism pervasive in the contemporary philosophical landscape. On closer inspection, however, this could not be farther from the truth, since a basic tenet of Fichte's theory is that even the most elemental conditions of willing, such as feeling, longing, and desire, bear an essential connection to the free activity of the I. Nor should this be surprising, since this anti-naturalistic view of agency is of a piece with Fichte's idealism in general, his view that what is seemingly brute and given in experience is intelligible only in relation to the I and its free activity. I emphasize this from the outset because it helps to explain why Fichte develops his drive theory in the *System of Ethics* in accordance with the principles of the "doctrine of science [*Wissenschaftslehre*]." The drive theory we shall discuss in this essay is not a departure from these idealist principles

[4] Russell 1945: 718.

but a clear instance of their application. For Fichte, the original reciprocity present in the natural drive is already a form of freedom that our ethical vocation bids us to cultivate, develop, and bring to perfection.

2 Fichte's Drive Theory

According to Fichte's drive theory in the *System of Ethics*, my nature is originally undivided as a "fundamental drive [*Urtrieb*]." When this fundamental drive is represented as non-conscious activity, it appears as a lower capacity of desire, which manifests itself as a natural drive for enjoyment. When this same drive is represented as self-conscious activity, it appears as a higher capacity of desire, which manifests itself as a pure drive for independence. Yet Fichte's point is that there is no basic difference between the two. The "dividing line," he says, is "reflection": it is only by becoming aware of my natural drive that I can step back from it and posit myself as free (*SE*, 125; *SW*, IV: 131). Reflection allows me to fashion a concept of my freedom as an "end [*Zweckbegriff*]," separate from the natural drive and its *Zweckbegriff* of enjoyment. But again, this very separation of a lower and higher capacity only exists in the emerging conditions of time that mark the development of my self-consciousness. When we abstract from these emerging conditions and take up a properly transcendental viewpoint, Fichte argues, we have only one single activity manifested in different forms. My nature is originally whole, and only reflection separates me from this original wholeness.

But how does any of this address the question of moral content? Fichte's first answer is that the pure drive alone cannot yield determinate courses of action. The pure drive, he explains, only appears in consciousness as a restraint of the natural drive and its striving for enjoyment. Considered in isolation, then, the end of the pure drive is without material application, for it cannot specify what actions I ought to perform in striving for independence. And Fichte notes that this stands in tension with the character of morality, its character of requiring that I do something here and now. Morality obliges me to action, but the pure drive alone only obliges me to the omission of action, to what I ought not to do. Were we to develop a theory of ethics on the basis of the pure drive alone, we would be led to what Fichte calls a theory of "continuous *self-denial*," which he suggests is the shortcoming of Kant's own metaphysics of morals (*SE*, 140; *SW*, IV: 147). The question then becomes: If we cannot specify determinate courses of action on the basis of the higher capacity of desire, where can we derive the content of our duties? Fichte's reply, and what I am calling the first derivation, is that we can derive this content from the natural drive itself. What I ought to do from a moral standpoint is, in a sense, what I am already doing in exercising my lower capacity of desire.

To be clear, Fichte is not saying that morality directs me to the end of the natural drive, enjoyment, since the natural drive only relates this end to myself as the subject of the drive. Nor is he saying that morality requires that I give up the end of my pure drive, independence, since the concept of independence as such is precisely what morality requires of us. The solution, Fichte explains, is to remember that these drives are but expressions of one and the same activity, the fundamental *Urtrieb*, and that actualizing the demands of morality is a project of reuniting the two:

> These two drives, however, constitute only one and the same I. The I must therefore be united within the sphere of consciousness. We will see that in this unity the higher drive must surrender the *purity* of its activity (that is, its non-determination through an object), while the lower drive must surrender enjoyment as its end. (*SE*, 125; *SW*, IV: 131)

In this way Fichte wants us to think of the project of morality as a project of self-unification. Fulfilling the demands of morality requires that I reintegrate my natural drive for enjoyment and my pure drive for independence in the right way. Yet this mandate for self-unification is only valid as a prescription, as something I ought to do, because it accurately describes my original wholeness, my nature prior to the self-division brought about by reflection. This is important to bear in mind, for otherwise we shall be at a loss to understand Fichte's claim that our higher vocation is to bring our actual willing into harmony with our original drive:

> [M]y foundational drive [*Grundtrieb*] as a pure and as an empirical being, the drive through which these two, very different components of myself become one [*zu Einem werden*], is the drive toward agreement between the *original* I, which is determined in the mere idea, and the *actual* I. Now the original drive [*Urtrieb*] – i.e., the pure drive and the natural drive considered in their unity with one another – is a determinate drive. (*SE*, 137; *SW*, IV: 143–4)

This striving to become one manifests itself to consciousness in what Fichte now calls our "ethical drive [*sittliche Trieb*]," which he characterizes as a synthesis of the pure and natural drives. Like the former, the ethical drive strives for independence, and in this regard, it has the end of independence. But unlike the pure drive, the ethical drive does not strive for complete non-determination through an object, and so it does not seek complete independence from the natural drive. On the contrary, the natural drive supplies the ethical drive with its content. But unlike the natural drive, it does not restrict itself to actions that relate objects of nature merely to myself as the subject of the drive. The ethical drive cancels out the end of the natural drive but preserves its material, and it cancels out the material of the pure drive but preserves its end. That is why Fichte defines it as a mixed drive: "from the natural drive," he explains, the ethical drive "obtains its material. Yet it obtains its form merely from the pure drive" (*SE*, 144; *SW*, IV: 152).

According to Fichte's first derivation, then, the natural drive supplies morality with its content, thereby allowing us to specify actions I ought to perform in striving for self-sufficiency. But to what extent does this derivation work? One worry is that extracting moral content from the natural drive alone is not inclusive enough for specifying a complete division of duties, which is Fichte's larger aim in Part III of the *System of Ethics*. And this worry is only compounded by the fact that Fichte ends up drawing a close connection between the natural drive and the "body [*Leib*]" as a system through which I exercise my causality in the world. My body, he explains, can be understood as a microcosm of the system of nature I represent outside of me: each part of the body strives to preserve the body as a whole, and the whole strives to preserve each part, in a relationship of reciprocal interaction (*SE*, 121–2; *SW*, IV: 127–8). Since moral laws, for Fichte, are valid only as prescriptions to perfect what I am already doing, it appears that this line of argument can only yield a material norm to preserve and perfect my body as a self-organizing system. Yet that falls short of a complete division of duties, which Fichte later presents in terms of the obligations I have to the mind and to others as well. By drawing such a close tie between moral content and the body, then, it appears that Fichte's first derivation in the *System of Ethics* is too limited.

3 Embodiment, Intelligence, and Sociality

Let us turn now to consider Fichte's second derivation of moral content, which appears in Part III. What is immediately evident when we turn to read these later sections is that Fichte's strategy is no longer the narrow one presented above, the strategy of extracting content for morality from the body as a self-organizing system. Instead, Fichte's new starting point is the broader notion of our individual "I-hood" or "selfhood" (*SE*, 200–1; *SW*, IV: 211). As we soon discover, the condition of my embodiment is but one of three transcendental conditions of selfhood, that is, one of three conditions necessary for my agency as a rational yet finite being. In my view, the initial advantage of this approach is that by starting with the notion of individual selfhood as such, Fichte has the means of presenting a comprehensive division of duties. As he explains, the goal is to provide "a complete presentation of the conditions of I-hood and show how these conditions are related to the drive for self-sufficiency as well as how this drive is determined by these conditions" (*SE*, 201; *SW*, IV: 212). If we can accomplish this, Fichte adds, "we will have provided an exhaustive account of the content of the moral law" (*SE*, 201; *SW*, IV: 212).

Fichte only takes steps toward this exhaustive account until he has derived duties to the body, and what he says there is instructive:

> To facilitate our survey, one should note that the condition of I-hood that was just indicted is a condition for the I's causality [*Kausalität*], a causality that is demanded by

> the moral law. It will become evident that there is also a second condition, one concerning the substantiality [*Substantialität*] of the subject of morality, as well as a third condition, one concerning a certain, necessary reciprocal interaction [*Wechselwirkung*] of the latter. (*SE*, 205–6; *SW*, IV: 216)

What makes this second derivation promising is that it approaches the notion of my individual selfhood under the category of relation: first, as a finite rational being who is embodied (under the category of causality), second, as a finite rational being who is intelligent (under the category of substantiality), and third, as a finite rational being who stands in community with others (under the category of reciprocal interaction).

To start with, Fichte's analysis of the first condition of selfhood is the most straightforward, since it follows the pattern of the first strategy discussed above. He begins by claiming that my actual willing requires my natural drive, reminding the reader of the close connection between the natural drive and the body: "The natural drive addresses itself to me only through my body, and this drive is realized in the world outside me only through the causality of my body" (*SE*, 204; *SW*, IV: 215). Fichte's point now is that a relationship with my body is a transcendental condition of my selfhood, a condition necessary for me to exercise my causality in the world. When we then step back and relate this condition to the drive for self-sufficiency, he argues, we get the following result: that I have a duty to preserve and perfect my body as a means of fulfilling my ethical vocation. That is to say, I can approximate the goal of my ethical vocation only by acting, and acting requires my body. I ought to preserve and perfect my body, then, but not for the sake of seeking my enjoyment. Rather, I ought to preserve and perfect my body as a means for realizing my ethical vocation (*SE*, 204–5; *SW*, IV: 215). "The sole end of all my care for my body," Fichte writes, "must be to transform this body into a suitable instrument of morality [*Werkzeuge der Moralität*] and to preserve it as such" (*SE*, 205; *SW*, IV: 216). Cultivation of the body therefore gives us a substantive obligation.

It is relatively easy to follow Fichte's next point, that I also have a duty to cultivate my mind, since this rests on the claim that my capacity to form concepts is a transcendental condition of selfhood too. Yet it is far less obvious how he derives a duty to others, given that the supporting line of argument moves us into unfamiliar territory. At this juncture of the text, rather than appeal to the empirical fact that I depend on others for my existence and continued survival, Fichte advances the much stronger claim that my individuality – my capacity for free agency as such – has an intersubjective "root [*Wurzel*]." While a detailed examination of this claim goes beyond the scope of my essay, three points are relevant for our present discussion. The first point is that I lack the resources to determine myself on the basis of reasons, so that I cannot become a self-governing agent all on my own. The second is that I can become a self-governing agent only by being called, invited, or summoned to realize my spontaneity. The third and final point is that recognizing this summons requires that I posit the existence of a being outside of me, a being who wishes to invite me freely into a space of mutual reason-giving. It is therefore a "condition of self-consciousness, of I-hood," Fichte argues, "to assume that there is an actual rational being outside of oneself" (*SE*, 210; *SW*, IV: 221).

In a captivating turn of argument, then, Fichte argues that "my I-hood, along with my self-sufficiency in general, is conditioned by the freedom of the other" (*SE*, 210; *SW*, IV: 221).[5] But how, we must ask, does this third transcendental condition of selfhood give content to the moral law? The answer we receive in the context under discussion is that "my drive to self-sufficiency absolutely cannot aim at annihilating the *condition of its own possibility*, that is, the freedom of the other" (*SE*, 210; *SW*, IV: 221). Here Fichte's point rests on a principle of consistency, that I have a duty to respect others because doing so is consistent with the reciprocal interaction at the root of my individuality (*SE*, 210; *SW*, IV: 221). Yet the force of his argument runs deeper than this, I believe, since Fichte also claims that in contrast to my body and my mind, the social whole of which I am a part instantiates the "final end" (*Endzweck*) of my ethical vocation, and to that extent it specifies the domain over which the moral law applies (*SE*, 244; *SW*, IV: 255). In this light I have a duty to preserve and perfect the freedom of others, not because doing so is a means for attaining some other end, but because doing so embodies the very essence of my higher vocation in the sensible world. As Fichte writes: "The object of the moral law, i.e., that in which it wants its end to be presented, is by no means anything individual" (*SE*, 243; *SW*, IV: 254). And that is why "I posit this reason as such as something outside me" (*SE*, 243; *SW*, IV: 254). What the transcendental condition of sociality reveals, therefore, is the proper object of my own striving, the "entire community of rational beings outside me" (*SE*, 244; *SW*, IV: 254).[6]

[5] As Fichte writes: "It follows that my drive to self-sufficiency absolutely cannot aim at annihilating the condition of its own possibility, that is, the freedom of the other . . . I am not allowed to be self-sufficient at the expense of the other's freedom" (*SE*, 210; *SW*, IV: 221). This yields a material duty to others, of which Fichte distinguishes three kinds: (1) a *negative* duty: "never disturb the freedom of the other; never use the other as a mere means to your own end"; (2) a *positive* duty: "cultivate the freedom of the other as much as you can. Help, support, and encourage the freedom of the other to the extent that it is within your power"; and lastly (3) what Fichte calls a *limitative* duty: "support for the other that cannot be related, with sincere conviction, to the other's freedom is impermissible and contrary to the law" (*SE*, 210; *SW*, IV: 221).

[6] Here I think Hansjürgen Verweyen is right: "Embodiment and intelligence condition the drive for self-sufficiency, not [next to] the interpersonal constitution of freedom – which would give in this connection three self-standing parts in the division of a material ethics – but within this most fundamental structure of the I. The *System of Ethics* as a whole thereby shows itself as an ethics of society [*Gesellschaftsethik*]" (Verweyen 1975: 146).

4 The *Bildungstrieb*

The results of this second derivation are on track to secure a complete division of duties, which Fichte will elaborate upon for the remainder of the *System of Ethics*. However, rather than conclude that his first strategy failed, I wish to return once again to Fichte's notion of a natural drive to support a more charitable interpretation. Upon a careful re-examination of the text, we shall see that the elements of Fichte's discussion of embodiment, intelligence, and sociality are implicit in our original drive, and what our ethical vocation requires of us, to unite with the community of rational beings, is a requirement to unfold our original drive for wholeness. The key to this re-examination lies in Fichte's claim that the natural drive for enjoyment is not, as one might expect, a drive merely to satisfy objects of desire. Fichte does not regard desire-satisfaction understood in terms of consuming objects to capture the end of enjoyment itself. On his view, the character of this end must be akin to the character of nature represented as an organic whole, whereby all parts strive to unite with the whole and the whole in turn strives to unite with all parts (*SE*, 110–1; *SW*, IV: 114–15). According to this organic model of nature, Fichte argues that enjoyment consists of striving to unite with an object, to relate to it, and not to absorb it straightaway (as one absorbs food and drink through digestion). The natural drive, he explains, is a drive for mutual *Bildung*, "to form and to be formed [*zu bilden und sich bilden zu lassen*]," or what Fichte now calls a "formative drive [*Bildungstrieb*]" (*SE*, 116; *SW*, IV: 121).

As this last turn of phrase makes clear, Fichte conceives of the *Bildungstrieb* as displaying a form of *primitive reciprocity*. It is a drive not just to relate to an object, but to relate to it both actively and passively: to shape and to be shaped. It is therefore a form of striving that is, according to Fichte's organic model of nature, thoroughly relational. In striving to relate an object to my natural drive in a relation of mutual *Bildung*, I am not striving to subordinate the object to my efficacy, nor am I trying to subordinate my efficacy to the object, as would be the case if we viewed this connection under the category of causality. Rather, Fichte is reframing this connection under the category of "reciprocal interaction [*Wechselwirkung*]," whereby the drive and its object are co-ordinated and brought into community with each other. Indeed, the underlying model of organicism that Fichte draws upon in the *System of Ethics* to explain the structure of desire, even in its lower capacity, is precisely the model of a holistic community between parts of nature and their whole, the dynamic of which allows us to think of nature as a community of self-organizing and mutually interactive systems. For Fichte, the natural drive qua *Bildungstrieb* is simply a way of understanding this form of primitive reciprocity within us, namely, as a striving for self-organization that brings us into community with objects that help sustain our self-organization.

Given this richer conception of the natural drive, we can begin to see the extent to which Fichte's later discussion of embodiment, intelligence, and sociality unpack elements already contained in the drive theory sketched above:

- *The causality of the body*. In the first case, what the condition of embodiment highlights is the causality by which I strive to shape and be shaped in a relationship. As a self-organizing system, I seek to coordinate all the parts of my body and maintain their equilibrium, and to do that I seek to bring myself into community with objects of nature that contribute to this equilibrium. My body then serves as the locus by which I exercise my willing, both as a means of organizing myself, so to speak, and of interacting with the environment around me in ways that support my ongoing self-organization. When Fichte speaks of enjoyment as the *Zweckbegriff* of the natural drive, I do not take him to mean that I strive to consume an object, to subordinate it to my willing, or any other mode of action that would link desiring with the negation of an object. Instead, "enjoyment" refers to the *Zweckbegriff* of mutual formation, whose attainment produces a feeling of harmony (pleasure), and whose frustration produces a feeling of disharmony (displeasure). Already at this fundamental level of agency, then, Fichte wants us to think of the natural drive in terms of a reciprocal dynamic, both at the intra-embodied level (how the parts of my body relate to my body as a whole) and at an inter-embodied level (how my body as a part relates to the environment as a whole).
- *The substantiality of the intellect*. In the second case, what the condition of intelligence highlights is the substantiality by which I actively prefigure enjoyment as the end of my striving for self-organization. As a self-organizing body with the capacity for reflection, I determine myself to action on the basis of conceptually mediated ends, all of which require free acts of self-positing to be possible. In the same way that embodiment is a transcendental condition of my causality as a finite I, intelligence is a transcendental condition of my substantiality as a finite I too, even in its lower expression of desire. "And I must have a capacity for reflection in order to pre-figure something given through an inner act of freedom," Fichte writes, including those objects of nature (food, drink, an extensive view) that support my drive for self-organization (*SE*, 206; *SW*, IV: 217). While my body is the locus through which I exercise the causality of my natural drive in the world, I remain the subject of my natural drive as a free intelligence. In this way the category of causality makes salient the objective side of the I as a self-organizing body capable of articulating a variety of

actions in space, whereas the category of substantiality makes salient the subjective side of the I as a self-positing intellect capable of prefiguring such actions through concepts. But again, Fichte's point is that these are one and the same "I" simply viewed from different standpoints.

- *The sociality of the individual.* In the third and final case, what the condition of sociality highlights is the reciprocal interaction by which I actively determine my sphere of embodied articulation vis-à-vis those spheres marked out by other finite rational beings. As a self-organizing system with the capacity for reflection, I determine myself to action on the basis of conceptually mediated ends. Yet this very capacity for prefiguration is itself conditioned by a finite rational being outside of me. As we have seen, it is conditioned by another being who, in limiting her own sphere of articulation, left space open for me to determine my mine, freely and without coercion. On the basis of this summons or "invitation [*Aufforderung*]" to exercise my capacity for reflection and to prefigure an end of action, the self-limitation of another rational being turns out to be the most foundational condition of my selfhood. Viewed through the category of causality, the I is a self-organizing body capable of articulating a variety of actions in space; and viewed through the category of substantiality, the I is an intelligence capable of prefiguring such actions through concepts. However, it is only by introducing the category of reciprocal interaction that the "root" of my individuality as such comes to light, namely, in the original connection of my self to another.

It is only thanks to another rational being, and her invitation for me to exercise my free efficacy, that I can fashion concepts of ends and determine myself on the basis of them. My "first state," Fichte explains, "is not determined through my freedom, but is determined through my connection with another rational being" (*SE*, 211; *SW*, IV: 222–3). My original sociality therefore reveals another dimension of the natural drive that was only implicit in Fichte's initial discussion. The capacity of reflection that allows me to enter into a reciprocal relationship with my body and the natural world – the capacity, that is, that allows me to pursue the end of enjoyment – points outside my finite I and exposes, at the root of my being, a connection to another finite I. That is not to say I am mechanically "compelled" to be free, which Fichte notes is a contradiction. Rather, the point is that another's summons clears room for me to engage my capacity of reflection. The *Aufforderung* itself performs this room-clearing activity, not by presenting me with an impression of causality, but by presenting me with an impression of rationality (interestingly, Fichte writes elsewhere that the schema of this impression lies in the shape of the human body, particularly in the human "face," whose expression intimates another's intelligence, rationality, and freedom, a point we shall return to below) (*FNR*, 78; *SW*, III: 84).

I have taken time to unpack this line of argument in order to show that the primacy of other-regarding duties in Fichte's system mirrors what he takes to be an accurate depiction of how my capacity for reflection is first activated. An obligation to serve the community above my interests is valid as a prescription of what I ought to do because it speaks to the intersubjective basis of my existence, of who I am. Among the three transcendental conditions of selfhood, then, sociality takes pride of place because I could not be an embodied intelligence without that invitation, communicated to me by another, to exercise my free efficacy. For this reason, Fichte subordinates duties to the body and duties to the mind, as material commands of self-cultivation, to the social whole of which I am a part. I ought to cultivate myself and nurture the causality and substantiality of my original nature, but only in the service of the community; hence all duties to self acquire their normative orientation from my reciprocal connection with others. In this respect, the only immediate moral reasons I have are other-regarding, since I cannot take the cultivation of my body or my mind as the "final end [*Endzweck*]" of my willing – not because that would violate a norm *external* to me, but because that would contradict *who I am*. Thus, the only *Endzweck* reflective of my selfhood is that of entering into free, reciprocal interaction with others in society, of which my own perfection is a means, but never a final end.

Looking back, what the foregoing sections of this chapter bring to light is a striking set of parallels between the way Fichte conceives of nature and community as self-organizing systems, and the way he relates each of these systems to the drives of the individual. First, an organic model of nature brings to light its holistic structure, whereby each part strives to preserve itself and to preserve the whole to which it belongs. This allows Fichte to specify the character of our natural drive as displaying a form of primitive reciprocity, which reframes the end of enjoyment in terms of seeking harmony between objects of the sensible world and our striving for self-organization. In the second case, an organic model of rational beings brings to light its holistic structure as well, whereby each individual member strives to preserve itself and to preserve the social whole to which it belongs. This allows Fichte to specify the character of our ethical drive as displaying a form of reflective reciprocity, which reframes the end of morality in terms of seeking harmony between objects of the sensible world (now including others) and our original nature. In other words, both the natural drive and the ethical drive amount to drives for reciprocal interaction; and in this respect both display the character of a *Bildungstrieb* as Fichte understands this term. The difference is that the natural drive limits this formative-relation to objects that serve my own body as a self-organizing system; whereas the ethical drive proper extends this formative-relation to all the conditions of my selfhood, including my connection to the entire community of which I am a part.

5 Fichte's Ethical Holism

Let me conclude by highlighting two virtues of the interpretation I have begun to develop here. The first is that it gives us a footing to distinguish the self-organizing activity of living organisms from the self-determining character of rational agents. The second virtue, which I shall discuss afterwards, is that it helps makes sense of Fichte's puzzling claim in the *System of Ethics* that we are mere "instruments" of morality.

5.1 The Social Vocation of Human Beings

Much of the blueprint for what I am calling Fichte's ethical holism was anticipated in a set of public lectures he delivered in 1794 on the vocation of scholars. What is clear when we read these lectures is that Fichte wants to be mindful of a distinction between the question of our "final end [*Endzweck*]" and the question of our higher "vocation [*Bestimmung*]." The former is none other than the fantasy of subordinating the not-I to the I, which Fichte links to the fantasy of "becoming God." The latter, by contrast, is a matter of working toward "perfection [*Vollkommenheit*]," which Fichte defines in terms of achieving "complete agreement with oneself [*völlige Uebereinstimmung mit sich selbst*]" (*VBG*, VI: 300). As a way of motivating this distinction, Fichte calls attention to the fact that the concept of perfection just introduced only reveals the vocation of human beings considered in isolation. This means the concept is incomplete, since it does not consider the "general connection between rational beings," which Fichte observes raises a difficult topic. Once we introduce the concept of rational beings in society, we must ask: "How do we come to assume that there are rational beings outside of us, and how do we recognize them?" (*VBG*, VI: 303). The fact that I possess representations of other rational beings is not in dispute, for even the skeptic will grant me this. The question before us is one of entitlement: By what right do I possess such representations?

As a first step, Fichte reminds the reader that one's "highest drive" is the "drive toward identity [*der Trieb nach Identität*]," where identity is again understood in terms of perfection or "complete agreement with oneself" (*VBG*, VI: 303). What he now adds is that this highest drive is not fulfilled by avoiding a contradiction between the concepts one possesses and the objects to which they are meant to correspond. Rather, one's drive toward identity is the drive for a real correspondence between the two. Because of this, Fichte argues, all concepts found within one's I "should have an expression [*Ausdruck*] in the not-I, a counter-image [*Gegenbild*]" (*VBG*, VI: 303). This means that if we can find the counter-image of the concept of a rational being in the sensible world, then we can justify our possession of it. Where, then, does this concept find expression outside of us? Fichte begins by calling our attention to "activity according to ends [*Thätigkeit nach Zwecken*]," which he says is a sensible expression of rationality. However, he points out that the concept of "purposiveness [*Zweckmässigkeit*]" is ambiguous. Its distinguishing character is "harmony of multiplicity in a unity [*Uebereinstimmung des Mannigfaltigen zur Einheit*]" (*VBG*, VI: 304). But that, Fichte points out, is the very character of organisms as living, self-organizing systems, none of whom enjoy our capacity to reflect and act according to concepts. So where does this leave us?

On the one hand, living organisms are self-organizing systems, and that means their striving for self-organization brings them into reciprocal interaction with the natural environment, exactly as human beings behave in relation to their formative drive. Human beings are, considered objectively, nothing more than nature, whose entire system can only be understood, Fichte claims, through the formative laws of organization. On the other hand, human beings are also more than nature. Viewed subjectively, they are also intelligent, reflective, and capable of directing their willing according to concepts. In this respect there is no outward difference between human beings and natural organisms: both display purposive activity, reciprocal interaction with the natural environment, and a striving for harmonious self-organization. One real contrast is that human beings have the capacity to reflect upon the end of self-organization and fashion a concept of it, the concept of enjoyment. The result is a form of self-determination that is materially equivalent to the purposive activity of living organisms, but now this activity is freely structured around a goal. Whereas non-reflective living organisms have no choice in what they do, human beings enjoy a range of options for relating objects to their drive for self-organization. And that gives us a clue for finding the right counter-image of freedom in the sensible world: "The freely achieved harmony of multiplicity in unity," Fichte writes, "would thus be a certain and non-deceptive distinguishing feature of rationality in appearances" (*VBG*, VI: 305).

Fichte clarifies that this distinguishing feature does not amount to consciousness of another being's freedom, since freedom is not an object of consciousness at all, either in myself or in others. Freedom as such is the "ultimate explanatory ground of all consciousness," Fichte writes, "and thus freedom itself cannot belong to the realm of consciousness" (*VBG*, VI: 305). What I can become conscious of is a certain lack of determination, a lack of determination from any cause external to myself, which Fichte notes is how I fashion a concept of my own self-determination. On the basis of my consciousness of non-determination, I have no explanatory ground of my willing other than myself. Were I to find myself interacting with another being who also gave sensible expression to this consciousness of non-determination, then I would not have a basis to connect this appearance to another cause (according to a natural law). Consequently, I would be forced to lend the concept of my own self-determination to this appearance, to regard (without ever cognizing) the source of this appearance in the other being's freedom. In other words, I am able to distinguish a naturally governed expression of purposive activity from a freely governed expression on the basis of the latter's indeterminacy. Without a rule to connect one articulation of this activity to another, the only way I can comprehend the appearance and determine it is by turning within, appealing to the concept of my own freedom, and lending that concept to the other.

In a revealing turn of phrase, Fichte describes this process in terms of "reciprocal interaction according to concepts [*Wechselwirkung nach Begriffen*]," the result of which lays the foundation for "purposive community [*zweckmässige Gemeinschaft*]" and "society [*Gesellschaft*]" (*EPW*, 156; *SW*, VI: 306). The counter-image of the concept of a rational being like myself is found precisely in the appearance of the other's purposive yet indeterminate activity, the other's free movement, whose sensible expression admits of no explanation on the basis of a natural law, organic or otherwise. The only way I can comprehend such purposive yet indeterminate activity is by lending the concept of my own self-determination to it; and that is why, as Fichte explains elsewhere, I am compelled to recognize other rational beings as equals to myself, even though I am at liberty to act against this recognition (*FNR*, 74; *SW*, III: 80). The positive character of society, therefore, is what Fichte calls "reciprocal interaction through freedom [*Wechselwirkung durch Freiheit*]," which is, he adds, the true end of our ethical vocation (*VBG*, VI: 306). Only now can we see that the concept of perfection is not personal, but social. The perfection of our drive for identity is, for Fichte, a form of *Bildung*, but *Bildung* now understood as the shaping of free, mutual interaction between myself and others in community. Our ethical vocation is complete self-harmony, to be sure, but self-harmony made possible through "*reciprocal interaction*, *mutual* influence, *mutual* give and take, *mutual* passivity and activity" (*VBG*, VI: 308).

5.2 *Instruments of Morality*

One implication of the social character of our ethical vocation, which Fichte develops further in the *System of Ethics*, is the manner in which I ought to relate to the community of others – namely, as an "instrument [*Werkzeug*]":

> I am *for myself* – i.e., before my own consciousness – only an instrument, a mere tool of the moral law, and by no means the end of the same. – Driven by the moral law, I forget myself as I engage in action; I am but an instrument in its hand. (*SE*, 244; *SW*, IV: 255)

Now the idea that we are instruments of the moral law has been cited by critics like Schopenhauer as yet another instance of how Fichte's exposition of ethics "crosses over into the comical," and it has elicited puzzlement even among his more sympathetic readers today.[7] The frequency with which this proposition appears in the *System of Ethics* suggests Fichte thought seriously about the matter (*SE*, 204; cf., 220, 225, 244, 248, 258, 267, 296; *SW*, IV: 215; cf., 231, 236, 255, 259, 270, 280, 311). But, the difficulty is plainly visible. To be nothing more than instruments of the moral law suggests that we are not recognizing our dignity as ends, contrary to Kant's Formula of Humanity (FH): "So act that you use humanity, whether in your own person or in the person of any other, always at the same time as an end, never merely as a means" (*GW*, 4: 429). To make matters more complicated, Fichte himself appears unaware of this tension: "Kant has asserted that every human being is an end in itself [*Jeder Mensch ist selbst Zweck*], and this assertion has received universal assent," to which he adds: "This Kantian proposition is compatible with mine" (*SE*, 244; *SW*, IV: 255).

Fichte goes on to say that the key to reconciling his position with FH lies in taking up the right point of view. From my perspective, he explains, I am torn away from myself in the moment of moral deliberation, and the focus of my deliberation is guided by the concerns of other people. In my eyes I am nothing more than an instrument for the community outside of me, and the members of this community appear to me as ends. "Within me and before my own consciousness," Fichte writes, "these others are not means but the final end" (*SE*, 244; *SW*, IV: 255). At the same time, the way in which I experience the moral law must be the same for every other member of the community. "For every rational being outside me, to whom the moral law certainly addresses itself in the same way that it addresses itself to me, namely, as the tool of the moral law, I am a member of the community of rational beings" (*SE*, 244; *SW*, IV: 255–6). This means that from the perspective of another person, the situation is reversed: I appear as an end, and he (in his own eyes) is nothing more than an instrument for the moral law. As Fichte puts it: "I am, from his viewpoint, an end for him, just as he is, from my viewpoint, an end for me. For everyone, all others outside of oneself are ends, only no one is an end for himself [*nur ist es keiner sich selbst*]" (*SE*, 244; *SW*, IV: 255–6).

If this last claim is true, however, how is Fichte's position supposed to be compatible with Kant's? Far from alleviating the tension at hand, he seems to have left us with a contradiction, with FH affirming the thesis, that "Everyone is an end for himself," and Fichte affirming the antithesis, that "Nobody is an end for himself." In the next paragraph Fichte acknowledges the presence of a contradiction and he proposes the following solution. We can concede the basic point of FH, and agree that everyone is an end, but only if we qualify this

[7] Schopenhauer 2009: 178.

to hold that everyone is a "means [*Mittel*]" for realizing the self-sufficiency of reason as such (*SE*, 245; *SW*, IV: 256). It is by virtue of approximating this aim, and by gradually overcoming our individuality, that everyone becomes "a pure presentation of the moral law in the world of sense and thus becomes a pure I, in the proper sense of the term" (*SE*, 245; *SW*, IV: 256). As I understand his response, Fichte is telling us here that the standpoint of our highest moral goal removes the impression of a conflict between the affirmation and denial of FH. The thesis is true, since striving for the self-sufficiency of reason as such transforms us into an end in itself (a "pure" presentation of the moral law), but the antithesis is also true, since a total transformation is unattainable, a goal to which we can only ever aspire as the limited beings we are.

There is, I believe, an important piece of evidence in the *System of Ethics* for understanding this solution better. When Fichte introduces FH for the first time, he adds a small yet important remark: that FH is compatible with his position "when the latter has been further elaborated" (*SE*, 244; *SW*, IV: 255). What exactly does he mean by this? When we look back to the ground covered so far, I think the answer is as follows. The standpoint of our highest moral goal brings to light our common duty to care for the rational community: "Everyone is, for himself and before his own self-consciousness, charged with the task of achieving the total end of reason; the entire community of rational beings is dependent on the care and efficacious action of each person" (*SE*, 245; *SW*, IV: 256). In this way the claim that no one is an end for himself is compatible with FH, but only when we extend the latter to encompass the Kantian ideal of our union under moral laws, in other words laws founded upon mutual interaction, mutual recognition, and mutual respect in a possible "kingdom of ends [*Reich der Zwecke*]" (*GW*, 4: 433). As Kant describes this ideal in the *Groundwork*, such a kingdom conveys the thought of every rational being as a co-legislator of the moral law, "a whole of all ends in systematic connection (a whole both of rational beings as ends in themselves and of the ends of his own that each may set himself)" (*GW*, 4: 433).

This is far from the end of the story, however. When we pause to reread the stretch of text under consideration (*SE*, 243–5; *SW*, IV: 255–6), signs of a shift in meaning begin to appear, at first hardly detectable, between the thesis of FH that Kant originally formulates and the version Fichte eventually accepts. What is important to bear in mind is that Kant makes room for FH by first asking us to suppose that "there were something the being [*Dasein*] of which in itself has absolute worth" (*GW*, 4: 428). In this being, he goes on to say, we would find the "ground of a possible categorical imperative, that is, of a practical law" (*GW*, 4: 428). Shortly afterwards Kant identifies this concept with human beings in particular and rational beings in general, that is, beings he says count as "persons" in a technical sense "because their nature [*Natur*] already marks them out as an end in itself [*Zwecke an sich selbst*]" (*GW*, 4: 428). In saying this, however, Kant is resting upon an assumption he nowhere defends in the *Groundwork*: namely, that a multiplicity of beings originally exist as self-standing ends, that is, myself, other finite rational beings, and God. And this explains why he phrases FH as a disjunctive proposition: that I ought to use humanity, whether in my own person or in the person of any other, always at the same time as an end, never merely as a means (*GW*, 4: 429). Put simply, this is the assumption behind Kant's moral pluralism, the assumption that more than one "end in itself" exists.

The position Fichte takes up in the *System of Ethics* appears to challenge this assumption. When he discusses how agents engaged in moral action must view each other, he is careful to say that they must view each other as "ends [*Zwecke*]," not as "ends in themselves [*Zwecke an sich selbst*]." To quote him again: "For everyone, all others outside of oneself are ends," to which he adds: "only no one is an end for himself" (*SE*, 244; *SW*, IV: 256). One exception to this claim appears when Fichte writes that "everyone expressly ought to be an end for himself [*für sich selbst Zweck*]" (*SE*, 245; *SW*, IV: 256). Yet this is ambiguous, since Fichte accepts the statement only on the condition that it says "everyone is a *means* for realizing reason" (*SE*, 245; *SW*, IV: 256). What is more, when he later argues that the goal of realizing reason outside of us, in the form of caring for the rational community, is how we become a "pure" presentation of the moral law, the point is not that we actually become "ends in ourselves," but that progressing toward this goal gives us a higher vocation. For Fichte, there is only one "viewpoint" in which "all individuals without exception are a final end," but it is, he claims, not accessible to us. It is the "viewpoint from which the consciousness of all rational beings is united into one, as an object. Properly speaking, this is the viewpoint of God" (*SE*, 245; *SW*, IV: 256).

It could be objected that I have overlooked an important qualification in what Fichte says, that no one is an end "for himself [*sich selbst*]." Once we emphasize the reflexive, it seems we can accept FH as a proposition about how things are (objectively speaking) and Fichte's denial of FH as a proposition about how things appear (subjectively speaking). Granted, on this alternative reading the gap between Kant and Fichte would be less wide than I am hinting at. But I find this alternative difficult to accept, since to make it work we would have to show that Fichte is only committed to a perspectival claim, that we are not ends in ourselves relative to our own points of view. However, there is evidence to suggest that Fichte is committed to an additional claim, that everyone outside me should be viewed as a tool for the moral law. "[I]f I have a dutiful disposition," he writes, "then I consider the other person to be a tool not, as it were, of mere legality, but of morality" (*SE*, 270; *SW*, IV: 283). Other statements to this effect run throughout Part III: "I am required to regard the other person as a tool of the moral law" (*SE*, 276; *SW*, IV: 290);

"within the domain of the moral law, I should view my fellow human beings only as tools of reason" (*SE*, 296; *SW*, IV: 311); "we are obliged to regard everyone with a human face as a tool of the moral law" (*SE*, 297; *SW*, IV: 312). This is quite a departure from Kant's position, on my reading.[8]

Once we have an eye for it, evidence of Fichte's rejection of moral pluralism appears throughout the *System of Ethics*. In one place, for instance, he writes: "If all of the authors who have treated ethics merely *formally* had proceeded consistently, then they would have had to arrive at nothing but a continuous *self-denial*, at utter annihilation and disappearance – like those mystics who say that we should lose ourselves in God (a proposition that is indeed based upon something true and sublime, as will become evident later)" (*SE*, 140; *SW*, IV: 147). One can hardly doubt that Fichte is referring to his novel appropriation of FH, and he comes close to foreshadowing this appropriation when he speaks of the "error of the mystics [*Der Irrthum der Mystiker*]" (*SE*, 143; *SW*, IV: 151). The error, he explains, "is that they represent the infinite, which cannot be attained in any time, as something that can be attained in time. The complete annihilation of the individual and the fusion of the latter into the absolutely pure form of reason or into God is indeed the ultimate goal of finite reason; but this is not possible in any time" (*SE*, 143; *SW*, IV: 151). Statements like these are by no means rare in Fichte's corpus. In an earlier text, to take one example, he writes that "reason is the only thing-in-itself, and individuality merely accidental; reason the end, and individuality the means; the latter merely a special way of giving expression to reason, and one which must increasingly lose itself into the universal form of the same" (*IW*, 90; *SW*, I: 505).[9]

While readers may feel inclined to dismiss such comments as odd or unusual, I believe they reveal an important feature of Fichte's moral

[8] I believe Wood underplays this departure, although he correctly emphasizes the fact that Fichte describes our status, not as mere tools, but as "active tools" (Wood 2016: ch. 7). As Fichte puts it: "I am an instrument of the law, *as an active principle*, not as a thing serving the law [*Ich bin Werkzeug des Gesetzes, als thätiges Princip, nicht Mittel desselben als Sache*]" (*SE*, 258; *SW*, IV: 270).

[9] Citing this passage, Robert Pippin writes: "If there is a 'monism' emerging in the post-Kantian philosophical world, the kind proposed by Fichte (and that decisively influenced Hegel, as this passage especially reveals) is what might be called a normative monism, a claim for the 'absolute' or unconditioned status of the space of reasons" (Pippin 2001: 164). While I agree that the "Second Introduction" gives evidence of Fichte's commitment to monism (see *IW*, 90; *SW*, I: 505), and while I believe it is correct to describe this monism as "normative," Pippin's appeal to "the space of reasons" requires fleshing out. My worry is that this Sellarsian notion is too thin to capture that kind of reason-giving that Fichte ascribes to the idea of striving for self-sufficiency. For this reason, as much as I am sympathetic to Pippin's reading, I prefer to speak of Fichte's ethical holism rather than his normative monism, as the former expression captures the part-whole relationship of the I and the rational community. I develop this point further in Ware 2020.

philosophy, which brings us back to my opening suggestion. When Fichte refers to the complete "fusion" of the individual I into the pure form of reason (represented by the mystics as "God"), we hear a strong claim: that such fusion "is indeed the ultimate goal of finite reason" (*SE*, 143; *SW*, IV: 151). Every finite I strives to become one with the absolute I, to transcend limitations of every kind, including the limitations of individuality itself. That is the "true and sublime" proposition Fichte sees in the mystics, their recognition that every finite self yearns for the infinite. Their "error," in his view, was to think that such self-overcoming is possible in time (*SE*, 143; *SW*, IV: 151). What then informs the basis of Fichte's moral philosophy is the insight that while every finite self yearns for the infinite, the goal of such yearning is impossible to realize, and that orients the activity of the finite I toward the gradual approximation of "becoming one" with the pure I, which in the *System of Ethics* is equivalent to the absolute self-sufficiency of reason as such. If there is an element of truth to the figure of Fichte the mystic, then, it is this. We all yearn to become God, to become infinite – in a word, to overcome our individuality. But since this is not possible, our ethical vocation requires that we cultivate our individuality, not for its own sake, but for the sake of the social whole to which we belong.

9 Jacobi on Revolution and Practical Nihilism

Benjamin Crowe

Hegel encapsulates his view of the French Revolution in two dramatic passages from the *Philosophy of Right*, in which the language of annihilation is particularly striking:

> [I]f it turns to actuality, [abstract freedom] becomes in the realm of both politics and religion the fanaticism of destruction, demolishing the whole existing social order, and annihilating any organization which attempts to rise up anew. Only in destroying something does this negative will have a feeling of its own existence . . . it is precisely through the annihilation of *particularity* and of *objective determination* that the self-consciousness of this negative freedom arises. (*PR* §5; emphasis added)

> [W]hen these abstractions were invested with power, they afforded the tremendous spectacle, for the first time we know of in human history, of the overthrow of all existing and given conditions within an actual major state and the revision of its constitution from first principles and purely in terms of *thought*; the *intention* behind this was to give it what was *supposed* to be a purely *rational* basis. On the other hand, since these were only abstractions divorced from the Idea, they turned the attempt into the most terrible and drastic event. (*PR* §258)

In these passages, Hegel is describing how the intellectual foundations of the old order were destroyed under the onslaught of critical reason, leading to a revolution that annihilated traditional social, material, and political institutions. The problem with this, for Hegel, is that the assertion of abstract freedom by itself runs directly counter to the existence of functioning rational institutions. For this reason, the "fanaticism of destruction" was unable to yield to the positive task of constructing institutions appropriate for a free society. F. H. Jacobi (1743–1819) first used the label "nihilism" for the impoverished, abstract conception of reason that he (like Hegel afterwards) understands as being realized in politics, philosophy, and Enlightenment culture more

Earlier versions of this paper were presented at the Boston University's Workshop on Late Modern Philosophy (April 2017), the Southwest Seminar in Continental Philosophy (June 2017) (California State University, Northridge), and the workshop on Reason, Revolution, and Rights (December 2018) (University of York). Thanks to participants in each for comments and criticisms on these drafts. Thanks to Reidar Maliks for bringing these Hegel passages to my attention.

generally. Jacobi identified and analyzed both the *theoretical* and the *practical* sides of nihilism. The former afflicts metaphysics and is the outcome of reason's drive for ultimate explanation; the latter is characteristic of the search for a purely rational foundation of moral judgment. Most contemporary scholarship deals with theoretical nihilism, with work by Karin Nisenbaum and Paul Franks being standout recent examples.[1] Yet, as Franks reminds us, Jacobi introduces the charge of "nihilism" in a discussion of Kant's moral theology.[2]

This primary, "practical" sense of nihilism consists of a model of ideal practical rationality as equating to a pure form, either consistency or correct calculation of advantage, minus the "way of sensing [*Sinnesart*]" that makes it possible for us to see what is at stake in a situation. Our "way of sensing" is also the source of our individuality and our irreplaceable value as persons, and it requires specific loyalties for its formation.[3] Jacobi's claim is that practical nihilism characterizes a broad swathe of eighteenth-century philosophy, including French *philosophes*, Kant, and Fichte. For ease of reference, I'll call this target group "the Enlightenment." My reconstruction of Jacobi's account begins with his initial and ambivalent response to the French Revolution, captured by an addition to the 1792 edition of *Edward Allwill's Collection of Letters* entitled "To Erhard O." Having established the core of Jacobi's objection to Enlightenment thought, I next turn toward the open letter "To Fichte" (1799) in which the charge of nihilism is actually made. Ranging over other writings from the 1790s, I show how Jacobi takes on overly formalist accounts of practical rationality and develops an argument for the centrality of a developed *Sinnesart* to ethical life.

1 See Franks 2005 and Nisenbaum 2018.

2 Franks 2005 finds a contemporary analogue to Jacobi's account of nihilism in Bernard Williams's argument that philosophical reflection undermines our "thick ethical concepts" and destroys "*individual character*, the enduring ground of immediate commitment." On Franks's reading, the sinister protagonist of Jacobi's novel *Edward Allwill* is an "ethical nihilist" because "his will is entirely perspectival, flowing entirely into passions that are relative to given situations and lacking any genuine individual character" (Franks 2005: 168–9). The parallel to Williams is instructive. For an attempt to draw a different analogy between Jacobi's worries about Kantian ethics and Williams's criticisms of the "peculiar institution" of morality, see Crowe 2014.

3 The term "*Sinnesart*," which Jacobi employs in "To Erhard O.," could be translated variously as "mode of sensing," "way of sensing," or "sensibility." "Sensibility" has acquired a close association with Kant in English-language scholarship due to its use as a translation of "*Sinnlichkeit*," and so could be potentially misleading. What Jacobi has in mind is, broadly speaking, the notion of a receptive faculty of perception common to all organic beings (see, for example, remarks in *David Hume* [*MPW*, 321; *JWA*, 2.1: 90]). In *David Hume*, he argues that the passive and active (or spontaneous) sides of the mind necessarily work in tandem with one another, forming a dynamic whole of sorts. The emphasis, however, is on the mind's productive capacity: "I do not allow the concept of an exclusively passive faculty, but only as a modification of an active principle" (*MPW*, 328n; *JWA*, 2.1: 98). The important conclusion that Jacobi wants to draw from all this is that one's "way of sensing," while certainly rooted in natural endowments, can be formed and developed.

1 Jacobi on Revolution

In the brief piece, "To Erhard O.," one learns a lot about Jacobi's response to the Revolution in France in a way that turns out to directly illuminate his conception of nihilism. Jacobi himself licenses this interpretation, for in "To Fichte" (1799), the work that introduces his notion of "nihilism," he reproduces a substantial excerpt from "Erhard O." as a "Supplement" designed to clarify his position. In the main body of the response to Fichte, Jacobi is even more direct about the link:

> The mystery of the identity and difference between Fichte and me, of our philosophical sympathy and antipathy, ought to be apparent (so it seems to me) to everyone willing to make the effort of reading correctly, and thoroughly understanding, just the one Epistle to Erhard O*, at the back of *Allwill's Collection of Letters*. (*MPW*, 506; *JWA*, 2.1: 200)

In a less visible way, this passage connects the composition of the open letter to Fichte to a period of intense engagement with Kant's philosophy during the early 1790s. An almost identical passage appears in the much earlier letter of February 11, 1790 to Reinhold, except instead of referencing Fichte, Jacobi cites his "sympathy and antipathy with regard to Kant's doctrine" (quoted in *JWA*, 2.2: 458). While he occasionally complains that "political" affairs – in other words, events in France – are distracting him from carrying out plans to write a great work on Kant, it is clear from his correspondence that Jacobi's interest in Kant was closely linked to his attempts to grapple with the moral and political views of the "Enlightenment." For example, he tells J. L. Ewald in December 1790 of his New Year's resolution to complete a treatise on "freedom, natural right, civil legislation, and religion, in which I aim to definitively [*auf das Bestimmteste*] differentiate my way of thinking from Kant's" (*JBW*, I.8: 454).

A letter to his close friend Schlosser from 1792 suggests that one of the things Jacobi found important about the Revolution was the way it involved a kind of experiment in government according to "pure reason": "Since the unrest in France I have had no peace from the idea of properly clarifying the extent to which human reason *in Praxi* is practical. The point I need to make must be made in a striking manner, since I'll have the ardor of the *genius saeculi* in its full fury against me" (*JWA*, 2.2: 460). Of course, Jacobi had prejudged the result of the trial to a certain extent.[4] More important for the present discussion, what these remarks from his correspondence show is that Jacobi had begun to connect Kantianism with the French Revolution almost from the latter's inception. The letter to Fichte that introduces the issue of

[4] He tells Countess Von Reventlow in November 1790 that, based on Hume's account in the *History of England*, he expects extralegality to give way to dictatorship (*JBW*, I.8: 447).

nihilism thus reflects issues that had been of deep concern to Jacobi for nearly a decade.

The Revolution itself first appears in Jacobi's correspondence in September 1789. While some of his close friends, such as Count Stolberg, welcomed the events with joy, Jacobi was ambivalent (*JBW*, 1.8: 284).[5] He nevertheless plunged into the study of French political thought with, as he saw it, somewhat immoderate verve (see, e.g., *JBW*, 1.8: 293–4). Jacobi became increasingly alarmed as more radical elements came to power. Already in October of 1789, Jacobi exclaims in a letter to Georg Forster (among other things, future member of the Revolutionary government in Mainz) "may God preserve us Germans from the *manière fixe d'être gouverné par la raison*" that Mirabeau is already trying to "inflict" on his own nation (*JBW*, I.8: 303).[6] As Revolutionary violence broke out in parts of Brabant and in Liège, Jacobi began to fear more for his personal and financial interests, and began to have darker suspicions about the nature of the Revolution. Still, in November, Jacobi can say to Forster that "this French business has thrown me completely into the field of politics [*in die politische Fach*]; I basically read nothing else now and I am not a little curious to see the end of my [writing] efforts" (*JBW*, I.8: 318). Unfortunately, the work on the Revolution that Jacobi planned to write, and on which he worked assiduously for several years, never appeared, largely because, by his own admission, Burke in England and Rehberg in Germany beat him to the publisher (*JBW*, I.9: 14).[7] He occasionally calls the missing work his "treatise on the philosophy of the new French legislation" (*JBW*, I.8: 441).

The fictional piece, "Erhard O.," nonetheless preserves some of Jacobi's line of thinking from this period, in which Kant and revolutionary politics were simultaneous preoccupations. The piece is first mentioned by name in a letter from March 1791 to Lavater:

> I'm now writing a couple of pages against the philosophy *du jour* in the broadest sense, entitled "To Erhard O," just as if from Allwill's papers. I'll send it to you as soon as I've finished it. The other day I had to let something drop. It pertained to the "manner of

[5] See Jacobi to Forster on November 24, 1789: "Yesterday I received a four page letter from Laharpe in Paris. Everything looks very ambiguous [*zweideutig*] there. I am taking the most lively interest in what is going on there, and I am ruining myself with newspapers and pamphlets" (*JBW*, I.8: 331).

[6] This phrase recurs in a letter of November 7, 1789 to Reinhold: "The tremendous arrogance of 1200 Lycurguses wanting to create a constitution that, according to the definition of Count Mirabeau, would be a *manière fixe d'être gouverné par la raison*, has set all of my vital spirits into an uproar" (*JBW*, I.8: 317).

[7] Jacobi first mentions Burke in a letter to Müller of May 1790 (*JBW*, I.8: 393) in connection with his own concerns about "French Purism and Hyperidealistic Materialism." By January of the following year, Jacobi is praising Burke's *Reflections* in high terms to some of his close associates (*JBW*, 1.9: 13–14).

being governed by reason alone." But – dear God! What counsel [is there] for the eighteenth century? Whither can one look for help? (*JBW*, I.9: 20)

While it is not immediately clear what "philosophy *du jour*" means, it is noteworthy that Jacobi says that he intends the phrase "in the broadest sense." In his own German context, there can be little doubt that Jacobi meant the term to refer to Kant and some of his followers. Even before Fichte arrived there, Jacobi had taken to calling Jena the "Kantian Republic" in his letters. As I'll set out in more detail below, the actual text of "Erhard O." deals more directly with a proto-utilitarian strand within the French Enlightenment that influenced some members of the National Assembly than with Kant or any other German philosopher. Jacobi's concern is therefore less with specifics such as substantive normative claims than with a more general commonality. Later on, I'll show that this commonality lies in a model of ideal practical rationality.

In a different letter, to his friend Kleuker, Jacobi also describes the target of "Erhard O." as the "philosophy *du jour*." While he leaves the label unexplained here as well, he does tell of how he wrote the piece in part to champion "the Socratic 'I know *nothing*'" against this otherwise unnamed philosophy. Importantly, it is likewise "non-knowing" whose cause he takes up in the open letter to Fichte on nihilism from nearly a decade later. Indeed, he says that Socratic non-knowledge is the Archimedean point of all his intellectual labor, telling Kleuker that it "is my vocation, perhaps my divine mission" to move the intellectual world by asserting "human truth" against abstract and impoverished rationality. In "Erhard O." itself, he echoes this, proclaiming how "great" it is to "lead non-knowledge to battle against insolence and lie" (*MPW*, 493; *JWA*, 6.1: 236). We are meant to read "Erhard O." as a dialectical challenge to the pretensions of Jacobi's more rationalist contemporaries to have transformed morals into a science.

Jacobi, signing his own name to "Erhard O.," writes of a previous conversation in which "Erhard" had cast aspersions upon his "struggle for a secure conviction," strangely contented by the "eternally ruminating monster" of skeptical doubt (*MPW*, 485; *JWA*, 6.1: 224). Yet it is not his friend's doubt, but rather the "wisdom of the present age" that Jacobi takes on directly in the letter (*MPW*, 486; *JWA*, 6.1: 225). Going beyond criticism of the traditional sources of moral authority, the "wise" offer a reductive explanation of morality "[b]y grounding [*ergründet*] what is living on the non-living, what is rational on the irrational, the moral on the animal" (*MPW*, 486; *JWA*, 6.1: 224).[8]

[8] These remarks are also similar to a passage at the end of Jacobi's 1799 letter to Fichte, in which he adopts the point of view of a well-intentioned *Aufklärer* who sets out to demolish superstition and to free humanity from "servility to a being *outside*" itself by "finding its ground" or explaining it (*MPW*, 524; *JWA*, 2.1, 221).

Passing over the claim that the "wise" have successfully overcome the "twilight of error and illusion," Jacobi takes aim instead at their "*positive non-knowledge*" (*MPW*, 486; *JWA*, 6.1: 225). He cites Gibbon as the source of this paradoxical phrase, adding his own emphases in the quotation: "The opinion of the Academics and Epicureans were of a less religious cast (than those of the Stoics and Platonists); but whilst the *modest science* of the former induced them to doubt, *the positive ignorance* of the latter urged them to deny, the providence of the Supreme Ruler" (cited by Jacobi at *MPW*, 486; *JWA*, 6.1: 225). That is, while the "wisdom of the age" may dissolve prejudice, it also constructs a "positive" (i.e., dogmatic) worldview meant to *replace* the grounds of moral authority that have been swept aside – in particular, the "way of sensing" that grounds judgment.

This part of the discussion evokes the constellations of ancient philosophical schools in a way not unfamiliar from the writings of other eighteenth-century philosophers. Jacobi's goal in doing so is to distinguish himself from *both* traditionalists and radicals. While later in the nineteenth century, conservative German thinkers adapted personalist themes partly inspired by Jacobi's critiques to defend the Prussian monarchy, Jacobi himself adopts a non-dogmatic stance.[9] This is what the emphasis he places in the citation from Gibbon regarding the "modest science" of the Academics is intended to highlight. By way of summarizing a very complex stretch in the history of philosophy, the relevant point is that the "New Academy" under Carneades and his successors developed a dialectical method of "internal" criticism targeting the different dogmatic schools in an open-ended quest for the truth. In doing so they took themselves to be authentically "Socratic," while the preceding "Old Academy" has lost its way in the thicket of dogmatism. One of Jacobi's favorite writers, Cicero, whom he cites at the beginning of "Erhard O.," was a kind of Academic skeptic who enshrined this approach in his dialogues. The Academics (at least after Carneades) also maintained that, while certain knowledge is impossible, we ought to have enough confidence in our beliefs to act and to investigate nature scientifically. The Academic method clearly had some influence on Jacobi's writing, for he frequently adopts dialogical and epistolary formats for exploring a given issue.

The task of championing the "Socratic" cause against his era's own dogmatism takes on special urgency for Jacobi because of events in France and the political ascendancy there of Enlightenment thought. But before he clarifies this connection, he rhapsodizes about a "star of rapturous non-light" that leads "to the *barren* jubilation of the golden wedding feast of Erebus with the Night, without the offspring of a new heaven and a new earth" (*MPW*, 486;

[9] For a superb examination of the period that examines the role of Jacobi's thought in political debates of the 1830s and 1840s, see Breckman 1999.

JWA, 6.1, 225). According to the original story in Hesiod, Night and Erebus, the deepest darkness, give birth to the ether, the source, in turn, of light. But for Jacobi, Enlightenment thought is a parody of these primal nuptials, since no element of "light" issues from the darkness. We might say these days that, like a black hole, the force of rational criticism allows nothing to escape its reach, not even the belief that overturning error will lead to the truth. But perhaps, Jacobi suggests, there is a kind of "light" emanating from the Enlightenment after all. Yet, he likens it to a false star that only leads us into deeper darkness. What is this false light?

In the act of writing these thoughts down, a convenient answer happens to come across Jacobi's desk, in the form of a report on the doings of the *Assemblée nationale* (in the January 1791 issue of the *Journal de Paris*).[10] The report's author criticizes Burke's account of the virtues of a free citizenry as being grounded on error and sheer illusion, which must be replaced by the newly discovered "lights" of the principles of human nature. Invoking the authority of Locke against Burke's celebration of tradition, the author proclaims that only "the eternal rocks of nature which the rigorous demonstrations of reason have, so to speak, laid bare" can ground a society of free individuals (*MPW*, 487; *JWA*, 6.1: 225–6). In other words, once tradition and privilege have been cleared away, the residue *must* be the truth about human nature, upon which a rational system of morals and natural law can be constructed. The metaphorical bedrock is just the "plain, bare egoism" most obviously characteristic of people in the state of nature. Once sentiment or submission to God's will have melted away in the sunlight of reason, one can see that virtue can only mean correct calculation of advantage. Jacobi sarcastically takes the Parisian author to be arguing that people ought to live a kind of lie – appearing virtuous, but all the while acting according to reason, which means acting purely self-interestedly. Doing so will lead us to a this-worldly utopia of "one general state of contentedness which is called *happiness*; the *pure and fulfilled* happiness of *mortal* man" (*MPW*, 487; *JWA*, 6.1: 226–7). Echoing Stoic criticisms of the Epicureans, Jacobi writes of how this triumph of utility strips "honor" of its status as an independent value, and turns love into a "weakness" that must be replaced by "correct insight into the order of advantages" (*MPW*, 487; *JWA*, 6.1: 227).

[10] Jacobi's discussion of this article echoes an earlier passage in *David Hume* (1787), showing that the political and social implications of Enlightenment thought were very much on his mind even before the Revolution. Having earlier shown that reason is necessarily grounded in "sense [*Sinn*]," Jacobi and his interlocutor challenge any notion of a "pure" or autonomous reason. This turns out to have *political* implications. Jacobi's interlocutor says, "Supposing that this is our own case, it offers a peculiar contrast to the philosophical Gospel which proclaims that we are well on the way to being governed by reason *alone* and to inaugurating the Golden Age" (*MPW*, 325; *JWA*, 2.1: 194). He goes on to contrast "genuine reason [*eigentliche Vernunft*]" and an impoverished, abstract "pure" reason.

So what does this say about the identity of the "false star" from France? The following rehearsal of another stretch of the history of philosophy fills in the answer. Seventeenth-century philosophers like Hobbes constructed naturalistic (i.e., non-God-requiring) accounts of morality and right, while thinkers more friendly to traditional theism, such as Locke, likewise relied on the rational reconstruction of the state of nature to account for moral authority. Both wedded these accounts to instrumentalist conceptions of practical rationality to account for things like political authority and other-regarding duties. After Mandeville and others drew radical conclusions from rational egoism, this strand of British moral thought was domesticated in France in works like *De l'esprit* (1758) of Claude-Adrien Helvétius (1715–71). Incorporating Spinozistic premises, his posthumous *De l'homme* (1772) further developed his mechanistic moral psychology. While Helvétius is not mentioned directly in "Erhard O.," Jacobi identifies him elsewhere as a paradigm of the very same "wisdom of the present age" he finds expressed in the report from Paris (*Spinoza Letters*, 1785). Another figure relevant to this line of thought and quite familiar to Jacobi is d'Holbach, whose *Système de la nature* (1771) presents a similar view of virtue as rational self-interest, while his *La Politique naturelle* (1773) offers a proto-utilitarian theory of the state.[11] This stream of Enlightenment thought blended what Jacobi saw as a highly abstract conception of human nature with a hyper-rationalist view of practical reason in an account that claimed to settle all the issues of morality and politics. As he correctly recognized, many Revolutionaries in Paris viewed their task as bringing to pass a society grounded solely on these principles.

Jacobi's understanding of this particular line of Enlightenment thinking can also be made clearer with help from an essay called "Concerning Man's [*sic*] Freedom" that was included in the 1789 reissue of the *Spinoza Letters*. "Concerning Man's Freedom" is also referenced in the open letter to Fichte, establishing the links between the arguments of these three pieces. The essay is arranged in a series of numbered propositions split into two dialectically opposed sections advertising different positions on free will. The first side develops a theory of ethics in terms of rational egoism and correct reasoning. Like some key figures in the radical tradition (Spinoza, Hobbes, Helvétius, d'Holbach), this account begins by attributing to every organism an "original 'impulse'" whose principal function is "to preserve and augment the faculty of

[11] While Jacobi was deeply influenced by Rousseau, who was of course the source of an alternative strand of naturalistic thinking in the Revolutionary mix, he shows no trace of sympathy for the primitivist ideology behind some of the more extreme events of the Revolution. Both of Jacobi's novels, *Woldemar* and *Edward Allwill*, reveal a debt to Rousseau, but also a wariness of the cult of sentimentality that flowed from his writings. For a general account of this connection, see Christ 1998.

existing of the particular nature of which it is the impulse." Human rationality reflects this primal conatus, as he goes on to explain:

IX. The existence of rational natures is said to be "personal," as distinct from all other natures. This personal existence consists in the consciousness that a particular being has of its identity, and results from a higher degree of consciousness in general.
X. The necessary impulse of a rational being, or rational desire, is therefore necessarily directed to the enhancement of the degree of personality, i.e., the degree of living existence itself.
XI. Rational desire in general, or the impulse of the rational being as such, we call "will." (*MPW*, 342; *JWA*, 1.1: 159)

The text details how rationality preserves the integrity of the organism by arranging one's desires instrumentally in relation to what Jacobi calls "the enhancement of the degree of personality." Elaborating the implications of Propositions IX–XI above, Jacobi explains how what makes certain desires irrational is that they disrupt or impair the identity of the person, diminishing the "quantity" of consciousness or personality (*MPW*, 342; *JWA*, 1.1: 159). Because a person is by definition conscious of his enduring identity, he is able to take responsibility for acting on irrational impulses, and so feel regret, or "the unpleasant situation in which . . . he must experience a most embarrassing discord with himself" (*MPW*, 343; *JWA*, 1.1: 160). While an individual has many inconsistent desires, on the view represented in this essay they are all modifications of the single desire for self-preservation. Thus, it turns out, the latter "provides the principle according to which different desires can be weighed against one another, and the relation determined according to which they can be satisfied without the person running into contradiction and enmity with itself" (*MPW*, 343; *JWA*, 1.1: 160–1). The key to discovering this principle is to first abstract away from the particularity of given desires and take the result as the common currency (personality enhancement) for assessing every desire. This method of resolving conflict by abstracting away from particularity and deriving universal principles can also be handily applied to "[e]xternal right" (*MPW*, 343; *JWA*, 1.1: 161). Indeed, there is an explicit analogy between the particular desires of the individual and the particular individuals within the social whole.

According to this perspective, morality can be grounded on "rational desire in general" plus the correct application of a formal standard to the pursuit of satisfaction. No more illusions of the sort denounced by the author of the *Journal de Paris* article! "The beginning (or the *a priori*) of principles in general is the original desire of a rational being to preserve its own particular existence, i.e., the person, and to subjugate anything that would injure its identity" (*MPW*, 343; *JWA*, 1.1: 161). By adopting the initial premises of this view the unaccountable particular solidarities between actual human beings no longer need to be considered in grounding moral and legal obligations:

> XXIII. From this very impulse [toward self-preservation as a rational creature] there flows a natural love and obligation to justice towards others. A rational being cannot distinguish itself *qua* rational being (abstractly) from another rational being. The I and Man are one; the He and Man are one; therefore the He and I are one. The Love [*sic*] of the person therefore limits the love of the *Individuum*, and necessitates my not holding myself in high regard. (*MPW*, 344; *JWA*, 1.1: 161–2)

This love is "natural" just as the principles of justice discussed in the citation from the *Journal de Paris* are natural; both rest solely on the facts of human nature as disclosed by critical reason. This "natural" love is grounded on the abstract, universal desire for self-preservation, which is abstract because it leaves aside the specific constitution of the individual whose preservation is at stake. Rationality thus requires a demanding transition from particular interests to universal principles, one that is nonetheless deemed to be "natural" on this theory. The problem is that the former are what constitutes the self as an individuum, as a particular person with a particular way of looking at the world; more than that, Jacobi hints that one's "esteem" for oneself is intimately bound up with this particularity. What makes someone a unique, valuable individual is precisely that person's distinctive way of sensing (*Sinnesart*).

As he puts it in "Erhard O.," "[a]s little as infinite space can determine the particular nature of any one body, so little can the *pure* reason *of man* constitute with its will (which is evenly good everywhere since it is *one and the same* in all men) the foundation of a particular, *differentiated* life, or impart to the *actual person* its proper individual value" (*MPW*, 488; *JWA*, 6.1: 228). When I take someone at his word, I don't trust his *pure reason*, rather I trust *him* – the kind of person he is overall. "What gives me assurance in him is his manner of sensing, his taste, his mind and character" (*MPW*, 489; *JWA*, 6.1: 230).[12] The hyper-rationalist account of moral authority is unable to ground the value of the individual as such, and is also unable to orient moral judgment. Both of these require not the "faculty . . . of syllogism" but "*sense-dispositions* [*Gesinnungen*]" or "*affect*" (*MPW*, 488; *JWA*, 6.1: 229).[13] "Sense-dispositions" reflect the way that a living creature's "principle of self-determination," which takes the form of a drive "to *preserve* a certain cohesion, to *promote* it,

[12] In the 1789 edition of the *Spinoza Letters*, Jacobi makes the point in similar terms:

> It is just as impossible for a man of *pure reason* to lie or to cheat, as for the three angles of a triangle not to equal two right angles. But will a real being endowed with reason be so driven into a corner by the *abstractum of his reason*? Will he let himself be made such a total prisoner through a mere play of words? Not for a moment! If honour is to be *trusted*, and if a man can *keep his word*, then quite another spirit must dwell in him than the spirit of syllogism. (*MPW*, 347; *JWA*, 1.1, 166)

[13] Here I happily adopt di Giovanni's somewhat non-standard translation of "*Gesinnungen*," which I think brings out the connection with "sense [*Sinn*]" and "way of sensing [*Sinnesart*]" nicely.

and *enlarge* it," takes shape in specific circumstances (*MPW*, 489; *JWA*, 6.1: 230). Each organism, including the human one, strives to preserve its integrity as a particular kind of thing with a given "form." But it is not possible for there to be a "form" of nothing, a "form which would be *just* form" (*MPW*, 490; *JWA*, 6.1: 231). Jacobi's point is that views like that of the Parisian author (or that defended in "Concerning Man's Freedom") claim to be able to ground morality in something like a "form which would be *just* form."

2 Jacobi on Nihilism

Jacobi's assertion of the key role of our "way of sensing," disregarded by Enlightenment thinkers, furnishes an argumentative link between "Erhard O." and "To Fichte." Remember that the former was composed in 1791 and published the following year, and the open letter "To Fichte" was written and appeared in 1799. This time lag provides an indirect illustration of Jacobi's manner of working and of constructing arguments – he tends to range back and forth in time across his own writings, correspondence, and notes. The letter as a whole, including the preface, the supplements, and some of the surrounding unpublished correspondence, is a key document not only of Jacobi's thought but also of the history of post-Kantian philosophy more generally. My topic, however, means that I'm going to focus only on one aspect of this material.

Previously I showed how Jacobi's intense engagement with Kant in the early 1790s forms part of the concatenation of ideas linking "Erhard O." and the letter to Fichte. Here I want to draw attention to a feature of Jacobi's dialectical staging in the letter. In the preface that Jacobi added for publication, he tries to separate his specific criticisms of transcendental idealism (in the following correspondence with Fichte) from his views regarding Kant. The purpose is for Jacobi to align himself with what he took to be valuable aims in Kant's work. Since the 1760s, Jacobi had been well disposed toward Kant's efforts to limit the scope of reason in morals and theology. Using language that links the letter to Fichte with the aims of "Erhard O.," and alluding to Kant's famous claim to "make room for faith," Jacobi writes:

> For since I regard the consciousness of *non-knowing* as what is highest in man [*sic*], and the place of this consciousness as the place of *the true* inaccessible to science, so I am bound to be pleased with Kant that he preferred to sin against the system rather than against the majesty of the place. (*MPW*, 499; *JWA*, 2.1: 192)

By praising Kant for preserving the sanctity of "non-knowing," Jacobi connects the point of view of the letter to Fichte with the goal of his earlier criticisms of the "philosophy *du jour*." The difference is that, in the case of "Erhard O.," the target would seem to include Kant. The strategy in 1799 is to employ the authority of the "master" against the less restrained views of the erstwhile "disciple" in a bid to occlude the fact that both are equally worthy of opprobrium. But it is particularly important for the present discussion that Jacobi explicitly integrates his argument with Fichte into his larger skeptical project.

This skeptical framework is hinted at about halfway through "To Fichte," where Jacobi switches from his fluid epistolary style to what he advertises as a more fragmentary, "more rhapsodic, more grasshopper-like" approach modeled on Hamann (*MPW*, 506; *JWA*, 2.1: 199). Jacobi cites illness for the abrupt change, and for the fact that he wrote to Fichte "incompletely and rhapsodically," providing more of a "*narration* [*nur erzählt*] of my doctrine of non-knowledge [*UnWißenheitslehre*] than a philosophical exposition" (*MPW*, 526; *JWA*, 2.1: 232). Still, the buried reference to Hamann and the explicit mention of "non-knowledge" gives the strong suggestion that Jacobi's stylistic shift indicates something about the argument. The text largely consists of brief passages selected and grouped here, some drawn from elsewhere in Jacobi's personal writings and correspondence. For example, Jacobi provides Fichte with the modified borrowing from the 1790 letter to Reinhold that I discussed at the beginning of the paper. More substantial is a passage, perhaps written for the 1799 piece, describing how he is able to sympathetically "transpose" himself into Fichte's *Wissenschaftslehre*, and yet still experiences a sense of inner resistance toward it. Perhaps this is "from lack of patience," he writes, "almost furious at [Fichte's] *artificial way of taking leave of his senses* [*künstliches Von-Sinnen-Kommen*] in virtue of which I, following his example, am to be liberated from my natural *lack of sense* [*Wahn-Sinn*]" (*MPW*, 506; *JWA*, 2.1: 200). Fichte, like the speaker in the *Journal de Paris* cited in "Erhard O.," would have one take up the abstract, critical standpoint of "pure" reason in order to emancipate oneself from illusion and superstition. Also, as in "Erhard O.," *David Hume*, and elsewhere, Jacobi exploits the polysemy of the term "*Sinn*," the primary sense of which he takes to be perception, to make his point that being rational, being sensible, is a matter of one's "way of sensing."

The desire to construct an all-embracing, encyclopedic science is another characteristic of the Enlightenment as Jacobi understands it, and it is something that he lingers over in the letter to Fichte. Laying out what he tells Fichte is their shared conception of "science as such," Jacobi describes the goal as nothing less than the construction of "the one and only true philosophical shape of reality" (*MPW*, 502; *JWA*, 2.1: 195). The problem, says Jacobi later on, is that an all-embracing science incorporating morality winds up resembling a game of peg solitaire [*Nürnberger Grillenspiel*] (or tic-tac-toe, as di Giovanni's translation puts it). Once all the possible moves have been thoroughly understood, playing the game becomes pointless. If, *per impossible*, there ever really were an *Encylopédie*, the whole "game" of life would be spoiled (*MPW*, 512; *JWA*, 2.1: 206).

Jacobi goes on to maintain that an all-embracing science of this sort first requires something like a "chemical process through which everything outside reason is changed into nothing, and reason alone is left" (*MPW*, 507; *JWA*, 2.1: 202). As he puts it later, "[a]bstraction lies at the basis of all reflection" (*MPW*, 509; *JWA*, 2.1: 202). What remains is variously characterized as an indeterminacy that "cannot itself *be*" (*MPW*, 507; *JWA*, 2.2: 201), a "*mere schema*" (*MPW*, 508; *JWA*, 2.2: 202), or an absence where there should at least be a "*caput mortuum*" (*MPW*, 509; *JWA*, 2.2: 202). Jacobi also describes this "annihilation" process in more positive terms as a progression "through ever more universal concepts" (*MPW*, 209; *JWA*, 2.2: 203). While the process does generate new concepts, it also annihilates specifying determinations in the very act of generating universals. Jacobi is saying that Fichte's aim of building the science of science embodies this pure philosophy that is itself just the natural *terminus ad quem* of all human striving to know (*MPW*, 507; *JWA*, 2.1: 201). Simply by pursuing its natural drive, reason reaches a state of "*pure logical enthusiasm*" in which one can proclaim that "even if body and soul were to fail us, we would not care because of this lofty love for knowledge *merely of knowledge*, the insight *merely into seeing*, the doing *merely of doing*" (*MPW*, 511; *JWA*, 2.2: 205; translation modified). Taken to the point of "pure logical enthusiasm," a natural drive collapses into incoherence. Ascending by way of "universals ever more universal" strips away determinate content leaving behind an empty universal. Considered as the goal of an activity, an empty universal is a bad candidate. One acts, Jacobi supposes, by doing specific things. Just acting isn't an activity that anyone could undertake. To be sure, Jacobi is happy to grant that even just acting may have rules, above all the demand for consistency. But apart from the determinate "way of sensing" left behind in the conceptual ascent, no one has any reason to care about the rules. For instance, in a simple counting game, it would be "quite silly, laughable ... detestable, even to ask for a *meaning* of numbers, or a *content* for them" (*MPW*, 512; *JWA*, 2.1: 207).[14]

Jacobi eventually turns to the manifestation of this logical enthusiasm in moral philosophy and theology. On his reading of Fichte's works, including some of his ill-judged rebuttals of the recent charges of atheism, the "good in itself" is to be thought of as the pure "will that wills nothing" – "this hollow

14 Cf. these remarks about speculative philosophy in an October 21, 1797 letter to Jens Baggesen: "It's a calculating, merely for the sake of [discovering] new propositions to keep on calculating, never for the sake of discovering a *Facit* [*I do*]; altogether just a simple number game with pure, empty numbers" (*JBW*, 1.11: 248). A much earlier letter of March 1793 to Reinhold is, if anything, less charitable. Regarding transcendental idealism, he writes, "I really sometimes think I discern something akin to the sin of Onan in the goings on of this philosophy, which has from the beginning held me back from accepting it as a philosophy of truth, at least in a practical regard" (*JWA*, 2.2: 672). See Genesis 38: 8–10.

shell of self-subsistence and freedom in the absolutely indeterminate" (*MPW*, 515; *JWA*, 2.1: 210–11). Jacobi does not object to conceiving of God in terms of ideal rationality, as Fichte indeed does in relevant writings from the late 1790s. The difficulty is with the model of ideal rationality that is used to define the notion of God. Echoing "Concerning Man's Freedom," Jacobi glosses Fichte's conception of it as an "*impersonal personality*, that naked *I-hood* [*Ichheit*] of the I without any *self*" (*MPW*, 516–17; *JWA*, 2.1: 212; translation modified). In both texts, Jacobi uses loosely synonymous terms (person, personality, I, self, individual) to capture what he sees as the self-defeating or inherently unrealizable character of the Enlightenment conception of ideal rationality. As he had explained in "Erhard O.," Jacobi tells Fichte that the form of a living thing, its "I-hood" or principle of identity, is an "urge for identity [*Identitäts-Trieb*]" or "the necessary urge to be consistent with ourselves [*der nothwendige Trieb der Uebereinstimmung mit uns selbst*]" (*MPW*, 518; *JWA*, 2.1: 214).[15] Considered in the abstract as "the *a priori* of principles" this "urge" lacks the determinate content. Jacobi agrees with the hyper-rationalists that the "*accord of a man* [*sic*] *with himself*" is a desideratum of rationality (*MPW*, 517; *JWA*, 2.1: 212). Yet he insists that it is not the totality of it. The "Kantian moral law" simply states this "necessary urge" in the form of a rule of judgment, which, without the "way of sensing" that gives the will something to will, lacks content.

Having explained thus far his "identity and difference" with Fichte, Jacobi introduces the term "nihilism" as a label for what characterizes moral theories committed to this abstract conception of rationality. Clarifying the source of his resistance to Fichte's philosophy, he writes: "I feel a terrible horror before the *nothing, the absolutely indeterminate, the utterly void* (*these three are one*: the Platonic infinite!), especially as the object of philosophy or *aim* of wisdom" (*MPW*, 519; *JWA*, 2.1: 214). And so, he says, Fichte ought to excuse Jacobi for opting for a "philosophy of non-knowledge" against this "philosophical *knowledge of the nothing*" that he calls "*Nihilism*" (*MPW*, 519; *JWA*, 2.1: 214). Why "nihilism"? Here, it is useful to remember that the term had yet to acquire the more apocalyptic connotations that long usage, and the likes of Nietzsche and Heidegger, have lent it. The key to understanding what Jacobi

[15] In a passage from the 1796 edition of *Woldemar* that Jacobi included as a supplement for Fichte, the title character muses in a similar vein:

> [W]as this will [for the good] perhaps only the immediate consequence of a *personal consciousness attached to universal concepts and images*? Only the *striving for self-preservation* essential to all natures but in *pure rational form*? – It then had no object except its own activity, and the prototype and origin of all virtues was the pure empty form of *being in thought – personality without person or distinction of persons*. (*MPW*, 534; *JWA*, 2.1: 256)

means is his reference to Plato. In "Erhard O.," Jacobi had maintained that all rational creatures, insofar as they strive for their own self-sufficiency, have an intimation of perfection (*MPW*, 490; *JWA*, 6.1: 231). But he cautions against attempting to transform this obscure intimation into a clear concept, recommending that one hold back in Socratic reserve (*MPW*, 493; *JWA*, 6.1: 236). This is because reflection is liable to transform the idea of perfection into the idea of the infinite or unbounded. But, citing *Philebus*, Jacobi reminds Erhard O. of Plato's view of the infinite as the indeterminate nothing. Elsewhere in notes on *Philebus*, Jacobi discusses how the Platonic infinite is the *indefinite* (*apeiron*) or the *indeterminate*, and as such it cannot have any "objective existence"; the *apeiron* is unreal. According to one of the notes, "[t]he infinite is rightly dismissed by Plato because the human intellect can only think of it as the indeterminate" (see *JWA*, 2.2: 681).

"Impersonal personality," "personified nothingness," the Platonic infinite – these are all Jacobi's terms for characterizing what nihilistic models of ideal rationality ultimately provide by way of a ground for moral judgment and personal dignity. The lack of content means, for Jacobi, that the model contains no account of the sources of commitments, no anchor for judgments. Against this ideal of the "will that wills nothing" (*MPW*, 516; *JWA*, 2.1: 211), Jacobi offers Fichte a series of exemplary people who each *virtuously* violated a moral duty. He mentions, inter alia, Pylades, Desdemona, Timoleon, Epaminondas, and King David. The important point isn't that sometimes there are exceptions to the rules, but rather that "the *privelegium aggratiandi* [right to immunity] for such crimes . . . is man's true *right of majesty*, the seal of his worth, of his divine nature" (*MPW*, 516; *JWA*, 2.1: 211). The point is that sound judgment is something that Jacobi reserves for human beings, not "personified nothingness."

The judgments made in each of these cases do not rest on an abstract model of ideal reasoning, but on the whole *Sinnesart* of the individual. As he'd put it previously, we trust these judgments not because we trust the rules to lead to good judgments, but because we trust the people who are making the judgments. With this in mind, we can glean a bit more about Jacobi's own positive alternative to Enlightenment nihilism. In each of the examples Jacobi cites one could point to the complex role of particular solidarities. Desdemona, whose only "sins" were her "loves" for Othello, tells a lie on her deathbed to shield her guilty husband. Pylades passes himself off as his dear friend Orestes when they find themselves marooned in hostile territory. In the cases of Timoleon and Epaminondas, the circle of solidarity extends to their fellow citizens in the comparatively small Greek states. Timoleon's misdeed was to murder his own brother, Timophanes, whom he'd previously saved in battle, but who now threatened tyranny over Corinth. Epaminondas, a Theban statesman who defeated mighty Sparta and encouraged independence for subject states, was later put on trial for extending his term of office beyond what was allowed. David (1 Sam. 21: 2–7) appropriated the Bread of the Presence for his famished men. In addition to providing grist for the particularist mill, these examples also accentuate the social dimension central to the formation and realization of a *Sinnesart*. Jacobi is trying to avoid a different kind of abstraction, namely the reduction of moral judgment to private feeling. His primary literary works, *Woldemar* and *Edward Allwill's Collection of Letters*, chronicle the effort involved in shaping youthful sentiment into mature judgment. In *Allwill* (to which "Erhard O." was added in 1792), while the title character remains a sinister outsider, another character moves from embittered alienation to a kind of reconciliation through the ministrations of a small, tightly knit family. This example helps to bring out the complexity involved in Jacobi's conception of an individual *Sinnesart* by showing how the latter includes affective shifts of perspective. In both works, it is when characters are cut off from the group or something goes awry in a key relationship that they lose perspective and quickly take up extreme stances.

It would take me very far afield to develop these thoughts about Jacobi's novels and their bearing on his critique of what he viewed as the hyper-rationalists of the day. This critique was carried out in a Socratic or, perhaps, Academic mode, in order to champion humble ignorance against dogmatism. During the Revolutionary decade of the 1790s, Jacobi's thinking returned again and again to the *practical* meaning of the ideal of rationality advocated by many important contemporaries, and by 1799 it had crystallized around the catchy, yet terrifying term "nihilism." The nihilism of practical reason means that it has been reduced to formal consistency (or some other formula) stripped of the way of sensing that provides content to and orients judgments. The "nihil" – nothing – captures various elements of Jacobi's position at once. First, ideal rationality rests on an abstractive move that "annihilates" determinate features of things (in this case, for example, specific feelings about specific people or groups). What remains is, second, "nothing" in the Platonic sense, in other words sheer indeterminacy (in this case, what is there to make me care about being consistent?). Finally, nothing can be done with this sort of rationality; there's nothing to deliberate about, as in a game of peg solitaire.

To be sure, this *is* an abstract issue being taken with a theory charged with itself being too abstract. One wonders where Jacobi's own "star" is to lead next. To stick with practical ethics (there are also important political questions one could ask) for now, how does Jacobi's own account of how to make judgments resolve tensions between particular obligations and more universal ones? That is, what if you're not David or Desdemona, but you have to figure out what you owe someone else's kids versus your own? Jacobi nowhere argues that there are no universal duties, nor that particular ones outweigh them by default. One gets the sense that, for Jacobi, one can't really be David or Desdemona without recognizing both kinds of obligations (otherwise, why would we trust their judgments?). This is an example of the kind of issue that arises for Jacobi's view. There is reason to suppose that exploring such questions sheds light on more details of his highly eclectic, skeptical contribution to the intellectual treasury of a tumultuous age. For now, non-knowledge will have to suffice.

10 The Political Implications of Friedrich Schlegel's Poetic, Republican Discourse

Elizabeth Millán Brusslan

> Poetry is republican discourse: a discourse which is its own law and end unto itself, and in which all the parts are free citizens and have the right to vote.
> (*PH*, 8. Translation modified; *KFSA*, 2: 155)

As John Stuart Mill pointed out in his path-breaking essay, "The Subjection of Women" (1869), laws would never be improved if we did not have people with *better* moral sentiments than the existing laws. Even earlier, Mary Wollstonecraft argued for the rights of women in her *A Vindication of the Rights of Women* (1792). At the time Wollstonecraft and Mill wrote their treatises on women, the Glorious Revolution had long since established democracy as the ruling system of government in England. Meanwhile, in German-speaking lands, there were attempts to bring attention to social injustice and the deleterious effects of narrowly scripted gender roles.[1] However, in contrast to the situation in England, at the time that Friedrich Schlegel was attempting to defend the rights of women, the leading philosophers in German-speaking lands were still arguing that democracy was necessarily despotic. Such claims kept power in a limited number of, mostly male, hands.

In what follows, I shall explore Schlegel's efforts to weave social reform into his thought and to apply his better moral sentiments to the cause of greater freedom for all. Schlegel's push to include women in political decision-making and to recognize their equality as free thinkers was a necessary, even if, alas, not a sufficient condition to create the enlightened society envisioned by Kant.

To unpack the details of the story of Schlegel's progressive political views, we have to look at the relation between early German Romanticism and the Enlightenment. The early German Romantics were not opposed to the Enlightenment project, but they did critique certain limitations of the

With thanks to Gabriel Gottlieb and James A. Clarke and to the participants of the Cincinnati workshop, whose comments on a draft of this paper helped me to sharpen several points.

[1] While I will not discuss his writings in defense of the rights of Jews, Schlegel was an early defender; see *KFSA*, 7: 470–82.

Enlightenment thinkers.[2] Indeed, as Frederick Beiser has made clear in his work, while the Romantics were critics of the *Aufklärung*, they were also its disciples.[3] A closer look at Schlegel's critique of Kant will bring the relation between early German Romanticism and the Enlightenment into sharper focus.

Kant penned definitive defenses of freedom, yet he did not push for the social enactment of freedom in regard to the emancipation of women. Schlegel in his fragments, in his novel, *Lucinde*, and in some of his essays makes an explicit call to redress the exclusion of women from education and from participation in the philosophical world. Why does Schlegel pick up on, while Kant ignores, the subjection of women as a problem that philosophers should address?

To address this question, I will focus upon what was unique about Schlegel's philosophical lens, a lens uniquely suited to capture social injustice. I shall do this by examining the roots of his philosophical pluralism and his project of blending philosophy and poetry. Schlegel's push to blend disciplines was part of a project to reform our approach to truth, a topic that I will explore in Sections 1 and 2 of this paper. The new philosophical lens developed by Schlegel allowed him to see what other thinkers overlooked and to address urgent social issues that needed attention. The reforming spirit of Schlegel's thought is most systematically developed in an essay on Kant's *Toward Perpetual Peace*, and so in Sections 3 and 4, I will analyze that essay and Schlegel's critique of it to more clearly present the political implications of Schlegel's thought.

1 Romantic Critique and the Revolutionary Power of the Call for a New Relation between Poetry and Philosophy

Friedrich Schlegel was the leading philosopher of the movement that came to be known as *Frühromantik* or early German Romanticism, which blossomed between 1794 and 1808. The hybrid identity of early German Romanticism has made its reception more difficult, for a philosophy modeled on the natural sciences was and remains a reliable way to distinguish philosophy from *mere* poetry. The early German Romantics, however, resisted such distinctions between philosophy and poetry. Many of the fragments published in *Das Athenäum*, the short-lived journal edited by Friedrich and August Wilhelm Schlegel between 1798 and 1800, reflect a view of philosophy that embraces uncertainty, openness, and poetry, and rejects a view of philosophy as modeled on a science offering final words. A more intimate relation between philosophy and poetry is part of a project to step out of mastery and domination and open

2 See Cassirer 1968; Starobinski 1983; Frank 1993.

3 Beiser 1996: 318.

more space for freedom, not only in our search for knowledge, but also in our lived social lives.

As Rüdiger Bubner points out, the work of the early German Romantics is set against a backdrop of hermeneutical challenges posed by the forces of social transformation, forces which he claims upset our understanding of how the new relates to the old.[4] The challenge of understanding the new in relation to the old, a challenge most urgent within the context of the revolutionary zeal sweeping through continental Europe during the 1700s, was one to which the early German Romantics enthusiastically rose. Schlegel emphasizes philosophy's role as a cultural tool: political, literary, and philosophical events mark the age to which he belonged, and he firmly believed that philosophers must be prepared to respond to the transformation of culture in innovative and socially progressive ways. In *Athenäum Fragment* Nr. 216, where Schlegel claims that, "The French Revolution, Fichte's philosophy, and Goethe's *Meister* are the greatest tendencies of the age," he is calling for attention to be paid to the transformation of culture as a whole, a culture informed not only by a major political event (the French Revolution), but also by innovations in philosophy (Fichte's *Wissenschaftslehre*) and literature (Goethe's *Wilhelm Meister*) (*PH*, 46; *KFSA*, 2: 198). The "age" is the whole of which political, philosophical, and literary events are parts, parts that should come together to form some sort of cohesive unity.[5] The call to unify poetry and philosophy in the service of social change developed in a period of revolution and radical revolutions.

Schlegel dismissed as historically myopic any view of philosophy that laid claim to having established truth with absolute certainty. As he was fond of reminding his readers, the search for truth involved an infinite progression, one without end or closure: indeed, one could not *be* a philosopher, but only *become* one.[6] Change, openness, and uncertainty are hallmarks of Schlegel's thought.

Part of what distinguishes the philosophical contributions of the early German Romantics from their idealist counterparts is a move away from the comfort of final words. In his recent book, Fred Rush nicely contrasts German Idealism and early German Romanticism, noting that the cultural stability sought by the German Idealists, and their "obsession with rigorous systematicity" were their coping mechanisms to deal with the philosophical anxiety in the wake of political and philosophical revolutions of the period.[7] As Rush

[4] Bubner 2003: 185ff. [5] For more on Schlegel's tendencies fragment, see Saul 2003: 57–101.

[6] In *Athenäum Fragment* Nr. 54, Schlegel writes: "One can only become a philosopher, not be one. As soon as one thinks one is a philosopher, one stops becoming one" (*LF*, 24; *KFSA*, 2: 173). This theme of becoming is part of the Romantic project to make philosophy an infinite task. See Frank 1997.

[7] Rush 2016: 99.

notes, the early German Romantics were not as concerned with cultural stability as their Idealist counterparts:

> The overall impression one takes from Schlegel is that he is intent on holding in abeyance any rush to false stability and insisting that one adopt an explicitly experimental attitude towards life and mind. He is content to allow German intellectual life in the wake of Goethe, Fichte, and the French Revolution to messily develop from out of its historically contingent native internal conceptual resources without antecedent philosophical gerrymandering. More generally one can say that the Jena circle is primarily interested in the phenomenon of how thought and value *emerge* from their historical context.[8]

With this characterization, Rush offers us invaluable signposts for understanding Schlegel's Romantic philosophy. The avoidance of philosophical gerrymandering referenced by Rush was part of the Romantic move from artificial and sometimes unjust boundaries that hampered the development or cultivation of members of the societies they were seeking to reform.

Schlegel dedicated many fragments and several essays to the unjust treatment of women, both in philosophy and in life. As he noted in *Athenäum Fragment* Nr. 49, "Women are treated as unjustly in poetry as in life. If they're feminine, they're not ideal, and if ideal, not feminine" (*PH*, 24; *KFSA*, 2: 172). Schlegel argues that looking anew at the history of women in philosophy and art would liberate them from the narrowly scripted roles that confined them to the private, domestic sphere with little public presence or power, and certainly with no affinity for the discipline of philosophy. In *Über die weiblichen Charaktere in den griechischen Dichtern* (On the Female Figures of the Greek Poets) and *Über die Diotima* (On Diotima), Schlegel observes that the Greeks were able to provide a community that enabled individual women to progress and to attain high levels of *Bildung* (*KFSA*, 1: 45–115). According to Schlegel, the Greeks' higher level of *Bildung* is reflected in their art, an art in which both men and women are represented as fully developed human beings, an art in which humanity is the genus to which both men and women belong and participate equally. To support this point, Schlegel provides a detailed analysis of several female characters from Greek drama and poetry (e.g., Helen, Penelope, Circe, Calypso, etc.) and discusses the strengths and virtues accorded to them by their authors. He contrasts this to the way in which women were presented in Germany during his lifetime, as domestic, limited beings. Schlegel claims that the ancients offered a broader vision of the talents and possibilities of women than the pathetically narrow one offered by his contemporaries.

[8] Rush 2016: 99.

Penelope, for example, is lauded by Homer for her loyalty and forbearance and represents the beloved homeland for which Ulysses yearns, thereby giving the poem continuity and center (*KFSA*, 1: 54). Although Penelope embodies some domestic virtues, these do not limit her influence or the sphere of her power. In *Über die Diotima*, Schlegel emphasizes that "femininity and masculinity should be subsumed under the higher category of humanity" (*KFSA*, 1: 54). Schlegel condemns the practice of characterizing humans by emphasizing their gender-specific characteristics. He writes: "What is uglier than overdone femininity, what is more repulsive than exaggerated masculinity, which dominates our customs, our opinions, and our best art ... Only independent femininity, only soft masculinity is good and beautiful" (*KFSA*, 1: 92–3). With a bit of the sort of playfulness that often led others to misunderstand his work, Schlegel emphasizes that both men and women should be liberated from narrow gender-based views and that the way toward this liberation is opened by an ideal of humanity that supersedes narrow gender roles. He chides Schiller and Jacobi for creating portraits of women that were woefully restrictive.[9] A leading culprit in the narrow script for women was the view of marriage at the time.

Schlegel's own view of marriage is developed through his fragments and in his novel, *Lucinde* (1799).[10] *Lucinde* is essentially an anti-*Woldemar* novel and as such a feminist novel. One of Schlegel's most important objectives in this novel is to present a true partnership between a man and woman, and in so doing, to criticize conventional concepts of love and marriage, which placed women in a subservient role to men. *Lucinde* is a type of *Bildungsroman*; it is the story of how one character, Julius, develops into a human being. Although the narrator is Julius, the novel carries the name of Julius' beloved, Lucinde. The title underscores the important role that Lucinde plays in Julius' development. In order to develop into a cultivated human being, Julius needs the relation of love he shares with Lucinde. Their marriage is one of mind, soul, and body – of two free individuals, not two narrowly scripted roles. Julius does not need Lucinde to knit his socks (one of the images from Schiller's poem, *The Worth of Women*); he needs her in order to develop into a developed human being, to cultivate himself.

[9] He found Schiller's "The Worth of Women" (1796) to be a laughable depiction of women as merely domestic beings meant to serve men. In *KFSA*, 2: 6, he writes that men like those depicted by Schiller should be bound. Schlegel also objected vehemently to the view of marriage and women presented in Jacobi's novel, *Woldemar*. See his review of *Woldemar* (*KFSA*, 2: 57–77). In particular, Schlegel cannot understand why Jacobi believes that friendship and marriage are mutually exclusive.

[10] *KFSA*, 5: 1–92. *Lucinde* was written from November 1798 to May 1799. The first printing was in 1799. It has been translated by Peter Firchow in *LF*.

For Schlegel, the ideal of humanity is a unity, a seeing of the self in the other. In *Lucinde*, genders are presented as roles that we take on, even play with, not as categories that determine and dominate us. In a section entitled, "A Dithyrambic Fantasy on the Loveliest Situation in the World," Julius reflects upon the interplay between gender roles in the following way:

> When we exchange roles and in childish high spirits compete to see who can mimic the other more convincingly, whether you are better at imitating the protective intensity of the man, or I the appealing devotion of the woman. But are you always aware that this sweet game still has quite other attractions for me than its own – and not simply the voluptuousness of exhaustion or the anticipation of sweet revenge? I see here a wonderful, deeply meaningful allegory of the development of man and woman to full and complete humanity. (*LF*, 49; *KFSA*, 5: 18)

Schlegel's goal was to help both genders overcome the confines of the gender scripts that prevented their full cultivation, confines that also stood in the way of social progress. An important document in Schlegel's battle against the customs and caprices that limited both men and women in their development is an open letter he wrote to his wife, Dorothea – *Über die Philosophie: An Dorothea* (1799). In this letter he presents his arguments concerning the reasons why the study of philosophy is indispensable for women. The letter is a reaction against views like Schiller's and Jacobi's, which confined women to the private realm of the home. In the letter to Dorothea, Schlegel argues that philosophy is indispensable for women and that the domestic confines of women are unacceptable. Schlegel argues that society has made a mistake in confusing the contingent, socio-politically orchestrated situation (*Lage*) of women for their vocation (*Bestimmung*). Schlegel recognized that the *Lage* of women was one of limitation, oppression, domesticity, but that this was not the proper way to define the capacities and potential of women. His view that women should study philosophy is part of his attempt to open space for the *Bestimmung* of women in society. For Schlegel, philosophy deals with the unconditioned in human knowledge, it abstracts from all limitations, therefore it is an important tool in combatting the social ills that plagued women at that time, a narrow, confined realm of intellectual activity.

In varied literary forms – his letter to Dorothea, in his novel *Lucinde*, and in his fragments – Schlegel pushed for the recognition of women as equal intellectual partners in society. Schlegel's critique of culture was far-reaching, and he was frustrated by any work of critique that did not address the pressing issue of women's rights.

Schlegel held Kant's *Critique of Pure Reason* in high esteem, regarding it as an intellectual guidepost. In a letter to his brother August Wilhelm from 1793, he claims that "the Critique of Pure Reason is eternal" and that "Kant's theory is the first I could understand something of and the only one from which I hope to learn much" (*KFSA*, 18, xxi). These words of praise notwithstanding,

Schlegel was frustrated by the limitations of Kant's work. Indeed, in a set of fragments on Kant from 1796–7, he writes, "Kant is in principle highly uncritical [*Kant im Grunde höchst unkritisch*]" (*KFSA*, 18: 21). Kant's critical philosophy provided the tools necessary to submit claims of knowledge and values to critique, in other words to delineate the kinds of claims that could be justifiably made, but it did not go far enough in looking critically at philosophy itself or at some of the unjust distributions of power in society. I will now present a brief overview of the Enlightenment project through the lens of Kant, a thinker who not only shaped Enlightenment thought in German-speaking lands, but who also had a strong influence upon the development of German Romanticism in general, and on Friedrich Schlegel's thought, in particular.[11]

2 Away from Kant: Schlegel's Historical Turn and Its Implications

In his essay on Kant's *Toward Perpetual Peace*, Schlegel develops his critique of Kant's limitations. In his rather impudent essay, "On Incomprehensibility," Schlegel expresses his discontent with the achievements of the "Critical Age": "[We] have the honor to live [in] that age which has, in a word, earned the modest but highly suggestive name of the Critical Age, so that soon everything will have been criticized – except the age itself" (*OI*, 120; *KFSA*, 2: 364). A Critical Age that criticizes everything except itself is not a fully critical age; one could say that it is "half-critical." Schlegel is after a critique of critique, a philosophy of philosophy, attempting, through his conception of historical critique, to achieve a meta-philosophy, a way of looking critically at philosophy itself, as a discipline that has developed through history. The very first fragment of the *Athenäum* gives expression to Schlegel's concern with making philosophy the subject of philosophy: "Nothing is more rarely the subject of philosophy than philosophy itself" (*PH*, 18; *KFSA*, 2: 165). With characteristic irony (of just the sort that led so many of his contemporaries to misunderstand him), in *Athenäum* Nr. 56, Schlegel describes his push to criticize philosophy as just retaliation for the failure to develop a robust meta-philosophy: "Since nowadays philosophy criticizes everything that comes in front of its nose, a criticism of philosophy would be nothing more than justifiable retaliation" (*PH*, 25; *KFSA*, 2: 173).[12]

Schlegel's charges against the limits of Kant's "critical philosophy" are rooted in his desire to develop a critical philosophy of philosophy itself. Just as the Critical Age criticizes all but itself, Kant does not criticize his "critical philosophy," and so Schlegel calls Kant a "half critic," later explaining that:

[11] For more of Kant's influence on the early German Romantics, see Kneller 2007.

[12] Cf. *KFSA*, 18: 40, Nr. 228.

"[A] critique of philosophizing reason cannot succeed without a history of philosophy. [This] is proved to us by Kant himself. His work as a critique of philosophizing reason is not at all historical enough even though it is filled with historical relations and he attempts to construct various systems" (*KFSA*, 12: 286; my translation).

When Schlegel calls Kant a "half critic [*halber Kritiker*]," he is pointing to the limitations of Kant's critical project. Without a historical perspective, claims Schlegel, when we come to judge other systems we can only judge them according to our own system. Hence, all assessments of other systems ultimately presuppose the validity of one's own systems and are self-referential. So, Kant is unable to critique his critique: he can claim the legitimacy of scientific knowledge only within his own system. Schlegel believes that the philosopher must also be a philologist and a historian in order to be a good critic.[13] Kant, he claims, failed to incorporate history and philology into his critique:

> The critic has much in common with the polemicist; only he is not concerned with destruction but rather merely with sifting [*sichten*], with cleansing prior philosophies of their slag [*Schlacken*]. Kant's aim is not polemical; he says that the critic must attempt to place himself, with greatest versatility and universality, in the standpoint of each system, must grant each system its due rights, yet this does not often occur in Kant's work. The idea, nonetheless, that a critique must precede philosophy itself is entirely Kant's discovery and is certainly useful: he approximated his ideal here and there; this would have happened much more often had he been more of a philologist and had paid more attention to the philological, critical history of philosophy. (*KFSA*, 12: 291; my translation)

Schlegel exhibits sympathy and praise for the path opened by Kant's critical philosophy and yet he offers a clear criticism of Kant's failure to develop "critique" fully enough – to connect philosophy to history, to develop a historical critique, in short, to develop a comparative framework for philosophy. Kant's historical myopia is what leads Schlegel to claim that "Kant is in principle highly uncritical"[14] and that "philosophy must be critical but in a much higher sense than in Kant."[15] Recall that Schlegel's essay on Diotima and on the feminine characters of Greek poetry expanded his historical horizon to uncover new insights that were meant to shed light on how utterly unenlightened the present view of women was. Schlegel believed that to be fully (as opposed to half) critical, philosophers had to engage in wide-spanning historical investigations.

[13] Cf. *KFSA*, 18: 34, Nr. 163: "The critical method is at one and the same time philosophical and philological."
[14] *KFSA*, 18: 21, Nr. 35. Cf. *KFSA*, 18: 21, Nr. 36.
[15] *KFSA*, 19: 346, Nr. 296.

Schlegel's notion of critique opened his thought to a consideration of groups that had been neglected by Kant's critique. Far from being unphilosophical and politically irrelevant because of its push toward poetry, early German Romanticism, precisely because of its emphasis on poetry, became a potent political tool of social change. Emphasizing the connection between poetry and politics in early German Romanticism, Nicholas Saul writes:

> Whenever Romantic writers use the term "Poesie," it connotes this implicit critique of philosophy. In the end, poetry becomes for the Romantics a mythical entity. Their texts are not only to realise philosophy's project, but also to incarnate absolute poetry. In this sense poetry becomes a cult, and the cult of poetry comes to embody Germany's post-revolutionary answer to the French religion of reason. The abstract quality of some of these procedures should not mask their political status as a response to the Revolution. "Poesie," said Friedrich Schlegel, is a republican discourse.[16]

One way to unveil what Schlegel meant when he claimed that poetry is republican discourse is to take a close look at the political implications of his response to Kant's essay on perpetual peace. I turn now to a brief overview of Kant's essay, to provide context for Schlegel's conception of republican discourse.

3 Kant, Schlegel, and Democracy

The publication of Kant's *Toward Perpetual Peace* was occasioned by the peace treaty signed between Prussia and France on April 5, 1795. Kant opens with a grim, yet witty description:

> *Toward perpetual peace*
>
> It may be left undecided whether this satirical inscription on a certain Dutch innkeeper's signboard picturing a graveyard was to hold for human beings in general, or for heads of state in particular, who can never get enough of war, or only for philosophers, who dream that sweet dream. (*TPP*, 8: 343)

In the essay, Kant's goal is to provide a concrete political consideration of peace that is in keeping with his principle of right. The six preliminary articles provide a list of what is to be prohibited if enduring peace between states is to be achieved. Implicit in this list are certain premises from Kant's critical philosophy, his moral philosophy, and his philosophy of right. The definite articles develop the positive side of Kant's plan for the possibility and guarantee of peace. Here the six preliminary articles find their systematic unity in the answer to the question concerning what the a priori conditions of the possibility of perpetual peace are. This is a question concerning not only the theoretical possibility, but the historical realizability of the guarantee of perpetual peace.

[16] Saul 2003: 72.

In the *Idea for a Universal History from a Cosmopolitan Point of View* Kant claims that: "[T]he problem of the erection of a perfect civil constitution . . . is dependent on the problem of the lawful external relations among states and cannot be solved without [a solution to] the latter" (*UHC*, 8:24, seventh thesis).

Therefore, a theory of the republic must be built into a theory of the international order of right. Kersting observes that Kant makes an important contribution to political philosophy because he argues for the realization of the overcoming of the natural condition not only of individuals, but of each state.[17] The natural condition is one of independence from external law – a condition of lawless or senseless freedom (*gesetzlose Freiheit*). This is opposed to the state of right that is ordered by laws and rational freedom. Only in a republic does a state overcome its natural condition; only when all states of the world have overcome this natural condition can peace reign.[18] Until all states have become states of right, there will always be a threat of war and this threat can lead to an enduring arms race. Kant envisions and outlines a plan for peace that is based on a balance of right. This is possible only if all states are organized according to the principle of right. According to Kant, pure practical reason demands that we work for perpetual peace. Perpetual peace rests in turn upon the ideal of the republic.

Kant claims that the classification he gives of the forms of state (*civitas*) will help us to avoid the common confusion of the republican with the democratic constitution (Schlegel will point out that a relation between a constitution and the state is here presupposed, but never explicated). Kant never tells us why these are commonly confused. We can surmise a possible source of confusion stemming from the political transformations of the late 1700s. The American Revolution of 1776 and the French Revolution of 1789 called into question the tradition of one ruler standing above the power of the people, that is, the vertical structures of power were called into question, making way for a shift to a horizontal structure of political power, an architecture of power that does not place one person or group at the top of a ladder of power, but rather allows all groups to share the power equally, which is the model for democracy, and the view of power that fueled the American and French Revolutions. In the late 1700s, the idea and practice of a democratic republic became more attractive and the voice of the "people" became more powerful. The legitimacy of an enlightened despot such as Frederick the Great lost its firm grounding. Kant, however, continued to hold him in great esteem. In *What Is Enlightenment?* (1784) he calls the "Age of Enlightenment" the "Century of Frederick" (*PP*, 8: 40).

[17] Kersting 1992: 342–66. [18] Cf. *CJ*, 5: 432–3.

In *What Is Enlightenment?* Kant makes it clear that he does not place much faith in the power of the "people" to rule. In this essay, he insists upon the distinction between the public and private use of one's reason: there are many cases in which "argument is certainly not allowed – one must obey" (*PP*, 8: 37). The goal of enlightenment is the "release from one's *self-incurred* tutelage," a task, we are told, that women, that fair sex, consider very dangerous, as do the greater portion of mankind (*PP*, 8: 35; my emphasis). Kant does not consider the conditions of tutelage that may not be self-incurred, but are rather imposed by the existing structures of society. His project of enlightenment is aimed at transforming the individual, not the society. For Kant, a transformation of society amounts to anarchy, chaos, violent revolution. In *Toward Perpetual Peace*, Kant claims that he is providing a classification of the forms of state so that we can avoid confusing the republican and democratic forms of constitution; perhaps it is more accurate to read this characterization as an attempt to delegitimize democracy, condemning it to despotism.

According to Kant, the form of a state is divided according to its sovereign power (*forma imperi*), that is the number and kind of people who rule, or according to the mode of administration exercised over the people (*forma regiminis*), that is the way the state makes use of its power. There are three forms of sovereignty: autocracy, aristocracy, and democracy. These are characterized respectively as the power of the monarch, of the nobility, and of the people. There are only two forms of government: republican and despotic. These are based on the way a state makes use of its power; this in turn is based on the constitution, which is the act of the general will through which a multitude (*die Menge*) becomes a people (*Volk*).[19]

The issue of the administration of will is critical. Freedom involves following laws we have given ourselves; a person pursues freedom by being her own law-giver. When we are citizens of a state we must, however, submit to external laws: How can this be done without infringing upon our internal freedom? According to Kant, if the state is organized according to the rights of equality, independence, and political freedom, and if the structuring principle is a collectively universal will (the will of reason), then political freedom will not infringe upon internal freedom; legal duties will not conflict with moral

[19] This may not be the best translation of Kant's parenthetical clarification of what a constitution is. Kant writes that it is, *den Akt des allgemeinen Willens, wodurch die Menge ein Volk wird* (*AA*, 8: 352). Lewis White Beck translates this as "the act of the general will through which the many persons become one nation." Hans Reiss, however, translates this as "an act of the general will whereby the mass becomes a people," and Gregor translates as I have it above (*PP*, 324). A constitution is a unifying force, through which a collection of individuals becomes a unified group. It seems not unimportant to question whether we will call this group "a people" or "a nation." I think that for purposes of clarity, the German term *Volk* should be used instead of either of these translations.

duties – the two will be harmonized. The issue of the organization of the state for the prevention of war is the issue of how the general will of the people should be legislated. This is the problem of right: how the arrangement that establishes that the free actions of one individual can be reconciled with the freedom of the other in accordance with a universal law is to be attained. The universal principle of right establishes the condition of external freedom. The principle is the following: "Every action which by itself or by its maxim enables the freedom of each individual's will to coexist with the freedom of everyone else in accordance with a universal law is right" (*MM*, 6: 231).

Why doesn't democracy allow this? According to Kant, only a separation of executive power from the legislative power qualifies a form of government for inclusion in the class of republicanism. The public will must be administrated or executed by a will other than the public will, that is, by the ruler, but not as his own will; he must represent the will of the people. Schlegel criticizes Kant here for assuming that a division of power implies representation of the will of the people. One can easily imagine a case in which two wealthy landowners share power; one executes power, and the other legislates. According to Kant's weak criteria, we then have a republic. But we certainly do not necessarily have the representation of the will of the people. Neither the relation between the division of power nor the issue of just representation are adequately elucidated by Kant. He claims that a government must be representative, but a mere division of power does not insure this.

Kant also claims that it is logically impossible that one and the same person could be legislator and executor of his/her will. He writes:

> Every form of government which is not representative is, properly speaking, without form. The legislator can unite in one and the same person his function as legislative and as executor of his will just as little as the universal of the major premise in a syllogism can also be the subsumption of the particular under the universal in the minor. (*TPP*, 8: 352)

All dictators are counterexamples to this claim; this is not logically impossible as the analogy suggests. But the analogy does suggest something that is most revealing of Kant's view of power within a state; again the force of the doctrine of absolute sovereignty presents itself. The structure of government upon which Kant bases his classification is built upon an idea of power in which power comes from the top down, in a hierarchy: one in which the will of the people is subsumed by the laws of the ruler. Kant's idea of government structure can only lead to a state with a vertical structure of power. He claims, in fact, that the best form of republicanism is the form in which one rules over many. When one ruler represents the will of the people, we maintain order, as we do in a logical deduction. Only if we move from the "all" form, embodied in the ruler down to the "some" or "each" form, that is, to the people, do we preserve the essential feature of a republic, that is, a rule of law guaranteed by a constitution and the separation of legislative and executive powers, based upon the consent of the governed. The will of the people must not only be "represented" but must also be rationally and impartially executed. Democracy is anarchy, with "each" against "each" and no division of power possible. Democracy is despotic because it represents a horizontal structure of power, the power *of* the people, as opposed to the power *over* the people by a monarch or a group of aristocrats.

Despotism is "the autonomous execution by the state of laws which it has itself decreed" (*TPP*, 8: 96). In a democracy, everyone wishes to be master and because democracy establishes an executive power in which "all" decide for or even against one who does not agree – that is, "all" who are not quite all decide (a contradiction of the general will with itself and with freedom) – democracy is necessarily despotic (*TPP*, 8: 352). There are several problems with this "deduction": the most serious problem is that if Kant wants to claim that democracy and republicanism are mutually exclusive and bases this claim upon the fact that there exists within the structure of democracy the possibility of the struggle between the "one" and the "all," he has to show that this cannot be otherwise. Democracy can be despotic, but Kant has not shown that it *must* be. Schlegel, in reaction *against* Kant's view of democracy as necessarily despotic, attempts to show that republicanism must be democratic, and that democracy is *not* necessarily despotic.

4 Schlegel's Republican Discourse

Schlegel's critique of Kant's concept of republicanism, which is the subject of his "Essay on the Concept of Republicanism Occasioned by the Kantian Tract 'Perpetual Peace'" (*Versuch über den Begriff des Republikanismus veranlaßt durch die Kantische Schrift zum ewigen Frieden*) (1796) can be understood as an attempt to uncover some of the shortcomings of Kant's view of the Enlightenment and of Kant's generally dismissive view of democracy and the implications of that dismissive view for women. In a fragment from 1796–8, found in one of his many notebooks (First Epoch II), Schlegel tells us that, "A person can endure everything, even suffering, better than truth. One lives not to be happy, also not to fulfill one's duty, but to cultivate oneself" (Nr. 697).[20] As we have seen, *Bildung* is a theme that runs throughout Schlegel's work. Schlegel's aesthetic philosophy and the political critique performed by him in his "Essay on the Concept of Republicanism" – a critique that challenged Kant's view that democracy is necessarily despotic – takes

[20] Beiser 1996: 162.

shape against the backdrop of his view that human cultivation (*Bildung*) was central to the progress of society. And this *Bildung* needed human relationships of friendship and love, and a society that valued art. As Schlegel writes: "The only valid political fiction is that based on the law of equality: the will of the majority should be the surrogate of the general will. Republicanism is therefore necessarily democratic, and the unproven paradox that democracy is necessarily despotic cannot be correct" (*ECR*, 102). In this context, the fiction is the form of representation, and it is related to political power: "The power of the majority of the people, as an approximation to universality and as a surrogate of the general will, is the *political power*" (*ECR*, 104).[21]

We do well to keep in mind Schlegel's *Bildungs*-project and the value he placed on cultivation, while also considering how this project guided Schlegel's critique of Kant's essay. For if Schlegel is correct, that we live not to be happy or to fulfill our duty, but to cultivate ourselves (much of his philosophical work was carried out in this spirit of cultivation or *Bildung*), then it is with the notion of *Bildung*, I would like to suggest, that we find the guiding concept to understand Schlegel's political critique and the guiding force of much of the aesthetic and philosophical tasks he set for himself.

Schlegel begins his review with praise for the spirit of Kant's project in *Toward Perpetual Peace*. Schlegel opens his "Essay on the Concept of Republicanism" without a trace of the impudent spirit of his claims that Kant is not critical enough. In the opening lines we find the sort of praise of Kant we saw in Schlegel's letter to his brother, in which he declared that Kant's *Critique* was eternal. He writes:

> The spirit that breathes in the Kantian essay *Perpetual Peace* must benefit every friend of justice, and even our most distant progeny will admire in this monument the elevated frame of mind of the venerable sage. His bold and dignified discourse is unaffected and candid, and it is spiced with a biting wit and a clever spirit. It contains a rich abundance of fruitful ideas and new insights for politics, morals, and the history of humanity. For me, the opinion of the author concerning the nature of *republicanism*, and its relations to other kinds and conditions of the state, was especially interesting. The examination of it occasioned me to think through the subject anew. Hence arose the following remarks ... (*ECR*, 95)

While Schlegel is effusive about the "spirit" of Kant's *Toward Perpetual Peace*, the "letter" of the essay is another matter, and it is with the letter or the specific arguments that Schlegel begins his critique: a critique of Kant's definition and deduction of the concept of republicanism. As I discussed in Section 3, this deduction leads Kant to the conclusion that democracy is necessarily despotic. Schlegel reveals this to be an unsubstantiated paradox that cannot be right.

[21] Schlegel says this explicitly at *ECR*, 103.

According to Kant, the civil constitution of every state should be republican because only this type of constitution is based upon freedom, equality and the principle of dependence of all upon a single common legislation (note here that Kant does not follow the triad established by the French Revolution of freedom, equality, and fraternity) (*TPP*, 8: 350). Kant claims that the republican constitution is practically necessary because it is the only one that springs forth from the idea of the original contract. But what is the idea of the original contract grounded upon if not the principles of freedom and equality? If this is the case, then, claims Schlegel, Kant is caught in a circle. Moreover, Kant claims that "no definition of juridical [rightful] dependence [*rechtliche Abhängigkeit*] is needed, as this already lies in the concept of a state's constitution as such" (*TPP*, 8: 350n. 2). But if juridical dependence is already contained in the concept of a civil constitution then it cannot be a characteristic of the republican constitution. In light of these problems, Schlegel suggests that the practical necessity of political freedom and equality must be deduced from another, "higher position." Schlegel's point is that the concept of a republican constitution is not exhausted by the characteristics of freedom and equality as Kant has presented them. An interesting parallel is found in the *Oldest Systematic Program of German Idealism*. The author writes that:

> Only that which is the object of *freedom* is called *idea*. We must therefore go beyond the state! – Because every state must treat free human beings like mechanical works; and it should not do that; therefore it should *cease*. You see for yourself that here all the ideas, that of eternal peace, etc., are merely *subordinate* ideas of a higher idea. At the same time I want to set forth the principles for a *history of the human race* here and expose the whole miserable human work of state, constitution, government, legislature – down to the skin. (*OSP*, 161–2)

Tendencies toward strands of anarchism in Romantic thought notwithstanding, it is not Schlegel's goal to destroy the state. Schlegel *does* want to subordinate Kant's postulate that all constitutions must be republican to a higher principle, namely to the political imperative that we should strive for the establishment of a community of humanity (*Gemeinschaft der Menschheit*).

Schlegel claims that Kant's analysis of republicanism is limited. According to Schlegel, when we speak of freedom as manifested in the state, we are speaking of a progression with a beginning, a middle, and an end. Kant remains at the beginning of this progression, and the conclusions he reaches concerning the nature of republicanism reflect this short-sightedness. Schlegel first draws our attention to the limitations of Kant's concept of external (juridical or rightful) freedom (*rechtliche Freiheit*). Kant claims that to understand external freedom to be the privilege (or warrant) "of doing anything one wills so long as he does not injure [or does no injustice to] another" is an empty tautology. Properly understood, juridical or rightful freedom is the privilege (or warrant) "to lend obedience to no external laws except those to which

I could have given consent" (*ECR*, 96–7). According to Schlegel, these claims are only partially right. For Schlegel, freedom is an idea that can only be actualized in a process of infinite approximation; it is an unfolding process and not a static concept. In the first moment of this progression, freedom is considered in terms of the individual within a state with only the properties of reason available to make the concept of external freedom determinate. In the first moment of this progression, external freedom should be understood in terms of lending obedience to no external laws except those to which one could have given one's consent. But we must go beyond this if we are to come closer to the ideal of freedom. In the second moment, we have a concept of freedom that involves our direct relation to others, and not merely to the laws that connect us to them indirectly. In the second moment, we overcome the differences that exist between citizens concerning rights and have a society in which the only differences in rights are those that the majority has chosen; in this moment the idea of freedom considered as the privilege to do something so long as it does no harm to another is not an empty tautology, for in this moment, human needs and interests are essential to the concept of freedom. In the second moment, we are dealing with a historical concept of freedom. In the third or final moment, we achieve an absolute equality of rights and obligations (*Verbindlichkeiten*) amongst citizens; here all structures of domination (*Herrschaft*) and dependence are overcome: solidarity is absolute; the individual wills freely endeavor to satisfy each other's needs without governance of external authority.[22] This final moment is unrealizable, it serves as the ideal to which all societies should strive. The second moment, however, is realizable; it is the democratic moment.

Paul Kluckhohn defends the thesis that the Romantic concept of the state rests upon the concepts of personality and community (*Persönlichkeit* and *Gemeinschaft*).[23] Beiser makes a similar point in the introduction to his volume on the political writings of the German Romantics, emphasizing the organic conception of the state developed by the Romantics to solve the problems of the tension between absolutism and liberalism, which Beiser describes as forces that "undermined a differentiated society for the sake of centralized authority."[24] He writes: "The romantic critique of the liberal and absolutist traditions then left them with an apparently irresolvable problem. If the absolutist underestimated the value of liberty, and if the liberal underrated the need for community, then it was necessary to reconcile two seemingly irreconcilable ideals: individual liberty and community."[25] The Romantic embrace of community and the development of the Romantics' concept of an organic state marks an important shift from the focus on the individual and

[22] Only in this moment does the state become superfluous, for all power structures are overcome.
[23] Kluckhohn 1925. [24] Beiser 1996: xxvi. [25] Beiser 1996: xxvi.

the relation between the individual and the state that guides Kant's political writings.

Schlegel's view of freedom as an idea that can only be actualized in a process of infinite approximation puts him in a position to uncover the problems with Kant's characterization of democracy as despotic. Schlegel begins with the premise that the realization of the ideal of political freedom is an infinite progress with a beginning, middle, and unrealizable (asymptotic) end. The problem of the state is that there is a gulf between the individual will of each citizen and the universal or general will of the "people." This insurmountable gap cannot be crossed except by some kind of *salto mortale* or by means of a fiction, a surrogate for the universal will that we can locate in history. Schlegel turns to the majority as the surrogate of the universal or general will. Instead of taking a leap of faith, the majority allows us to move from individual wills to the universal will via a process of infinite approximation. If one person presumes to represent the general will or if a group of nobles does, this process of approximation ceases. A political system should be continually evolving, moving toward a state in which the general will and the will of the individual become one and the same; this occurs if we take the empirical majority as the surrogate for the universal or general will and develop a system of representation (power to vote) that allows each citizen to participate in this process of approximation. Schlegel claims that though it may be the case that some voices carry more political weight, so that in some cases votes could be determined not by number but by weight (the degree to which a given individual approximates the general will), this kind of inequality cannot be presupposed, but must be demonstrated. Kant presupposes it. We cannot, without a demonstration, presuppose that certain groups – Schlegel mentions women and the poor – remain outside the realm of political decision-making (Kant holds that only property owners can vote, therefore, the power of indirect representation is not equally accessible to all).

To include more individuals in the *civitas* is Schlegel's goal; his model is one that moves toward inclusiveness in the public sphere. Kant's model is one in which the majority is a political null (*politische Null*), with the result that the majority is treated as a thing (*Sache*) rather than a person. Schlegel shows that the arguments Kant uses in his deduction of republicanism bring him into conflict with the categorical imperative. We have, then, precisely that conflict that a republic is supposed to prevent, a conflict between political and moral duties. Moreover, we have none of the values needed for social change that would help subjugated women, for example, and other groups for whom tutelage was not self-incurred and who were, as a matter of law, excluded from full participation in society. By now we are painfully aware of the results of failing to include all humans under the protective shield of humanity: unjust exclusions of certain groups of humans, unjust distributions of opportunities and power in society, are just a few of the terrible consequences of this failure. Schlegel's essays, novels, fragments, and his Romantic blending of disciplines created a republican discourse that was and remains an important tool for the project of creating a just, inclusive society.

11 The Limits of State Action
Humboldt, Dalberg, and Perfectionism after Kant

Douglas Moggach

1 Introduction

Current research depicts the early German idealists as advocates of sweeping programs of cultural and political reform, introducing new conceptions of freedom, personhood, and community.[1] For all their innovative features, however, these programs have deep roots in the earlier thought of the German Enlightenment. Political theories inspired by Kant emerge through a long process of engagement with the heritage of Leibniz, represented especially by Christian Wolff and his school.[2] In the course of these contestations, two conflicting positions on the nature and aims of the state come to be articulated. On the one hand, Wolff and his followers develop a comprehensive theory of political perfectionism, according to which the state ought authoritatively to prescribe a substantive vision of the good life for its subjects. The function of the state, according to these theorists, is actively to promote the happiness or thriving of its members, including the satisfaction of their material needs, but also the fulfillment of the putative higher, intellectual and spiritual, requisites of human nature. The state is to be the agent of a comprehensive vision of the human good, to be achieved by wide-ranging interventions in the activities of its members. On the other hand, theorists who take their lead from Kant contend that the state ought instead to leave the quest for felicity to individual initiatives, and ought to limit its scope to the preservation of internal and external security and the protection of rights, though these are conceived in various ways, more or less expansively or restrictively. The essence of the diverse Kantian programs formulated in this process is the defense of the principle of spontaneous, self-determining activity, and the derivation of spheres of rightful action that respect this principle. The state is to be the vehicle of freedom. The effect of this shift in orientation is

The author acknowledges the support of the Social Sciences and Humanities Research Council of Canada for this project. He expresses his thanks to Dr. Birsen Filip for ongoing research assistance.

[1] Jaeschke 1990: 2. [2] Cassirer [1917] 2001.

to divest politics of its older perfectionist aims in the pursuit of a particular conception of the human good.

These debates in the German Enlightenment are thus activated by the tension between the contending political aims of perfection and freedom. And yet these two objectives are not mutually exclusive but can be combined in various ways. Therein lie the genius, and the variety, implicit in these arguments. The central claim to be developed here is that a renewal of perfectionist ethics is not precluded, even after Kant. This renewal occurs not as an extraneous development, but through the efforts of committed Kantians themselves, once the ethical and political goal to be promoted is conceived in a fundamentally different way: not as the political prescription of the good life (along with the paternalistic implications of this view that Kant cogently decried), but rather as the institutional and intersubjective conditions for the exercise of freedom itself. Furthering, consolidating, and extending the possibility of free self-determination, and not any given substantive end, define the objective of post-Kantian perfectionism.[3] The aim is to perfect the sphere of rights and of rightful interactions, and to eliminate obstacles to their exercise. Here we cannot analyze closely the systematic issues raised in this transition, nor canvass all the available options. The intent is rather to examine a particular moment in the evolution of the post-Kantian perfectionist approach. Two major interlocutors will be introduced, one from the school of Wolff, the other inspired by Kant. Their thought will be situated in the context of a broader (but far from exhaustive) range of theoretical contributions, which experiment with various combinations of freedom and perfection. This contextualization clarifies both the sources and specific usages of concepts deployed in the particular debate on which we focus, as well as alternate positions against which our two central protagonists will define their own stances. The confrontation between the two positions that we will describe here clearly exposes distinctions between pre-Kantian and post-Kantian versions of perfectionist ethics and their political applications, while also revealing significant differences within each respective school.[4]

2 The Protagonists: Humboldt and Dalberg

A particularly illuminating moment in the confrontation between the old and the new perfectionism occurs in the debate, in 1792–4, between two friends and associates within the circle of the playwright, historian, and philosopher Friedrich Schiller (1759–1805), namely Wilhelm von Humboldt (1767–1835)

[3] Moggach, Mooren, and Quante 2020.

[4] The distinction here is conceptual, not chronological. Kant's canonical position is fully defined only in 1797 (*MM*, 6: 243–493).

and Karl von Dalberg (1744–1817). This debate, concerning the nature and limits of the state and the extent of its legitimate role in promoting the welfare of its subjects, represents a confrontation between one branch of the Kantian school, strenuously occupied in working out the implications of Kantian morality for political life, and advocates of the school of Leibniz (1646–1716) and Christian Wolff (1679–1754). The latter approach had long been dominant in German intellectual life, but was now experiencing serious rifts and inner tensions, and was losing its primacy in theoretical and practical philosophy. Humboldt and Dalberg differ sharply at the normative level, the latter advocating a strongly interventionist state, the former seeking to circumscribe the scope of rightful political action; and while they also diverge in their respective meta-ethical views (their overall theoretical conceptions about persons and their actions), they nevertheless significantly share common sources in Leibniz. Each theorist appropriates Leibniz in a distinctive way, and utilizes the resources he provides in defense of a contrasting normative account of the extent and purposes of politics. The persistence of the Leibnizian heritage is a key to deciphering the complexities of post-Kantian political thought.

Prussian censorship regulations prevented Humboldt from publishing in its entirety his early text, *Ideen zu einem Versuch, die Grenzen der Wirksamkeit des Staates zu bestimmen* (*Ideas for an Attempt to Determine the Limits of the Effectiveness of the State*; hereafter *The Limits of State Action*). However, his friend Schiller succeeded in inserting chapter II and part of chapter III into his journal *Neue Thalia* in 1792; while chapters V, VI, and VIII also appeared in that year in the *Berlinische Monatsschrift*.[5] The complete German edition was prepared posthumously by Humboldt's brother Alexander (1769–1859), and published in 1852.[6] An English translation appeared in 1854 under the title *The Sphere and Duties of Government*.[7] The text was appreciatively cited by John Stuart Mill in *On Liberty*, and in his *Autobiography*.[8] In making Humboldt's central ideas his own and securing their wide dissemination among Anglophone readers, Mill helped to guarantee Humboldt's place in the history of developmental liberalism.[9] Recent research has shown the depths of the young Humboldt's opposition to the repressive cultural policies pursued by the Prussian regime, especially under the minister Johann Christoph von Wöllner (1732–1800), who had introduced stringent regulatory and coercive measures to ensure religious conformity in universities and other public institutions.[10] It is opposition to these retrograde policies, as well as to the absolutist state in

5 Burrow 1969: xvii. 6 Humboldt 1851; Humboldt 1969. 7 Humboldt 1854.

8 Mill [1859] 1991: 64; Mill [1873] 1960: 179.

9 Taylor 1997: 25–54, contrasts developmental or perfectionist liberalism with procedural liberalism. The former focuses on the conditions of human thriving, the latter on institutional checks upon interference in individual activities.

10 Schui 2013: 178–85.

general, that Humboldt articulates in *The Limits of State Action*, defending freedom of thought and expression, and promoting a vigorous cultural flowering which, he contends, such untrammeled freedom would initiate. Although he would later revise his conclusions on some of these subjects, as is evidenced by his leading role in the Prussian reform movement and in the promotion of public education (an aim expressly disavowed in 1792), our attention here is confined to his early text on the limits of the political realm.[11] The particular implications that he draws from his reading of Kant, and his underlying commitment to a Leibnizian sense of persons and their activity, mark out Humboldt's position as distinctive within the Kantian school.

Even in its initial truncated form, Humboldt's ideas proved controversial. The publication of parts of *The Limits of State Action* provoked an almost immediate critical reply from an advocate of much broader interventionist powers for the state from Karl von Dalberg's (anon.) *Von den wahren Grenzen der Wirksamkeit des Staats in Beziehung auf seine Mitglieder* (*On the True Limits of the Effectiveness of the State in Relation to Its Members*).[12] Both Dalberg and Humboldt frequented Schiller's circle in Jena, and Dalberg's critique presupposes familiarity with Humboldt's entire text, not only with what was then publicly available. Dalberg himself encouraged the young Humboldt to set down his thoughts about the limits of permissible state action.[13] He then composed his own response, inspired by the works of Christian Wolff. In retaining a strongly reformist orientation, Dalberg's Wolffianism is distinct from that of other contemporary offshoots, such as the staunchly conservative Historical School of Law, an issue to which we shall return.

Dalberg was the scion of a prominent aristocratic lineage in the Holy Roman Empire, so prominent indeed that a member of the family customarily officiated at imperial coronations.[14] While authoring a number of theoretical texts, Dalberg enjoyed a successful and varied ecclesiastical and political career.[15] Among other distinctions, he served as co-adjutor Bishop of Mainz (1787), as the last *Reichskanzler* (1802–6) of the Empire before its dissolution by Napoleon, and subsequently as prince-primate of the Confederation of the Rhine (1806–13). As the presiding officer of the *Rheinbund*, he was

[11] Beiser 2011: 167–213, on Humboldt's "Protean" changes of position.

[12] Dalberg (anon.) 1793/4, reproduced in Leroux 1932a: 45–54. Attribution of this anonymous text to Dalberg was made by his first biographer, August Krämer, in 1821 (cited in Leroux 1932a: 1); and his authorship is reaffirmed in the detailed study by Beaulieu-Marconnay 1879: 168–200. Grounds for secure attribution are laid out by Leroux 1932a: 2–3.

[13] Gleichen-Russwurm n.d.: 10.

[14] Hill 2011: 9, in a biography of Dalberg's famous nephew, John Emerich Dalberg Acton, First Baron Acton (1834–1902).

[15] Among other texts, Dalberg 1791.

responsible for introducing and carrying out wide-ranging Napoleonic reforms in those territories.[16] Clearly, Dalberg identified Napoleon as an enlightened despot whose role had been foreshadowed in his critique of Humboldt in 1793/4, and whose salutary interventions would promote the happiness and unity of his subjects. For his collaboration with the French, Dalberg himself earned the opprobrium of later German nationalist thinkers.[17] In the 1790s, as an active participant in the Schiller circle, he illustrates through his amicable but fundamental critique of Humboldt the complex trajectories of German political thought at the origins of idealism.

3 The Wolffian School: Enlightened Absolutism and Political Perfection

Beyond its immediate instigation in his adverse reaction to the Wöllner edicts, Humboldt's polemic against the interventionist state has a specific target: the model of enlightened absolutism defended by Christian Wolff. According to the Wolffian school, predominant throughout much of the German Enlightenment, the aim of the state is to promote the perfection of its subjects.[18] In accord with modern European conceptions of natural law, Wolff describes an original, apolitical state of nature as a primitive community without private property, from which the state derives by means of a contract. What is peculiar to Wolff is the view that the original condition is characterized not by the constant threat of conflict and violent death, as in Hobbes, but by mental and physical stagnation, and the inability to cultivate latent capacities for self-improvement and cooperation. He argues for the moral necessity of leaving this torpid natural state in order to develop our higher powers as persons and as contributors to the collective good. Political society thus arises through a social compact, whose aim is not mere self-preservation, but the perfection of our faculties in collaboration with others.[19] In the absence of intelligent political stimulus and oversight, human capacities remain dormant or inefficacious: individuals and households cannot independently secure the conditions of their own sustained thriving.[20] The state is to initiate, coordinate, and direct the activities of its members toward a common goal. Reminiscent of Aristotelian *eudaimonia*, perfection for Wolff, as the *telos* of politics, has physical, intellectual, and spiritual dimensions. In its physical aspects, it involves a number of natural-law duties, notably to labor, and legitimate claims to the preconditions of labor: he stresses the provision, under the aegis

[16] Boyle 2000: 32–3; Völker 2006: 57–208.
[17] Weigend-Abendroth 1980. Another assessment is offered by Färber 1995.
[18] On perfection, Wolff [1754] 1969: 43, 106–8; Wolff [1758] 1988: 16, 41.
[19] Wolff [1754] 1969: 186–9; Wolff [1758] 1988: 88–9. [20] Wolff [1754] 1969: 972.

of the state, of adequate food, housing, and living conditions.[21] Wolffian perfection has a marked material, economic, and demographic content. His thought has affinities with contemporary doctrines of political economy designated as cameralism, an alternative to the mercantilist policies pursued by those centralized European states that could draw on colonies for materials and markets.[22] In the absence of external outlets, the state, for cameralists and for Wolff, is required to mobilize available natural resources and to foster their use by skilled populations: hence, in conjunction with material well-being, Wolff prescribes that education, training, and intellectual cultivation are among the functions of the enlightened state. In less clearly defined ways, Wolff would also have the state solicitously oversee the spiritual thriving of its members, though early in his career his defense of the possibility of a non-ecclesiastical, purely rationalistic ethic led to a serious embroilment with German Pietists, and his temporary exile from Prussia.[23]

The highly interventionist order that Wolff promotes has certain limits, which depend not on an idea of individual rights retained against the state,[24] but on pragmatic considerations, such as the fiscal interests of government and population. He argues that local forms of redress of social ills, being attuned to specific needs and circumstances, are often more efficacious than standardized, central interventions, and hence more conducive to the general interest in progress.[25] He thus heralds what has been described in modern European usage as the principle of subsidiarity,[26] or the proximity of administrative agencies to the source of the problem addressed. But Wolff argues consistently from likely consequences,[27] not from an idea of fundamental right, as Kantians will later do.

The meta-ethical basis of Wolff's normative platform lies in a particular appropriation and reformulation of Leibniz. He broadly follows Leibniz in equating happiness and perfection, giving Aristotelian *eudaimonia* a particular Leibnizian inflection by focusing on activity as constant mobilization and application of forces, but he significantly modifies how these forces operate. In private correspondence to Wolff, Leibniz had outlined his doctrine of perfection as the unity of unity and multiplicity.[28] Elaborating here and elsewhere,[29] Leibniz explained that such an articulated unity occurs when each constitutive element achieves its full and individualized expression, while

[21] Wolff [1754] 1969: 112–16; Wolff [1758] 1988: 32, 36–9. See also Wolff [1721] 1971: 224.
[22] Tribe 1988; Backhaus 1998. [23] Schneewind 1998: 442–4. [24] Klippel 1998: 81.
[25] Wolff [1721] 1971: 383–5. [26] Backhaus 2001. [27] Schneewind 1998: 432–44.
[28] Leibniz to Wolff, May 18, 1715, in Leibniz 1887: Bd. III, 233–4, cited and translated in Beiser 2009: 35 n. 16: "Perfection is the harmony of things, that is, the state of agreement or identity in variety."
[29] Leibniz 1969: 167: "By perfection I mean every simple quality which is positive and absolute, or which expresses whatever it expresses without any limits."

being harmonized and balanced by a singular directive principle, which endows the whole with form and coherence. In the subsequent development of Leibnizian thought, the two dimensions of perfection come to be distinguished more clearly: an absolute or qualitative notion as the achievement of implicit potential, which remains closer to the Aristotelian position, and a relative or quantitative notion of unifying difference.[30] The stress on the multiplicity of interests and perspectives, and the ways in which it can be rendered compatible with social unity, become central issues in the philosophical and political debates of the later eighteenth century, and beyond.[31] Unlike the position adopted by Humboldt, it is not clear that Wolff values diversity in its own right. His emphasis is on the achievement of social unity, and the awakening of dormant potentialities, thus on perfection in the absolute sense.

Wolff's principal departure from Leibniz consists in the insistence that the undirected, spontaneous actions of particular subjects are not conducive to an order of maximal happiness, either for the individual or for the collectivity.[32] Leibniz had developed a dynamic account of the individual (or monad) as the source of self-directed change, in constant transition through states of awareness and perception, whereby its inner content is progressively revealed. This sequence is governed by a unique internal law of development, distinct for every self.[33] Spontaneity is the capacity of subjects to be the self-initiating cause of change, enacting inner imperatives, and not simply determined by external natural causality, as Enlightenment materialism holds. The perfection of the monadic order is constituted by this ceaseless exposition of implicit properties, and by the irreplicable character of each agent, its complete distinctiveness, making its specific contribution to the universe of striving.

From his early work onwards, Wolff introduces a significant revision, seeking to reconcile two conflicting theories of force and motion, Leibnizian spontaneity and Newtonian inertia.[34] For Wolff, the initial impetus for the motion of a body (or a substance) derives from an external force, not from self-initiation; once activated, motion continues unless blocked or hindered by another force. In its application to political theory, this kinetic function is precisely the role that Wolff attributes to the state: to overcome the stagnation of the natural condition of mankind, to awaken its latent possibilities, and then to direct the ensuing activities of subjects in ways that avoid collisions and maximize beneficial results. Spontaneity is not denied, in that subjects' activities follow teleological principles and not merely mechanical laws, but it is

[30] Hernández Marcos 2020. [31] Moggach, Mooren, and Quante 2020.

[32] Wolff [1721] 1971: 264.

[33] *Leibniz-Thomasius* (Leibniz 1993: 55–117); Leibniz [1720] 1991: esp. section 11–13; Rutherford 2005: 156–80.

[34] Wolff [1723] 2010.

now linked to an external, kinetic cause. This necessity for an outside stimulus and continuous harmonization of spontaneous actions is the key Wolffian idea. Hence arises the normative requirement for individuals to relinquish rights enjoyed in the natural condition insofar as these are inimical to personal and social betterment; contrary to Locke, such primitive rights are not retained against the state as limits on its power.[35] This might be taken to suggest a Hobbesian conception of the renunciation of original rights. However, unlike Hobbes, these original rights must be renounced in the interests of *perfection*, both individual and collective, and not of *security*.[36] Wolff thus defends a tutelary state, which, for all its positive intentions, becomes the target of Kant's denunciation as the greatest despotism: by conceiving happiness rather than freedom as its aim, it reduces its subjects to the status of dependent minors, rather than recognizing them as autonomous agents (*TP*, 8: 290–2).[37] In answer to Kant's critique, the idea of right must be vindicated anew.

4 Kantian Responses

Wilhelm von Humboldt was among the participants in such a vindication. The problem confronted in the *Limits of State Action* is that posed by the publication in 1785 of Kant's *Groundwork of the Metaphysics of Morals*, the injunction never to treat rational beings as merely means, but always as ends in themselves. In this text, Kant also outlines a critique of Leibniz's perfectionist ethical system, a system Wolff developed into a defense of enlightened absolutist politics. Though the explicit condemnation of Wolff's position as particularly noxious would await Kant's "Theory and Practice" of 1793 (*TP*, 8: 290–2), its meta-ethical foundations had already been undermined in the 1785 text, where Kant rejects perfectionist doctrines under the rubric of rational heteronomy (*CPrR*, 5: 33–42; *GW*, 4: 441). Accounts such as Leibniz's and Wolff's posit an order of perfection independent of, and prior to, the moral wills of subjects. In such accounts, the will determines itself teleologically in respect to an external end to be attained, rather than deontologically, through inner self-legislation and prescription of unconditional maxims. Leibniz's rationally heteronomous ethical system differs from the empirical heteronomy of Hobbes or the French materialists, because it is not based on gratifying sensuous impulses, but on contributing to the overall perfection of the cosmological order. But Kant further distinguishes Leibniz's system from his own deontological position because the former orients itself to the production of an extrinsic state of affairs, rather than to the quality of the moral will (*GW*, 4: 441).

[35] Locke [1690] 1980: esp. chs. 2, 3, 8. [36] Klippel 1998: 81.
[37] On the Kant–Wolff relation, see Grapotte and Prunea-Bretonnet 2011.

Both Kant's repudiation of perfectionism, and his moral rule prohibiting instrumental treatment of other human beings, posed a challenge to members of the Kantian school, who were anticipating the elaboration of a properly critical political theory: if a political order rests necessarily on the possibility of coercion, and if coercion of a moral being is ethically reprehensible, how is a social order possible? Are there any grounds on which some forms of coercion could be deemed legitimate? The young jurist Gottlieb Hufeland (1760–1817) was among the first to intervene.[38] Combining Kantian and Leibnizian perspectives, he justified the coercion of individuals by juridical authorities on the grounds of social perfection, in its first, absolute sense, as fulfillment of potentiality. The punishment of transgressors by the responsible guardians of public security was a necessary condition for the maximal development of all the members of the political community.[39] Hufeland, as Kant and other critics like K. L. Reinhold (1757–1823) immediately recognized, produced an unstable combination of deontological and teleological ethical principles (*BKP*). Hufeland conflates right and morality, or rights and duties, giving the claims of right an unconditional, peremptory status, so that the possession of a right would imply its obligatory exercise. In his review of Hufeland, Kant himself resists this interpretation (*PP*, 8: 127–130), anticipating a distinction fully elaborated only a decade later in the *Metaphysics of Morals* (*MM*, 4: 385–463). Here Kant roots the necessity for a sphere of right in the moral law, while maintaining that the exercise of any specific right is never a matter of duty. The existence of a juridical space for the spontaneous pursuit of personal ends is a demand of pure practical reason. But, since rights concern actions only in their external aspect, and not in their motivating maxims, they can in individual instances be subject to pragmatic constraints. It may be that his response to Hufeland sparks Kant's further reflection on this issue. Secondly, Hufeland wishes the principle of right to be categorical, thus binding in itself, without regard to its empirical consequences; but he offers a teleological justification of this principle through its desired pragmatic outcome in social harmony and progress. In his contribution to this debate, Reinhold, distinguishing material and formal principles of right, argued that a Kantian juridical order could not be based on Hufeland's consequentialist and perfectionist foundations. The only possible justification of political coercion would be its elimination of obstacles to the *freedom* of others, not its enhancement of their moral capacities or material satisfactions (*BKP*, 445–60). The premise of Humboldt's argument is announced in Reinhold's critique of Hufeland.

[38] Rohls 2004: 41, n. 121; 49. [39] Hufeland 1785.

5 Schiller's Contribution

The early stages of the German debate on the state are conducted in the name of the absolute concept of perfection, the full realization of implicit content, which Hufeland had invoked as the basis for legitimate coercion. In its subsequent development, in Schiller and Humboldt, the absolute concept is depoliticized; it remains a moral goal, but one that ought to be posed by individuals for themselves, without state sponsorship. The relative concept of perfection, the unification of the manifold, retains however its political relevance as a directive ideal. The task of the state is to sustain the conditions for diversity, and thus for untrammeled expression; and social unity is to be achieved in free mutual accord, and not imposed from above. The inflection of Kantian political debates toward the problem of diversity may be due to the influence of Friedrich Schiller, though the publication of his own views occurs in parallel with the Humboldt–Dalberg controversy. Some of his ideas on forms of unity, and the specific disparities between differentiated modern and homogeneous ancient societies, were already in circulation,[40] but his fullest account of modern diversity is reserved for his *Aesthetic Education* text (*AEM*), which postdates Humboldt's intervention. It is clear, however, that in 1792–4, Schiller focuses on the concept of *relative* perfection, the unity of unity and multiplicity. He seeks to attain a unity compatible with difference, or a harmony without uniformity.[41] His starting point is the recognition of distinct and opposing interests in modern society, but he seeks a possible compatibility or mutual adjustment among them; he seeks a universal interest, a commonality of purpose, not through imposition from above, as in Wolff, but by individual effort and virtue. Schiller's politics are attuned to the problem of difference and its accommodation.[42]

Together with other German idealists like Fichte, Schiller understands modernity as characterized by a tension between difference and unity. Modern life appears as a culture of diremption or separation, marked by deeply opposing interests; but it also contains a new emancipatory potential. Having discarded traditional relations and institutions, it now offers possibilities for a renewal of social and political life, based on republican virtue.[43] The emergent division of labor in manufacturing and trade partakes of the same dialectic of constriction and liberation (*AEM*, Letter VI). While the growing specialization of labor is restrictive for individuals, whose repetitive and enervating tasks render them incapable of exercising a broad range of skills, it represents a necessary historical development for humanity, massively expanding

[40] For example, *DGG*, 163–9. See Chytry 1989: 92–103.
[41] Wilkinson and Willoughby 1967: lxxxviii. [42] Moggach 2008.
[43] Beiser 2005: 124–5, 163–4.

cumulative productive forces and knowledge (*AEM*, Letter VI). Yet this tragic recognition contains the possibility of cathartic resolution, not in romantic nostalgia for irretrievable forms of social life, but in a redefined sense of community: an aesthetic political state of harmonized life-conditions, reposing on the virtue of its members, their aesthetic self-limitation, and freely undertaken mutual adjustment of interests (*AEM*, Letters XIV, XVI). This aesthetic-republican state is an idea in the Kantian sense, an object of permanent striving; it is not a pre-established harmony, but an accord created and sustained by conscious effort.

In contrast to this ideal stand two other forms of political association. One, the dynamic or mechanical state, is characterized by the collision of rights (*AEM*, Letter XXVII). Here opposing interests, shaped largely by the modern division of labor, are litigiously affirmed, and cannot be reconciled except by external constraint. Such an association of egoists is not a genuine unity but an aggregate, the political expression of the culture of diremption under the primacy of narrow private interest; perhaps critique of emergent utilitarianism as the politics of self-interest is intended here. A second unacceptable alternative is the Wolffian tutelary state, which seeks to secure perfection through constraint rather than consent. It thus cuts perfection off from its sources in freedom. The unity it effects is brittle and lifeless, because it is not animated by an internal energy, but juxtaposed from without (*AEM*, Letter XVI). As Schiller puts it, the perfect may achieve its complete concept, but only in the beautiful is form determined by inner essence, "The perfect, represented with freedom, is transformed directly into the beautiful" (*LK*, 169; translation modified). If perfection remains a goal for the political community, Schiller contends that it must result from an inner-directed source, that it must be the manifestation of the freedom of subjects seeking accord and mutual accommodation. Schiller's contribution is to acknowledge modern diversity, and to make its recognition the central political task.

6 Humboldt's Synthesis

Wilhelm von Humboldt's own approach to politics shares with Schiller this recognition and affirmation of diversity. It is, moreover, in a Reinholdian spirit that Humboldt writes: justifiable coercion must contribute to freedom, not perfection. He clearly differentiates concepts that Hufeland had conflated. Humboldt continues to draw on both Kant and Leibniz, but he combines these sources in a distinct synthesis. Humboldt stresses the uniqueness and irreducibility of each subject's perspective on the world, rather than the overall perfection of the system. For Hufeland, systemic perfection remains the purview of the state; for Humboldt systemic perfection is not to be brought about by political interference, but is uniquely the result of spontaneous individual activity.[44] Humboldt's originality lies both in his radical normative anti-interventionism, and in his theoretical conception of personhood, which demonstrates a Leibnizian provenance.

Humboldt reads the Kantian critique of Wolffian perfectionism as raising a categorical prohibition against state intervention in the activities of its members, except to protect individual rights and property. Thus precluded are political prescriptions of religious practices and beliefs, and state economic undertakings to stimulate trade and production or to redistribute resources, such as had been promoted by cameralism. The young Humboldt even denounces the prospect of national, state-sponsored systems of education, as inducing conformity and blind compliance. The idea of right is to be purged of any welfare implications. The state ought not to concern itself with its citizens' happiness, but only with the preservation of their proprietary and civil rights. In this regard, economic inequalities are irrelevant to right. Kant too will assert in his "Theory and Practice" of 1793 that political equality does not imply economic equality (*TP*, 8: 290–6). Hence Humboldt's Kantian anti-interventionism is not an entirely implausible interpretation, but it is far from exhaustive, and will soon be vigorously contested by Fichte in *The Closed Commercial State*. Humboldt formulates an early version of the liberal minimal state that was to attain prominence in the nineteenth century.[45] State provision of security enables the spontaneous activities of individuals to occur with minimum external interference, and with maximum conformity to the intentions of their originators. On Humboldt's reading, right is a condition for spontaneous freedom or independent goal-setting by individuals, who are to act with minimal constraint within their own designated spheres, and in pursuit of their own private conceptions of happiness. These choices ought not to be coerced or homogenized by the state, which is to uphold the juridical order, but not to intrude into it.

If Humboldt mounts a case against Wolffian interventionism in its material dimensions as promoter of social welfare, he also offers a sustained critique of its intellectual and spiritual aspects. On Humboldt's reading, right is a condition not only for the freedom and independence of individuals, but of their moral perfection and virtue itself.[46] He argues that statist promotion of perfection is necessarily misconceived. Individual spontaneity, where unconstrained by external forces, is most conducive to the optimal development of the powers and capacities of each person, and of all persons collectively. Only on the condition of rightful interaction can individuals realize their true potential, and express their unique properties and perspectives. Perfection remains a moral goal, but it must be self-induced and self-directed: in

[44] Humboldt 1969: 32. [45] See, for example, Mack and Gaus 2004: 115–30.
[46] Humboldt 1969: 10, 32, 48.

opposition to Wolff, Humboldt contends that perfection is the result of freedom, never of tutelage.

Humboldt's account is premised on the idea that freedom is the key to the two dimensions of Leibnizian perfection. "Freedom is the first and indispensable condition" to achieve both the "infinite potentialities" of one's capacities, and also the "richest diversity."[47] Such perfection is open-ended: it describes a process, and not a final result. The achievement of perfection is described as a limitless, infinite process.[48] "There is no point at which perfectibility reaches its ultimate aim or exhausts its measure; it has the energy of living power and life grows through living."[49]

First, as realization, perfection for Humboldt entails perpetual activity, exploring and expressing the unique set of possibilities possessed by each self. "The highest ideal, therefore, of the co-existence of human beings, seems to me to consist in a union in which each strives to develop himself from his own inmost nature, and for his own sake."[50] Liberty entails "the possibility of a various and indefinite activity."[51] He stresses the vital importance of inner causation, not of mere imitation or external pressure, in the initiation of action.[52] Such spontaneous unfolding of one's distinctive, implicit powers must be allowed the broadest possible scope consistent with the freedom of all. The specific developmental trajectory of each individual is jeopardized by collectivist projects and centralized control. He contends that:

> [W]hatever man receives externally, is only as the grain of seed. It is his own active energy alone that can convert the germ of the fairest growth, into a full and precious blessing for himself. It leads to beneficial issues only when it is full of vital power and essentially individual.[53]

Humboldt's idea of spontaneous freedom thus remains close to Leibniz's: it posits a law of individual (quasi-monadic) development that ought not to be hindered by external impediments, that is unique and irreducible, and that is, in principle, harmoniously orchestrated with the development of others (or at least capable of such mutual adjustment).[54] Such a self is in manifold relations with others, and is constantly adjusting to their actions; however, such adaptations ought not to be imposed from without, but should respond to inner motivations and insights, and thus be internally caused. This inner causality is the meaning of spontaneity here. Accordingly, each person ought to enact his or her own endogenous law of evolution, constantly modifying states of consciousness and perceptions. In this formative process, implicit content is

[47] Humboldt 1969: 10, 48. [48] Humboldt 1963: 153. [49] Humboldt 1963: 153.
[50] Humboldt 1969: 18. [51] Humboldt 1969: 4.
[52] Humboldt 1969 : 13; cf. Leroux 1932b: 109, 110. [53] Humboldt 1969: 36.
[54] Leibniz [1720] 1991: sections 10–22, 49, 50.

made manifest, and perfection in its first sense is achieved. As external interference in individual actions hinders the development of conscious selfhood, it is a bar to perfection. In adopting this fundamentally Leibnizian view of spontaneous self-activity, Humboldt resists the Wolffian revision of this concept. He is thus able to repudiate the interventionist political consequences that Wolff draws from his reformulation, and to defend instead a spontaneous order.

Yet his conception of personality is not purely derived from Leibniz. In this first dimension of perfection, Humboldt combines a Leibnizian sense of the originality and activity of the self with a recognition of juridical personhood and its inviolability in a Kantian sense. Persons are ends in themselves, and must never be treated as means for the satisfaction of others, even in the name of some collective benefit; this is the error made in different ways in both Wolff's tutelary state and in Hufeland's principle of coercion. Humboldt described the legitimate juridical order as one in which "no single agent would be sacrificed to the interest of another."[55] He pronounces the Kantian moral law as an imperative of right.

In its second dimension, as difference-in-unity, the goal of perfection is advanced through maximal diversity rather than homogeneity. In opposing self-activity to paternalistic provision by the state, Humboldt evokes the Leibnizian unity of unity and multiplicity, an idea whose political ramifications Schiller was simultaneously exploring. On the one hand, multiplicity is simply the recognition of the specific and irreplicable life-perspectives of each individual, and thus is itself an aspect of freedom; on the other hand, it also contributes to personal and collective betterment. Humboldt considers diversity of outlook and expression as a necessary condition of historical and social progress, because the confrontation of views presents energizing challenges and opportunities, opening new horizons for change.[56] In contrast, homogenization or uniformity is inimical to perfectionist striving.[57] In making this argument, Humboldt construes this relative sense of perfection, the unification of the manifold, as the basis for the absolute sense, the complete exposition of content. He also accords with Schiller in recognizing the political problem of accommodating diverse interests in the modern state. The result would be an accomplished if not a pre-established harmony among these interests, but, as in Schiller, this harmony must be achieved in freedom, and not through imposition or standardization.

Like Leibniz, Humboldt regards harmony as unity in variety: "nature maintains both unity and richness."[58] Oneness and differentiation are not opposed, but "closely related qualities."[59] In a complex unity, "[d]issimilar materials

[55] Humboldt 1969: 32. [56] Burrow 1969: liv. [57] Humboldt 1969: 10.
[58] Humboldt 1963: 332. [59] Humboldt 1963: 332.

relate themselves to one another; the resultant relationship again becomes part of a greater whole and up to infinity each new union comprises a richer content, each new manifoldness serves a lovelier unity."[60] Humboldt's view of the spontaneous political order is characterized negatively by the relative absence of political interference, and positively by a pluralistic vision of free association in civil society. Mutually enhancing relationships display the invigorating effects of difference for personal growth when individuals coalesce in "open communication between them."[61] According to Humboldt, "the very variety arising from the union of numbers of individuals is the highest good,"[62] as opposed both to narrow self-containment, and to coercive arrangements that "transform one being into another,"[63] imposing conformity rather than respecting individual choice. Cooperation and agreements among "enlightened men, fully instructed in their truest interests, and therefore mutually well-disposed and closely united together" are definitely to "be preferred to any State arrangements."[64] "This variety is undoubtedly merged into uniformity in proportion to the measure of State interference."[65]

Humboldt also offers a historical perspective on the growth of civil society and the management of its disputes. He contends that depending on the level of development of individuality, human forces would "either merge in union" or "clash in direct collision" in war or unbounded competition.[66] The progress of civilization and refinement of taste and manners would have a transformative effect on conflicts of interest, both within states and in the international order. While such differences remain an ineradicable aspect of multiplicity itself, cooperation would increasingly displace struggle and warfare as a means of conflict resolution.[67] Hence the coercive role of the state in maintaining security, in both domestic and international relations, could be expected to diminish as a result of the advance of enlightenment. Humboldt does not merely presuppose that interests are compatible, but like Schiller he considers that the harmonious composition of such interests, rather than their elimination, is the main political issue.

Humboldt's political views are thus a composite of Leibnizian and Kantian elements. The normative conclusions that he draws from Kant are not, however, undisputed, and Kantian debates continue to occupy the public stage. Despite his own distinction between political and economic equality, which might seem to align him with Humboldt, Kant himself provides a more expansive account of legitimate state functions. In 1793 he admits interventions in education, in welfare measures needed to secure the loyalty of the population in the context of international rivalries, and in ongoing legal

[60] Humboldt 1963: 332.
[61] Humboldt 1969: 27.
[62] Humboldt 1969: 18.
[63] Humboldt 1969: 27.
[64] Humboldt 1969: 92.
[65] Humboldt 1969: 22.
[66] Humboldt 1969: 47.
[67] Niezen 2009: 192.

reforms, as gradual approximations to the ideal of reason (*TP*, 8: 299).[68] Kant's position represents neither the moralization of politics, nor a reversion to Wolffian consequentialism, but the progress of freedom. So Fichte will understand Kant, as enjoining processes of social transformation whereby the domain of right is reconfigured and extended, and its prevailing injustices redressed. For Fichte, the purpose of political intervention is to make freedom accessible to all.

7 Dalberg's Revised Wolffianism

In his critique of Humboldt, Karl von Dalberg defends the tutelary state as a necessary condition for personal and collective perfection (*TLS*, 45–53). While Kantians continue to argue among themselves about the meaning of a genuinely critical political philosophy, Dalberg offers an external perspective. He is responsive neither to Kant's critique, nor to contemporary endorsements of modern diversity. Yet he does not merely restate discredited older positions but offers significant refinements. Even before Schiller, he had already written on the relation of aesthetics and politics in his 1791 book, *Grundsätze der Ästhetik, deren Anwendung und künftige Entwickelung* (*Principles of Aesthetics, Their Application and Future Development* [*GDA*]). Here Dalberg follows Leibniz and Wolff in taking perfection as the full and explicit manifestation and configuration of content. He considers art to be the medium for this expression, and politics to be a field of application for it, to be guided in its practice by the aim of the aesthetic fashioning of the societal whole. Such (absolute) perfection as realization of implicit possibilities also implies its relative sense, a multiplicity of elements so arranged that they reveal their underlying unity, while evincing the primacy of the whole over its parts. Diversity, however, does not constitute an independent value for Dalberg; the value lies in their harmonious integration. The question of how this order is to be achieved, and its underlying principle, will be the issue in contention with Humboldt.

That this integration is the work of an external force, that it represents the perfect, in Schillerian terms, but not the beautiful, is the principal consideration. Dalberg's objective in his 1794 rebuttal of Humboldt, *Von den wahren Grenzen der Wirksamkeit des Staats in Beziehung auf seine Mitglieder* [*On the True Limits of the Effectiveness of the State in Relation to Its Members*], is to reinforce Wolff's affirmation of the absolutist state, on the grounds that, in the absence of direction by competent state authorities, a spontaneous order of the kind described by Humboldt cannot achieve maximal happiness, or perfection;

[68] Kaufman 1990: 28–30.

in other words, Schiller's self-determining republican ideal is unattainable. To this end, Dalberg develops an anthropological account that stresses the concept of *Eigennutz*, or self-interest, and illustrates its debilitating effects. Dispensing with the Wolffian supposition of a state of nature, Dalberg describes the individual actors in civil society as characterized by torpor and indolence. A basic need may momentarily activate them to seek satisfaction, but once sated, they immediately fall back into idleness. They are indifferent to the public good, nor can they be easily roused to promote it. The gratification of immediate self-interest occurs at the expense of the duty to perfect oneself and others (*TLS*, 46). Without state initiation, enterprises flounder; without state oversight, cooperation fails, and the course of perfection is blocked.[69]

It is this absence of initiative that marks the limits of spontaneity in Dalberg's account. Departing from Leibniz, but concurring with Wolff, he asserts that bodies at rest remain at rest unless prodded from without (*TLS*, 46, 48). This external stimulus is provided the state, directing actions toward the common good, and promoting advances in the arts and sciences as well as economic progress.[70] Only on this condition can the movement toward perfection, the realization of implicit possibilities, be sustained.

In its wide-ranging interventions, however, the state is to employ a minimum of coercion.[71] Moreover, while a uniformity of morals is more conducive than sectarian divisions to mobilizing contributions to the public good, the state must never compel consciences, but only outer behavior. Yet if inner freedom lies beyond the ambit of political authority, the state retains an important ethical role in discouraging immoral and egoistic actions, which not only undermine social unity, but also hinder the best possible flowering of personality. For Dalberg, individuality achieves its highest form through its integration and coordination in a social whole, through active participation in social betterment. To further this end is the mission of the enlightened state.[72]

In its promotion of the general welfare, the state should rely as much as possible on the salutary effects of a public system of education (that Dalberg defends over Humboldt's objections), regular religious instruction, and the provision of energizing opportunities and exemplary behavior to its people (*TLS*, 50–1). The state is absolute because it represents and enacts the ultimate social good, but not because it is the source of omnipresent coercion. It ought never to oppress or tyrannize, but to lead as far as possible by inducement and incentive rather than by force, and to comply with constitutional principles and

[69] Leroux 1932a: 34–41 suggests that Dalberg's administrative experience in petty German states might account for this pessimistic view.
[70] Leroux 1932a: 6.
[71] Leroux 1932a: 11–15 notes Dalberg's concern with reform of the penal system.
[72] Leroux 1932a: 7.

public law.[73] As in Wolff's advocacy of subsidiarity, there is scope for civil freedom in Dalberg, even if this does not translate into political liberty in a Kantian, republican sense (*TP*, 8: 289–97).

But here too, the ideas of inertia and *Eigennutz* impose limits on this freedom. Like Rousseau,[74] Dalberg is highly suspicious of partial associations within the state that may militate against a general interest; here is none of Humboldt's pluralism, but a concern with close political supervision and regulation of civil society (*TLS*, 47). While allowing its subjects, in principle, a broad range of choice in private matters, the state must also be cognizant of the distorting and immobilizing weight of private interest in these choices, and be prepared to overrule them in order to optimize social benefits. Individual liberties cede to social perfection as the directive principle of state action. But Dalberg sees no true incompatibility between these ends, because the advance of social welfare is also the basis for the fullest development of individuality. If they lacked authoritative direction and had nothing but their own limited spontaneity to draw on, individualities would remain rudimentary, static, or perverse. This is the fundamental meta-ethical claim that distinguishes Dalberg from Humboldt.

In assessing Dalberg's contribution, it is important to recognize that he maintains the Wolffian heritage in still another way, namely in his commitment to *reformist* absolutism. Though he rejected the Kantian turn and its associated republican orientations, Dalberg continued to insist that the tutelary state is the necessary condition for historical progress. He remained faithful to this commitment in his Napoleonic phase as leader of the Confederation of the Rhine, instituting significant legal and economic reforms.[75] In this reformist bearing he differed from many former Wolffians, who in the 1790s inaugurated the Prussian Historical School of Law. Resisting the French Revolution, the Historical School conceived of natural law as descriptive rather than normative, offering no directives toward change or amelioration, but merely cataloguing existing rights and privileges.[76] Most significantly, the Historical School ceased to champion the Wolffian activist, reforming state, but largely defended the pre-Revolutionary political order, with its juridical and social inequalities.[77] The Historical School of Law sacrifices Wolff's political perfectionism in the name of institutional continuity or imperceptibly slow change. In strenuous opposition to this school, the idealist current inspired by Kant understands history critically, not as the empirical record of enduring systems of power and hierarchy, but under the ideal of the progressive

[73] Leroux 1932a: 26–7. [74] Rousseau [1762] 1963: Livre III, ch. 13.
[75] For a recent assessment, see Aaslestad and Hagemann 2006: 547–79, esp. 559–64.
[76] De Pascale 1994: 489–505. [77] Beiser 2011: 214–52.

conquest of freedom.[78] Dalberg's position as a reforming Wolffian differs from many of his contemporaries. The debate in the German territories is conducted not only between rival schools, but within them.

8 A Fichtean Alternative

Illustrating further the internal divisions at work, an alternative Kantianism, that of Fichte's 1800 *Closed Commercial State*, should be understood in this polemical context (*CCS*, 73–199; *SW*, III: 387–513). So Fichte himself informs us in his preface, where he calls for a reconsideration of the basis of state intervention, in light of current misunderstandings. Previous authors had incorrectly attributed to the state the tutelary function of promoting happiness and beatitude among its subjects; Dalberg is clearly the unnamed adversary here. Other theorists had correctly grasped the role of the state in defending freedom and rights, but had misconstrued these concepts (*CCS*, 91–4; *SW*, III: 399–403). Freedom for Fichte is the independent causality of each subject in the objective world, in pursuit of self-determined goals (*SE*, 14; *SW*, IV: 9). To exercise this causality, all subjects must be equipped by right with the necessary material and instrumental means to change the sense-world in light of their needs and ideas, in their spontaneous pursuit of happiness; and all must possess this right equally, so that a social order that condemns some to penury while others live in idleness or superfluity is fundamentally unjust. The role of the state is to promote freedom in this sense, distributing and guaranteeing to each individual citizen the conditions for the effective exercise of right. The right to labor, and to live from the fruits of one's labor, is for Fichte the fundamental right. For him, this requires close state regulation of economic relations and transactions, not, as in Wolff or Dalberg, in order to foster happiness or maximize production, but in order to sustain the environment for the practice of individual rights by all citizens. Fichte thus follows the Kantian turn in political thought, but differs from Humboldt because he stresses egalitarian access to the material conditions of freedom. Humboldt's emphasis on the absence of external constraints on the self-development of each person is not misplaced, for Fichte, but Humboldt's error is to suppose that the existing distribution of property meets the critical standards of distributive justice.

Fichte's post-1800 texts are reflective of the Humboldt–Dalberg debate in other ways. Combining the Humboldtian emphasis on modern diversity with a problematic of egoism, Fichte comes to describe modernity, as Schiller had done, as a culture of diremption or alienation. The "characteristic trait of the

[78] E.g. in Fichte (*EPW*, 162; *SW*, VI: 313–14).

present age" is the egoistic incapacity of individuals to elevate themselves to the standpoint of morality (*GGZ*, VII: 3–265). This egoism consists in the litigious affirmation of freedom as particular interest, which Schiller had also decried; or it is the treatment of private right as paramount and peremptory, to be inflexibly asserted at the expense of general interests. Such an attitude Dalberg had characterized as an anthropological constant. In his *Addresses to the German Nation*, Fichte continues to describe his times as the era of absolute sinfulness, of unchecked egoism, where universal interests are overwhelmed by particularism and heteronomy (*AGN*, 9–21; *SW*, VII: 262–74). Freedom consists in exertion, not in passive enjoyment. Egoism represents a blockage of spontaneous energy, a submission to the merely given rather than a tireless process of engendering the new. It is a clinging to particularity and finitude. In thus characterizing egoism as idleness, Fichte recuperates something of Dalberg's idea of inertia within his own system (*AGN*, 3ff.; *SW*, VII: 257ff.).

However, for Fichte egoism is a historical product, and not a permanent feature of human nature. He describes history as a process of decadence and renewal, in which the period of narrow particularism and moral decline can and ought to be followed by the reaffirmation of self-conscious reason, enriched and enlightened by its struggles. The current historical period is not irredeemably corrupt, since it contains the possibility of redress and of passage to higher levels of awareness and freedom. In experiencing and overcoming alienation, the rational self recovers its endangered autonomy. Fichte thus inscribes egoism and inertia as transitional moments within his own, post-Kantian historical perfectionism. For all their intrusive and coercive features, Fichte views his *Closed Commercial State* as a defense of the institutions enabling the universal practice of freedom. Its pervading spirit is Kant's, not Wolff's.

9 Conclusion

This examination of German political debates at the turn of the nineteenth century illustrates the confrontation between two competing visions of the state, as the source of *eudaimonia* or of freedom. These controversies, of enduring historical relevance, demarcate authoritarian regimes from liberal and social-interventionist forms. Neither theoretical approach is, however, homogeneous, but characterized by marked inner divisions: in the former case, by the conflict between conservation and reform; in the latter, by widely differing assessments of the legitimacy and scale of state interventions. If, moreover, freedom and perfection are contending aims, they are not mutually exclusive. Advocates of the minimal state like Humboldt, who combines a Leibnizian meta-ethic with (putatively) Kantian normative restrictions on political authority, uphold the ideal of continuous self-perfecting. Here spontaneity is the essential precondition for perfection: the Leibnizian self achieves its full reality only in a Kantian juridical order, which secures the possibility for free self-determination. Advocates of the tutelary state like Dalberg stress the important of *prudent* political interventions, which avoid onerous and unnecessary impositions, and which lead by example and education, not by force. Each approach shares certain theoretical preoccupations with its adversary. The emergence of post-Kantian perfectionism does not represent a radical rupture in the history of ethics, but a series of complex syntheses and gradations, in which the new appears imbricated in earlier forms. The blending of Leibnizian and Kantian themes constitutes the central theoretical interest in this transitional period.

12 Echoes of Revolution

Hegel's Debt to the German Burkeans

Reidar Maliks

The French Revolution began in 1789 as a liberal project defending liberty, equality, and constitutional monarchy. Three years later, in 1792, radical factions took over, introduced the republic, massacred suspected enemies, executed the king, and imposed a dictatorship and rule of terror. Hegel claims that the liberal principles of 1789 motivated the radicals of 1792. Their "abstract" and individualistic concept of freedom, found in Kant and the philosophy of the Enlightenment, inexorably led to terror and an endless cycle of revolutions. Hegel's still compelling account of the Revolution is a powerful and enduring indictment of a certain kind of liberalism.

Although Hegel's account has been influential, its originality may have been overstated. In this paper, I argue that Hegel echoes key tenets of the "German Burkeans" – authors that included Friedrich Gentz, August Wilhelm Rehberg, and Justus Möser, all of whom argued against Kant in an influential debate triggered by an essay on theory and practice Kant published in 1793, at the height of the French Revolution. The debate turned on whether politics should be guided by abstract principles of natural right, as Kant had argued, or whether principles of law and politics should be rooted in social institutions and traditions, as the conservatives contended. The debate about Kant intersected with the broader debate about the French Revolution. Radicals like Johann Gottlieb Fichte and Johann Benjamin Erhard attacked the conservatives, who considered France's troubles to have been caused by an appeal to a priori principles of equal liberty similar to those defended by Kant. Hegel, whose earliest philosophical attempts were Kantian but whose path in the 1790s led away from Kant, was indebted to both sides to the debate.

I am grateful to Elias Buchetmann, James A. Clarke, Gabriel Gottlieb, and Sebastian Stein for very helpful comments on the chapter, and to Katherine Pettus for skillful copyediting. An earlier version was presented at the workshop on "Reason, Right and Revolution" at the University of York on December 9, 2018; I am grateful to James A. Clarke and Gabriel Gottlieb for the invitation. Parts of the paper were presented at the conference "The Early Critique of Kant's Moral Philosophy" at the University of St Andrews on September 14, 2019; I am grateful to Antonino Falduto and Jens Timmermann for the invitation.

Scholars have neglected Hegel's intellectual links to the conservatives. The most obvious reason is that Hegel mostly does not reference them. This does not mean absence of influence – he often failed to provide references – but it does mean that any case for influence must be built on textual interpretation and contextual analysis. Yet, Hegel studies have largely neglected contextual methods and typically ignored the ideological and philosophical controversies of the contemporaneous German public sphere.[1] Since the German Burkeans were not major philosophers, they have attracted little attention among philosophers and there are few modern editions of their writings. The scholarly neglect may also be explained by the dominant tendency to interpret Hegel as a liberal, who was critical of ancient conventions and practices.[2] Although this line of research has advanced our knowledge in some domains, it has downplayed the conservative elements in Hegel's writings.

James Schmidt has questioned the value of comparing Hegel to the German Burkeans, because, unlike them, he situated the Revolution in a historical teleology that identified the Terror as a necessary step toward Spirit's realization.[3] Schmidt points to an important feature of Hegel's theory of the Revolution, which most of the literature highlights.[4] I am not situating Hegel in the German Burkean context in order to argue that they foreshadowed all his seminal contributions, but to elucidate his perception of the challenges to be resolved by his philosophy. Hegel took up what the German conservatives had diagnosed as a serious problem with a modern philosophical view of freedom, and defined it in terms of his view of the development of reason in history.

To ignore this context is to omit both an important source that illuminates the problems to which Hegel was responding, and an important example of how his method reconciled the tension in apparently opposite philosophical positions. My goal in showing Hegel's debt to the conservatives is not to argue for an interpretation of Hegel as a conservative, but to demonstrate that he sought to transcend, refine, and reconcile the opposing parties to the *Theory and Practice* debate – to "sublate" (*aufheben*) them, as Hegel would put it. In seeking to reconcile these tensions, Hegel (like Kant) adopted a metaphysical justification for law and politics while (like the conservatives) rejecting the appeal to abstract freedom. The Revolution's challenge drove Hegel to develop a theory of law and politics that conceived of freedom as "concrete": embedded in social and political institutions and based on immanent historical values. Although it is beyond the scope of this essay to fully substantiate this ambitious claim, I will describe how it elucidates a key Hegelian claim, the so-called *Doppelsatz*: "What is rational is actual; and what is actual is rational"

[1] For two exceptions, see Lee 2008 and Buchetmann 2020.
[2] For an overview of the literature, see Stern 2006. [3] Schmidt 1998: 18.
[4] Hyppolite 1973: 61–2; Habermas 1974: 121; Ritter 1982: 52, 59; Smith 1990: 220.

(*PR*, 20; *HW*, 7: 24). This enigmatic sentence in the *Philosophy of Right*, which both conservatives and radicals claim as an endorsement, is actually Hegel's answer to the *Theory and Practice* debate. It steers a middle way between the extremes of utopian rationalism and conventionalist empiricism.

J. F. Suter claims that the lack of references notwithstanding, Hegel was probably familiar with, and influenced by, Edmund Burke.[5] While this is probably true, Hegel's knowledge of Burke was likely mediated by the German Burkeans such as Gentz, Rehberg, and Möser. Hegel would have been familiar with Gentz's (1793) annotated translation of Burke's 1790 *Reflections on the Revolution in France*. Gentz's essays, appended to that translation, formulated a conservative position that was highly critical of the Revolution. Gentz can shed more light than Burke on the kinds of questions Hegel was asking, not just because he was part of the same public sphere, but because Burke's book was published in 1790, three years before the Terror, which was Hegel's particular concern.

Hegel's mature critique of Kant and the ideal of abstract freedom attempted to substitute proper reasoning for the visceral backlash and polemics of the 1790s. I analyze his debt to the Burkeans by flagging the philosophical similarities and historical links between Hegel's arguments and their published opinions. I will proceed by first reviewing Hegel's experiences of the French Revolution and the debates of the 1790s, second by exploring his argument challenging the rights of man, third by exploring his argument against popular sovereignty, and, finally I will discuss the implications for his philosophy of right as a whole.

1 Hegel and the 1790s Debate

Hegel's best-known accounts of the French Revolution are found in his 1807 *Phenomenology of Spirit* and the 1820 *Philosophy of Right*, as well as in the more historical writings, to which we will return. Since these philosophical works reflect on historical events of his youth, we can begin with his own views and experience of the Revolution during the 1790s, which follow a common German trajectory.[6] In 1789, the largely liberal leaders of the Third Estate in France spearheaded a revolution that ended absolutism, established a national assembly, abolished feudalism, and declared the rights of man and the principle of popular sovereignty. They then tried to establish a constitutional monarchy. These early events were followed keenly in the German public sphere, where the question of whether the philosophy of the Enlightenment causes revolution had been debated since the 1780s.[7] When the Revolution in

[5] Suter 1971. [6] Valjavec 1951; Epstein 1966; Gooch 1966.
[7] See, for example, Schmidt 1996.

France took place, liberal doctrines like Kant's were immediately considered to have played a major role in causing it.[8] As a seminary student in Tübingen, Hegel, along with his friends Friedrich Schelling and Friedrich Hölderlin, who were devoted to Kant's philosophy, welcomed the Revolution.[9] He joined a political club to discuss it and to read revolutionary writings, including the liberal journal *Minerva: Ein Journal historischen und politischen Inhalts*, edited by Johan Wilhelm von Archenholz. Founded in 1792, *Minerva*'s main focus was the news about, and discussions of, the French Revolution.

The attempt to establish a constitutional monarchy in France failed: war and a second revolution in 1792 empowered the radical factions that introduced the republic, orchestrated massacres of suspected enemies of the Revolution (the "September massacres"), and executed the king. The Jacobins, the most radical of these groups, reigned until mid-1794, imposing dictatorship and the Terror. German intellectuals turned against it, and disappointment with the Revolution became a disappointment with Enlightenment philosophy. Hegel's enthusiasm for the Revolution survived the massacres, the proclamation of the republic in 1792, and the trial and execution of the king.[10] His views during the subsequent two years of terror are not clear, but at Christmas 1794 – by which point Robespierre had been guillotined and the Jacobins were banned in Paris – he wrote a letter to Schelling emphasizing the importance of Jean-Baptiste Carrier's trial. Carrier was a Jacobin official who had ordered the execution of 4,000 civilians during the terror in the Vendée, and in Hegel's view, the trial exposed the "ignominy" of Robespierre's party (*Schändlichkeit der Robespierroten*) (*L*, 29; *BrH*, 11). So it is reasonable to conclude that he welcomed the liberal 1789 French Revolution, but was repelled by the post-1792 radical phase.

Although Hegel wrote his legal and political philosophy during the post-revolutionary period, his early unpublished work bore the seeds of his skepticism about Kant and the Enlightenment principles of right. Although initially committed to Kant's philosophy in his early theological writings, by the mid-1790s he had become increasingly skeptical about legislation as a tool for the creation of social order (*HW*, 1: 285). He began to develop the concept of culture as the source of social stability and idealized the classical Greek city-state, articulating this view in the 1796/7 "Oldest Systematic Program," the product of a spirited collaboration with Schelling and Hölderlin.[11] France's experience of political instability generated by attempts to re-create society from basic principles made him wary of applying "abstract" and individualistic

[8] Fink 1992: 18. [9] Harris 1997. [10] Harris 1997: 2; Pinkard 2000: 24.

[11] "Every state must treat free human beings like mechanical works; and it should not do that; therefore it should cease." See "The Oldest Systematic Programme," in Beiser 1996: 4; *HW*, 1: 234–5.

principles to governance, and led to the search for more communitarian alternatives to Enlightenment liberalism.

Such criticisms were common in the German public sphere. Justus Möser, the doyen of German conservatism, was among the most critical voices. He had published a piece in *Berlinische Monatsschrift* in 1791, claiming that the "scholarly theory [*Buchtheorie*] of the rights of man" was responsible for the excesses of the French Revolution and that cultural conventions and "common practice,"[12] should guide society, not abstract theory. Kant responded in the *Theory and Practice* essay, by arguing for *more* theory, not less. He used the analogy of general mechanics and the mathematical doctrine of ballistics applied by engineers and artillerymen, arguing that an artilleryman who fails to predict the parabolic arc of a bullet in an empirical experiment would not conclude that the theory of ballistics works in theory but not in practice. He would add *more* theory, not less, such as the theory of atmospheric pressure (*TP*, 8: 276). This line of argument implied that the successful revolutions need better theories of law and politics. In the 1790s, Kant accepted the challenge of developing a principled defense of the liberal arguments of 1789.

Möser, Gentz, and Rehberg remained unconvinced. They considered Kant's metaphysical principles valid only for moral theories of individual agency. Principles for social practice in a political community had to be derived from empirical practice.[13] Rehberg's response to Kant was conventionalist: he argued that existing traditions were the source of justice in the political sphere, which was directed toward the regulation of ends, and Kant's formal principles are silent about the nature of ends (*ÜTP*, 117–20). Existing institutions such as the estates and guilds to which individuals belonged, determined the scope and content of rights. Since estates are hereditary, persons are born with unequal rights (*ÜTP*, 125). Humans are not metaphysically free in the Kantian sense, and criticizing institutions threatens the civil constitution (*ÜTP*, 128). Here Rehberg was drawing on earlier anti-Kantian arguments he had published as a critique of the French Revolution.

Several scholars, including Johann Gottlieb Fichte, Karl Heinrich Heydenreich, Johann Benjamin Erhard, Johann Adam Bergk, and Friedrich Schlegel, came to the rescue of Kant and the Revolution. They upheld the liberal principles, and sometimes also practices, of the Revolution, even though Kant had explicitly rejected a right of rebellion. Bergk considered it the duty of an oppressed people to change the constitution by revolution if necessary, and considered the claim that writers who promote enlightenment cause revolution an "honorable reproach" (*D*, 230). To be sure, the results in France were becoming increasingly bloody, but that should be attributed to

[12] Möser 1965: 290. [13] *N*, 103.

centuries of oppression, not to the principle of freedom. In 1793, Fichte, presumably addressing Rehburg, wrote: "You point to a gentle people, reduced to the rage of cannibals; to how they thirst after blood not water; to how they surge more avidly towards executions than toward the theatre. Yet, this is not the fruit of freedom, but the result of a previous long slavery of the spirit" (*R*, 133). Kant himself responded to the conservative objections by refining his legal and political philosophy in the *Metaphysics of Morals*, a more extensive and systematic work.[14] Although he started out as a disciple of Kant, and later became a critic, Hegel was indebted to both sides of the debate, which determined the contours of his mature philosophy.

Much like the Burkeans, Hegel's earliest statements on the Revolution in the essay *The German Constitution*, written between 1798 and 1802 and published posthumously, concluded that it was caused by "would-be philosophers and teachers of human rights" engaging in a vast political experiment, where the idea of unrestrained individual freedom eventually gave birth to the terror (*GC*, 21; *HW*, 1: 479). Yet unlike them, he venerated metaphysical principles as long as they were immanent in a historically developing social structure that also included principles of individual freedom.

In the following, I will emphasize Hegel's account of the Revolution in the *Philosophy of Right*, although most of the arguments can also be found in the *Phenomenology of Spirit*. His account in these books is mono-causal, emphasizing only the power of ideas, and does not mention other causes such as financial turmoil, war, and oppressive social structures. This approach situates Hegel closer to conservatives such as Gentz and Rehberg, who also sought to blame the Terror on the ideas of 1789, and further from radicals like Fichte, who blamed it on the old regime oppression. Although Hegel's account emphasized the power of ideas, it did not exclude other contributory causes, which appeared in his more historical writings. Contributing factors such as the economy, inequality, the repressive old regime, and the rising middle class, appear in the post-1820s' *Lectures on the Philosophy of History* (*LPH*, 214–15; *HW*, 12: 527–9). Here he argues that the Revolution benefitted society by ridding it of feudal institutions that undermined legitimate demands for freedom and rational social organization, and considered France's old regime a "chaotic aggregate of privileges contrary to all thought and reason, a senseless state of affairs which was at the same time associated with extreme ethical and spiritual corruption" (*LPH*, 214; *HW*, 12: 528).

Schmidt has suggested that the mature Hegel changed his mind.[15] Elements of this more conventional explanation, however, can be found in the early long essay the *German Constitution*, which maintained both the idea-centered

[14] Maliks 2014. [15] Schmidt 1998: 25.

account and the more conventional one (*GC*, 65–6; *HW*, 1: 535–7). There is no necessary contradiction between the two accounts, since idea-centered explanations can align with exogenous (economic and structural) causes. The difference can probably be explained by the fact that the more complex causal account is found in his social and historical writings. I will now turn to the German Burkean critique of the rights of man and popular sovereignty, and trace echoes of it in Hegel's writings.

2 Against the Rights of Man

The 1789 *Declaration of the Rights of Man and of the Citizen* claimed that men were born free and equal with regard to rights. Rights were "natural, imprescriptible, and inalienable," and valid independently of the positive law of any society.[16] These principles were quickly subjected to Burke's harsh criticism that "liberty in the abstract" is inherently worthless, and that principles derive their content and value from circumstances and consequences.[17] He supported a "manly, moral, regulated liberty," aligned with the social order as a whole, not limited to government, a public force, and public revenue, but including, morality, religion, and manners.[18] Burke's warnings about the disorder and social breakdown that would flow from appeals to natural rights seemed to have been confirmed by the Revolution's development.

Gentz built on this view, promoting a theory of the destructive consequences of the fanaticism of "absolute freedom," which foreshadows Hegel's later approach (*ÜPF*, 405). The argument partially restates the moderate liberal position: he supports political, but not unlimited freedom, by which he meant the freedom of the state of nature, unrestricted by law. Yet, his view developed into an account of a personality type that regards any restrictions at all, including those imposed by a constitution, as an absolute bad (*ÜPF*, 414). "Fanatical worshippers of freedom are never good citizens. As long as they see limits [*Schranken*], they are drawn to destruction" (*ÜPF*, 430). Rehberg singled out Rousseau's idea of individuals as free and equal and therefore as the supreme judges of right and wrong, as particularly destructive. No one may force such an individual to act against his conscience and reason, and everyone is the judge on what the laws of nature decree (*UFR*, 6). Leaving positive law behind and seeking government by natural laws opens the floodgates for the brute masses (*rohe Haufen*), who have nothing to lose by tearing down existing institutions (*UFR*, 78). The Revolution wiped out the legitimacy of all existing arrangements, and an arbitrary fury destroyed everything that contradicted the Revolution's "abstract" foundations (*UFR*, 21).

[16] National Assembly of France: 1961.
[17] Burke 1987: 7; Burke and Gentz 1991: 56–7.
[18] Burke 1987: 7.

Hegel singled out the rights of man for critique in the *Philosophy of Right*. The Revolution's core value was an "abstract" or "universal [*Allgemein*]" will that conceived persons in abstraction from social values and individual concepts of the good (*PR*, 38; *HW*, 7: 49). Originating in Rousseau, the Kantian version is clearly modeled on the formalism of pure practical reason, which Hegel says fills the will with entirely universal content that is undetermined by anything specific in the world. Borrowing a Kantian term, Hegel refers to this as "negative freedom." It is the core idea of self-assertion, freedom from anything that actually exists:

> The will contains (a) the element of pure indeterminacy or of the "I"'s pure reflection into itself, in which every limitation, every content, whether present immediately through nature, through needs, desires, and drives, or given and determined in some other way, is dissolved; this is the limitless infinity of absolute abstraction or universality, the pure thinking of oneself. (*PR*, 37; *HW*, 7: 49)

This abstract will is the source of all moral value, and since it legitimates all social, cultural, legal, and political institutions, it must *de*legitimate many features of the old regimes, such as social and economic status. But the ideal quality and formality of this concept of individual agency *also* derails attempts to build *new* institutions, because the process of setting up those institutions entails choices that limit "negative freedom," and abstract freedom must remain unlimited:

> [I]f it turns to actuality, it becomes in the realm of both politics and religion the fanaticism of destruction, demolishing the whole existing social order, eliminating all individuals regarded as suspect by a given order, and annihilating any organization which attempts to rise up anew. Only in destroying something does this negative will have a feeling of its own existence [*Dasein*] ... This is why the people, during the French Revolution, destroyed once more the institutions they had themselves created, because all institutions are incompatible with the abstract self-consciousness of equality.[19] (*PR*, 38–9; *HW*, 7: 50–2)

In one sentence Hegel captures the 1789 Revolution's rationale for destroying social institutions such as feudalism and the Church, *and* the post-1792 fanaticism of the Jacobins and others. The purely negative concept of freedom leads inexorably to chronic destruction of existing institutions, even those that represented the Revolution's ideals of equal freedom.

Hegel's theory is puzzling, in part because it is embedded in a complex theory of the development of individual human agency (the will). One way to understand this idea is to examine how Gentz foreshadowed it in his (1800) book *The Origins and Principles of the American Revolution, Compared with the Origin and Principles of the French Revolution*, which discusses the social

[19] Hegel first made the argument in the *Phenomenology of Spirit*. See *PhS*, 359; *HW*, 3: 435–6.

impacts of the rights of man. He argued that the 1793 Terror flowed naturally from the introduction, in 1789, of abstract morals into politics. Once the appeal to natural rights discredited positive law, the Estates-General rejected the traditional forms of assembly, the king's right to veto their decisions, and the obligation to abide by the rules of local assemblies. It didn't matter that these moves had no legal foundation: the radicals simply appealed to the moral notion of the rights of man. The people could agree only on destroying existing institutions, not on what to replace them with. Unlike the American Revolution, whose only objective was to liberate the colony from British rule, the French Revolution had no objective goal. The French revolutionaries attacked and dismantled the old regime, including feudal privileges, the Church, some property rights, and eventually the monarchy. But they couldn't agree on what to create instead: "The republic had been proclaimed; but this republic was a word without definitive meaning, which everyone believed he might explain, according to his inclinations, and according to the fantastic whims, which he called his principles" (Gentz 1800: 65). Because the Revolution's only purpose was the negative goal of destroying the old regime in order to liberate individuals, its very logic empowered the most extreme faction, which sought a complete break with the past. This authorized Robespierre and led to the Terror. According to this logic, appealing to absolute principles triggers unlimited destruction of existing institutions.

Gentz foreshadows an argument about factionalism developed later by Hegel in the *Phenomenology of Spirit*. Any attempt by defenders of the rights of man to build new institutions must go beyond the establishment of formal freedoms: it must also articulate public priorities aligned with a standard of the good. The catch is that all such attempts fall prey to suspicions of factionalism (*PhS*, 360; *HW*, 3: 437).[20] Since freedom's defenders obstruct *any* such constructive attempts, the result is permanent revolution. As Gentz had argued, the Revolution had only one purpose, which was negative: to destroy the old regime in order to liberate individuals. By definition that purpose benefitted the most radical and destructive factions.

Hegel's interpretation of the doctrine of abstract individual freedom as inherently destructive relies on a misinterpretation of Kant's concept of right as the limitation of freedom:

> In the Kantian definition [*Bestimmung*] of right (see the introduction to Kant's *Theory of Right* [*Metaphysische Anfangsründe der Rechtslehre*]), which is also more widely accepted, the essential element [*Moment*] is "the *limitation* [*Beschränkung*] of my freedom or arbitrary will in such a way that it may coexist with the arbitrary will of everyone else in accordance with a universal law." ... The definition of right in

[20] He repeats the idea in *Lectures on the Philosophy of History* at *LPH*, 219; *HW*, 12: 534–5.

question embodies the view, especially prevalent since Rousseau, according to which the substantial basis and primary factor is supposed to be not the will as rational will which has being in and for itself or the spirit as true spirit, but will and spirit as the *particular* individual, as the will of the single person [*das Einzelnen*] in his distinctive arbitrariness [*Willkür*]. Once this principle is accepted, the rational can of course appear only as a limitation on the freedom in question, and not as an immanent rationality, but only as an external and formal universal. This view is devoid of any speculative thought and is refuted by the philosophical concept, and has at the same time produced phenomena [*Erscheinungen*] in people's minds and in the actual world whose terrifying nature is matched only by the shallowness of the thoughts on which they are based. (*PR*, 58; *HW*, 7: 80–1)

Since freedom of the external use of choice is the key value to be protected in Kant's legal and political philosophy (by contrast to his ethics, which is concerned with morality as autonomy), Hegel mistakenly thinks Kant saw law as a shackle, a limitation on what really matters. Just as in the 1790s theological writings, Hegel sees Kant through a Hobbesian lens, depicting individuals as pursuing private interests under externally imposed laws whose obligations they avoid whenever possible.[21]

Hegel's interpretation of Kant leaves something to be desired. Kant did not defend the kind of "abstract freedom" Hegel found to have led to the revolutionary terror. Hegel comes to his erroneous conclusion because he misquotes and ignores significant parts of the theory. The quote above shows that Hegel thought it significant that Kant had defined right as a "limitation [*Beschränkung*]" of freedom in the *Metaphysics of Morals*, yet the word does not appear in the definition in the *Metaphysics of Morals* Hegel cites. The source of his misquote may have been the earlier *Theory and Practice* essay, where Kant did use the word: "Right is the limitation [*Einschränkung*] of the freedom of each to the condition of its harmony with the freedom of everyone insofar as this is possible in accordance with a universal law . . ." (*TP*, 8: 290).

Since Hegel was in the habit of quoting from memory, it is possible the *Theory and Practice* essay and the conservative polemics surrounding it had stuck in his mind. Yet, by misquoting he unreasonably weakened his opponent. Had he focused on the more comprehensive *Metaphysics of Morals*, he would have found it difficult to make the argument that Kant considered law a limitation on freedom. In that book, Kant defined freedom as "independence from being constrained by another's choice" (*MM*, 6: 237). Freedom is not merely maximizing choice, or avoiding interference, but having the status of being one's own master, of not being subject to domination. As Arthur Ripstein has demonstrated, this concept of freedom as independence aligns Kant with the republican or neo-Roman concept of liberty.[22] In line with that

[21] See *HW*, 1: 292–3, 324–6. [22] Ripstein 2009: 43.

tradition, Kant argued that individual freedom was compatible with law: persons who enter the state do not *lose* their freedom but rather gain a *full* freedom, which is defined by legal rights and duties. Natural rights (to bodily integrity, and acquired rights to things, contracts, and a social status) are valid only under positive law that respects the separation of powers, representation, due process and so on. Kant developed this theory over time, and eventually dropped the word *limitation* in the *Metaphysics of Morals* definition of right. In so doing, he adopted a positive concept of freedom realized through law that reflects the individual's rational will, inherent in the ideal original contract.[23] Yet, Hegel also had misgivings about the social contract.

3 Against Popular Sovereignty

Hegel's second line of critique challenged the idea of popular sovereignty as a source of political legitimacy. He knew full well that the Enlightenment philosophers had sought to avoid anarchy and re-establish authority on a contractualist foundation, in particular through the notion of the general will. Emmanuel Joseph Sieyès, the main intellectual architect of the 1789 Revolution, had developed Rousseau's idea into the principle of the nation as the *pouvoir constituant*. Seeking to avoid the potentially destabilizing consequences of popular sovereignty, Sieyès proposed representation as a means of institutional mediation, and a limited franchise of "active citizens" who were also taxpayers.[24] The 1791 French constitution included the limited franchise,[25] and the 1793 constitution was ratified by popular referendum. Since Kant had argued that a constitution's justice is a function of its congruence with the ideal original contract, he defended a similarly circumscribed franchise (*TP*, 8: 294; *MM*, 6: 314) while his more radical followers like Fichte (*B*, 97, 120ff.) and Bergk (*U*, 48–9) defended a universal one. Fichte appealed directly to Kant's moral theory to develop a view founded on individual moral conscience that made the state's authority contingent on consent, which individuals could withdraw at any time (*B*, 51ff.).

The Burkeans had already criticized consent as a source of authority. Gentz identified the problem as the fact that both justice and legitimacy – the right to rule – were predicated on the absolute freedom of equal individuals. This undercuts the authority of any new government because individuals always

[23] In the *Metaphysics of Morals*, Kant wrote:

> And one cannot say: the human being in a state has sacrificed a *part* of his innate outer freedom for the sake of an end, but rather, he has relinquished entirely his wild, lawless freedom in order to find his freedom as such undiminished, in a dependence upon laws, that is, in a rightful condition, since this dependence arises from his own lawgiving will. (*MM*, 6: 316)

[24] Sewell 1994: 176–7. [25] See "Constitution of 1791" in Baker 1987: 254.

have the right to withdraw consent. Rehberg also saw consent as useless in founding authority. He pinpointed the source of this problem in the second paragraph of the *Declaration of the Rights of Man and the Citizen*, which listed a right of resistance to oppression as among the natural and imprescriptible rights of man: "Each makes himself of course judge over what oppression [*Unterdrückung*] is, and thereby all administration of justice and civil order is cancelled [*aufgehoben*]" (*UFR*, 121 and *ÜTP*, 126–7). Anyone disagreeing with the republic's politics could claim, based on subjective interpretation of the abstract principles of justice, that the rulers were tyrants, and could justify resistance by appealing to the rights of man. Legal permissiveness that prioritized the moral judgment of the people could only produce a cycle of revolutions. The lawlessness and cruelty of the subsequent years seemed to confirm that hypothesis.

Hegel pursued a similarly skeptical line of argument. He thought that the kind of abstract freedom promoted by Rousseau and Kant implied a form of voluntarism, legitimizing only the state authority to which citizens had consented. That rendered authority only instrumentally valid, invited disobedience and rebellion, and doomed future attempts to establish order. Hegel considered Rousseau's notion of the general will as the source of new legitimacy to be problematic because it was based on "abstract" will. This meant the general will could only be an aggregate of individual, abstract, atomistic wills. Hegel's uncharitable interpretation of Rousseau describes "the general will" as simply "the will of all"[26] that grounded the state in a contract of atomistic individuals. Such a contract lacked authority because its genesis was arbitrary individual consent that could be withdrawn at any time.

> The union of individuals [*der Einzelnen*] within the state thus becomes a *contract*, which is accordingly based on their arbitrary will and opinions, and on their express consent given at their own discretion; and the further consequences which follow from this, and which relate merely to the understanding, destroy the divine [element] which has being in and for itself and its absolute authority and majesty. Consequently, when these abstractions were invested with power, they afforded the tremendous spectacle, for the first time we know of in human history, of the overthrow of all existing and given conditions within an actual major state. (*PR*, 277; *HW*, 7: 400–1)

Hegel's influential critique of contract theory situates the problem in the absence of a prior moral commitment of contractual obligation. Since nothing prevents individuals from abandoning their obligation once the community no longer serves their interests (calculated in cost-benefit terms), any secure ("divine") authority can be dissolved at any time. Hegel argued that this is exactly what happened in the French Revolution. By contrast, his *Philosophy*

[26] This is emphasized by Robert Wokler in Wokler 1998.

of Right is holistic and teleological, in the sense of being oriented to the realization of a concept of the good defined partly in terms of an ethical life expressed through culture. Since the agents who belong to this culture experience their freedom through membership in a community, they will consider law not as a limitation but as a precondition for their flourishing. This argument echoes Hegel's 1790s writings, which praised the communitarianism of the classical Greek city-state.

This is also a powerful critique of voluntarist contract theories like Fichte's. As a critique of Kant though, it is not as persuasive. Kant did not postulate entry into the state as voluntary, but as an obligation derived from a pre-existing concept of public right.[27] Actual consent plays no moral role once individuals have submitted to a public authority. Hegel was correct in identifying Enlightenment philosophical ideals as inspirations for the liberal revolutionaries in 1789: Sieyès explicitly built on Rousseau's *Social Contract.* Yet blaming these liberal principles for the Terror ignores the fact that it arose in a highly specific context: a society with no experience of political freedom, threatened by internal and external enemies, including the king. As Robert Wokler emphasizes, the Terror obviously contradicted the deep respect for legal procedure that Sieyès and the other representatives of the third estate – the majority of them lawyers – had emphasized all along.[28] While Sieyès' debt to Rousseau is indisputable, he contributes to the theory of sovereignty by introducing the concept of representation as an antidote to the revolutionary danger of direct democracy. Sieyès believed representatives should mediate popular preferences, deliberating and acting in the assembly for the good of the country. There was no question of making decisions contingent on the arbitrary will of aggregated private persons acting as a mob in the way Hegel describes.

Hegel's account of the Revolution is significant because it insisted on ideas as causal historical forces. Perhaps he sometimes interpreted philosophies unfairly in order to make sense of this narrative and it is indeed absurd to blame Kant's philosophy for the Revolution or the Terror, considering that Kant's political philosophy was not even in print in France until the mid-1790s. Hegel's goal was in fact to identify broad intellectual approaches (*Standpunkte*) that existed relatively independently of the philosophers who formulated them theoretically. Indeed, he was committed to the view that theoretical formulations can only follow a "life form" that has already

[27] "When you cannot avoid living side by side with all others, you ought to leave the state of nature and proceed with them into a rightful condition, that is, a condition of distributive justice" (*MM*, 6: 307).

[28] Wokler 1998: 44–9.

peaked – or in his words: “the owl of Minerva begins its flight only with the onset of dusk.”[29]

4 An Attempt at Reconciliation

It is easy to see resonances of the conservative arguments from the 1790s in Hegel’s philosophy. They all argued for the continuity between the liberal ideals of 1789, and the Terror of 1793, depicting the new ideas of Rousseau and Kant as the sources of a concept of individual freedom as arbitrary choice, which in turn undergirded a voluntarist view of political legitimacy, all of which ensured a continued cycle of revolutions. But Hegel refines these critiques and embeds them in a philosophical vision. His account of the French Revolution is complex and multidimensional: it is a causal account of a historical event. It is also philosophical and critiques a new type of subjectivity.

As Schmidt rightly pointed out, Hegel’s account diverged from the Burkeans in that he situated the Revolution and the Terror in a context of teleological development, thereby bestowing on events a quality of necessity. In an 1807 letter, he says: “Thanks to the bath of her Revolution, the French Nation has freed herself of many institutions which the human spirit had outgrown like the shoes of a child.”[30] This teleological account distanced him from the skepticism to metaphysics of someone like Rehberg. Moreover, his later account of the fully developed “substantial will” in the modern state included a commitment to modern constitutionalism that rejected the kind of hereditary institutions defended by the conservatives.

Hegel believed that philosophy’s distinctiveness lay in its power to reconcile opposites: his mature *Philosophy of Right* reconciled the key opposites of his youth – the Kantian Enlightenment and the Burkean response. This justifies our deeper consideration of the work as a whole in the context of the 1790s. Although this is not the place for a well-deserved reinterpretation, two things stand out. First, in terms of moral justification, Hegel’s theory of rationality as immanent in real, already existing institutions can be seen as an attempt to reconcile both sides of the debate. Like Kant, by insisting that just and binding institutions had to be rationally justified, he avoided the conventionalism of the German Burkeans. He is highly critical of Savigny’s legal positivism, which by abandoning all criteria of right and wrong save those manifest at a particular time and place, ended up in relativism (*PR*, 29–30; *HW*, 7: 35). But like the German Burkeans, he insisted that legal and political principles develop *in history*, and always express the ethical life (*Sittlichkeit*) of a particular

[29] *PR*, 23; *HW*, 7: 28.
[30] See Hegel’s letter to Christian Gotthold Zellman on January 23, 1807 (*L*, 123).

context.[31] The tendency of this necessary development in history of "objective spirit" in the direction of the modern constitutional state, avoids relativism.

Hegel's famous dictum in the *Philosophy of Right*: "What is rational is actual; and what is actual is rational," can be seen as an attempt to reconcile the tensions in the *Theory and Practice* debate (*PR*, 20; *HW*, 7: 24). Its emphasis on the actual is sometimes taken as a conservative endorsement of the existing German, particularly Prussian, state. Its emphasis on the rational can also be interpreted as critical because it affirms a rational ideal that can be used to critique any political arrangement.[32] Such an ideal, however, must be discerned within a contextually situated discourse – rooted in a particular time and place. This view of historically embedded reason led Hegel to conclude that philosophy's ambitions to direct society must be modest, because philosophy can only judge properly *after* ideals have been fully realized in history. The task of philosophy is not to issue instructions about how the world ought to be, because ideals only become apparent, and reflection mature, once a society has fully advanced to a new stage. Wisdom arrives at the scene later. This is what Hegel meant by his metaphor describing the owl of Minerva, which quoted in full, reads: "When philosophy paints its grey in grey, a shape of life has grown old, and it cannot be rejuvenated, but only recognized, by the grey in grey of philosophy; the owl of Minerva begins its flight only with the onset of dusk" (*PR*, 23; *HW*, 7: 28).

Hegel's constitutionalism was likely an attempt both to pay tribute to the liberal ideals of the Enlightenment, and to the hesitations of the German Burkeans. Like Kant and his idealistic followers, Hegel defended representative government as a system where the People expressed its will indirectly through representatives.[33] He had little respect for France's old regime, and unlike Burke and his German followers, rejected feudal revival as the solution. He remained deeply concerned about the unmoored individualism identified by Gentz and Rehberg as a cause of the Revolution's anarchy and terror, and sought numerous remedial constitutional innovations that included some of his

[31] By contrast, Kant considered that human societies go through a development where ethical and juridical principles are *discovered*, while their nature and justification is a priori and independent of specific social constellations. See Kleingeld 1999.

[32] See Stern 2006.

[33] He argues this as early as *The German Constitution*:

> the people must take part in the making of laws and in the most important affairs of the state. In the organization of a body which represents it, the people has a guarantee that the government will act in accordance with the laws, and (it can observe in this body) the participation of the general will in the most important matters of general concern. (*GC*, 94; *HW*, 1: 572–3)

In the late *Lectures on the Philosophy of History*, he commends the "general opinion" of his time, that "the people must express its will, not directly but indirectly through its representatives" (*IPH*, 50–1; *HW*, 12: 67).

best-known innovations: ethical life as a context for individual perfection and corporations as the context for integrating individuals into the economic sphere. By articulating common goals, these would offset and stabilize the allure of abstract individualism. Hegel frames the three estates' revival in economic terms: agriculture, trade and industry, and administration (*PR*, 234–7; *HW*, 7: 354–9). Their explicit purpose was to offset the atomism spawned by the "abstract thinking" of the *Theory and Practice* Kantians (*PR*, 238–9; *HW*, 7: 359–60).

5 Conclusion

Hegel's words about the owl of Minerva flying at dusk are usually interpreted as a defense of the age of reconstruction that followed the French Revolution and the Napoleonic wars. Driven by abstract ideals of freedom and equality, French liberals had rushed into the 1789 Revolution, torn down the remains of feudalism, and sought to establish a new constitution, only to touch off terror and civil war ending in dictatorship and imperialism. Hegel claimed this was caused by philosophy arrogating to itself the right to instruct the world in abstract principles, thereby rendering all institutions insecure. In future, theory should play a more muted role. The experience of the revolutionary age paved the way for Hegel's reconstruction of an ideal of freedom embedded within historical institutions and culture, organized and safeguarded by a corporate state.

Yet, there is a more personal story behind Hegel's musings on the goddess of wisdom and her owl. As a young man sympathetic to the Revolution, Hegel had been an avid reader of Archenholz's liberal literary journal *Minerva*, dedicated to news from France. At some point Hegel turned away from his youthful defense of the Revolution and decided that abstract individualism of the kind Kant had supported was responsible for the French anarchy. I have argued that the conservative debates of Hegel's youth frame his mature critique of Kant and the Revolution. This mature philosophy unfolded in response to questions that arose in the 1790s from the debates about Kant and the Revolution. Hegel's youthful companions would have understood the reference to Minerva as a personal reflection.

13 Public Opinion and Ideology in Hegel's *Philosophy of Right*

Karen Ng

In the final paragraphs of his discussion of the internal constitution in the *Philosophy of Right*, Hegel turns to the problem of public opinion as an expression of formal subjective freedom. Hegel's account of public opinion is striking for several reasons. First, it appears to be a classic example of a "dialectical" concept: Hegel claims that public opinion expresses at once the universal and the particular, that it contains both truth and endless error in equal measure, and finally, that it "deserves to be *respected* as well as *despised*" (*PR*, §318). Second, Hegel suggests that public opinion exists as a self-contradiction, and more specifically, that it exists as a kind of collective self-deception on the part of a people with respect to how it knows and judges its own essential character. Third, public opinion is self-destructive, and tends toward the dissolution of the state. Indeed, apart from the external threat posed by other nation-states, public opinion appears to be one of the most significant internal threats faced by the modern, rational state. Hegel's highly ambivalent treatment of public opinion has not gone unnoticed by some of his most famous readers. Adorno, for example, strongly concurs with Hegel's discussion, and associates public opinion with ideology and even "necessary false consciousness."[1] Similarly, Habermas, in his consideration of the transition undergone by the concept of public opinion from Kant to Hegel, writes: "[i]n Hegel's concept of opinion the idea of the public of civil society was already denounced as ideology."[2] Thus, despite Hegel's infamous and widely criticized identification of the modern state with the actuality of reason itself, both Adorno and Habermas contend that there is not only room in Hegel's social

[1] Adorno writes:

> For the findings of what is called – not without good reason – "opinion research" Hegel's formulation in his *Philosophy of Right* concerning public opinion is generally valid: it deserves to be respected and despised in equal measure. It must be respected since even ideologies, necessary false consciousness, are a part of social reality with which anyone who wishes to recognize the latter must be acquainted. But it must be despised since its claim to truth must be criticized. Empirical social research itself becomes ideology as soon as it posits public opinion as being absolute. (Adorno 1976: 85)

[2] Habermas 1989: 117.

and political philosophy for a concept of ideology, but that a concept of ideology emerges as necessary and internal to Hegel's broader institutional theory of ethical life.[3] On their reading, the problem of ideology coalesces around the emergence and existence of public opinion, in which reason and unreason combine to threaten the unity and stability of society from within.

The aim of this paper is to investigate whether there is indeed room for a concept of ideology in Hegel's *Philosophy of Right*, and more generally, in his distinctive approach to theorizing the ethical domain of human action.[4] My discussion will focus on two sets of questions in order to investigate this possibility. The first set of questions concerns whether or not what Hegel calls public opinion indeed qualifies as ideology under existing definitions. To assess this question, I will draw on Raymond Geuss' definition of ideology as operating along three interconnected dimensions: the epistemic, the functional, and the genetic.[5] I argue that Hegel's concept of public opinion touches upon all three of these dimensions, and moreover, that the *Philosophy of Right* provides a sophisticated conception of social practices that helpfully contributes to contemporary debates concerning the status of ideological beliefs.

The second set of questions concerns the larger significance of the transition that takes place from Kant to Hegel, specifically concerning changes to the method of social and political theorizing and what the development of a concept of ideology contributes to these methodological changes. A major concern in the midst of this transition is the relation between theory and praxis: Kant, for example, felt the need to defend his moral, political, and cosmopolitan theories against the charge that they exist merely as "empty ideas" (*PP*, 8: 276); Fichte had asserted the primacy of the practical as against the theoretical in his doctrine of infinite striving (*SK*, 233; *SW*, I: 264); Hegel's absolute idea is likewise conceived in part as consisting of the unity of theoretical and practical reason (*SL*, 735; *HW*, 6: 548). These concerns about the relation between theory and praxis arguably culminate in Marx's famous pronouncement that theory, and more broadly, philosophy itself, can be realized as part of revolutionary, emancipatory praxis. One of the central issues

[3] Axel Honneth also follows the critical theory reading of the *Philosophy of Right*, identifying in Hegel's text a diagnosis of the social pathologies associated with the one-sided emphasis on individual freedom (Honneth 2010 and 2014).

[4] For recent discussions of Hegel on ideology, see Jaeggi 2009 and 2018: chs. 5 and 6. Jaeggi argues that ideology critique can be understood as a form of immanent criticism, where her account of immanent criticism is largely inspired by Hegel's method in the *Phenomenology of Spirit*. See also Ng 2015, where I defend a Hegelian-Marxian approach to ideology critique, drawing on the dialectic of life and self-consciousness in Hegel's notion of the "idea" and Marx's notion of "species-being." Morris 2016 defends a "neo-Hegelian" version of epistemic ideology critique against traditional problems that arise in strictly functional accounts. Novakovic argues against the possibility of ideology in Hegel's philosophy, writing: "Hegel does not have a conception of ideology, nor does he have room for one" (Novakovic 2017: 154). I discuss Novakovic's position in Section 1 below.

[5] See Geuss 1981.

at stake in this transition, particularly in the works of Hegel and Marx, is the appropriate method of social and political theorizing, and more specifically, a critique of a certain approach to this theorizing that is now often referred to as "ideal theory." I argue that the emergence of a concept of ideology is crucial for understanding this transition, and that Hegel constitutes an important stage in this transition that is often overlooked and undertheorized. To understand Hegel's contribution, I will turn to his *Natural Law* essay of 1802/3 to assess certain methodological commitments that help to bring the concept of ideology into relief. What the *Natural Law* essay reveals is that Hegel's ambivalent treatment of public opinion reflects his methodological commitment to a dialectic of the ideal and the real, one that renders the concept of ideology central to social and political theorizing.

Section 1 of the paper discusses Hegel's concept of public opinion in the *Philosophy of Right*, highlighting a number of ways in which Hegel's conception departs from Kant's. In particular, I argue that Hegel's ambivalent position regarding the positive and negative sides of public opinion stems from their being mediated through civil society and the estates, which proliferate private interests based on social status and class that can come into conflict with the public good. With the concept of public opinion in view, Section 2 assesses whether or not Adorno and Habermas are correct to identify this concept with a concept of ideology. To address this question, I draw on Raymond Geuss' account of ideology, developed as part of his assessment of critical theory, and conclude that public opinion indeed represents the development of a concept of ideology, one that emerges for Hegel as a central aspect of his institutional theory of modern ethical life. Section 3 turns to Hegel's *Natural Law* essay in order to shed further light on the methodological commitments of his social and political philosophy, arguing that his opposition to both *formalism* and *empiricism* signal the development of a nascent critical theory.[6] Although critical theory as a research program is most frequently associated with the thinkers of the Frankfurt school (of which Adorno and Habermas are prominent representatives), for the purposes of this paper, critical theory refers simply to approaches to social and political theorizing in which the concept and critique of ideology play a central role.[7] I argue that the problem of public

[6] Benhabib 1986 also argues that Hegel's contributions to the development of critical theory can be gleaned from the *Natural Law* essay. She focuses on two issues in particular: Hegel's development of the idea of immanent critique, and his principled opposition to counterfactual argumentation in political theory. Although she is also interested in the connections between Hegel and Marx, especially concerning what she calls "defetishizing critique," which she traces to Hegel's *Phenomenology*, her account omits a discussion of ideology, which I think is key to Hegel's rejection of both formalism and empiricism (Benhabib 1986: 44–69).

[7] For Geuss, "[t]he very heart of the critical theory of society is its criticism of ideology" (Geuss 1981: 2–3).

opinion for Hegel is the problem of ideology critique, a problem that challenges traditional understandings of his theory of the modern, rational state.

1 Public Opinion: Context, Origins, and Concept

Hegel's treatment of publicity and public opinion takes its point of departure from broadly Kantian themes concerning the importance of the public use of one's reason in the promotion and advancement of enlightenment. Although Hegel is no straightforward proponent of enlightenment ideals, his commitment to at least some of its core values is most clearly discerned in his discussion of positive laws in the *Philosophy of Right*, where he argues that there is a "right of publicity" with respect to the administration of justice (*PR*, §224A).[8] This right of publicity, in which the law's binding force stems from its being "*universally known*" by citizens, is itself derived from the right of formal subjective freedom, which acknowledges the right of individuals to determine for themselves, according to reason and conscience, what they take to be good (*PR*, §§132, 215, 224, 228A). However, although Hegel respects the importance of subjective freedom alongside publicity as a condition of its rightful exercise, subjective convictions are, even under conditions of publicity, liable to all sorts of error and caprice. Far from being a reliable path to enlightenment, Hegel offers a different diagnosis of the combination of publicity and subjective freedom, a diagnosis that revolves around an account of public opinion (*öffentliche Meinung*) in connection with the legislative power of the state.

Hegel's departure from Kantian themes is most clearly discerned in his investigation into the formation and function of public opinion, which traces its origins to the estates (*die Stände*) in their role of mediating between the government and the people (*PR*, §302). The estates were first introduced in the section on "Civil Society [*die bürgerliche Gesellschaft*]," where Hegel presented his analysis of the system of needs (essentially his contribution to a theory of political economy), a sphere of action in which private, self-interested individuals pursue the satisfaction of needs by means of work and the acquisition of property. Within the context of civil society, the estates are differentiated masses to which individuals belong, in part due to the division of labor and one's profession, and in part due to one's social standing, status, class, and position. One's particular estate is determined initially by "natural disposition, birth, and circumstances," but, and respecting the importance of individual free choice, the ultimate and essential determining factor is "*subjective opinion*" and "*arbitrary will* [Willkür]" (*PR*, §206). More than simply

[8] See also *PR*, §228A and Habermas' discussion at Habermas 1989: 106. Compare also with Kant's discussion of public right in *TPP*, 8: 381–6.

furnishing a name for one's profession or social status, however, the estates also serve an important ethical and educative function. In addition to helping one acquire a set of skills that are specific to one's estate, one also acquires a specific ethical disposition (*sittliche Gesinnung*) in which rectitude and honor for one's estate allow individuals to gain recognition from others, as well as self-respect and self-esteem. To stress the importance of the estates for the development of one's social identity, Hegel writes: "When we say that a human being must be *somebody*, we mean that he must belong to a particular estate; for being somebody means that he has substantial being. A human being with no estate is merely a private person and does not possess actual universality" (PR, §207A).

The discussion of the estates within the context of civil society is primarily positive, and membership in an estate forms an essential aspect of one's ethical and social identity. However, once we enter into the domain of the political state, the role of the estates becomes somewhat more ambivalent.[9] In the context of the legislative power, the estates, operating primarily through elected deputies, serve the function of bringing "the universal interest [*Angelegenheit*] into existence," establishing a "public consciousness" in which "the views and thoughts of the *many*" are expressed (*PR*, §301). Immediately after introducing the political function of the estates, Hegel expresses some doubts and concerns. On the one hand, in mediating between the government and the people, the estates serve an important role in educating the public, as well as ensuring something akin to democratic accountability. Indeed, part of the political function of the estates is to engage in "public criticism [*öffentliche Zensur*]," offering insight into the activities and specialized needs of those groups whose interests may not be visible to higher state officials (*PR*, §301A). On the other hand, Hegel also simply denies that the estates or "the people" in general have some special insight into what is in their own best interest, suggesting instead that "'the people' . . . refers to that category of citizens *who do not know their own will*." Thus, although the estates are supposed to serve the function of bringing the universal, public interest into existence, there is also a tendency in their functioning toward disintegration, a tendency toward retreat into particular interests and private points of view. Indeed, Hegel associates the tendency of the estates toward disintegration with the negative viewpoint of the "rabble," who automatically assume ill-will on the part of the government.[10] When the outlook of the rabble gains "*self-sufficiency*," the result is nothing less than "the destruction of the state" (*PR*, §272A).

In tracing the formation of public opinion to the political functioning of the estates, Hegel is claiming that individuals form their judgments concerning

[9] See Habermas' discussion in Habermas 1989: 118–22.

[10] On the "rabble," see *PR*, §244.

matters of public concern primarily from their position within civil society, and more specifically, from the position of their social status or class. Importantly, Hegel emphasizes (in a somewhat sexist formulation) that public opinion should be distinguished from "man's imaginings at home in the company of his wife and friends," which is meant to suggest that the opinions in question are not simply the ones shared within the private sphere of the family (*PR*, §315A). Instead, public opinion takes shape under the conditions of publicity combined with one's participation in an estate. Individuals form their judgments concerning public matters on the basis of their social and ethical identities, identities whose public existence is fundamentally shaped by the formal and informal education provided within civil society. Thus, whereas for Kant, the combination of publicity and subjective freedom is sufficient for securing the path to enlightenment, for Hegel the combination of publicity and subjective freedom is importantly mediated through participation in civil society and the estates, which generates a diverse sphere of private interests that have disintegrative effects for the public good. Public opinion, the formation and function of which are mediated by the estates, manifests the unstable push and pull between private and public interests, representing a site of enlightenment as much as a site of ignorance and false public consciousness.

Before turning to the question of whether and how public opinion may qualify as ideology, let me return briefly to its three chief characteristics that I mentioned in the introduction. First, public opinion appears to be a classic example of a Hegelian, dialectical concept. Public opinion brings universal, public consciousness into existence, and yet, it also tends to disintegrate into private and particular points of view. This is due primarily to its functioning through the estates, which represent the interests of civil society within the context of the political state. Public opinion is also capable of expressing "*true thoughts* and *insight*" and is able to form "*rational judgments*" concerning the state and its affairs (*PR*, §315). In its modern shape, Hegel emphasizes that public opinion gains recognition primarily through "insight and reasoned argument" rather than through habit or custom (*PR*, §316A). However, in virtue of its disorganized, subjective basis, public opinion also contains "ignorance and perverseness," "false information," and "errors of judgment" (*PR*, §317). In fact, the worse the opinion, the more distinctive it will be, which increases the likelihood that it will be taken up by others. Given its dialectical character, Hegel claims that public opinion deserves to be "*respected* as well as *despised*" (*PR*, §318). Public opinion must be respected not only because it is capable of forming rational judgments, but because even within its erroneous judgments, there is some truth to be found, more or less obscured. It deserves our contempt, however, when it operates under the guise of universal authority, and rising above public opinion is also a condition of "achieving anything great or rational."

The second feature of public opinion concerns the problem of self-deception and how this relationship can be understood as a large-scale rather than merely individual phenomenon. Indeed, Hegel had already claimed earlier that "the people" consist precisely in that group of citizens who do not know their own will. The idea that public opinion should be understood specifically as *self*-deception echoes a feature that Geuss will also identify with ideological false consciousness, namely, that it is "a form of *self-imposed* coercion" or "a kind of *self-delusion*."[11] Here is the key passage where Hegel discusses public opinion as the problem of self-deception:

> A leading spirit [*ein großer Geist*] set as the theme of an essay competition the question "whether it is permissible to deceive a people." The only possible answer was that it is impossible to deceive a people about its substantial basis, about the *essence* and specific character of its spirit, but that the people is deceived *by itself* about the way in which this character is known to it and in which it consequently passes judgments on events, its own actions, etc. (*PR*, §317A)

Regarding the character of deception at work in public opinion, Hegel begins by claiming that it is "impossible" to deceive a people regarding certain matters, specifically, matters pertaining to the essential ethical character of a people, or what we might call, the "spirit" of a people. The kind of deception that Hegel has in mind here is explicit and deliberate deception from a source external to the people, and it is Hegel's contention that such a complete deception of a people regarding their own ethical character is not a real possibility that we should even entertain, for to do so would be to misunderstand the way in which public opinion is constituted. Note that Hegel is *not* suggesting that such deliberate, external deception is never at work in the operations of state and civil society, but only that public opinion should not primarily be understood along these lines. There are at least two reasons why public opinion must be understood as self-deception in contrast with deliberate deception from an external source. First, public opinion is formed via participation in the estates, whose assemblies must operate under conditions of sufficient publicity in order to fulfill their educative function for the people (*PR*, §315A). Hegel thus understands these institutions to be sufficiently open and democratic (without the need for any official democracy), such that consensual participation is what sustains their continual operation. Thus, the people participate in these institutions willingly, and the participation in question is manifest primarily through the exercise of judgment and reasoned argument – public, rational debate – rather than unreflective habit or custom. Any deception that results from this process is therefore by definition self-imposed, and will consist of errors of judgment whose source is nothing but

[11] Geuss 1981: 58. See also Geuss 1981: 60.

the willing participation of the people in public debate regarding their own affairs. Second, the *content* of public opinion concerns the essential character and ethical identity of a people – for example, self-conceptions concerning what it means to be American, British, etc. Although the judgments in question may indeed contain factual errors of all kinds (ones that may result in part from deliberate forms of deception), these errors of judgment are ultimately all about the people themselves, in which the mistaken attitudes and beliefs in question are inseparable from the people's identity and collective sense of self. The mistaken attitudes and beliefs of public opinion thus necessarily involve an element of self-deception, and moreover, individuals will generally be invested in maintaining those mistaken attitudes and beliefs on pain of losing some essential part of their social and ethical identities. A people's belief in American exceptionalism, for example, may be fueled by misinformation and even propaganda, but it is a belief that can be difficult to correct simply by offering better information, since giving up this belief would involve a fundamental change in a people's understanding of who they are, of what it means to be American.[12] In stressing the element of self-deception, Hegel is arguing that deliberate, external forms of deception are never sufficient for the kinds of errors of judgment involved in public opinion, which always involve the question of a people's essential ethical identity.[13]

In her book, *Hegel on Second Nature and Ethical Life*, Andreja Novakovic offers a different interpretation of this crucial passage at §317A, arguing instead that this passage is "a clear statement against the possibility of ideology as a form of false consciousness."[14] She contends that while Hegel suggests "that a people can become the source of its own confusion," he also flatly denies that a people can ever be deceived about its substantial basis. Moreover, although Hegel accounts for the possibility of confused self-conceptions, these confusions lack the functional character of ideology, which is to say that they do not function to justify and maintain certain (unjust) social relationships. In the next section, I will take up the functional dimension of public opinion and address the question of whether and how this can be understood in terms of

[12] Compare this with the example of a government lying to the people that the water in their town is potable. The people can receive new and better information that allows for the false belief in potable water to be corrected for, without requiring a fundamental change in their ethical identity.

[13] In the *Phenomenology of Spirit*, Hegel makes a similar argument in the context of commenting on enlightenment's mistaken critique of faith: the accusation that people of faith are simply victims of deception on the part of a priesthood misunderstands entirely how faith is essentially bound up with the self-knowledge of the faithful (*PhS*, ¶¶542, 550; *HW*, 3: 401, 407–8). I take it that here, too, Hegel is not at all ruling out the possibility of deliberate deception on the part of the priesthood, but simply arguing that such deception is neither necessary nor sufficient to account for the self-understanding of the faithful.

[14] Novakovic 2017: 156.

ideology, but for now I want to add one more point of clarification regarding the nature of self-deception. Novakovic argues that "public opinion cannot be deceived, but it can be self-deceived," and suggests that self-deception is better understood as a kind of self-forgetfulness that emerges through habitual participation in ethical life.[15] Although habitual participation forms a large part of Hegel's understanding of ethical action, earlier I noted that the formation and proliferation of public opinion does *not* primarily operate by means of habit and custom, but instead, that it operates "mainly through insight and reasoned argument" (*PR*, §316A). Thus, rather than passive and unreflective self-forgetfulness, Hegel appears to be claiming that the self-deception in question is *active*, a result of the relatively disorganized way in which opinions are articulated, exchanged, and reflected upon. Instead of the self-forgetfulness of habituated and unreflective participation, the active self-deception of public opinion is better understood in terms of what Hegel calls "common sense [*der gesunde Menschenverstand*]," a public consciousness and ethical foundation that exists in the shape of prejudices (*PR*, §317).[16] These prejudices of common sense manifest themselves by distorting the explicit judgments that people make concerning their own essential character, their actions, and the events that take place within ethical life. The prevalence of prejudice in public opinion appears to rest on a combination of two factors: its inchoate mixture of true and false judgments on the one hand, and its lack of any reliable criterion for distinguishing between such judgments on the other. Self-deception in the shape of prejudice thus appears to be an essential rather than contingent feature of public opinion, and here, the best we can hope for appears to be establishing the *right* prejudices, rather than eliminating prejudice altogether.

Third and finally, public opinion is self-destructive, and tends toward the dissolution of the state. This was suggested by Hegel's earlier discussion of the tendency of the estates toward disintegration, which at its most extreme, is associated with the negative, oppositional, and private point of view characteristic of the rabble (*PR*, §§301A, 272A, 244). In the concluding paragraph of the section on the internal constitution, Hegel reiterates the destructive character of public opinion, claiming that it manifests a kind of formal, subjective freedom that is "the dissolution of the existing life of the state by opinion and argument [*Räsonieren*]" (*PR*, §320). As Hegel continues his discussion of international law and world history, he continues to stress that states – even if they are maximally rational ethical totalities – are continually exposed to contingency: to the external contingency resulting from relations with other states, and to the internal contingency of "inner particularity," a contingency

[15] Novakovic 2017: 203–4.

[16] See also the discussions of "common sense" in *D*, 98–103; *HW*, 2: 30–5. In the *Differenzschrift*, Hegel also discusses "common sense" in connection with problems related to faith.

that asserts itself most forcefully in public opinion (*PR*, §340). In fact, the more rational the state, and the more developed its recognition of the principle of formal, subjective freedom, the more public opinion emerges as a threat from within, as a source of internal unrest and turmoil. Public opinion thus poses an especial threat for modern states, and in particular, for functionally differentiated societies in which economic and political spheres of action are distinguished in principle.

2 Public Opinion as Ideology

With Hegel's understanding of public opinion in view, how should we assess the contentions of Adorno and Habermas that this notion already represents the development of a concept of ideology? To address this question, I want to turn now to Geuss' conception of ideology in order to assess whether Hegel's concept of public opinion qualifies as such according to his definition. Geuss' account is an appropriate point of reference here for two reasons: first, he develops his concept of ideology drawing primarily from Habermas and Adorno; second, he helpfully distills the methodological innovations of critical theory through the concept of ideology. In the next section, I will also discuss Hegel's methodological innovations by turning to his essay on *Natural Law*, and argue that his methodological commitment to a dialectic of the ideal and the real render the concept of ideology essential for social and political theorizing, representing a nascent critical theory. Thus, despite his reputation for defending the state as the actuality of reason itself, I will argue that Hegel's social and political philosophy contains a concept and account of ideology as a necessary feature of modern ethical life.

Geuss begins with a very general definition of ideology in a pejorative sense as a form of delusion or false consciousness, where a form of consciousness refers to "a particular constellation of beliefs, attitudes, [and] dispositions."[17] A form of consciousness can be ideologically false on account of three potential factors: first, on account of certain *epistemic* features; second, on account of certain *functional* features; and third on account of certain *genetic* features.[18] *Epistemologically*, a form of consciousness can be false in a variety of ways: by confusing the epistemic status of a belief (for example, confusing a value judgment with a statement of fact), by making an objectification mistake (for example, taking a social, historical phenomena as natural and unchangeable), by mistaking a particular interest for something universal and general (for example, taking the interests of the estate of trade and industry as the

[17] Geuss 1981: 12. Geuss also discusses two further senses of ideology as descriptive and positive (see Geuss 1981: 4–12).

[18] Geuss 1981: 13.

universal interest of all human beings), and finally, by not recognizing self-fulfilling or self-validating beliefs *as* self-fulfilling or self-validating (for example, not understanding that identifying some individual or group as lazy has effects upon how that individual or group is treated, and thereby, has further effects upon their possibilities for actions and their self-understanding).[19]

A form of consciousness can also be ideologically false on account of certain *functional* properties. For instance, a form of consciousness can serve the function of "supporting, stabilizing, or legitimizing certain kinds of social institutions or practices."[20] In particular, ideology serves the function of justifying "reprehensible social institutions, unjust social practices, [and] relations of exploitation, hegemony, or domination." Additionally, forms of consciousness can also serve the function of "masking social contradictions."[21] Finally, certain *genetic* features concerning origins and history can also potentially render a form of consciousness ideologically false (some classic examples here might be Marx's suggestion that the ruling ideas of a period are always the ideas of the ruling class, or Nietzsche's genealogy of morals that traces Christian morality to "hatred, envy, resentment, and feelings of weakness and inadequacy"[22]). One of the virtues of Geuss' account is his proposal that all "interesting" accounts of ideology, and more specifically, what he calls, following the Frankfurt School, "dialectical" accounts of ideology critique, will combine two or more of these three modes of analysis.[23] This is important, not only because it identifies what is distinctive about ideology critique, but moreover, because each mode of analysis on its own very quickly produces some potential problems. For example, the most obviously non-self-sufficient form of critique is the genetic one, where identifying certain genetic features of a form of consciousness is neither necessary nor sufficient to render it false. The epistemological critique, while crucial, is not sufficient to render a form of consciousness ideological, since there are many instances of such errors that are innocuous, merely incidental, and easily corrected for. The problems concerning the functional critique are more complex, but broadly speaking, when it is not supported by epistemological concerns, there is a danger that the exclusive focus on the functional properties of a form of consciousness

[19] Geuss 1981: 13–14. On self-fulfilling beliefs, see Fricker's discussion of constitutive and causal construction, and her example of how one can be constructed as a "hysterical female" (Fricker 2007: 55–8, 88). Haslanger 2012 also discusses a number of helpful examples of self-fulfilling phenomena in connection with ideology.

[20] Geuss 1981: 15.

[21] Geuss 1981: 18. On the connection between the epistemic and functional dimensions of how ideology can mask social contradictions, see Mills' discussion of "cognitive dysfunctions (which are psychologically and socially functional)" in Mills 1997: 18.

[22] Geuss 1981: 44. [23] Geuss 1981: 22.

undermines the commitment to truth that ought to guide philosophical and social critique. Recently, Michael Morris has argued that the functional critique of ideology, on its own, leads to a general skeptical attitude that "breeds apathy, cynicism, fideism, and nihilism," and in extreme cases, can lead to the glorification of violence.[24] Geuss' three-fold approach to ideology critique thus avoids the potential pitfalls of taking these modes of critique in isolation.[25]

Are Adorno and Habermas correct, then, to suggest that with the concept of public opinion, Hegel has already developed a concept of ideology as a form of self-deluded false consciousness? Does a concept of ideology arise as a necessary feature of Hegel's theory of the rational state? The case seems fairly easy to make if one considers the epistemological features of public opinion identified by Hegel. As he suggests, "every kind of falsehood" is present in public opinion (*PR*, §318A). However, falsity alone does not capture what is distinctive about the modern phenomenon of public opinion as arising from the education and political functioning of the estates. In describing the modern version of this phenomenon, Hegel stresses that it operates within the context of the heightened awareness of agents as participants within a space of reasons.[26] Errors in judgment, which surely include the common kinds of epistemological mistakes noted by Geuss, increase alongside the increasing importance of reasoned argument, and the more rational argument permeates the spheres of ethical life, the more errors of judgment will proliferate. But beyond these kinds of errors of judgment, there is a further feature of public opinion that many have identified as a distinctive feature of *ideological* forms of consciousness, namely, that they are particularly recalcitrant, stubborn, and resistant to change, even in the face of clear evidence or good arguments. I take it that this is why Hegel describes public opinion not only in terms of reasoned argument, but also in terms of prejudice and common sense. The kind of false consciousness at stake, then, is a kind of prejudicial self-deception, where commonly held prejudices adversely affect agents' abilities to judge themselves, their actions, and their form of life accurately.

Public opinion also has several functional features. As noted above, its political function is to mediate between the government and the people: from a top-down perspective, publicity is a means of educating the public concerning the state and its laws, serving as a force of societal integration; from a bottom-up perspective, publicity functions as a source of democratic

[24] Morris 2016: 30.

[25] Geuss also claims that it is important to establish which of the three modes is "basic" to a theory of ideology (Geuss 1981: 22). For Habermas, according to Geuss, the epistemic dimension is basic (Geuss 1981: 69).

[26] Habermas calls this "the subjection of domination to reason" (Habermas 1989: 117). See also Honneth 2007 who also argues that ideology operates within "the space of reasons."

accountability, affording the opportunity for citizens to criticize the government. However, insofar as public opinion stems from the estates, its most important function is to represent the interests of civil society, a function that on Hegel's own account, comes into conflict with the more integrative aims of the state. If we combine its function of representing the interests of civil society with the epistemological critique whereby public opinion contains falsehoods that are stubbornly supported by prejudice, its potential ideological status becomes more evident. In a widely known and much commented upon discussion in "Civil Society," Hegel suggests that the proper and normal functioning of civil society necessarily leads to a disproportionate inequality of wealth and the creation of a rabble (*der Pöbel*). In a famous line, he writes: "despite an *excess of wealth*, civil society is *not wealthy enough* – i.e., its own distinct resources are not sufficient – to prevent an excess of poverty and the formation of a rabble" (*PR*, §245). Thus, the institutions and practices of civil society lead to excessive inequality and poverty, and yet, the function of public opinion is to represent the interests of civil society with its prejudicial blending of falsity and truth. Arguably then, public opinion serves the function of supporting, stabilizing, and legitimizing the unjust institutions of civil society, and its prejudices and erroneous judgments make it more difficult for citizens to see relations of exploitation and domination for what they are. Habermas, commenting on the same passage, states the following:

> [In his analysis of civil society, Hegel] diagnosed a conflict of interests that discredited the common and allegedly universal interest of property-owning private people engaged in political debate by demonstrating its plainly particularist nature. The public opinion of the private people assembled to form a public no longer retained a basis of unity and truth; it degenerated to the level of a subjective opining of the many.[27]

In representing the interests of civil society, public opinion functions to stabilize and legitimate the excessive inequality and poverty generated by the institutions and practices of that sphere; combined with its falsehoods, prejudices, and epistemological errors, public opinion appears to be a form of ideological false consciousness that arises as a necessary feature of Hegel's rational state.

With regard to the genesis of public opinion, I noted above that one of Hegel's most important departures from Kant on this topic is to trace its origins explicitly to the education of the estates. Although the genetic argument is subject to worries surrounding the genetic fallacy, when coupled with the epistemological and functional critiques, the genetic account serves as a helpful general reminder concerning the embeddedness of forms of consciousness – our ideas, beliefs, attitudes, and dispositions – in particular and concrete

[27] Habermas 1989: 119.

social practices. In more recent discussions surrounding the concept of ideology, a debate has arisen concerning whether or not ideology is best understood primarily as a set of beliefs, or more fundamentally as a set of practices, attitudes, social meanings, and material conditions that operate in mutually reinforcing ways.[28] For example, Sally Haslanger has argued against Tommie Shelby's strongly *cognitivist* approach to ideology in which ideology is primarily understood in terms of a set of shared beliefs.[29] Instead, Haslanger argues that "practices are logically prior to the behavior and states of mind of the participants; they provide a 'stage setting' for action; they render our action meaningful; they constitute reasons for action. For example, Akna performs a ritual with maize *because* this is a way to worship. The practice constitutes her reason."[30]

This "practice-first" approach, in which attitudes, beliefs, and reasons are opened up by social practices further explains why the epistemological errors that are characteristic of ideology are so stubborn, and why the mere pointing out of these errors often seems to miss the point (not to mention, generates such ire).[31] Hegel makes a similar argument in the context of enlightenment's mistaken critique of faith in the *Phenomenology*: pointing out that objects of religious practices are merely "stone or wood or dough," and not, for example, literally the body of Christ, misunderstands entirely how agents participate in social practices (*PhS*, ¶553; *HW*, 3: 409). The logical priority of social practices is even more evident in the *Philosophy of Right*, where specific ethical dispositions, along with their requisite attitudes and beliefs, develop *only* within the context of specific institutional spheres of action such as the family, civil society, or the state. For example, in addition to the disposition of rectitude and honor for one's estate that one acquires through participation in civil society, participation in the family develops the ethical dispositions of love, trust, and living a shared existence, and participation in the state develops a distinctly political disposition that Hegel calls patriotism. Thus, although the genesis of public opinion in the estates is surely not a sufficient condition for rendering it a form of ideological false consciousness, Hegel's insistence on this origin serves as a reminder that the specific content of these opinions is no accident, for the opinions are deeply embedded in the specific practices surrounding one's profession and social status within civil society. These practices are themselves reasons, and so even when one's opinions are full of ignorance and falsehoods, public opinion is difficult to change or correct, without the requisite changes within the social practices from which they arise.

28 See Shelby 2003, 2014 and Haslanger 2017.

29 Haslanger argues that ideology critique "needs to be *less* cognitivist [my emphasis]," but I do not take her account to be *anti*-cognitivist (2017: 3).

30 Haslanger 2017: 13.

31 Haslanger 2017: 15.

In tying the formation of public opinion to the estates, Hegel is suggesting that our beliefs and attitudes – as much as our social and ethical identities – are fundamentally bound up with concrete material conditions, emerging as a result of education through and participation in social practices and institutions.

Employing Geuss' three-fold model of ideology, I have argued in this section that Hegel's concept of public opinion operates as a form of ideological false consciousness that emerges as a necessary feature of his theory of modern ethical life. In exploring the epistemological, functional, and genetic features of public opinion, I further suggested that Hegel's philosophy provides us with a sophisticated account of how forms of ideological false consciousness, as constellations of beliefs, attitudes, and dispositions, are embedded in social practices operating within civil society. In presenting the formation of public opinion, and more importantly, our ethical dispositions, as essentially bound to the practices and institutions of ethical life, Hegel is operating with a method of social and political theorizing that, departing from the approaches of both early modern thinkers and the approaches of Kant and Fichte, he developed as early as 1802/3 in his essay on *Natural Law*. In the following section, I will propose that the *Natural Law* essay throws the concept of ideology into relief in two ways: first, in laying out certain methodological commitments that are sustained in the *Philosophy of Right*, providing further context for the ambivalent treatment of public opinion; and second, in showing that Hegel's methodological commitments already express, in nascent form, the methodological commitments of a critical theory, which he formulates in opposition to both *formalism* and *empiricism*.

3 Hegel's Critical Theory

Although it appears that the concept of public opinion is only restricted to the several paragraphs that conclude the discussion on the internal constitution, its importance in relation to Hegel's method in the *Philosophy of Right* is quite evident if one turns to the preface of that text. In the preface, Hegel presents the problem faced by social and political theorizing as, in part, revolving around the problem of public opinion: on the one hand, the truth concerning matters of "*right, ethics, and the state*" are already present in the "*public laws and in public morality and religion*," which are "universally acknowledged and valid"; on the other hand, that which is universally and publicly acknowledged likewise presents itself as a "jumble of truths," "an infinite variety of opinions," and as merely "subjective convictions" (*PR*, 11, 19). Sorting through the thicket of what is publicly acknowledged to arrive at the truth concerning matters of right, ethics, and the state is thus a central problem for social and political theorizing, and resolving this problem largely hinges on approaching such matters with the appropriate philosophical method, a method that, as I have tried to show, involves ideology critique. In the preface, however, Hegel largely refers his readers to the speculative method developed in his *Science of Logic*, a suggestion that has generated much dispute within the scholarship.[32] Although I believe that the *Logic does* matter for thinking about the *Philosophy of Right*, Hegel's methodological considerations in the *Natural Law* essay provide a more generally helpful sketch of the issues at stake, particularly as they concern sorting through the thicket of public opinion.

Hegel's essay on *Natural Law* was written during a period in which much of his work still employed Schellingian concepts and language. Although it is the case that Hegel at this time had not yet fully worked out his own philosophical system, it would be a mistake to read Hegel's mature work in terms of a full "break" with the Schellingian view, particularly as it concerns his use of the term "absolute." In the *Natural Law* essay, the terms "absolute" and the "idea" stand in for what, in principle, cannot be captured by the prevailing theories of natural law, which are one-sided in different ways. Whereas *formalism* (roughly attributed to the philosophies of Kant and Fichte) follows the path of a priori theorizing at the expense of attention to existing institutional realities and practices, *empiricism* attends haphazardly to experience in uncritical and unsystematic ways that tend to obscure the aims of human activity as well as the unity of ethical life. What emerges in his criticism of both formalism and empiricism is that what is "absolute," or "absolute ethical life," can appear as both "distorted [*verzogen*]" and "inverted [*verkehrt*]" and, thus, that we require a critical method that allows us to see such distortions for what they are.

Hegel's objection against formalism is better known, and the *Natural Law* essay presents a classic version of Hegel's critique of purely a priori theorizing concerning ethical matters. "Formalism," he writes, "asserts its formal principles as the *a priori* and absolute, and thus asserts that what it cannot master by these is non-absolute and accidental" (*NL*, 62; *HW*, 2: 443). Hegel has two kinds of worries in mind. First, formalism creates a fundamental and ultimately unbridgeable gap between its formal, a priori principles and the empirical reality (here: the ethical domain of human action) that these principles are meant to govern. Referring to Kant's fundamental law of pure practical reason, Hegel objects that the mere form of universal law cannot by itself generate any

[32] Wood argues that Hegel's *PR* should be completely severed from his "speculative logic"; and Neuhouser refers to Hegel's understanding of social freedom in the *PR* as "quasi-logical" (Wood 1990: 4–6; Neuhouser 2000: 31). For defenses of a "systematic" approach that stress the inseparability of Hegel's logic and his theory of objective spirit, see Brooks 2007 and Brooks and Stein 2017. For defenses of a balanced approach to the issue that draw insights from Hegel's logic without insisting that the *PR* can *only* be judged in connection with Hegel's larger philosophical system, see Kervégan 2018: xii and Novakovic 2017: 5–12, 164–7, 186–8.

ethical content. Rather than explaining why, for example, it is wrong to steal, formalism generates nothing but tautologies: "this tautological production is the legislation of this practical reason; property, if property *is*, must be property. But if we posit the opposite thing, negation of property, then the legislation of this same practical reason produces the tautology: non-property is non-property" (*NL*, 78; *HW*, 2: 463). In other words, stealing is non-universalizable only if we assume the institution of private property ("property is property"). If we negate the institution of private property, surely "stealing" (if it still makes sense to talk of stealing) *is* universalizable ("non-property is non-property"). Formalism's principles are not only parasitic upon an institutional context, but more importantly, they provide no guidance with respect to explaining or evaluating that institutional context as a sphere of human action. Second, the a priori approach of formalism leads to a "mechanical" conception of ethical life, in which the absolute gap between the ideal and real generates a situation in which the political domain, in sharp contrast to the moral domain, is governed ultimately by coercion and force. In the *Differenzschrift* from the same period, Hegel refers to Fichte's conception of the state as a "machine . . . an atomistic, life-impoverished multitude" (*D*, 149; *HW*, 2: 87). Far from a necessary feature of ethical life, this sharp separation of morality and politics is a result of formalism's absolute separation of the ideal and the real, one that masquerades as a so-called realism concerning political affairs.

Hegel's critique of empiricism is less often discussed, and perhaps surprisingly, his assessment of empiricism is not entirely negative. In fact, in agreement with empiricism against formalism, Hegel writes, "[empiricism] rightly demands" that social and political theorizing "should take its bearings from experience [*Erfahrung*]" (*NL*, 69; *HW*, 2: 451). His objection to empiricism is that it relies on experience in unsystematic, haphazard, and reductive ways. Two tendencies appear to be particularly problematic. First, empiricism tends to choose *one* feature out of a multitude of possibilities to do its explanatory work. For example, to explain punishment, empiricism focuses exclusively on the "criminal's moral reform," excluding all other relevant considerations (*NL*, 60; *HW*, 2: 441); or, in state of nature theories, there is an exclusive focus on chaos and conflict ("a war of all against all"), which abstracts from all other relevant features of human behavior and interaction (*NL*, 63–6; *HW*, 2: 444–9).[33] The decision to focus on this *one* empirical feature is either arbitrary, or a kind of cherry-picking where one simply chooses the evidence that best fits the view that one is trying to prove. Second, when empiricism does focus on a multiplicity of factors as explanatory, it still lacks the resources to grasp

[33] See also *NL*, 67; *HW*, 2: 449: "*one facet* . . . must be given primacy over the other facets of the multiplicity."

the multiplicity as a non-arbitrary, non-aggregated whole. It approaches its explanations of society in an atomistic and piecemeal fashion, staying at the level of "superficial points of contact," without being able to grasp the essential connections between the parts that make up the whole (*NL*, 65; *HW*, 2: 447). Later in the essay, Hegel defends his own philosophical approach against the "positive sciences" by suggesting that empiricism lacks a sufficiently nuanced concept of experience, anticipating the development of his more sophisticated account of experience in the *Phenomenology*. He writes: "Philosophy can exhibit its ideas in experience; the reason for this lies directly in the ambiguous nature [*zweideutigen Natur*] of what is called experience" (*NL*, 118; *HW*, 2: 511).[34]

To be sure, although there are rejoinders that could be made on behalf of defenders of formalism and empiricism, for the purposes of this paper, I will focus instead on what Hegel's critiques tell us about his *own* philosophical commitments.[35] What I want to suggest is that Hegel's position against formalism and empiricism in the *Natural Law* essay reveals that his methodological commitments are quite close to the methodological commitments of a *critical* theory and already represent the development of such a theory in a nascent form. To conclude, I will again draw from Geuss in order to point out three ways in particular that Hegel's methodological commitments point in the direction of a critical theory. First, Hegel's objections against both formalism and empiricism mirror critical theory's objections against both ideal theory and the position they refer to as positivism. In line with Hegel's worries concerning formalism, critical theorists contend that ideal theories such as Kant's theory of morality depend upon concrete, historical institutions and practices for their ethical content. Taking this one step further than Hegel, critical theory contends that Kantian morality reflects a specifically bourgeois morality that is deeply embedded in bourgeois institutions and practices. In line with Hegel's objections against empiricism, critical theory directly opposes itself to a position it refers to as positivism. Positivism holds: "(a) that an empiricist account of natural science is adequate, and (b) that all cognition must have

[34] In the introduction to the *Phenomenology*, Hegel also refers to the dialectical movement of the experience of consciousness in terms of ambiguity or *Zweideutigkeit* (*PhS*, ¶86; *HW*, 3: 79). There, the ambiguity in question concerns the distinction between *an sich* and *für sich*, and how this distinction generates knowledge for consciousness. Although it is beyond the aims of this paper to elaborate on Hegel's concept of experience, what I am suggesting is that Hegel's mixed treatment of empiricism in the *Natural Law* essay anticipates this later development.

[35] Two recent helpful essays cataloguing and assessing the various objections and replies on the issue of Hegel's empty formalism charge are Freyenhagen 2012 and Stern 2012. On the essential connection between Hegel's critique of empiricism and his criticism of Kant's formalism, see Sedgwick 1996. In her interpretation of Hegel's *Natural Law* essay, Sedgwick argues that a priori formalism and empiricism about content ultimately imply one another in Hegel's critique of Kant.

essentially the same cognitive structure as natural science."[36] Like Hegel then, critical theory defines its method in contrast to both ideal theory and positivism or empiricism, contending that an adequate understanding of society or "absolute ethical life" requires a more complex philosophical method.[37]

Second, once both formalism and empiricism are rejected, social and political theorizing consists of a mutually beneficial relationship between philosophy and empirical social research, one in which the concept of ideology plays a central role.[38] Of course, Hegel did not have access to what we understand today as empirical social research, but his attention to the need to orient ourselves through experience and his reference to both the importance and shortcomings of the "positive sciences" suggest that there is room in his method for this kind of development.[39] In the *Natural Law* essay, Hegel argues that formalism and empiricism offer distorted and inverted views of ethical life, and moreover, emphasizes that ethical life itself is subject to a number of social pathologies. He expresses concern that our philosophical theories can themselves become sources of ideological distortion, where these distortions should not simply be viewed as contingent or accidental epistemological errors. Rather, our philosophical errors can reflect tendencies and pathologies of ethical life itself, described by Hegel as "sickness and the onset of death" brought forth especially by the "isolation" of particular spheres of action from the whole (*NL*, 123; *HW*, 2: 517). He writes: "Thus it may happen that, in the general system of ethical life, the principle and system of civil law, for example, which is concerned with possession and property, becomes wholly absorbed in itself, and in the diffuseness in which it loses itself takes itself to be a totality supposedly inherent, absolute, and unconditioned" (*NL*, 123; *HW*, 2: 517–18). Our philosophical and conceptual errors, then, are not immune to the general tendencies of the age. Rather, certain one-sided ways of thinking reflect certain social pathologies.

Finally, Hegel's approach to social and political theorizing shares a third feature with critical theories: it is a fundamentally reflexive approach in which critical, philosophical reflection must be able to account for itself as part of its object of investigation. This sheds some light on why the problem of public opinion, which plays such a prominent role in the methodological reflections in the preface of the *Philosophy of Right*, is also the problem with which Hegel

[36] Geuss 1981: 2. [37] And as mentioned above, a more complex concept of experience.

[38] See Horkheimer's inaugural lecture in Frankfurt where he presents this relationship between philosophy and empirical social research in essentially Hegelian terms (Horkheimer 1993).

[39] Indeed, Hegel's debt to the British political economists in developing his own ideas surrounding labor, property, and the system of needs is undeniable. This is just to say that Hegel was deeply engaged with the nascent empirical social science of his own time. Thanks to the editors of this volume for emphasizing this point.

concludes his theory of the rational state. Sorting through public opinion, criticizing its forms of ideological false consciousness, and discovering the truths behind its prejudices are not just problems for philosophers or philosophy. They are problems inherent to modern ethical life itself, and in the transition that takes place from Hegel to Marx, problems that point in the direction of revolutionary political praxis.

Bibliography

Aaslestad, Katherine and Hagemann, Karen (2006). "1806 and Its Aftermath: Revisiting the Period of the Napoleonic Wars in German Central European Historiography," *Central European History* 39:4: 547–79.

Achenwall, Gottfried and Putter, Johann ([1750] 1995). *Anfangsgründe des Naturrechts (Elementa Iuris Naturae)*, edited by Jan Schröder (Frankfurt am Main and Leipzig: Insel Verlag).

Adorno, Theodor W. (1976). "Sociology and Empirical Research," in *The Positivist Dispute in German Sociology*, translated by Glyn Adey and David Frisby (London: Heinemann Educational Books), 68–86.

Alexander, Gerhard (1985). "Johann Albert Hinrich Reimarus und Elise Reimarus in ihren Beziehungen zu Lessing," in Günter Schulz (ed.), *Lessing und der Kreis seiner Freunde* (Heidelberg: Schneider), 129–50.

Alexy, Robert (2002). *The Argument from Injustice: A Reply to Legal Positivism* (Oxford University Press).

(2012). "Law, Morality, and the Existence of Human Rights," *Ratio Juris* 25:1: 2–14.

Altman, Matthew (2014). *The Palgrave Handbook of German Idealism* (New York: Palgrave Macmillan).

Anderson, Frank M., ed. (1908). *The Constitutions and Other Select Documents Illustrative of the History of France, 1789–1907* (Minneapolis: H. W. Wilson).

Aquinas, Thomas (2002). *On Law, Morality, and Politics*, translated by Richard J. Regan (Indianapolis: Hackett).

Aris, Reinhold ([1936] 1965). *History of Political Thought in Germany from 1789 to 1815* (New York: Russell & Russell).

Backhaus, Jürgen, ed. (1998). *Christian Wolff and Law and Economics* (Hildesheim: Olms).

Backhaus, Jürgen, ed. (2001). "Subsidiarity as a Constitutional Principle in Environmental Policy," www.vonmisesinstitute-europe.org/wp-content/uploads/2018/11/Subsidiarity.Backhaus.pdf

Baker, Keith M., ed. (1987). *University of Chicago Readings in Western Civilization, Volume 7: The Old Regime and the French Revolution* (University of Chicago Press).

Batscha, Zwi (1972). "Johann Benjamin Erhards Politische Theorie," *Jahrbuch für Deutsche Geschichte* 1: 53–75.

Baumgardt, David (1963). "The Ethics of Salomon Maimon," *Journal of the History of Philosophy* 1:2: 199–210.

Beaulieu-Marconnay, Karl (1879). *Karl von Dalberg und seine Zeit*, Vol. I (Weimar: Böhlau).

Beck, Lewis White (1960). *A Commentary on Kant's* Critique of Practical Reason (University of Chicago Press).

Beiser, Frederick C. (1992). *Enlightenment, Revolution and Romanticism: The Genesis of Modern German Political Thought, 1790–1800* (Cambridge, MA: Harvard University Press).

ed. (1996). *The Early Writings of the German Romantics* (Cambridge University Press).

(2002). *German Idealism: The Struggle against Subjectivism, 1781–1801* (Cambridge, MA: Harvard University Press).

(2005). *Schiller as Philosopher: A Re-examination* (Oxford University Press).

(2009). *Diotima's Children: German Aesthetic Rationalism from Leibniz to Lessing* (Oxford University Press).

(2011). *The German Historicist Tradition* (Oxford University Press).

Benhabib, Seyla (1986). *Critique, Norm, and Utopia: A Study of the Foundations of Critical Theory* (New York: Columbia University Press).

Berlin, Isaiah (2014). *Freedom and Its Betrayal: Six Enemies of Human Liberty*, edited by Henry Hardy (Princeton University Press).

Beyleveld, Deryck and Brownsword, Roger (1986). *Law as a Moral Judgment*. (London: Sweet & Maxwell).

Bowie, Andrew (2002). *Schelling and Modern European Philosophy: An Introduction* (New York: Routledge).

Boyle, Nicholas (2000). *Goethe: The Poet and the Age*, Vol. 2 (Oxford: Clarendon Press).

Breazeale, Daniel (2016). "From Autonomy to Automata? Fichte on Formal and Material Freedom and Moral Cultivation," in Daniel Breazeale and Tom Rockmore (eds.), *Fichte's* Addresses to the German Nation *Reconsidered* (Albany, NY: State University of New York Press), 21–54.

(2021). "Formal vs. Material Freedom in the Jena *Wissenschaftslehre*." In Owen Ware and Stefano Bacin (eds.), *Fichte's System of Ethics: A Critical Guide* (Cambridge University Press).

Breckman, Warren (1999). *Marx, the Young Hegelians, and the Origins of Radical Social Theory: Dethroning the Self* (Cambridge University Press).

Brooks, Thom (2007). *Hegel's Political Philosophy: A Systematic Reading of the* Philosophy of Right (Edinburgh University Press).

Brooks, Thom and Stein, Sebastian, eds. (2017). *Hegel's Political Philosophy: On the Normative Significance of Method and System* (Oxford University Press).

Bubner, Rüdiger (2003). *The Innovations of Idealism*, translated by Nicholas Walker (Cambridge University Press).

Buchetmann, Elias (2020). "Hegel's Intervention in Württemberg's Constitutional Conflict," *History of European Ideas* 46:2: 157–74.

Burke, Edmund (1987). *Reflections on the Revolution in France*, edited by J. G. A. Pocock (Indianapolis: Hackett).

Burke, Edmund and Gentz, Friedrich (1991). *Über die französische Revolution: Betrachtungen und Abhandlungen*, edited by Herman Klenner (Berlin: Akademie Verlag, 1991).

Burrow, John W. (1969). "Editor's Introduction," in John W. Burrow (ed.), *Wilhelm von Humboldt, The Limits of State Action* (Cambridge University Press), vii–xliii.

Cassirer, Ernst (1968). *The Philosophy of the Enlightenment* (Princeton University Press).

([1917] 2001). *Freiheit und Form. Studien zur deutschen Geistesgeschichte* (Hamburg: Meiner).

Christ, Kurt (1998). *F.H. Jacobi, Rousseaus deutscher Adept: Rousseauismus in Leben und Frühwerk Friedrich Heinrich Jacobis* (Würzburg: Königshausen & Neumann).

Chytry, Josef (1989). *The Aesthetic State: A Quest in Modern German Thought* (Berkeley: University of California Press).

Clarke, James A. (2016). "Fichte's Independence Thesis," in Gabriel Gottlieb (ed.), *Fichte's Foundations of Natural Right: A Critical Guide* (Cambridge University Press), 52–71.

Clarke, Randolph (2005). "Agent Causation and the Problem of Luck," *Pacific Philosophical Quarterly* 86:3: 408–21.

Coffman, Eldon J. (2010). "How (Not) to Attack the Luck Argument," *Philosophical Explorations* 13:2: 157–66.

Colbois, Sylvie and Perrinjaquet, Alain (1994). "Recht zur Aufklärung und Sozialrechte. Zu J.B. Erhards Theorie der Menschenrechte," in Manfred Buhr (ed.), *Das Geistige Erbe Europas* (Biblioteca Europea 5, Naples: Vivarium), 558–72.

Coleridge, Samuel (1847). *Biographia Literaria* (London: William Pickering).

Crowe, Ben (2014). "Jacobi on Kant, or Moral Naturalism vs. Idealism," in Matthew C. Altman (ed.), *The Palgrave Handbook of German Idealism* (London: Palgrave Macmillan), 205–21.

Curtis-Wendlandt, Lisa (2012). "No Right to Resist? Elise Reimarus's *Freedom* as a Kantian Response to the Problem of Violent Revolt," *Hypatia* 27:4: 755–73.

(2013). "Legality and Morality in the Political Thought of Elise Reimarus and Immanuel Kant," in Lisa Curtis-Wendlandt, Paul Gibbard, and Karen Green (eds.), *Political Ideas of Enlightenment Women: Virtue and Citizenship* (Burlington, VT and Farnham: Ashgate), 91–107.

Dalberg, C. Th. [K. von] (1791). *Grundsätze der Ästhetik, deren Anwendung und künftige Entwickelung* (Erfurt).

Deligiorgi, Katerina (2017). "Interest and Agency," in Markus Gabriel and Moe Anders Rasmussen (eds.), *German Idealism Today* (Berlin: De Gruyter Verlag), 3–26.

De Pascale, Carla (1994). "Archäologie des Rechtstaates," in Manfred Buhr (ed.), *Das geistige Erbe Europas* (Naples: Vivarium, 1994), 489–505.

Di Giovanni, George (1994). "Introduction: The Unfinished Philosophy of Friedrich Heinrich Jacobi," in *The Main Philosophical Writings and the Novel* Allwill (Montreal: McGill-Queen's University Press), 1–157.

(2005). *Freedom and Religion in Kant and His Immediate Successors: The Vocation of Humankind, 1774–1800* (Cambridge University Press).

Eliot, George (2014). *Daniel Deronda*, edited by Graham Handely (Oxford University Press).

Epstein, Klaus (1966). *The Genesis of German Conservatism* (Princeton University Press).

Erhard, Johann Benjamin (1993). *Du droit du peuple à faire la révolution et autres écrits de philosophie politique* (1793–5), translated by Alain Perrinjaquet and Jeanclaude Berger (Lausanne: L'Âge d'Homme).

Färber, Konrad (1995). "Carl von Dalberg – Reichsverräter oder Reichspatriot?," in K. Hausberger (ed.), *Carl von Dalberg. Der letzte geistliche Reichsfürst* (Regensburg: Universitätsverlag), 153–75.

Ferry, Luc (1981). "Sur la distinction du droit et de l'éthique dans la première philosophie de Fichte," *Archives de philosophie du droit* 26: 287–301.

Fink, Gonthier-Louis (1992). "The French Revolution as Reflected in German Literature and Political Journals from 1789 to 1800," in Ehrhard Bahr and Thomas P. Saine (eds.), *The Internalized Revolution: German Reactions to the French Revolution, 1789–1989* (London: Routledge), 11–31.

Finnis, John (1996). "The Truth in Legal Positivism," in Robert P. George (ed.), *The Autonomy of Law: Essays in Legal Positivism* (Oxford University Press), 195–214.

(1998). *Aquinas: Moral, Political, and Legal Theory* (Oxford University Press).

(2011). *Natural Law and Natural Rights* (Oxford University Press).

(2018). "Natural Law Theories," in Edward N. Zalta (ed.), *The Stanford Encyclopedia of Philosophy* (Winter 2018 Edition), https://plato.stanford.edu/archives/win2016/entries/natural-law-theories/.

Fischer, Kuno (1900). *Fichtes Leben, Werken, und Lehre*, 4th ed. (Paderborn: Salzwasser Verlag).

Foot, Philippa (1981). *Virtues and Vices* (Berkeley and Los Angeles: University of California Press).

Förster, Eckart and Melamed, Yitzak Y., eds. (2012). *Spinoza and German Idealism* (Cambridge University Press).

Fraenkel, Carlos (2009). "Maimonides and Spinoza as Sources for Maimon's Solution of the 'Problem Quid Juris' in Kant's Theory of Knowledge," *Kant-Studien* 100:2: 212–40.

Frank, Manfred (1993). "Two Centuries of Philosophical Critique of Reason and its 'Postmodern' Radicalization," in Dieter Freundlieb and Wayne Hudson (eds.), *Reason and Its Other: Rationality in Modern German Philosophy and Culture* (Oxford: Berg), 67–85.

(1997). *"Unendliche Annäherung": Die Anfänge der philosophischen Frühromantik* (Frankfurt: Suhrkamp).

(2004). *The Philosophical Foundations of Early German Romanticism*, translated by Elizabeth Millán-Zaibert (Albany, NY: State University of New York Press).

Franklin, Christopher E. (2011). "Farewell to the Luck (and Mind) Argument," *Philosophical Studies* 156:2: 199–230.

Franks, Paul W. (2005). *All or Nothing: Systematicity, Transcendental Arguments, and Skepticism in German Idealism* (Cambridge, MA: Harvard University Press).

(2007). "Jewish Philosophy after Kant," in Michael L. Morgan and Peter E. Gordon (eds.), *Modern Jewish Philosophy* (Cambridge University Press), 53–79.

Freudenthal, Gideon, ed. (2003a). *Salomon Maimon: Rational Dogmatist, Empirical Skeptic* (Dordrecht: Kluwer Publishing Company).

(2003b). "Maimon's Subversion of Kant's *Critique of Pure Reason*," in Gideon Freudenthal (ed.), *Salomon Maimon: Rational Dogmatist, Empirical Skeptic* (Dordrecht, Boston, and London: Kluwer Academic Publishers), 144–75.

(2005). "Rabbinische Weisheit oder Rabbinische Philosophie? Salomon Maimon's Kritik an Mendelssohn und Weisel," *Mendelssohn Studies* 14: 31–64.

(2012). "Salomon Maimon's Development from Kabbalah to Philosophical Rationalism"; in Hebrew, "Hitpathutoh shel Shelomo Maimon mikabalah l'rationalizm filosofi," *Tarbiz* 80:1: 105–71.

Freyenhagen, Fabian (2012). "The Empty Formalism Objection Revisited: §135R and Recent Kantian Responses," in Thom Brooks (ed.), *Hegel's Philosophy of Right* (Oxford: Wiley-Blackwell), 43–72.

Fricker, Miranda (2007). *Epistemic Injustice: Power and the Ethics of Knowing* (Oxford University Press).

Friedman, Michael (1992). *Kant and the Exact Sciences* (Cambridge, MA: Harvard University Press).

Fuchs, Erich, ed. (1992). *Fichte im Gespräch*, Bd. 6 (Stuttgart-Bad Cannstatt: Frommann-Holzboog).

Gardner, Sebastian (2017). "The Metaphysics of Human Freedom: From Kant's Transcendental Idealism to Schelling's Freiheitsschrift," *British Journal for the History of Philosophy* 25:1: 133–56.

Gentz, Friederich (1800). *Origin and Principles of the American Revolution, Compared with the Origin and Principles of the French Revolution, translated by an American gentleman* [John Quincy Adams] (Philadelphia: Asbury Dickens).

Gesang, Bernward, ed. (2007). *Kants vergessene Rezensent: die Kritik der theoretischen und praktischen Philosophie Kants in fünf frühen Rezensionene von Hermann Andreas Pistorius*, Kant-Forschungen Bd. 18 (Hamburg: Felix Meiner Verlag).

Geuss, Raymond (1981). *The Idea of a Critical Theory: Habermas and the Frankfurt School* (Cambridge University Press).

Gleichen-Russwurm, Alexander, von (n.d.). "Einleitung des Herausgebers," in Wilhelm von Humboldt, *Ideen zu einem Versuch, die Grenzen der Wirksamkeit des Staats zu bestimmen* (Berlin: Deutsche Bibliothek), 9–15.

Gooch, George P. (1966). *Germany and the French Revolution* (New York: Russell & Russell).

Grapotte, Sophie and Prunea-Bretonnet, Tinca, eds. (2011). *Kant et Wolff. Héritages et ruptures* (Paris: Vrin).

Green, Karen (2014). *A History of Women's Political Thought in Europe, 1700–1800* (Cambridge University Press).

(2017). "Locke, Enlightenment, and Liberty in the Works of Catharine Macaulay and Her Contemporaries," in Jacqueline Broad and Karen Detlefsen (eds.), *Women and Liberty 1600–1800: Philosophical Essays* (Oxford University Press), 82–94.

Guyer, Paul (2010). "Moral Feelings in the *Metaphysics of Morals*," in Lara Denis (ed.), *Kant's Metaphysics of Morals: A Critical Guide* (Cambridge University Press), 130–51.

(2016). *Virtues of Freedom: Selected Essays on Kant* (Oxford University Press).

(2017). "The Struggle for Freedom: Freedom of Will in Kant and Reinhold," in Eric Watkins (ed.), *Kant on Persons and Agency* (Cambridge University Press), 120–37.

(2020). Introduction to *Natural Law: A Translation of the Textbook for Kant's Lectures on Legal and Political Philosophy*, by Gottfried Achenwall, edited by Pauline Kleingeld (London: Bloomsbury), xiii–xxxi.

Haasis, Hellmut G. (1970). "Nachwort," in Johann Benjamin Erhard, *Über das Recht des Volks zu einer Revolution und andere Schriften*, edited by Hellmut G. Haasis (Munich: Carl Hanser Verlag), 205–32.

Habermas, Jürgen (1974). *Theory and Practice*, translated by John Viertel (Boston: Beacon Press).

(1989). *The Structural Transformation of the Public Sphere: An Inquiry into a Category of Bourgeois Society*, translated by Thomas Burger and Frederick Lawrence (Cambridge, MA: The MIT Press).

Hammacher, Klaus (1969). *Die Philosophie Friedrich Heinrich Jacobis* (Munich: Fink).

(1971). *Friedrich Heinrich Jacobi. Philosoph und Literat der Goethezeit: Beiträge einer Tagung in Düsseldorf 1969 aus Anlaß seines 150. Todestages und Berichte* (Frankfurt am Main: Klostermann).

Hanna, Robert (2006). "Kant, Causation and Freedom: Review of E. Watkins, *Kant and the Metaphysics of Causality*," *Canadian Journal of Philosophy* 36:2: 281–306.

Harris, Henry S. (1997). *Hegel's Ladder: Volume I: The Pilgrimage of Reason. Volume II: The Odyssey of Spirit* (Indianapolis: Hackett).

Haslanger, Sally (2012). "Ideology, Generics, and Common Ground," in *Resisting Reality: Social Construction and Social Critique* (Cambridge University Press), 446–75.

(2017). "Racism, Ideology, and Social Movements," *Res Philosophica* 94:1 (January): 1–22.

Hay, Carol (2013). *Kantianism, Liberalism, and Feminism: Resisting Oppression* (New York: Palgrave Macmillan).

Henrich, Dieter (2003). *Between Kant and Hegel: Lectures on German Idealism*, edited by D. S. Pacini (Cambridge, MA: Harvard University Press).

(2004). *Grundlegung aus dem Ich: Untersuchungen zur Vorgeschichte des Idealismus* (Frankfurt: Suhrkamp).

Hernández Marcos, Maximiliano (2020). "Rights-Perfectionism, from Kant's *Grundlegung* to Politics: Kantian Debates," in Douglas Moggach, Nadine Mooren, and Michael Quante (eds.), *Perfektionismus der Autonomie* (Paderborn: Fink), 29–68.

Hill, Roland (2011). *Lord Acton* (New Haven, CT: Yale University Press).

Hill, Thomas E. (2000). *Respect, Pluralism, and Justice: Kantian Perspectives* (Oxford University Press).

Holzman, Gitit (2013). "R. Moshe Narboni's Commentary to Maimonides' *Guide of the Perplexed*," *Daat* 73: 197–236 (in Hebrew).

Homann, Karl (1973). *F. H. Jacobis Philosophie der Freiheit* (Freiburg: Alber).

Honneth, Axel (2007). "Recognition as Ideology," in Bert van den Brink and David Owen (eds.), *Recognition and Power: Axel Honneth and the Tradition of Critical Social Theory* (Cambridge University Press), 323–47.

(2010). *The Pathologies of Individual Freedom: Hegel's Social Theory*, translated by Ladislaus Löb (Princeton University Press).

(2014). *Freedom's Right: The Social Foundations of Democratic Life*, translated by Joseph Ganahl (New York: Columbia University Press).

Horkheimer, Max (1993). "The Present Situation of Social Philosophy and the Tasks of an Institute for Social Research," in *Between Philosophy and Social Science:*

Selected Early Writings, translated by G. Frederick Hunger, Matthew S. Kramer, and John Torpey (Cambridge, MA: The MIT Press).

Hufeland, Gottlieb (1785). *Versuch über den Grundsatz des Naturrechts* (Leipzig).

Humboldt, Wilhelm von (1851). *Ideen zu einem Versuch, die Gränzen der Wirksamkeit des Staats zu bestimmen* (Breslau: Trewendt).

(1854). *The Sphere and Duties of Government*, translated by Joseph Coulthard (London: John Chapman).

(1963). *Humanist without Portfolio: An Anthology of the Writings of Wilhelm von Humboldt*, edited and translated by Marianne Cowan (Detroit: Wayne State University Press).

(1969). *The Limits of State Action*, edited by John W. Burrow (Cambridge University Press).

Hyppolite, Jean (1973). *Studies on Marx and Hegel*, translated by John O'Neill (New York: Harper & Row).

Ivry, Alfred (2015). "Al-Ghazali, Averroes, and Moshe Narboni: Conflict and Conflation," in Georges Tanner (ed.), *Islam and Rationality: The Impact of al-Ghazali*, Vol. 1 (Leiden: Brill), 275–87.

Jaeggi, Rahel (2009). "Rethinking Ideology," in Boudewijn de Bruin and Christopher F. Zurn (eds.), *New Waves in Political Philosophy* (New York: Palgrave Macmillan), 63–86.

(2018). *Critique of Forms of Life*, translated by Ciaran Cronin (Cambridge, MA: Harvard University Press).

Jaeschke, Walter (1990). "Ästhetische Revolution: Stichworte zur Einführung," in Walter Jaeschke and Helmut Holzhey (eds.), *Früher Idealismus und Frühromantik. Der Streit um die Grundlagen der Ästhetik (1795–1805)* (Hamburg: Felix Meiner Verlag), 1–11.

Jaeschke, Walter and Sandkaulen, Birgit, eds. (2004). *Friedrich Heinrich Jacobi. Ein Wendepunkt der geistigen Bildung der Zeit* (Hamburg: Meiner).

Kane, Robert (1989). "Two Kinds of Incompatibilism," *Philosophy and Phenomenological Research* 50:2: 219–54.

(1996). *The Significance of Free Will* (Oxford University Press).

Kaufman, Alexander (1990). *Welfare in the Kantian State* (Oxford University Press).

Kelsen, Hans (1961). *General Theory of Law and the State*, translated by Anders Wedberg (New York: Russell & Russell).

(1967). *The Pure Theory of Law*, translated by Max Knight (Berkeley and Los Angeles: University of California Press).

Kersting, Wolfgang (1992). "Politics, Freedom, and Order: Kant's Political Philosophy," in Paul Guyer (ed.), *The Cambridge Companion to Kant* (Cambridge University Press), 342–66.

Kervégan, Jean-François (2018). *The Actual and the Rational: Hegel and Objective Spirit*, translated by Daniela Ginsburg and Martin Shuster (University of Chicago Press).

Kleingeld, Pauline (1999). "Kant, History, and the Idea of Moral Development," *History of Philosophy Quarterly* 16:1: 59–80.

Klippel, Deithelm (1998). "Der liberale Interventionsstaat. Staatszweck und Staatstätigkeit in der deutschen politischen Theorie des 18. und der ersten Hälfte des 19. Jahrhunderts," in Heiner Lück (ed.), *Recht und Rechtswissenschaft im mitteldeutschen Raum* (Cologne: Böhlau), 77–103.

Kluckhohn, Paul (1925). *Personlichkeit und Gemeinschaft. Studien zur Staatsauffassung der deutschen Romantik* (Halle: Niemeyer).

Kneller, Jane (2007). *Kant and the Power of Imagination* (Cambridge University Press).

Kosch, Michelle (2017). "Individuality and Rights in Fichte's Ethics," *Philosophers' Imprint* 17:12: 1–23.

(2018). *Fichte's Ethics* (Oxford University Press).

Kraut, Richard (1979). "Two Conceptions of Happiness," *Philosophical Review* 88:2: 167–97.

Kröner, Richard (1961). *Von Kant bis Hegel*, 2 vols. (Tübingen: Mohr).

Kurt, Christ (1998). *F.H. Jacobi. Rousseaus deutscher Adept. Rousseauismus in Leben und Frühwerk Friedrich Heinrich Jacobis* (Würzburg: Königshausen & Neumann).

Lachterman, David (1992). "Mathematical Construction, Symbolic Cognition and the Infinite Intellect: Reflections on Maimon and Maimonides," *Journal of the History of Philosophy* 30:4: 497–522.

Landau, Albert, ed. (1991). *Rezensionen zur Kantischen Philosophie 1781–87* (Bebra: Albert Landau Verlag).

Lee, Daniel (2008). "The Legacy of Medieval Constitutionalism in the *Philosophy of Right*: Hegel and the Prussian Reform Movement," *History of Political Thought* XXIX:4.

Leibniz, Gottfried (1887). *Die philosophischen Schriften von Gottfried Wilhelm Leibniz*, Vol. 3, edited by Carl I. Gerhardt (Berlin: Weidmann).

(1969). "Two Notions for Discussion with Spinoza," in *Philosophical Papers and Letters*, translated and edited by Leroy E. Loemker (Dordrecht: Reidel), 167–69.

(1989). *Philosophical* Essays, translated and edited by Roger Ariew and Daniel Garber (Indianapolis: Hackett).

([1720] 1991). *Monadology*, edited by Nicholas Rescher (University of Pittsburgh Press).

(1993). *Leibniz-Thomasius. Correspondance (1663–1672)*, edited by Richard Bodéus (Paris: Vrin).

(2004). "Principles of Nature and Grace Based on Reason," J. Bennett translation, www.earlymoderntexts.com

Léon, Xavier (1954). *Fichte et son temps,* Vol. 1 (Paris: Armand Colin).

Leroux, Robert (1932a). *La théorie du despotisme éclairé chez Karl Theodor Dalberg* (Presses universitaires de Strasbourg).

(1932b). *Guillaume de Humboldt: La formation de sa pensée jusqu'en 1794* (Presses universitaires de Strasbourg).

Locke, John ([1690] 1980). *Second Treatise of Government*, edited by Crawford B. Macpherson (Indianapolis: Hackett).

Mack, Eric and Gaus, Gerald F. (2004). "Classical Liberalism and Libertarianism: The Liberty Tradition," in *The Handbook of Political Theory*, edited by Gerald F. Gaus and Chandran Kukathas (London: Sage), 115–30.

Maimon, Salomon (1778). *Hesheq Shelomo* (*Salomon's Desire*) (Posen). National and University Library, Jerusalem (MS 806426).

(1791). *Philosophisches Wörterbuch*, Erstes Stück (Berlin: Johann Friedrich Unger).

(1793). *Streifereien im Gebiete der Philosophie*, Erste Teil (Berlin: Wilhelm Vieweg).
(1797). *Kritische Untersuchungen über den menschlichen Geist, oder der höhere Erkenntnis und Willensvermögen* (Leipzig: Gerhard Fleicher dem Jünger).
(1965). *Give'at ha-Moreh*, edited by Samuel H. Bergmann and Nathan Rotenstreich (Jerusalem: Israeli Academy of Science).
(1999). *Commentaires de Maïmonide*, translated and edited by Maurice-Ruben Hayoun (Paris: Cerf).
(2010). *Essay Concerning Transcendental Philosophy*, translated by Nick Midgley, Henry Somers-Hall, Alistair Welchman, and Merten Reglitz (New York: Continuum Publishing Company).
(2018a). "Attempt at a New Presentation of the Principle of Morality and a Deduction of Its Reality," translated by Timothy Sean Quinn. *British Journal for the History of Philosophy* 27:1: 1–27.
(2018b). *The Autobiography of Salomon Maimon: The Complete Translation*, translated by Paul Reitter and edited by Yitzhak Melamed and Abraham Socher (Princeton University Press).
Maimonides, Moses (1974). *The Guide of the Perplexed*, translated by Shlomo Pines (University of Chicago Press).
Maliks, Reidar (2012). "Revolutionary Epigones: Kant and His Radical Followers," *History of Political Thought* XXXIII:4: 647–71.
(2014). *Kant's Politics in Context* (Oxford University Press).
Manson, Neil A. (2002). "Formulating the Precautionary Principle," *Environmental Ethics* 24:3: 263–74.
Melamed, Yitzhak (2004). "Salomon Maimon and the Rise of Spinozism in Germany," *Journal of the History of Philosophy* 42:1: 67–96.
Mele, Alfred R. (2006). *Free Will and Luck* (Oxford University Press).
Mill, John Stuart ([1873] 1960). *Autobiography of John Stuart Mill* (New York: Columbia University Press).
([1859] 1991). *On Liberty and Other Essays* (Oxford University Press).
Mills, Charles (1997). *The Racial Contract* (Ithaca, NY: Cornell University Press).
Moggach, Douglas (2008). "Schiller, Scots, and Germans: Freedom and Diversity in *The Aesthetic Education of Man*," *Inquiry* 51:1: 16–36.
Moggach, Douglas, Mooren, Nadine, and Quante, Michael, eds. (2020). *Der Perfektionismus der Autonomie* (Paderborn: Fink).
Morris, Michael (2016). *Knowledge and Ideology: The Epistemology of Social and Political Critique* (Cambridge University Press).
Möser, Justus (1965). "Über das Recht der Menschheit, in so fern es zur Grundlage eines Staates dienen kann," in Georg Lenz (ed.), *Deutsches Staatsdenken im 18. Jahrhundert* (Neuwied and Berlin: Luchterhand), 273–91.
Murphy, Mark C. (2005). "Natural Law Theory," in Martin P. Golding and William A. Edmundson (eds.), *The Blackwell Guide to the Philosophy of Law and Legal Theory* (Oxford: Blackwell), 15–28.
Nance, Michael and Yonover, Jason (2020). "Introduction to Salomon Maimon's 'On the First Grounds of Natural Right' (1795)," *British Journal for the History of Philosophy*, published online 7 May 2020.

National Assembly of France (1961). "Declaration of the Rights of Man and the Citizen," in Marvin Harris, Sidney Morgenbesser, Joseph Rothschild, and Bernard Wishy (eds.), *Introduction to Contemporary Civilization in the West: A Source Book, Volume 2* (New York: Columbia University Press), 33–5.

Neuhouser, Frederick (2000). *Foundations of Hegel's Social Theory: Actualizing Freedom* (Cambridge, MA: Harvard University Press).

(2016). "Fichte's Separation of Right from Morality," in Gabriel Gottlieb (ed.), *Fichte's Foundations of Natural Right: A Critical Guide* (Cambridge University Press), 32–51.

Ng, Karen (2015). "Ideology Critique from Hegel and Marx to Critical Theory," *Constellations* 22:3: 393–404.

Niezen, Roland (2009). "The *Aufklärung*'s Human Discipline: Comparative Anthropology According to Kant, Herder and Wilhelm von Humboldt," *Intellectual History Review* 19:2: 177–95.

Nisenbaum, Karin (2018). *For the Love of Metaphysics: Nihilism and the Conflict of Reason from Kant to Rozenzweig* (Oxford University Press).

Novakovic, Andreja (2017). *Hegel on Second Nature in Ethical Life* (Cambridge University Press).

O'Connor, Timothy (2007). "Is It All Just a Matter of Luck?," *Philosophical Explorations* 10: 157–61.

Oncina Coves, Faustino (1997). "Wahlverwandschaften zwischen Fichtes, Maimons und Erhards Rechtslehren," *Fichte-Studien* 11: 63–84.

Pinkard, Terry (2000). *Hegel: A Biography* (Cambridge University Press).

Pippin, Robert (2001). "Fichte's Alleged Subjective, Psychological, One-Sided Idealism," in Sally S. Sedgwick (ed.), *The Reception of Kant's Critical Philosophy: Fichte, Schelling, and Hegel* (Cambridge University Press), 147–70.

Plato (1997). *Complete Works*, edited by John Cooper (Indianapolis: Hackett).

Pruss, Alexander (2006). *The Principle of Sufficient Reason: A Reassessment* (Cambridge University Press).

Redding, Paul (2009). *Continental Idealism: Leibniz to Nietzsche* (London: Routledge).

Reimarus, Johann (1803). *Entwurf eines allgemeinen Staats-Unterrichts für künftigen Bürger* (Hamburg: Campe).

Reinhold, Karl L. (2008). *Briefe über die Kantische Philosophie*, Bd. II (Basel: Schwabe).

Reiss, Han, ed. (1991). *Kant: Political Writings* (Cambridge University Press).

Ripstein, Arthur (2009). *Force and Freedom: Kant's Legal and Political Philosophy* (Cambridge, MA: Harvard University Press).

Ritter, Joachim (1982). *Hegel and the French Revolution: Essays on the Philosophy of Right*, translated by Richard Dien Winfield (Cambridge, MA: The MIT Press).

Rohls, Michael (2004). *Kantisches Naturrecht und historisches Zivilrecht. Wissenschaft und bürgerliche Freiheit bei Gottlieb Hufeland (1760–1817)* (Baden-Baden: Nomos).

Rousseau, Jean-Jacques ([1762] 1963). *Du contrat social* (Paris: Union Générale d'Éditions).

Rush, Fred (2016). *Irony and Idealism: Rereading Schlegel, Hegel, and Kierkegaard* (Oxford University Press).

Russell, Bertrand (1945). *History of Western Philosophy* (New York: Simon and Schuster).

Rutherford, Donald (2005). "Leibniz on Spontaneity," in Donald Rutherford and J. A. Cover (eds.), *Leibniz: Nature and Freedom* (Oxford University Press), 156–80.

Sandkaulen, Birgit (2000). *Grund und Ursache. Die Vernunftkritik Jacobis* (Munich: Fink).

Salmon, Wesley (1998). *Causality and Explanation* (Oxford University Press).

Saul, Nicholas (2003). "The Pursuit of the Subject: Literature as Critic and Perfecter of Philosophy 1790–1830," in Nicholas Saul (ed.), *Philosophy and German Literature 1700–1990* (Cambridge University Press), 57–101.

Schlegel, Friedrich (1882). *Friedrich Schlegel: Seine prosaische Jugendschriften 1792–1802*. 2 vols., edited by Jakob Minor (Vienna: C. Konegan).

Schmidt, James, ed. (1996). *What Is Enlightenment? Eighteenth-Century Answers and Twentieth-Century Questions* (Berkeley: University of California Press).

(1998). "Cabbage Heads and Gulps of Water: Hegel on the Terror," *Political Theory* 26:1: 4–32.

Schneewind, Jerome (1998). *The Invention of Autonomy* (Cambridge University Press).

Schopenhauer, Arthur (2009). *Two Fundamental Problems of Ethics*, translated by Christopher Janaway (Cambridge University Press).

Schottky, Richard (1995). *Untersuchungen zur Geschichte der staatsphilosophischen Vertragstheorie im 17. und 18. Jahrhundert (Hobbes-Locke-Rousseau-Fichte) mit einem Beitrag zum Problem der Gewaltenteilung bei Rousseau und Fichte* (Amsterdam: Rodopi).

Schui, Florian (2013). *Rebellious Prussians* (Oxford University Press).

Sedgwick, Sally S. (1996). "Hegel's Critique of Kant's Empiricism and the Categorical Imperative," *Zeitschrift für philosophische Forschung* 50:4 (Oct.–Dec.), 563–84.

Sewell, William H. (1994). *A Rhetoric of Bourgeois Revolution: The Abbé Sieyes and* What Is the Third Estate? (Durham, NC: Duke University Press).

Shatz, David (2005). "Maimonides' Moral Theory," in Kenneth Sesskin (ed.), *The Cambridge Companion to Maimonides* (Cambridge University Press), 167–92.

Shelby, Tommie (2003). "Ideology, Racism, and Critical Social Theory," *The Philosophical Forum* 34:2: 153–88.

(2014). "Racism, Moralism, and Social Criticism," *DuBois Review* 11:1: 57–74.

Siep, Ludwig (2002). "La systématique de l'esprit pratique chez Wolff, Kant, Fichte et Hegel," *Revue germanique internationale* 18: 105–19.

Sieveking, Heinrich (1940). "Elise Reimarus (1735–1805) in den geistigen Kämpfen ihrer Zeit," *Zeitschrift des Vereins für Hamburgische Geschichte* 39: 86–138.

Smith, Steven B. (1990). "Hegel and the French Revolution: An Epitaph for Republicanism," in Ferenc Feher (ed.), *The French Revolution and the Birth of Modernity* (Berkeley: University of California Press), 219–39.

Socher, Abraham (2006). *The Radical Enlightenment of Salomon Maimon* (Stanford University Press).

Spalding, Almut (2005). *Elise Reimarus (1735–1805): The Muse of Hamburg: A Woman of the German Enlightenment* (Würzburg: Königshausen & Neumann).

(2006). "Siblings, Publications, and the Transmission of Memory: Johan Albert Hinrich and Elise Reimarus," in Naomi J. Miller and Naomi Yavneh (eds.), *Sibling Relations and Gender in the Early Modern World: Sisters, Brothers and Others* (Aldershot and Burlington, VA: Ashgate), 216–27.

Starobinski, Jean (1983). *1789. Die Embleme der Vernunft* (Munich: Fink).

Stern, Robert (2006). "Hegel's *Doppelsatz*: A Neutral Reading," *Journal of the History of Philosophy* 44:2: 235–66.

(2012). "On Hegel's Critique of Kant's Ethics: Beyond the Empty Formalism Objection," in Thom Brooks (ed.), *Hegel's Philosophy of Right* (Oxford: Wiley-Blackwell), 43–72.

Suter, Jean-François (1971). "Burke, Hegel and the French Revolution," in Zbigniew A. Pelczynski (ed.), *Hegel's Political Philosophy: Problems and Perspectives* (Cambridge University Press), 52–72.

Taylor, Charles (1997). "Was ist Liberalismus?," in *Hegelpreis 1997* (Stuttgart: Suhrkamp), 25–54.

Tribe, Keith (1988). *Governing Economy: The Reformation of German Economic Discourse, 1750–1840* (Cambridge University Press).

Valjavec, Fritz (1951). *Die Entstehung der politischen Strömungen in Deutschland, 1770–1815* (Munich: R. Oldenbourg).

Verweyen, Hansjürgen (1975). *Recht und Sittlichkeit in J. G. Fichtes Gesellschaftslehre* (Freiburg: Karl Alber Verlag).

Völker, Martin (2006). *Raumphantasien, narrative Ganzheit und Identität. Eine Rekonstruktion des Ästhetischen aus dem Werk und Wirken der Freiherren von Dalberg* (Hannover: Wehrhahn).

Walz, Gustav A. (1928). *Die Staatsidee des Rationalismus und der Romantik und die Staatsphilosophie Fichtes* (Berlin-Grunewald: W. Rothschild).

Ware, Owen (2020). *Fichte's Moral Philosophy* (Oxford University Press).

Weigend-Abendroth, Freidrich (1980). *Der Reichsverräter am Rhein. Carl von Dalberg und sein Widerspruch* (Stuttgart: Deutsche Verlagsanstalt).

Wilkinson, Elizabeth M. and Willoughby, Leonard A. (1967). "Introduction," in Friedrich Schiller, *On the Aesthetic Education of Man in a Series of Letters*, translated by Elizabeth M. Wilkinson and Leonard A. Willoughby (Oxford: Clarendon Press), xi-cxcvi.

Wilson, Eric (2008). "Kantian Autonomy and the Moral Self," *The Review of Metaphysics* 62:2: 355–81.

Winegar, Reed. (2021). "Elise Reimarus: Reason, Religion, and Enlightenment." In *Women and Philosophy in Eighteenth-Century Germany*, edited by Corey W. Dyck. Oxford: Oxford University Press.

Wokler, Robert (1998). "Contextualizing Hegel's Phenomenology of the French Revolution and the Terror," *Political Theory* 26:1: 33–55.

Wolff, Christian ([1754] 1969). *Institutiones juris naturae et gentium. Gesammelte Werke*, Bd. 26, edited by M. Thomann (Hildesheim: Olms).

([1721] 1971). *Vernünftige Gedanken von dem gesellschaftlichen Leben der Menschen und insonderheit dem gemeinen Wesen.*

([1758] 1988). *Principes du droit de la nature et des gens, extrait du grand ouvrage latin*, par M. Formey, tome premier (Presses Universitaires de Caen).

([1723] 2010). *Vernünftige Gedanken von den Wirkungen der Natur. Gesammelte Werke*, Bd. 6 (Hildesheim: Olms).

Wood, Allen (1990). *Hegel's Ethical Thought* (Cambridge University Press).

(1999). *Kant's Ethical Thought* (Cambridge University Press).

(2016). *Fichte's Ethical Thought* (Oxford University Press).

Index

CPSIA information can be obtained
at www.ICGtesting.com
Printed in the USA
LVHW081704110321
681236LV00006B/176